£1.75

LABOUR IN THE TROPICAL TERRITORIES OF THE COMMONWEALTH

LABOUR IN THE
TROPICAL TERRITORIES
OF THE COMMONWEALTH

By

B. C. ROBERTS

*Professor of Industrial Relations at the London School
of Economics and Political Science*

THE LONDON SCHOOL OF ECONOMICS
AND POLITICAL SCIENCE
(*University of London*)
G. BELL AND SONS LTD
LONDON   .   W.C.2

Printed in Great Britain by Richard Clay and Company, Ltd.
Bungay, Suffolk

CONTENTS

Preface   vii

Introduction   xiii

PART I. THE DEVELOPMENT OF TRADE UNIONS

1 The First Phase of Development   3

2 The Growth of Unions since 1938   35

3 Trade Unions and Politics   85

4 Trade Union Organization   122

5 The Influence of the British Trades Union Congress   146

6 International Trade Union Organizations and Trade
  Union Development   157

PART II. THE DEVELOPMENT OF LABOUR POLICY AND
         ADMINISTRATION

7 The Evolution of Colonial Office Labour Policy   169

8 The Development of Labour Administration   201

9 The Influence of the International Labour Organization   241

PART III. THE DEVELOPMENT OF LABOUR LAW

10 The Legal Regulation of Trade Unions   259

11 The Legal Regulation of Industrial Relations   304

PART IV. THE DEVELOPMENT OF INDUSTRIAL RELATIONS

12 The Pattern of Employment   337

13 The Employers   365

14 The Development of Industrial Relations   381

Index   413

v

PREFACE

COLONIZATION involves not merely the imposition by the colonial power of political forms on dependent territories, and at a later stage, the imposition of political institutions, but also a transmission of social institutions and ideas. No doubt at all stages the colonial authorities tended to assume the virtues of the institutions with which they were familiar in the metropolitan country and, as occasion arose, tried to get them reproduced —no doubt generally with modifications—in the dependencies. As education was developed it equally naturally tended to spread knowledge of the metropolitan institutions and a disposition to imitate them. In earlier times these tendencies were unsystematic and almost unconscious; and in so far as any deliberate attempt was made to introduce into dependent countries institutions similar to those in their metropolitan countries, the initiative was apt to come from non-government sources and to be of spasmodic character. During the inter-war period, however, the process of transmission of ideas and institutions from Britain to her colonial dependencies became a good deal more conscious and more organized.

This is not to say that no analogous attempt had been made in earlier generations, but it was only after the first world war that something like a systematic movement began in the field of government. Various reasons can be seen for this. One, obviously, was the growing general acceptance that governments had to play a more positive role in general social and economic development or what can be called in very broad and diffuse terms a general acceptance of a 'socialist' approach. Secondly, the trend might be regarded as a fuller flowering of a more positive attitude towards colonial problems, which had begun to make itself felt about the turn of the century and was symbolized in political terms by Joseph Chamberlain's tenure of the office of Colonial Secretary. Thirdly, it is perhaps relevant that it was not until after the first world war that the larger territories of tropical Africa, which from then on became the centre of Colonial Office interest, began to reach a level of social sophistication at which it became sensible to think of importing into

vii

them institutions similar to those in the home country. The first stage in their development had been the simple establishment of order over vast areas and the laying of the foundations of economic growth, of establishing the first main lines of communication, and introducing or enlarging a few simple export industries.

At the first stage of this process of social transmission attention was concentrated primarily on the aspect of technical information; in the middle 20's the Colonial Office attached to itself specialist advisers in agriculture, education and medicine with whom were associated advisory committees which included experts in all the appropriate branches of knowledge in those fields. These became the central points to which the technical officers in agriculture, education or medicine looked for advice and information, while actually serving in the colonial dependencies. The second stage, which can be regarded as emerging only towards the end of the inter-war period and reaching its full development only during and after the second world war, involved much more of a conscious attempt to stimulate and advise upon the development of institutions and social devices on lines already developed in Britain, in such fields as social insurance and social administration generally, the development of co-operative societies, labour administration and trade unions. It is perhaps legitimate to argue that in the case of education the deliberate setting up of models derived from British practice had come very much earlier, at the level of school organization, but it is again noteworthy that it was primarily in the second period mentioned that a conscious effort was made to transmit British university institutions to the dependencies.

The second stage was marked by a conscious effort on the part of authority in the shape of the Colonial Office, acting of course where appropriate in consultation with 'expert' departments of the British Government such as the Ministry of Education or the Ministry of Labour, but an important part was also played by other organizations. In the field of labour and many areas associated with it, a significant part in stimulating various developments was certainly played by the International Labour Organization and by the various international agreements on labour matters negotiated during this period. A large part was also played, however, by purely non-government organizations; for example, the churches and missionary societies in school education and, at the later stage, by the universities in higher-level education. In relation to such matters as co-operative and trade union developments a considerable part was also played by the appropriate organizations in Britain who were themselves interested in analogous developments in colonial dependencies. In many cases the initiative came from them, but in others they might be approached for advice or assistance by people from the dependencies anxious to promote or undertake relevant developments. Thus it would be quite wrong to concentrate attention entirely on government activity in any examination of the general process of social transmission.

What was in view in all cases was imitation of institutions already developed to meet British conditions. The need for adaptation to local circumstances was always recognized, although inevitably it may be questioned whether sufficient modification was always made. A good deal of influence was also exercised by experience in other parts of the British Empire in its old sense. It was obviously reasonable to look for lessons from the much more sophisticated communities forming part of that Empire in considering lines of development in the comparatively primitive territories of, for example, tribal Africa. In general, conditions in the territories of European settlements in Australasia and Canada were far too different from those of the tropical dependencies for much to be learned from them, but a good deal of attention was paid to Indian experience, and codes of law and administrative practices developed in India, and in some cases in Ceylon, were adopted and adapted not only in the immediately neighbouring territories, such as those in South-East Asia, but also in many parts of Africa and elsewhere. A particular example was in the field of co-operation, where much of the model legislation prepared for the Colonial Office for use in the dependencies at large was based on Indian or Ceylonese models.

It is fair to say that in many cases, thinking about prospective social development was more advanced in the Colonial Office itself and generally in interested circles in Britain, than in colonial governments or in the then dominant circles in the dependencies.   Indeed, it was in many cases in advance of the thinking of the more progressive or revolutionary elements in the colonies.   This was perhaps particularly true in the whole field of labour legislation, in which much of the legislation resulted from the promptings of London rather than from initiatives developed in particular territories.

The development of trade unions in the colonies was a very typical part of this general process of transmission of institutions. It was in fact a comparatively late example, although the growth was vigorous in many territories once the seed was planted.   With the rapid growth of modern industry and modern practices of wage-employment there has been a parallel and consequential growth of trade unions.   Basically, trade union development represents in the field of employment what the extension of the franchise represents in the wider field of politics—the recognition of the right of the common man to a say in the settlement of the affairs that affect his livelihood and his life.

The story of that development has not hitherto been told comprehensively.   Indeed, little of it has been told at all save in patches and incidentally to other stories.   Besides telling in detail the story of the growth (and occasional decline) of trade unions in the individual territories concerned, this book analyses the various influences of Colonial Office policy, of suggestions and advice from the older trade union movements in Britain and elsewhere and of various international organizations.   It shows how the spontaneous urges towards organization which arose in some individual territories have been supplemented and moulded by the conscious attempts to stimulate trade union growth resulting from the kind of developments of thinking in the Colonial Office and in Britain generally which have been briefly described above.

Many of the territories that have been examined are no longer colonies but independent states.   In at least one case, that of Ghana, the pattern taken over from the United Kingdom has, soon after independence, been felt to be unsuitable to local circumstances and a degree of centralization and government control foreign to British trade union tradition has been established.

Undoubtedly the story is not complete.   Others of the newly independent countries will want to experiment with modifications of the structure they have inherited. Some may, after experimenting, return nearer to the pattern we know. Both in numbers and size and in type of organization we may expect much further development. But in understanding that further growth, students will need to come back to this account of the emergence of trade unions and the evolution of the colonial industrial relations systems.

SYDNEY CAINE

INTRODUCTION

LABOUR has always been one of the central problems of colonialism. The labour problem began with the need to obtain workers to cultivate the plantations, provide domestic service and do every other kind of physical task that had to be carried out to develop the economy and administration of the colonies. In the absence of an adequate supply of indigenous labour, the problem was solved in the pre-nineteenth century transatlantic colonies by the simple and effective means of buying workers in the markets in human beings that had long existed in Africa. The demand for labour produced a supply of slaves that satisfied the needs of the West Indian and American colonies until public opinion in Britain revolted against the system of slavery and the trade was brought to an end.

The need for labour in the West Indies continued and new needs arose in other territories. The cessation of slavery meant that other methods of supplementing local labour resources had to be found. Large numbers of labourers were recruited under indenture in India for work in the West Indies, Ceylon and Malaya. Labourers were also obtained from China for employment in Malaya and, to a small extent, in the West Indies. The essence of the indenture system was that labourers were recruited under a contract to work for a given period in exchange for the financing of their passages to the colony.

The indenture system was also eventually brought to an end, but migration continued; it is still one of the outstanding features of the labour problem in many territories. In the West Indies the main flow of migrants is now from these territories to the United Kingdom, and to a much smaller extent to the United States, Canada and Venezuela. In Africa there is a continuous movement of labour from the tribal areas to the towns and centres of industrial and agricultural development.

Migratory labourers are exposed to the danger of abuse to a far greater extent than are employees drawn from an indigenous population, and the first steps in the development of an official colonial labour policy were taken in connection with the protection of workers arriving from overseas to work in the colonies.

With the development of trade unions the 'labour problem' took on a new dimension which induced changes in official policy and exerted a powerful influence in many other directions. The establishment of an employed labour force is a fundamental development that must first take place before it is possible for trade unions to be created. Until this stage is reached there can be no trade unions, since these organizations are associations of employees who have banded together to advance their common interests. The motives which have inspired the growth of trade unions—now a world-wide phenomenon—have been the same everywhere. They have included the desire of work-people to protect themselves from the vicissitudes of employment by collective action and to render aid in times of adversity such as sickness, injury and death; a need to establish a system of rules that would reduce the arbitrary power of the employer to an orderly and predictable pattern of behaviour; a desire to improve wages and working conditions by the exercise of the bargaining power achieved by organization—directly through negotiation with the employer and indirectly through political pressure. Since the status of the employee at work cannot be divorced from his status in society, the establishment of trade unions has always been a manifestation of concern with issues of social as well as of industrial significance. The link between political activity and trade union organization was inevitably made close when the right of workers to protect their interests by the exercise of collective bargaining was intimately connected with the bringing about of changes in the prevailing political environment. Because trade unions can provide mass support for their objectives, radical political parties have often been ready to promote their development so as to use their industrial strength as a means of winning political power.

Trade unionism in the tropical Commonwealth territories has been stimulated by all of these factors. The organization of labour began in some territories, as it did on many occasions elsewhere, as a manifestation of the desire of groups of skilled workers to create unions of skilled men. In other places it was an outcome of political movements which appealed to the underprivileged indigenous employees. The emergence of trade unionism in the colonies, once an employed labour force had been created and the right to organize had been granted, is no more surprising than its emergence anywhere else, but what has been unique about the development of trade unions in these territories is the fact that they were actively promoted by the United Kingdom Government. At a time when there had been few manifestations of the desire to organize, the British Government introduced a policy which deliberately encouraged the growth of unions and the establishment of a system of industrial relations modelled on that which had emerged in Britain.

The circular despatch of Lord Passfield,[1] sent out in September 1930, was a milestone in the history of colonial social policy. It stated that a recent Colonial Office conference had shown that the problem of the regulation of organizations of wage labourers was already one of importance in some colonies. The despatch went on to emphasize that it was the duty of colonial governments to take such steps as might be possible 'to smooth the passage of such organizations, as they emerge, into constitutional channels'.

Many colonies in the next decade adopted the legislation called for by Lord Passfield. Labour administration was developed and the structure of the Colonial Office was reorganized to cope with the growing significance of the 'labour problem'. The second world war greatly speeded up the pace of this evolution; after the war was over, events moved even faster. By 1960 a large part of the old colonial empire had become self-governing independent nations and the course was firmly set for every territory to achieve that status as soon as possible. This political development owes a good deal to the growth of trade unions, which were often the basis of the parties responsible for the achievement of self-government.

Organized labour has today become enormously important in every territory of major significance. The effect of the unions on the level of wages, conditions of employment and the discipline of workers is now considerable—so considerable in fact, that in some territories it is feared that industrial development and economic stability may be jeopardized unless the activities of the unions are closely regulated by the government.

The fundamental principles that were followed by Britain in the colonies were naturally those distilled out of British experience. They may be summarized as the concept of the right of

[1] Sidney Webb.

work-people to form, freely, associations to protect their vocational interests by means of collective bargaining. Implicit in this notion was the belief that the interests of work-people could best be promoted by the initiative of their own independent organizations rather than by reliance upon the power of the state alone. Inevitably British practice was modified and altered to suit the needs of the territories; in this respect the influence of America, Australia and India has been important.

The concepts of trade unionism which have been fostered by Britain and which also underlie the principles of the International Labour Code, have recently been sharply challenged as being inappropriate to the conditions of the under-developed territories. It has been suggested by political leaders from a number of territories that freedom of association has led to the proliferation of weak and unstable unions, that collective bargaining is ineffective when unions are weak, and that the right to strike may lead to irresponsible behaviour that is a deterrent to economic growth. Justifying their action by these arguments the leaders of Ghana, on gaining independence, reorganized the trade unions of that country by legislation, and brought them under the control of the ruling Convention People's Party.

Many governments of developing territories, apart from Ghana, have also imposed severe restrictions on unions and employers. Egypt, Sudan, Libya, Turkey, Guinea and South Africa have, for example, all done so. There is nothing new in this course of action; communist and fascist countries have always denied the right of workers to belong to independent unions, and they have for similar political reasons been afraid to permit the existence of independent associations which might challenge the power of the state.

It remains to be seen whether the political environment will so change as to lead to the destruction of independent trade unions, the abolition of collective bargaining and the right to strike. There are bound to be changes after independence, but it is unlikely that the systems of industrial relations that take shape will be entirely different from those that exist elsewhere. They may become less like the British system, but they are bound to be long influenced by the principles and patterns originally followed. A viable, smooth-working system of industrial relations well founded on enduring principles is of great importance to developing territories, since whatever changes occur, wages will have to be settled, working conditions decided upon, grievances adjusted and laws relating to the worker and his environment passed.

The purpose of this study was to examine the growth of trade unionism; investigate the evolution of British policy and its legal and administrative interpretation; and to analyse the emerging pattern of industrial relations in territories that were, until recently, the responsibility of the Colonial Office. These include the West Indies, the East, Central and West African territories, Aden, Mauritius, Malaya, Singapore, Sarawak, Brunei and North Borneo, Hong Kong and Fiji. Though reference will be made to India and Ceylon and to other territories, these were not within the principal focus of attention.

In making a cross-section study of this kind it is impossible to do justice to every territory. The main objective was to discover the general trends and common factors. It would be interesting to compare the evolution of the institutions, policy and pattern of industrial relations investigated in these Commonwealth territories with those which formerly belonged to France, Holland and Spain. Unfortunately it was not possible to make this comparison, but others may be ready to take on the task.

An investigation of this kind cannot be undertaken without the aid and assistance of many people. It is quite impossible to thank all who have helped to provide the necessary information, but certain organizations and individuals must be mentioned, since their contribution has been of special importance. Invaluable help was given by officials of the Colonial Office; their interest in the study and their practical assistance in London and in the territories was a major contribution to the research. The Overseas Employers' Federation and the Trades Union Congress have both been most co-operative and permitted access to their private records. In the territories, governments, firms and trade unions were generous hosts who willingly provided every facility to enable a full and accurate picture to be obtained. Officers of the I.L.O. made a visit to Geneva a fruitful source of inspiration and information.

During a large part of the time I was assisted by Mr. W. A. Warmington, who was appointed junior (later senior) research

B

officer to the study. Mr. Warmington's knowledge of Africa was of great value and his contribution to this work has been a most important one. Unfortunately Mr. Warmington was not able to see the study through to its conclusion; in these circumstances he felt it not possible to accept the responsibility of joint authorship.

Others to whom much is owed include Sir Sydney Caine, Director of the London School of Economics and Political Science, whose knowledge and experience of colonial problems, both as civil servant and university administrator, was of great help; Mr. George Foggon, Labour Adviser to the Secretary of State for the Colonies, Mr. Meredyth Hyde-Clarke and Mr. Guy Shipp of the Overseas Employers' Federation, Mr. Walter Hood and Miss Marjorie Nicholson of the Trades Union Congress. Finally, mention should be made of the large number of students and colleagues of the London School of Economics and universities in the Commonwealth and the United States who have helped to accumulate the material and to understand its significance.

Responsibility for the final shape of this study lies entirely with the author.

B. C. R.

London,
June 1962

Part One

The Development of Trade Unions

Part One

The Development of Trade Unions

CHAPTER 1

THE FIRST PHASE OF
DEVELOPMENT

THERE is some dispute about the exact origins of trade unions in Britain and Europe. Combination for the purpose of advancing a vocational interest is certainly of considerable antiquity, but the mere fact of association to improve wages or working conditions is not of itself evidence of the creation of a trade union. As the Webbs pointed out, evidence of spontaneous revolt against oppressive employers goes back to ancient times.[1] An industrial revolt only becomes a trade union activity when the decision to act together as a combined force is given an institutional shape and a continuous existence; then it can be said that a trade union exists. Every organization of work-people is not, however, a trade union. A trade union, as its name suggests, is a body formed from work-people for the primary purpose of advancing their interests in their capacity as workers. To emphasize this point does not mean that an association which seeks, for example, to achieve major political ends can never be a trade union. It does mean, however, that a body of people which is primarily interested in attaining non-vocational objectives cannot be a trade union. It might well be a social club or political party, but it is not a trade union.

In Britain, trade unions grew out of a conjunction of factors in the eighteenth century in that period of British social history that we know as the 'Industrial Revolution'. With the breakdown of the domestic system of manufacture and the growth in its place of entrepreneurial enterprises, the necessary conditions for the development of trade unions were established. These were, firstly, the creation of an employer–employee relationship, and secondly, the congregation of numbers of employed workers in a common place of work and engaged on common or closely-related tasks. The emergence of the employmental structure of industry was accompanied by the decay of the long-established practice of state and customary

[1] See S. and B. Webb, *History of Trade Unionism* (London, 1910).

3

regulation of economic relations; in its place were substituted the principles of a *laissez-faire* labour market. Labour became a commodity to be bought and sold at a price determined by the law of supply and demand, established through the higgling process of the market, rather than by the rule of custom and magistrate.

The urge to combine was stimulated by the desire to re-establish the certainty and security that had been undermined by the development of new ideas, new methods and new values. In the first stage, trade union organization arose as a protest against change in the organization of production and exchange. In its next stage, it sought to cushion the impact of the new system of production on the workers and to make it tolerable to them by the adoption of common rules of employment and mutual assistance. Finally, groups of workers were persuaded to combine because organization offered them the opportunity to improve their lot at the expense of other groups who were not allowed access to employment in the organized industries and occupations.

The first permanent trade unions in Britain were formed by skilled craftsmen towards the end of the eighteenth century. They built up their unions around the common interest which they had in protecting the conditions of their employment as printers, carpenters, tailors, shoemakers and members of other skilled trades. The early trade unions satisfied other vital needs too. They were a source of sympathetic help and advice at all times, but especially in adversity, when they provided an important element of social security through the organization of friendly benefits. The union made it possible for a worker and his family to be decently buried on decease; it provided monetary assistance when a worker was ill or suffering from the effects of an accident; and when he was unemployed it helped him to find a new job. The trade union was much more than a mere economic device to bring about a more equal bargaining strength with employers; it was a social club which satisfied the skilled craftsman's need for comradeship and adjusted him to the harsh consequences of living in a *laissez-faire* society.

The growth of industry, and the new methods of manufacture, mining and transport, stimulated open and wide-embracing, as well as closed and narrowly-limited trade unions which sought to achieve improvements in the economic and social conditions of their members by the exercise of industrial and political pressure through mass membership. The most extreme manifestation of this broader form of organization was the Grand National Consolidated Trades Union, which failed because of over-ambitious objectives, a weak administration and an ineffective system of leadership. General unionism became successful when it was able to recruit a competent paid secretariat, develop an appropriate system of government and enjoy a favourable political climate.

Trade unionism in America began among skilled craftsmen, as it had done in Britain; the idea of collective organization as the panacea for this rapidly developing nation's ills was then taken up with fervour by all types of employees and farmers. Labour organizations were strong supporters of radical political policies and vigorously pursued utopian ideals for the reform of society. Most of these attempts to change the course of American history failed, and it was not until workers concentrated on building trade unions with more narrowly defined occupational interests that they succeeded in establishing themselves as stable organizations.

As the Industrial Revolution spread across the Channel from Britain, work-people responded to it in a similar way. There was, however, one important difference in the origins of trade unionism in Britain and in the continental countries. In Britain, trade unionism was an autonomous development; it grew spontaneously rather than out of an ideology. In Europe, trade union organization was sponsored by political parties as a means of organizing mass support for their objectives. British trade unions were from the first highly concerned with political issues, and they have become more so as time has passed but the core of their purpose and activity was from the beginning to be found in the narrow context of improving wages and working conditions and in safeguarding a worker from the vicissitudes of the industrial environment within which he worked.

Trade Unions Lineal Descendants of Guilds?

Trade unions in the tropical territories with which we are concerned had their origins in circumstances which were in many respects quite different from those which prevailed when unions in Britain, America or Europe were first created. In most of the territories there was, until recently, little or no industrial development of the type that rapidly developed in Britain in the eighteenth century. Except in certain territories most of the population in Africa, South-East Asia and elsewhere were engaged in subsistence agriculture, and their way of life was centred on traditional family structures and tribal patterns. In the West Indies a different situation existed; from the beginning the population had been employed, initially as slaves and later as paid labourers, on plantations owned by the British, Dutch and French. The system of employment in estate and plantation agriculture, also important in Ceylon, Malaya and East Africa, is in some ways similar to that in large-scale industrial undertakings, but there were many reasons why these employees did not turn to trade union organization until a relatively short time ago.

Although the pattern of life in West Africa and China differed considerably from that in Britain and Europe, an institutional development preceding trade unions common to each area was the emergence of craft guilds. This type of organization, which flourished in Britain and Europe from medieval times to the Industrial Revolution, had a counterpart in Nigeria and Ghana and, stemming from China, in Hong Kong and Malaya.

It was suggested in Britain in the middle of the nineteenth century by Lujo Brentano [2] that the trade unions were the lineal descendants of the craftsmen's guilds, but the Webbs, writing later, vigorously disputed this point of view. [3] The Webbs contended that there was no evidence to establish any organic link between the guilds and the unions, and their opinion has been generally accepted as closer to the truth than that of Brentano. There are clearly functional similarities which suggest a close relationship between guilds and trade unions, but there are also important differences of purpose. [4] The object of a guild is to protect the interests of independent craftsmen, whereas a trade union exists to protect the interests of employees. A trade

[2] See Lujo Brentano, *History and Development of Gilds and the Origin of Trade Unions* (London, 1870).
[3] See S. and B. Webb, *History of Trade Unionism* (London, 1919).
[4] For a study of the structure and functions of this type of guild organization in Nigeria see P. Lloyd, 'Craft Organisation in Yoruba', *Africa*, January 1953.

union can come into being only where a family structure of employment has given way to one in which there is a permanent labour force employed on a wage basis. But it can be suggested that though it is difficult to establish any direct link between the guilds and trade unions, it is quite possible, and perhaps even likely, that the early unions were stimulated to some degree by a desire to emulate their predecessors—the guilds. Whether or not there is any lineal descent of trade unions from guilds, it is clear that both types of organization are manifestations of the basic desire to regulate the economic and social factors that determine the rewards for work. The existence of guilds before trade unions were established indicates that the idea of combination and the social skill to give it an institutional shape are not entirely a modern notion.

It was suggested by the Census Officer of the Gold Coast in 1911 that the guilds were 'not dissimilar in objects and methods to a modern trade union.'[5] The goldsmiths' guild, which was the most powerful, 'professed to regulate wages, to make laws concerning apprentices, to guard against unfair competition, and to settle disputes among craftsmen'. Some of these guilds have become trade unions, but in most cases there was no continuous line of development from the guilds to the trade unions which have emerged in modern times.

Guilds have been a most important feature of life in China for over a thousand years, and wherever Chinese have settled overseas they have established their own associations.[6] In objectives and methods the craft guilds of China were similar to those which flourished in Britain until the industrial revolution. They sought to regulate entry into a trade by control of apprenticeship, to enforce trade customs, to fix prices and to protect their members from the activities of other guilds and the imposition of governments. The guilds in China differed in one important respect from those that existed in Britain and Europe, and this made for a considerable difference in their behaviour. In China the guilds were completely outside the law; they were purely private self-governing institutions without any legal status. Thus guilds often acted as if they were

[5] Census of Population, 1911, Gold Coast Colony.
[6] See H. B. Morse, The Gilds of China (London, 1932), and W. L. Blythe, 'Historical Sketch of Chinese Labour in Malaya', Journal of the Royal Asiatic Society, Malayan Branch. Vol. 20, Pt. 1, 1947.

secret societies, and it is perhaps not surprising that without the element of control that a legal framework and exposure to public opinion would have imposed, they sometimes degenerated into a vicious means of exploiting their members and other sections of society. Conflicts between rival triads (Chinese secret societies) have been a common feature in Hong Kong, Malaya and elsewhere in South-East Asia where Chinese have settled. In the nineteenth century there were fierce clashes between the different triads into which the Chinese employees of the tin mines in Malaya were organized. A particularly violent conflict between rival gangs of miners led in 1890 to the banning of Chinese secret societies in Malaya, but it was practically impossible to get rid of secret societies merely by making them unlawful.

The guild and its close relation, the secret society, are still highly influential among the Chinese in Hong Kong and South-East Asia. Most of the Chinese trade unions registered under the trade union acts have about them a considerable element of the guild and the secret society. It is quite common for a union to exercise the role of a 'labour boss'; to sell the labour of its members and to take from them a considerable levy for this service. The Chinese union, in the guild tradition, is also often much more interested in certain social functions, such as providing friendly benefits, schools and entertainment, rather than in collective bargaining or workshop representation. Therefore, whilst it may not be correct to say that the trade unions formed by the Chinese in Hong Kong and the South-East Asian territories are a continuous development of the craft guilds that have existed in China from the earliest times, they are certainly lineal descendants in terms of their functions and behaviour patterns. In this respect trade unionism among the Chinese can be said to be different in its origin from unions in the rest of the world. If the guilds are excluded, it is in the West Indies that the earliest manifestations of what can properly be termed trade unions occurred in the tropical Commonwealth.

Early Attempts at Labour Organization

The development of trade unionism in the territories with which this survey is concerned has inevitably been influenced by the social, economic and political factors peculiar to each of them. In the West Indies there was a large employed labour force, divorced from its traditional pattern of life, without status, forced to work under harsh conditions and severe discipline, and unable to escape by returning home. Many of the riots and disturbances which occurred in the West Indies in the nineteenth century had their origins in these social conditions. Most of the outbreaks of unrest were isolated eruptions of protest and they produced no lasting political or social organizations. The earliest attempts to create a social movement to improve conditions of employment of the working people of the West Indies were made in Trinidad and British Guiana.[7]

The sugar industry, on which most of the West Indies depended, was severely hit in the 1890's by the competition of state-encouraged European beet sugar. Estates were closed down, unemployment grew and wages were reduced to a point where they could be depressed no further. This unhappy situation in the West Indies caused the British Government to set up a Royal Commission to investigate the situation and to suggest such measures as appeared 'best calculated to restore and maintain the prosperity of those Colonies and of their inhabitants'.[8]

The establishment of the Royal Commission seems to have been responsible for stimulating the formation in Trinidad of two reform organizations that closely resembled the liberal–labour political reform organizations in Britain and America during the first half of the nineteenth century. The Working Men's Reform Club, founded by Charles Phillips, gave evidence to the Royal Commission when it visited Trinidad in 1897. The Club seems to have consisted mainly of artisans, dock workers and boatmen employed in Port of Spain. In its submission to the Royal Commission the Club drew attention to the effect which the depressed state of the sugar industry was having on the labouring classes in the island. A protest was made against the taxes that were levied on working men, and it was emphasized to the Commission that the workers of Trinidad had formed their own friendly societies. 'We support our sick and bury our dead; on wages that barely keep us alive we have to pay the government a tax of 5s. yearly for licences.'[9] After

[7] See F. Cundall, *Political and Social Disturbances in the West Indies*, 1906.
[8] See *West India Royal Commission*, 1897.
[9] See *West India Royal Commission*, 1897, Appendix C, Vol. II, p. 348.

this brief moment of public glory, the Club seems to have faded away, since no further evidence of its activities has been found. The Trinidad Working Men's Association, also apparently founded in 1897, had a much longer life and made a notable contribution to the evolution of the island's political and social affairs. This body was evidently more representative of the skilled craftsmen than the Working Men's Reform Club. Its president, giving evidence before the Royal Commission, claimed that its members were 'carpenters, masons, labourers, tailors and other trades, about 50 in all'.[10]   Under the leadership of Alfred Richards, who was elected president in 1906, the T.W.A. was registered as an incorporated body. Its activities were not so much those of a trade union as those of a liberal political reform association. The leaders of the T.W.A. entered into correspondence with British Labour Members of Parliament, to whom Richards looked for guidance and help. On the basis of this contact, it was locally claimed that the T.W.A. was affiliated to the British Labour Party. Thomas Summerbell, Labour M.P. for Sunderland, acted as a corresponent of the Association for many years. After he died in 1910 this duty was taken over by the Labour member for Attercliffe, who was nicknamed by his colleagues 'the Member for Trinidad'.[11]

The leaders of the T.W.A. frequently used their connections with Labour M.P.s to have questions raised in the House of Commons; by this means they sought to bring pressure to bear on the Trinidad Government. This policy had a limited degree of success, but the Association was not able to bring about any radical improvement in the social and economic conditions of its members. Demands for a more militant policy were made, but the leaders of the T.W.A. were not disposed to make use of such trade union tactics as strikes.

Attempts were made to found skilled workers' unions in Trinidad in 1910, but these came to little. At about the same time, efforts were being made in Jamaica and British Guiana to form unions of skilled craftsmen on the British model. For example, in 1907 and 1908, printers and cigar makers employed

[10] See *West India Royal Commission*, 1897, Appendix C, Vol. II, p. 301.

[11] See F. X. Marks, *The Rise and Development of Labour Movements in the British Caribbean, with particular reference to British Guiana, Jamaica and Trinidad* (an unpublished thesis in the University of Edinburgh, 1959).

in Jamaica organized unions and made contact with the American Federation of Labor. On 12th September 1908 the International Typographical Union of America issued a charter to a local with 24 members in Georgetown, Demarara (British Guiana). The *Typographical Journal* of March 1909 published the following item about the inauguration of this local:

> The Journal is in receipt of an article taken from the *Daily Argosy* of Georgetown, British Guiana, descriptive of the impressive dedicatory exercises which took place when the first charter from the International Typographical Union ever implanted in a jurisdiction in the South American continent was received and Typographical Union No. 666 duly instituted. The hall was decorated with flags, and the charter, handsomely framed, was hung over the platform, around it being draped the stars and stripes of the United States, which was borrowed for the occasion from the American consul in Demarara.

Such developments as those just mentioned were, however, isolated instances, and they generally failed to survive for more than a few years. Most of the craft skills, such as making textiles, clothing, footwear, furniture and buildings, were exercised by self-employed workers. Since there was little industrial development there were few communities of skilled employees with vital occupational interests to protect, as there had been in Britain, America and Europe during the period following the Industrial Revolution. The economic and industrial conditions which stimulated trade unionism in Britain, America and Europe, namely the development of paid employment, were first satisfied in the colonies in public service and on plantations. The modern trade union movement in the tropical territories did not, therefore, originate from skilled craftworkers, as was the case in Britain, America and Europe, but, as we shall see, from government employees, railway and port workers, school teachers and clerks.

There were many other reasons why trade unions did not develop in these territories until recently. The indigenous population living in cities before the first world war were mainly engaged in service occupations and as we know from experience in the more advanced countries, servants are too easily dominated by their close relationship with their employers to be attracted by unions.   Moreover, many of those who worked in cities retained a close link with their family and village community.   There was, at this stage, little or no vigorous town life which because of its different economic and social values usually provides the stimulus for collective organization.

The master–servant relationship was reinforced by the fact that most employees had no civic or political rights.   Furthermore, their education was rudimentary; most of them could not read or write.   Lacking literacy, and having little opportunity to acquire the social skills necessary to form and administer organizations, wage-earners did little more than resort occasionally to demonstrations of their feelings.   Protest against their lot took the form of non-co-operation and occasionally of riotous behaviour, but it was instinctive and spontaneous rather than organized and directed.

Until after the first world war most territories, with the possible exception of parts of the West Indies, Ceylon and India, were not ready for the emergence of trade unions.   Industrial developments had barely started, but communications were being improved, local governments were becoming more ambitious and educational opportunities were becoming available to a limited number of future indigenous leaders.

The Impact of the First World War

The first world war had a profound impact on social development over the entire globe.   In one way or another the revolutionary changes it promoted had repercussions in every country.   It gave a violent wrench to established ways of behaviour, upset traditional political patterns and led to new political boundaries.   The problems of colonial rule were highlighted by the need to decide the future of the former German colonies.   The emergence of the League of Nations, and with it the concept of trusteeship and the foundation of the International Labour Organization, introduced new elements into the colonial structure.   The Russian Revolution and the subsequent creation of the Third International whose avowed purposes were to overthrow imperialism and to promote communism in its stead, was perhaps an even more significant event. But probably the most important development of all, for the British colonies, was the growth of the labour movement in

Britain, with its promise of future labour governments which would have a new and radical approach to colonial problems. None of these factors had an immediate and decisive effect on the course of events in the British colonies, but cumulatively they exercised a profound influence during the next twenty years.

Army service in the first world war provided an opportunity for workers from the colonies to travel far afield. Others found employment building military bases. After the war was over they returned home with a new vision and a determination to build a better place in which to live. (The second world war was even more important in this respect.)

In Trinidad the Working Men's Association was re-formed in the years immediately following the first world war, by an ex-army officer named Captain Cipriani. The son of Corsican immigrants, Cipriani was a well-to-do cocoa planter and race-horse owner, but his interest in the welfare of the 'barefoot' man had been stimulated by war-time experience, and on retiring from the army he entered into politics. Under Cipriani's leadership the Trinidad Working Men's Association became a vigorous organization. Its policy was broadly that of a liberal reform movement concerned to advance the notion of self-government and to promote legislation that would benefit wage-earners and small property owners. It was especially concerned with the adoption of a system of social insurance, a legal minimum wage, land resettlement and various constitutional and civic reforms. The Association was for a time highly influential in Port of Spain, and Cipriani was elected to the Legislative Council as member for that constituency.

Although much concerned with labour matters, the T.W.A. was never a trade union. In 1919 a group of rebels who had come to the fore as militant leaders of unofficial strikes during the war, pushed the Association into organizing and supporting the waterfront workers in a claim for higher wages and shorter hours. The leaders of the T.W.A. issued a statement to the press in 1919 stressing the fact that the Association was 'a political organization for the furtherance of social reform. . . . It is not a Labour Union for gain.'[12] Alfred Richards, the President of the Association, was even moved to seek an

[12] See F. X. Marks, *op. cit.*, p. 191.

injunction to prevent the rebel group from acting in the name
of the T.W.A. The Association was compelled to support its
members in a series of other claims, but it is clear that its
official leaders had no stomach for full-blooded trade union
activities. The Association was also hurt by the activities of
Marcus Garvey's followers who were circulating literature advocating the overthrow of the white man and the establishment
of a negro republic (see p. 29). Allegations were made that
the leaders of the T.W.A. were implicated in a revolutionary
conspiracy against the government, but no evidence to sub-
stantiate the charge was produced. The government decided,
however, that it was necessary to pass a seditious publications
ordinance, and under it the importation of a number of
American negro publications was banned.

When Captain Cipriani became President of the T.W.A. its
membership had fallen to less than 100, but this decline was
rapidly remedied. Under Cipriani the T.W.A. concentrated
on the attainment of self-government, which Cipriani considered the primary condition for improving the wages and
conditions of employment of Trinidad workers. Nevertheless,
the branches of the T.W.A., which in Port of Spain were
organized on an occupational basis, very frequently acted like
trade unions. The association was also in favour of legislation
to legalize trade union activity. It was, in fact, the passing of
the Trinidad Trade Union Ordinance in 1932 which compelled
Cipriani to choose whether to register the T.W.A. as a trade
union or to confirm that the Association was a political
organization. After taking advice from friends in the British
labour movement, Cipriani decided to change the name of the
T.W.A. to that of the Trinidad Labour Party.

This step established beyond all doubt that although the
association had frequently acted like a trade union, it was
primarily concerned with the attainment of political objectives
by political means, as had been fairly obvious throughout its
history. It is difficult to say whether the foundations of a
durable trade union movement could have been laid in the
period of industrial unrest after the first world war, had the
T.W.A. not existed. The T.W.A. acted both as a vehicle for
the development of trade union ideas and activities and as a
barrier to their growth and development, as did the political

reform associations in Britain and America in the nineteenth century.

One of the most successful attempts to form a labour organization in the West Indies after the first world war was unquestionably the British Guiana Labour Union formed by Hubert Critchlow in 1919. Critchlow, the son of Barbadian parents, was a self-educated, quiet-spoken, but determined man. He was employed on the docks and had taken part, as a young man, in the great labour disturbances that had occurred in Georgetown in 1905 and 1906. These outbreaks of industrial unrest were a protest against unemployment, low wages and the generally bad social conditions under which large sections of the wage-earning population of Georgetown and the sugar estates were compelled to live. Critchlow was well endowed with the qualities required of a successful trade union leader. He had read widely and deeply and developed a keen interest in the British trade union movement. Critchlow also enjoyed fame and popularity in Georgetown as an accomplished local cricketer. Within a few months of its foundation in 1919 the British Guiana Labour Union had attracted a membership of 13,000, and 36 branches had been organized. After a hard struggle it was able to win a ten-hour day and higher wages for members employed on the waterfront. During the next few years the B.G.L.U. was involved in a series of struggles for recognition.

The most important victory of the B.G.L.U. was achieved when the Court of Policy decided to pass a trade union ordinance making it impossible for the employers to sue the members of the union for engaging in an illegal conspiracy. The ordinance did not, however, give the unions the right to engage in peaceful picketing without fear of legal reprisal, as did the law in England.

The B.G.L.U. found the major obstacle to its progress in the refusal of employers to recognize its authority to speak for the employees. This attitude was the response that employers throughout the world have given when first confronted by trade unionism, but the opposition of employers has never succeeded in doing more than temporarily check the growth of trade unions. In this instance the employers were able to recruit blackleg labour and defeat the attempts of the union to improve

c

wages and working conditions.   No doubt the employers were
satisfied with this result, but their negative attitude at this time
encouraged the resurgence of race consciousness; this was fed
by a religious fanaticism which embodied a strong anti-white
element.

Critchlow was not an aggressive union leader, but faced with
completely unyielding employers and influenced by the rising
fever of opposition to the 'white' domination of industry and
government, the B.G.L.U. was compelled to adopt a more
militant attitude.   In 1924 the casual labourers employed on
one of the wharves suddenly decided to go on strike.   The
union next day organized a demonstration in support of an
arbitration board to investigate their grievances.   The situation got out of hand, and Critchlow, who was against any resort
to violence, found himself unable to control his supporters.
The government at once declared martial law, and issued a
warning that it would use whatever force was necessary to
restore order.   Warnings did not, however, prevent several
thousand employees from neighbouring sugar estates from
marching on Georgetown when they heard of the strike on the
waterfront.   The police ordered them back, but the crowd refused to disperse and the police were eventually compelled to
fire on them, killing 12 and wounding 21.   It is almost certain
that had the police not taken a firm stand the consequences
would have been much worse.   But the riot might never have
happened if the union had been recognized and if the employers had adopted a constructive attitude towards the development of collective bargaining.

The B.G.L.U. differed considerably from the Trinidad
Working Men's Association in that it was a genuine trade
union primarily pursuing trade union aims rather than political
objectives.   Critchlow, unlike Richards or Cipriani, was a
worker motivated by a desire to bring about an improvement
in the wages and working conditions of his fellow members,
rather than the achievement of political independence.   Like
British unions in the mid-nineteenth century, the B.G.L.U.
received advice and assistance from a number of middle-class
friends, who remained, however, in a purely advisory capacity.
Critchlow, who became a paid full-time official soon after the
union was founded, ran his organization on lines similar to those

of the British unions which he had studied. Branches had a considerable degree of autonomy, but all contributions had to be paid into a central fund over which Critchlow, as secretary-treasurer, had control. The union was constitutionally governed by a general committee, and a smaller executive committee was responsible for its day-to-day affairs. The main branch of the union in Georgetown was divided into occupational sections, but the other branches were of a general character.[13] The foundations of the organization were well laid, for the B.G.L.U. has had a continuous existence to the present day.

Jamaica also experienced an outbreak of industrial unrest at the end of the first world war. A wave of strikes began with a stoppage of labourers in the West Indies Chemical Works and was followed by strikes among municipal employees, in the docks and on the railways, among the banana carriers, general labourers and employees on the sugar estates. These strikes were often accompanied by violence and irresponsible behaviour. The general cause seems to have been the attempt by the government to prevent inflation by trying to keep wages down in the face of a rising cost of living. Several unions seem to have been established at this time, the most important of which were the Longshoremen's Union, the Cigar Makers' Union and the railway employees' Workmen's Co-operative Association. A Montego Bay Labourers' Benevolent Union was also started. None of these organizations was very successful, but the government did respond to this development of trade unions by passing a law in 1919 to legalize combinations. The Jamaican trade union law did not, however, protect unions from actions for damage in tort, nor did it establish the legality of peaceful picketing. In these respects this law fell short of the standard which most trade unionists in Britain considered to be absolutely essential for the growth of a strong trade union movement.

Africa

Although the African colonies were less well developed than the West Indies, they too felt the social and economic effects of the first world war. During the war the demand for labour

[13] See F. X. Marks, *op. cit.*

rose, but despite the shortage of workers, the price of com-
modities went up faster than wages. Employees of the government, which was by far the largest employer of labour, began
spontaneously to protest collectively against the fall in real
wages.

An organization of civil servants existed before the war in
Sierra Leone, and a Nigerian Civil Service Union had been
founded in 1912 'to promote the welfare and interests of native
members of the Civil Service'.[14]   This union, in the manner of
most British Civil Service unions, rejected the strike as an instrument of policy and concentrated on presenting petitions to
the Governor and the Secretary of State for the Colonies as a
means of securing improvements in staff conditions.

Employees in the Public Works Department and railway
workers in the Gold Coast were more ready to take strike action,
and in 1920 they threatened to withdraw their labour if
the government did not do something about the cost-of-living
and wage levels.   As the government's employees were pro-
testing against the high cost of living, the economic situation
was starting to change.   The world-wide post-war slump had
begun and the cocoa boom which followed the war collapsed.
In 1921 the government sought to reduce wages, and the public
works and railway employees affected came out on strike,
following exactly the same pattern as in Britain.   In the same
year an Artisans' and Labourers' Union had been founded in
Accra, and this body called a strike of mechanics employed in
the city.   A few weeks later an attempt was made by the
authorities to suppress the union by charging its members,
under native law, with uttering unlawful oaths.   This action,
Roper states, has 'a striking parallel with the case of the famous
Tolpuddle martyrs in Britain in 1834'.[15]   Fortunately the outcome was less depressing than in the case of the Dorchester
labourers who were sentenced to deportation, since the charges
appear to have been withdrawn on appeal.

Thus, in West Africa, as in the West Indies, the concept of
trade unionism begins to take shape in the period of the first
world war and its aftermath.   In East and Central Africa,

---

[14] Quoted by T. M. Yesufu, *An Introduction to Industrial Relations in Nigeria* (an
unpublished thesis in the University of London, 1960).
[15] See J. J. Roper, *Labour Problems in West Africa* (London, 1958).

where the indigenous population was, generally speaking, at a
more primitive level of development, there were few signs of
trade union activity among Africans until twenty-five years
later.   The first steps to form unions were taken by European
workers in Northern Rhodesia around the end of the first world
war.   The oldest trade union in existence in this part of Africa
today is the Rhodesian Railway Workers' Union, founded by
Europeans, which has its headquarters in Southern Rhodesia.
Sir Roy Welensky, formerly the Prime Minister of the Federation of Central Africa, was a prominent member of this union
for many years.   Among the European mineworkers in
Northern Rhodesia, trade union organization was not estab-
listed until 1936; it was achieved after an attempt to found a
branch of the South African Mineworkers' Union had failed in
the previous year.

Mauritius

The first steps to form a trade union were also taken in
Mauritius immediately following the first world war.[16]   W.
Moutou, an employee of a printing firm in Port Louis, the
capital of Mauritius, asked a friend who was leaving for England
in 1917 to send him some information about trade union developments in Britain.   Some time afterwards Moutou received
a letter which mentioned the name of Arthur Henderson, who
was at that time one of the leaders of the British Labour Party.
Moutou wrote to Henderson and received a reply advising him
to start a trade union movement and then to ask the Government of Mauritius for its approval of the organization.   If the
government would not give its consent to the formation of the
union, Henderson advised Moutou to draw up a memorial and
send it to the Secretary of State for the Colonies, and at the same
time to despatch a copy to the British Trades Union Congress.
Moutou and several friends from the same printing firm discussed Henderson's letter and decided to follow his advice.
They secured the support of Dr. Edgar Laurent and Arthur
Rohan, a well-known local attorney, and launched an appeal to
every worker in Mauritius to join the union.   An inaugural

---

[16] I am indebted to Mr. Kenneth Baker, sometime Trade Union Adviser to the
Government of Mauritius, for much of the following material relating to the
origins of trade unionism in Mauritius.

meeting under the chairmanship of Dr. Laurent, was held in February 1921 in the Town Hall, Port Louis. Workers from all over the island attended the meeting and they agreed unanimously to form 'The National Trade Union of Mauritius'. Dr. Laurent was elected President; Mr. Rohan, Treasurer; and Mr. Moutou, General Secretary.

It was decided that the objects of the union should be:

(1) to extend trade union principles amongst the working classes of this Colony;
(2) to protect the interests of labour and of all members;
(3) to endeavour to obtain fair wages and reasonable hours of duty for all members;
(4) to provide funds for the relief of members during trade disputes;
(5) to regulate disputes between employers and employees.

A number of further meetings were held and rules were drawn up. In the meantime, the union found itself involved in a strike of railway workshop employees, which it had not called, but which it decided to support. The strike was not very successful, but it dramatized the existence of the union and also brought it to the notice of the authorities. When the rules of the union were submitted to the Procureur General's office for approval it was stated that, owing to the absence of any legislation authorizing the formation of trade unions, the government was unable to endorse the application of the National Trade Union of Mauritius. Faced by this impasse, the leaders of the union obtained an interview with the governor of the island, who advised them to approach individual members of the Legislative Council with a view to their pro-moting a private Bill. The union followed up this suggestion, but they were not successful in finding anyone who would initiate the kind of Bill the union wanted. It was then decided to pursue Henderson's other suggestion and send a memorial to the Secretary of State for the Colonies. In 1925 a new governor arrived in the island, and in his first speech to the Legislative Council he announced that he had received instructions from the Secretary of State to submit draft legislation to cover trade unions and employers' liability for compensation to workmen injured in their service. He added that both subjects had been raised in two draft conventions prepared by the International Labour Organization and submitted to the British Government in accordance with Article 421 of the Treaty of Versailles.

A Trade Union Bill was eventually presented to the Legislative Council on 31st August 1926. This Bill was based on the law as it existed in England, except that it provided for compulsory registration. Unfortunately, however, before the Bill became law the Government of Mauritius, influenced by the General Strike which had occurred in Britain in May of that year, changed its mind. It is not possible to say for certain whether the governor was actually instructed by the Secretary of State to delay the Bill, so as to take into account the revisions in the British law which the Government had decided upon following the Strike, but it is apparent that the Mauritius Government fully appreciated the hostility that existed towards trade unions in some official quarters in Britain following the General Strike.

Notwithstanding the memorandum from Lord Passfield (Secretary of State for the Colonies) in 1930, it was not until 1938, and then only after serious disturbances had led to the appointment of a Committee of Inquiry, that the government of Mauritius was persuaded to introduce legislation to legalize trade unions. A consequence of the Government's refusal to legislate in favour of unions was the foundation, in 1936, of the Mauritius Labour Party. One of the first acts of this body was to pass a resolution 'that legislation be introduced in Mauritius to secure the working classes the right of association by trade unions, old age pensions and other measures recommended by the International Labour Bureau'. This resolution was sent to the Secretary of State for the Colonies, who replied that the British Government had no objection to the introduction of legislation in connection with trade unions, and any practicable proposal would be given sympathetic attention. But the Mauritius Government made no effort to introduce the necessary Bill until after a storm of industrial unrest broke out in the following year.

The Influence of Revolutionary Nationalism and Communism in Hong Kong and South-East Asia

In the colonies of Hong Kong, Malaya and Singapore, the growth of trade unionism was greatly influenced by the Chinese revolutionary movement led by Dr. Sun Yat-sen. As we have noted earlier, there had been guilds in China from much earlier times, and after 1911 some of them began to turn into trade unions. The most important of the organizations to make this transition was the Kwangtung Mechanics' Association, founded in Canton in 1909. In 1918 this organization, which included employers as well as wage-earners, joined forces with the Hong Kong Mechanics' Association. The employers, in the following year, left the Mechanics' Association to form their own Machine Trade Mutual Benefit Guild. In 1920 the Hong Kong Mechanics' Union asked for a wage increase and called out its 9,000 members in an effort to win its demands. This is thought to be the first modern example of the use of the strike as a collective bargaining weapon by the workers of Hong Kong.

A much larger and more significant stoppage occurred two years later, in January 1922, when the Chinese Seamen's Union induced its members in Hong Kong to strike for a wage increase. The Chinese Seamen's Union had been founded in the British Colony of Hong Kong in 1920, but its headquarters were in the neighbouring Chinese city of Canton. The cause of the strike was resentment against an increase in wages which had been granted to British and European seamen, but not to Chinese seamen. The Nationalist followers of Dr. Sun Yat-sen rapidly whipped up indignation against the treatment meted out to Chinese seamen by foreign shipowners, and the strike spread to many other trades when the Governor of Hong Kong made the mistake of declaring the Seamen's Union an unlawful organization. It is estimated that 50,000 people were on strike before an agreement, which gave the Chinese seamen a substantial increase in wages, was reached. Immediately following the settlement, the governor rescinded his order and the name board which had been removed from over the door of the office of the union was restored. At this time there was no law in Hong Kong which gave unions a legal status and regulated their behaviour.

The first national labour conference organized by the nationalists was held in Canton shortly after the seamen's successful strike in 1922. It was, however, the decision of Dr. Sun Yat-sen to ask for communist help and the arrival in China in 1923 of Michael Borodin, that really gave the development of trade unions a fillip. The communists saw the trade unions as a means of achieving their political goals and they did everything they could to foster their growth.[17] By 1925 it was estimated that there were some 200,000 workers in unions in Hong Kong, but there had been little development of organized relations between unions and employers.

The second labour congress, held in Canton in May 1925, was the high point of communist influence in the Kuomintang. The congress decided to create an All-China Federation of Labour and to affiliate to the Red International of Labour Unions. The British authorities were decidedly hostile to these developments, but they were unable to insulate Hong Kong against the influence of communist-dominated Canton.

A major disturbance was engineered by the left-wing leaders of the Kuomintang when, in 1926, demonstrations were staged against the foreign powers enjoying privileged status in China, which ended with British and French troops firing on rioting crowds. On 30th June of that year a general strike against foreign domination was called, and all Chinese labour was withdrawn. In Hong Kong the volunteer force was mobilized and troops were deployed to keep essential services going. The strike eventually collapsed, but a boycott of British goods and shipping was continued until October 1926.

The situation changed with the breakdown of relations between the nationalist leaders of the Kuomintang and the communists. Alarmed at the control which the communists had obtained over the labour movement in China, the nationalist leaders had all the red unions raided; many union leaders were arrested and the headquarters of the All-China Labour Federation were seized. Borodin was compelled to flee from China and relations with Moscow were ruptured. New labour laws were passed and the policy of revolutionary

[17] The second, fourth and sixth World Congress of the Communist International stressed that the development of trade unions was the most important of the immediate general tasks of the communists in the colonies.

unionism was abandoned in favour of promoting co-operation in industry and peaceful industrial relations, rather than constant conflict. The effect of this change in policy on the development of unions in China was naturally felt in Hong Kong and throughout South-East Asia. But the unions in Hong Kong were too closely connected with the Kuomintang and too deeply influenced by guild ideas to develop a collective bargaining system on the British model. Unions and employers remained at arm's length, neither side much concerned with the other.

The Chinese Engineering Mechanics' Association had existed in Malaya for many years, but it was in 1916 that the first trade union, the Malay Seamen's Association, was established. In 1920 a Clerical Workers' Union was organized in Singapore. However, it was not until 1924, when the communists began in earnest to organize unions, that a significant growth of trade union activity occurred. In the spring of 1924 an Indonesian communist spent some time in Singapore on his way to a communist-sponsored Pan-Pacific Labour Conference to be held in Canton. A representative of the Chinese Communist Party was later sent to Malaya to make contact with potential communist supporters. Little headway was made with the Malays and Indians, but communist influence among the Chinese grew steadily. A number of violent clashes with the police were provoked when strikes were stimulated and disturbances occurred.[18]

In 1926 the communists set up the Nan-Yang (South Seas) Federation of Labour, with headquarters in Singapore. The object of the Federation was to unite the communist-dominated labour organizations in Sumatra, Borneo, New Guinea, Celebes, Burma, Siam and Indo-China. At first, the attitude of the British authorities towards this Federation was to permit it to operate freely in the British territories. Two annual congresses were actually held in Singapore before the authorities decided that its activities had become so obviously menacing that action had to be taken against it. The Federation was further weakened by the split in the Kuomintang and the fierce internecine struggle for power that was taking place in China. The British authorities decided that the time had come

[18] See G. Z. Hanrahan, *The Communist Struggle in Malaya* (New York, 1954).

to outlaw the Federation after it had encouraged a series of strikes in Singapore and instructed its supporters to employ such violent methods as home-made bombs and arson as weapons against the 'imperialists'. A good many of the Chinese leaders of the revolutionary unions were thereafter deported to China, and this drastic policy curbed the political stimulation of union growth for some time.

Communist activity continued, however, and in 1930 a leading French communist agent, Joseph Ducroux, who had been sent to Malaya to organize the development of the trade unions and the Communist Party, was arrested in Singapore. From this man information was obtained which revealed a network of communist agents and organizations in South-East Asia. Acting on this evidence, the British authorities arrested, among other leading communists in Malay, the secretary of the Malayan Seamen's Union, the secretary of the Malayan Labour Union and the secretary of the Chinese Labour Union. Further action taken on Ducroux's confession led to the closing down of the Communist Far East Bureau in Hong Kong, and the arrest by the Chinese nationalists of the secretary of the Pan-Pacific Federation of Trade Unions in Shanghai.[19] The communists once again set about the task of rebuilding their shattered organization, and in 1934 they sponsored a Malayan General Labour Union. The Communist Far Eastern Bureau, now located in Shanghai, also made attempts to promote a Malay–Chinese Seamen's Union as a means of introducing communist agents into Singapore, but this plan was again frustrated by police action. The growth in the influence of the communists was evident, however, in a strike which occurred at the Batu Areng coal mine in 1935. This strike was organized with the deliberate intention of crippling the power stations and railways, which depended upon the mine for their fuel supplies. The communist-led strikers actually occupied the mine and established a 'Soviet' to run it. It was only after an assault had been launched by the police that the armed strikers were compelled to evacuate the mine and the strike was crushed. Batu Areng was immediately dramatically exploited by the communists as a glorious defence of the workers against 'capitalist

---

[19] See G. Z. Hanrahan, *ibid.*, and R. Onraet, *Singapore: A Police Background* (London, 1947).

imperialism', and during the next two or three years every opportunity was taken to provoke industrial unrest. The aim of the communists was to build up discontent until it resulted in a general strike. Had the British authorities been less active in their opposition to the designs of the communists, it is probable that they would have succeeded in achieving their aims. The Malayan Communist Party was, however, also seriously weakened by the continuous twists and turns of the Communist Party line to suit the interests of its Russian leaders. In 1940 the Malayan Communist Party received orders to cease all anti-British activity and to offer no opposition to aid offered by the Chinese in Malaya to the British war effort.[20] This instruction was undoubtedly determined by Russian rather than by Malay interests. Nevertheless, in spite of continual set-backs, there is little doubt that 'when the Japanese invaded Malaya in December 1941, the Malayan Communist Party had probably the most effective organization there, outside of that of the British "colonial government" '.[21]

The Communist Party was without question the most important factor in the development of labour organization in the period before the second world war in Malaya and Singapore. Perhaps a majority of the associations registered under the Societies Ordinance were dominated by the Party, although it was in fact an illegal organization. It is clear, however, that without the existence of the Communist Party there would still have been industrial unrest, since many of the strikes that occurred in these territories were spontaneous expressions of protest by workers angered by wage cuts, generally bad conditions of employment, the widespread abuse of the contract system of hiring and racial discrimination. A weakness in the communist-led associations was their failure to organize the Malays and Indians. The communist-led unions were over-whelmingly Chinese, because the majority of urban employees were of that race, but this was not the only factor. The other races in Malaya and Singapore were afraid of Chinese domination and for this reason were generally reluctant to accept Chinese leadership of the trade unions. Outside Hong Kong and the areas in South-East Asia where the Chinese were influential the Communist Party had less influence on the growth

[20] See Hanrahan, *op. cit.*, p. 24.   [21] See Hanrahan, *op. cit.*, p. 26.

of labour movements in the colonial territories before the second
world war.

*The Influence of Changing Social and Economic Factors on
    Trade Union Development*

In the period between the two world wars the immense social
and economic changes which were to lead to the political independence of many of the territories within the next few decades
began to make their impression.   These developments fostered
the growth of trade unions and accelerated changes in British
policy that gave a further impetus to the organization of
labour.

In every territory the population was growing and urban
communities were expanding.   For centuries the population of
the colonial territories had been held in check by famine and
pestilence.   With the conquest of malaria and the control of
other tropical diseases, populations were increasing rapidly
everywhere.   In many of the territories there had formerly
been a great shortage of labour, and the problem of economic
development had been to find enough men and women able and
willing to work on the estates and plantations, in the mines and
on the roads, railways and other public services.   To meet the
needs of an acute shortage of labour, employers had been
allowed and encouraged to sponsor the migration of thousands
of labourers.   In certain areas in Africa over-population made
heavy demands on limited supplies of food, and taxoatin forced
many men to leave their villages to work on the plantations and
in the mines.   As the tradition of working for wages became
more and more firmly established, there was a growing drift to
the towns and compounds.

The development of transport facilities brought people who
had been remote from industrial civilization into contact with
employment opportunities.   Expansion of the copper, gold and
coal mines in Africa, the development of bauxite in the West
Indies, the discovery and exploitation of oil in Trinidad, Brunei
and Sarawak, the expansion of settler-farming, estate and
plantation agriculture, together with the building of com-
modity-processing plants created new opportunities for employment.   In the vanguard as a source of regular paid
employment were the governments of the territories themselves.

It was the governments that built roads and railways, developed ports and airfields, administered health and other social services.

As the working population grew larger and the need and desire to seek paid employment became a more significant factor, the gap between employers and employed created by differences in race, colour, language and social and political status grew more evident, and low wages, harsh discipline and arbitrary treatment became harder to bear. Employers, for the most part, may well have been decent, good-hearted men, but they tended to look upon their workers merely as labour, conceding them few rights and granting them only the lowest possible wages and conditions of employment. In these respects there was nothing to choose between expatriate British employers and those of local origin, but for the organizers of labour protests the white employer and the government were easily identified as the common alien oppressor.

In the early stages of their development in all the colonial territories, trade unions aroused the fear and opposition of employers and governing circles. In their reaction to the emergence of trade unions, employers in the colonies behaved in exactly the same manner as employers had behaved in Britain and other countries when trade unions first appeared to challenge their authority. They did their best to make union organization as difficult as possible, and they were generally supported by the governments of the territories until British policy and the trend of events compelled a change of attitude. Even when colonial governments changed their policy from hostility to qualified acceptance and then to the encouragement and assistance of trade unions, many employers still refused to recognize attempts to bargain collectively. Their reluctance to acknowledge the existence of trade unions tended to encourage an aggressive leadership as similar attitudes had done in Britain in the nineteenth century.[22]

---

[22] 'African workers, growing rapidly aware that it is in their interest to organize and act collectively and observing that European workers do exactly that, will organize and act collectively whether governments or employers or anybody else wish to permit it or not. And such non-permitted, possibly illegal collective action and organization, by virtue of being illegal or without recognition, tends to be led by men more revolutionary and more irresponsible and less reasonable than the accepted and recognized trade unions leaders would have been' (R. E. Luyt, *Trade Unionism in African Colonies* (South African Institute of Race Relations), New African Pamphlets no. 19, Johannesburg, 1949, p. 16).

Under the conditions of employment that existed in every territory there were ample grounds for protest and from time to time there were eruptions of discontent, but it was only when conditions became unbearable that demonstrations, and sometimes rioting and violence occurred. The transition from spontaneous demonstration to organized trade unionism began to develop with the emergence of leaders with the ideas and skills necessary to organize and administer continuing associations. This leadership was drawn from various fields; in the case of government employees, teachers and literate skilled workers such as printers, it emerged from within. In other cases the inspiration to form unions came from outsiders, from politicians and lawyers, ambitious businessmen and clerical workers; in short, from men who saw unions as a means to achieve ideological and personal ends.

The desire to emulate European and American standards and institutions such as trade unions was greatly stimulated by the growth of travel overseas. Jamaicans employed in the Panama Canal Zone and in the United States as agricultural labourers, returned home with eyes opened by their experiences. An important influence in the West Indies during the 1920's was the United Negro Improvement Association, an organization founded in the United States by a Jamaican, Marcus Garvey, for the emancipation of the negro throughout the world. Garvey was a messianic figure and his appeal was to the dreams of the coloured man everywhere. Although, on his return from the United States, he was not successful in building a viable organization in the West Indies, his influence on the mass of low-paid workers was considerable and his movement was, without question, a potent stimulus to their thought and action.

The communication of ideas which developed in Britain, Europe and America to the indigenous people of the colonies was perhaps most effectively conveyed through education. Mission and government schools brought the people of the colonies into touch with the ways of life of the more advanced white countries. The more intelligent pupils were often encouraged and helped to travel to Britain, America, Europe and the Antipodes to further their education. These colonial students returned to their own countries imbued with the ideas of liberal democracy and the revolutionary notions of Marxism.

They were greedy consumers of doctrines that had been distilled in the long transition from medieval feudalism to pluralistic democracy in Britain. They saw no reason why what was good for their colonial masters should not be good for them. They returned home to preach the gospel of freedom, the right to be independent, the right to organize, the right to strike and also the destructive doctrine that industrial development was merely capitalistic imperialism.

The determination of those who had been to Britain and the other white countries to achieve the self-respecting status of independence for their homelands was greatly enhanced by their experiences overseas. They were made painfully aware of the fact that coloured peoples were generally regarded as inferior. Although they did not experience in Britain the vicious colour discrimination that existed in the southern states of America, most of them were subjected to prejudice in some form. They also had the experience of being received on terms of complete equality in British universities. There they were treated like all the other students without discrimination and without being patronized. Often, however, when they returned home they found that British and American companies only employed expatriate foremen, supervisors and managers from their own countries and the government service was generally manned in all its higher reaches by non-local civil servants.

In these circumstances, the students who went overseas generally became lawyers rather than engineers or doctors. In the period between the two wars, law was the profession which promised the highest rewards; this is only now beginning to change. Since law is intimately related to politics, it was not surprising that lawyers frequently became the nucleus of unions and other groups bent on bringing about social and political change.

Those who went overseas naturally made contact with sympathetic left-wing groups in Britain and elsewhere. They were encouraged by left-wing socialists and communists to organize opinion and movements against the colonial power. Organized labour in Britain, which was beginning to take an interest in the affairs of Africans and Indians, Malays and Chinese, expressed goodwill and started to give constructive assistance. This began in a limited way in the period between the wars, but it was tangible enough to be felt and appreciated. It was not always necessary to travel overseas to be brought into contact with ideas that stimulated trade union development. With the gradual spread of literacy, books, pamphlets and newspapers became an increasingly important source of inspiration.[23] During the inter-war period in the West Indies, where literacy was probably the highest in the British colonies, labour papers were published in a number of territories. In Jamaica, *Public Opinion*; in Trinidad, *The Pilot*, *The Socialist* and *The People*; in British Guiana, *The Guiana Review*; in Barbados, *The Barbados Observer*.[24]

The great depression in the 1930's severely checked the economic development of the colonies and was a potent stimulant to agitation that culminated in the establishment of trade unions and political organizations. Falling wages and rising unemployment, brought about by the world slump in economic activity, stirred workers to protest in the West Indies, Africa, Mauritius and South-East Asia. Numerous strikes and demonstrations were organized and disturbances occurred on a widespread scale in the West Indies.[25]

The riots in the Caribbean were of great social significance, since they induced a somewhat complacent British Government to take major steps to discover the cause of the unrest and to make critical changes in policy that were to be of profound consequence.

---

[23] Mr. Christopher Loblack, one of the founders and first President of the Dominica Trade Union, has recounted to the author how he became interested in unionism through a book *The Martyrs of Tolpuddle* (published by the British Trades Union Congress), which fell into his hands during the war. After reading about George Loveless and his brave companions Loblack decided that he would form a union in Dominica. One year later, in 1945, with the assistance of one or two prominent figures in Dominican affairs, and after receiving guidance from a visiting British labour adviser, the first trade union in the island was founded. The Dominica Trade Union was, from the outset, a general union and it secured members from among field workers, port workers, masons and carpenters, shop assistants and government employees. Its objectives were to improve the wages and working conditions of these members, but the attainment of these objectives could not be divorced from the wider and deeper political aspirations of self-government and the social and political advancement of the coloured working man.

[24] See E. E. Williams, *The Negro in the Caribbean* (Washington, 1942).

[25] List of places and dates where serious disturbances occurred as given in the *Report of the West India Royal Commission*: May–July 1934, Trinidad; January 1935, St. Kitts; May 1935, Jamaica; September–October 1935, British Guiana; October 1935, Jamaica and St. Vincent; June 1937, Trinidad; July 1937, Barbados; May–June 1938, Jamaica; February 1939, British Guiana. (*The West India Royal Commission Report*, Cmnd. 6607, January 1945.)

D

The West India Royal Commission, set up in 1938 to investigate the social and economic conditions which had given
rise to the unrest and to make recommendations, was to produce
a report which had a powerful impact on official policy and it
proved to have as stimulating an influence on trade union development in the West Indies as its predecessor forty years
earlier.   To obtain an immediate report on the labour situation,[26] the British Government also decided to send out Major
Orde Browne, whose appointment as special adviser to the
Secretary of State for the Colonies on labour questions, in 1938,
had been brought about by the stirring of unrest in the West
Indies.

The Royal Commission stated bluntly in its report that the
'disturbances can only be regarded as a symptom of which the
principal causes are low earnings and irregular employment'.
A statement made by the Secretary of State for the Colonies,
Mr. Malcolm MacDonald, who had been responsible for the
appointment of the commission and its composition, is quoted
in the report as being 'entirely accurate' in its description of the
origins of the disturbances.   The Colonial Secretary had said
that 'these feelings of unrest are a protest against the economic
distress, uncertainty of employment, low rates of wages, bad
housing conditions in many cases, and so on'.

The effect of the economic depression on colonial development and the social and political pressures it generated speeded
up changes in policy that had gradually been gathering
momentum since the first world war.   Colonial governments
were urged by the Secretary of State to adopt social legislation
to improve housing, public health, conditions of employment,
and to encourage the orderly development of labour organization.   The Secretary of State also pressed the territories to
establish labour departments, where these did not exist, so that
the necessary legislation could be effectively administered.

These developments were of great importance, since they
gave a positive encouragement to the development of labour
organization.   Because they feared that this would be the case,
local interests were often strongly against following the advice
of the Secretary of State and they frequently procrastinated for
as long as they could, but caught between the pressures exerted

[26] *Labour Conditions in the West Indies*, Cmnd. 6070.

by events in the colonies and by Whitehall, they reluctantly and gradually conceded the case for new laws and new attitudes towards labour.

It is possible now to summarize the major factors responsible for stimulating the growth of trade unionism in the British territories overseas that we are examining. Essentially they were the same kind of factors that had been responsible for stimulating union growth in the older industrial countries. First and foremost was the emergence of an employed paid labour force. This did not follow the same pattern in every territory. In some, plantations were the first to provide large-scale employment; in others, it was in trade and transport and in the mines; in all of them the public service has been an important source of employment—industry was the least significant in the first period of trade union development.[27]

Before unions, as distinct from demonstrations, could be established, it was necessary to have a sufficient number of persons with the skills and knowledge to organize and lead them. As in the early British trade unions, some of the first leaders were skilled artisans, clerical employees and middle-class professional men interested in social reform. The growth of opportunities to acquire education, to travel and to make contact with trade unionists in other countries gradually increased the number of employees with the desire and the social skills to form unions.

In addition to the pressures on work-people, inducing them to organize, that were generated by the conditions of employment, unions were also stimulated by the subordinate state of employees, in the political, as well as the industrial structure of their country. In this respect the workers in British overseas territories were in a similar position to that in which workers in Britain had found themselves in the nineteenth century when they began to form their unions. There was, of course, the fundamental difference that in the colonial territories the workers were generally of a different race and colour from the men who were responsible for the government and industrial management.

In the first stages of union development in the West Indies, nationalism and racialism were probably factors of no more

[27] See Chapter 12.

importance in stirring the workers to take the initial steps to form unions than the absence of political democracy had been in Britain in the nineteenth century, but they became much more powerful elements, stimulating union growth and development in the later period.

CHAPTER 2

THE GROWTH OF UNIONS
SINCE 1938

THE development of trade unions in the past twenty years has been spectacular. At the outbreak of the second world war there were in all the colonial territories about 100 unions in existence, with probably not more than 50,000 members. By 1960[1] there were more than 1,500 unions, and membership numbered well over 1,000,000. The numerical increase is, of course, only one aspect of the evolution of trade unionism. The large increase in the number of unions, in one respect, indicates a weakness that prevails in a number of territories—too many small, inefficient and ineffective organizations.

The pattern of trade union development has not been uniform in spite of the common factors, such as British policy, that have exercised an influence on union growth. Local differences in tradition, racial composition, geography, politics and the pace and character of industrial and commercial expansion have all exerted their pressures. In this chapter, the main course of union development in each of the more important territories in the years since 1938 will be examined.

West Indies

By the end of the second world war, unions were well established throughout the West Indies. In a number of the territories the most vigorous organizations were large blanket-unions, ready to organize all and sundry, irrespective of grade, skill or industry. These unions began as movements of social protest led by messianic leaders such as Alexander Bustamante in Jamaica and Uriah Butler in Trinidad, who appealed to the mass of less-skilled, poverty-stricken labourers. It is a measure of the progress that has taken place that 'Busta', now Sir Alexander Bustamante, became the Prime Minister of an

---

[1] These figures of registered unions and their membership represent a true rate of growth, but they must be taken only as an approximate scale of development, since completely accurate figures cannot be obtained.

independent Jamaica, while Butler lost all influence in an equally independent Trinidad.   What these leaders had to offer was not trade unionism of a conventional kind, but an onslaught against the established authorities, the government, white men and employers.   Specific demands were often unclear, and when they were made they quite frequently bordered on the fantastic.   These were not the only unions in existence, but they were the ones that had attracted attention by the extravagant claims and violent methods advocated by their leaders.   The more orthodox unions of significance that were established in Jamaica and Trinidad catered for skilled workers, public service employees, school teachers, and dock and transport workers.

For a brief period Bustamante worked with the other organizations in the Jamaican Trade Union Advisory Council, but he failed to dominate this body and he withdrew his union. With the introduction of a new constitution for the colony in 1944, Bustamante formed the Jamaican Labour Party and won a sweeping victory in the elections of that year.   Formally, the Jamaican Labour Party was a separate organization from the Bustamante Industrial Trade Union, but in practice they were both ruled in the same interest and followed the same policy.

In 1949 the unions in the Jamaican T.U.C. amalgamated into one composite organization, linked closely with the socialist People's National Party.   In effect this meant that there were two large unions in Jamaica competing against each other. Three years later, Norman Manley, leader of the P.N.P., decided that it was necessary to form a new general trade union that would be more closely related to the People's National Party than the T.U.C. had been.   The decision arose out of an internal conflict between the moderate socialist Manley and his supporters in the People's National Party, and a group of communist leaders of unions that had formed and dominated the Jamaican Trade Union Council.   It was feared by Manley and his friends that this group of communist supporters might succeed in capturing power within the P.N.P., through their influence in the T.U.C.   The P.N.P. leader thus felt compelled to start a new union when the communist group of trade union leaders was expelled from the P.N.P.   The National Workers'

Union, created by the P.N.P., had a very shaky start, but after a difficult period made headway under the vigorous leadership of a number of very able young men. A large proportion of the membership of the T.U.C. and a certain number of the members of the Bustamante Industrial Trade Union were attracted, so that by 1959 the N.W.U. had grown as large as the Bustamante Union, while the T.U.C. had shrunk to a mere fraction of its former size.

In the smaller islands of Antigua, St. Kitts-Nevis, Dominica, St. Vincent, St. Lucia, Grenada and Barbados the course of union development was similar to that of Jamaica. In each case a blanket-union was organized, but there were important differences in the pattern of leadership. In Antigua and St. Kitts-Nevis the leaders of the all-embracing union emulated Bustamante, founding successful political parties with the difference that they were not troubled by a rival union and a rival party. In St. Vincent and Grenada, the more primitive, demagogic type of union leader emerged and without an educated middle class to influence the course of developments, unionism and politics in these two islands have been more raw and crude than anywhere else in the West Indies.[2]

Trade union developments in Barbados took a different course. Under the leadership of two intellectuals, educated in Britain and supported by a number of exceptionally able workers, a general union embracing engineers, painters, longshoremen, coopers, bakers and seamen was brought into being in 1941. The Barbados Workers' Union grew out of a political organization, the Barbados Progressive League, which subsequently became the Barbados Labour Party. What is interesting about these developments is that while the union and party had a common root, they developed as completely separate organizations. The clear distinction between the union and the party owed something to British experience and advice, but it was due even more to the personal incompatibility between the leader of the Barbados Labour Party, one of the founders and former president of the union, and the man who succeeded him as leader of the union. What was perhaps even more important was the fact that neither union

[2] See Simon Rottenberg, 'Labour Relations in an Underdeveloped Economy', *Economic Development and Cultural Change I*, December 1952.

nor party was dependent on the other for its success in its own sphere of activity.

The pattern of trade unionism that developed in Trinidad and British Guiana, in spite of the early development of large and important unions under the powerful leadership of Butler and Critchlow, turned out to be quite different from the other territories. Instead of one all-embracing general union and an intimately associated political party, a variety of unions emerged with a far from united political policy. A fundamental factor influencing the development of trade unions that differentiated Trinidad and British Guiana from the other territories was the multi-racial composition of their population. Since the political parties reflected these divisions, trade unions were compelled to avoid political commitments in order to preserve their non-racial character. In both Trinidad and British Guiana, trades union councils were established as independent bodies.

The fact that the unions in Trinidad and British Guiana have maintained a politically independent position does not mean that their leaders and members have not been politically active. For example, the leaders of the Trinidad Oil Workers' Union, which had been founded in 1938 by a well-known Marxist Indian lawyer, leaned towards the extreme left in the period after the second world war. John Rojas, the leader of the Oil Workers' Trade Union, was closely associated with the leader of the Federated Workers' Union, Quintin O'Connor, one of the oldest and best-known trade unionists in the Caribbean, who made no secret of his communist sympathies. The leaders of these two unions were active supporters of the West Indian Independence Party founded in 1952 under communist influence. In the event, Rojas and O'Connor both resigned from the W.I.I.P., and in 1954 the Oil Workers' Trade Union disaffiliated from the World Federation of Trade Unions; since that time the Oil Workers' Trade Union and the Federated Workers' Union have kept clear of political alliances. The determination of Rojas' and O'Connor's successor, Simeon Alexander, to maintain an independent position brought these leaders into serious conflict with Eric Williams, the socialist leader of the People's National Movement, who believed they should give him and his party their active support. After the

P.N.M. formed a government in 1957, the party's newspaper conducted a bitter campaign of vilification against Rojas and his associates in the Trinidad T.U.C. because they refused to ally themselves with the P.N.M. This breach between the Oil Workers' Union and the P.N.M. was eventually healed with changes in the leadership of the union and also in the party.

In spite of political difficulties, racial tensions and organizational weaknesses the economic growth of Trinidad has provided a favourable environment for the development of the trade unions. Under the leadership of able men, the Oil Workers' Trade Union became one of the best organized and administered unions in the tropical Commonwealth. By comparison, the organization of workers employed on the sugar estates was weak and largely ineffective until the British T.U.C. decided, in 1956, to provide the All-Trinidad Sugar Estates and Factory Workers' Union with substantial financial aid together with the help of an experienced British trade union official. By July 1957, membership had increased from 350 to 4,000; recognition was won, and in 1958 the employers agreed to check-off union contributions. Over the two decades from 1937 to 1957, unions in Trinidad increased from 5 to 67 and membership rose to over 50,000.

Trade unionism made considerable progress in British Guiana after 1937. By 1946 there were 27 unions registered with a notified membership of over 6,000. The largest union, the Manpower Citizens' Association, had its main support on the sugar estates, and its membership was mainly East Indian. The M.P.C.A. and the British Guiana Labour Union, after the failure of an initial attempt to found a central trade union body in 1944, succeeded in forming a T.U.C. with eleven other unions. Racial and political tensions disturbed relations between the unions and the M.P.C.A. withdrew from the T.U.C. two years later. Following this split in the trade union movement the leaders of the British Guiana Labour Union, a union with its main membership among the negro port workers in Georgetown, gave strong support to the British Guiana Labour Party; this party won five seats in the elections of 1947. The M.P.C.A., which had sponsored six of its own candidates, gained only one seat. However, the British Guiana Labour

Party leaders could not agree on policy, and the party soon collapsed as a result of internecine conflict.

Out of the wreck of the Labour Party, Cheddi and Janet Jagan, together with a number of young intellectual negroes, formed the People's Progressive Party in 1950. Most of the unions, with the exception of the M.P.C.A., after an initial period of uncertainty, gave their backing to the new party, which then commanded an impressive array of support. In the elections of April 1953, held under the new constitution of the colony, the P.P.P. had a sweeping victory. Unfortunately, in its eagerness to put its Marxist ideas into effect, the P.P.P. Government provoked a political crisis that resulted in the suspension of the constitution.

One of the major issues in the crisis was a Labour Relations Ordinance; this was to provide for the compulsory recognition by employers of any union that obtained, by ballot, the support of 52 per cent. of the employees in an industry. This procedure was borrowed from the United States, where it had been introduced as part of a comprehensive reform of the industrial relations system under the National Labour Relations Act of 1935. Had the Ordinance been submitted for the purpose of improving industrial relations, it could have been defended on its merits, but the motive behind its introduction lay in the conflict that was taking place between the M.P.C.A. and the Guiana Industrial Workers' Union.

The Guiana Industrial Workers' Union had been founded under the influence of Dr. Jagan, after he had failed to capture control of the M.P.C.A., of which earlier he had been the treasurer. The G.I.W.U. had sought to destroy the M.P.C.A. by promoting industrial unrest, but these efforts had not been rewarded by success either in terms of membership or recognition by the Sugar Producers' Association.[3]

When the P.P.P. was returned to office, official support was given to the G.I.W.U. and Dr. Latchmansingh remained President of the Union, in spite of his appointment as Minister of Health. The Minister of Labour pressed the Sugar Producers' Association to recognize the G.I.W.U., but the government was not satisfied with the offer of the Association to

[3] Cf. *Commission of Inquiry into the Sugar Industry* (H.M.S.O., Colonial no. 249, 1949) and Reports of Registrar of Trade Unions, British Guiana.

recognize both unions, and it promoted a strike of the employees in the sugar industry. Failing to secure the support of other workers, the Minister of Health ordered the sugar-estate employees back to work and announced that recognition would be achieved by legislation. The government sought to push this bill through in one day by organizing a mob demonstration in the Parliament Building and by seeking to suspend the Standing Orders. When the Speaker refused to accept this motion as contrary to parliamentary practice, he was forced to leave the Chamber, and the leader of the opposition had to be given police protection against the threats of the crowd which, exhorted by Ministers, had stormed the Chamber.[4] It was these incidents and the breakdown of the administration of the territory that led to the intervention of the British Government and the suspension of the constitution.

After the suspension of the constitution, political divisions appeared in the ranks of the P.P.P. and in 1955 a split occurred. Forbes Burnham, leader of the negro element in the P.P.P., broke away from the Jagans to form a new party. In the meantime the unions in the British Guiana T.U.C. adopted an independent position. The M.P.C.A., with the assistance of the British T.U.C., gradually built up its organization, which had suffered from the political turmoil, until it became without any doubt the most powerful union in the colony. By 1959 it had won substantial concessions from the S.P.A., including the check-off. Its membership in 1961 was probably about 20,000, of which three-quarters were employed by the sugar plantations. Several other unions in British Guiana were also able to show good progress, including the Civil Servants' Union, the British Guiana Mineworkers' Union and the Transport Workers' Union. These organizations had each established bargaining procedures and had negotiated collective agreements of an up-to-date kind. The unions in British Guiana, as in Trinidad and the other islands of the West Indies, still suffered from many organizational weaknesses, but by 1960 they had made remarkable progress and become important elements in the industrial and political life of the territories.

[4] See *British Guiana, the Suspension of the Constitution*. Report of a Commission of Inquiry, Cmnd. 8980, October 1953.

Unfortunately, with the entry of the leader of M.P.C.A. into active political association with the leader of a rival party, the P.P.P. once again gave its support to a new trade union, the Guiana Sugar Workers' Union, which was reported to have gained some 8,000 members by mid-1962.[5]

West Africa

The Gambia was the first African colony to adopt a trade union ordinance. This step was taken in 1932, but neighbouring Nigeria and Sierra Leone did not pass trade union legislation until 1938 and 1939, and Ghana followed suit only in 1941. A number of unions already existed in all of the West African territories before these ordinances were passed, but the legalizing of unions evoked an immediate response, and within the next few years a significant number of unions had registered.

The first trade union to register in Nigeria under the Trade Union Ordinance in 1938 was the Nigerian Railway Workers' Union. This organization had been founded in 1931 as a 'breakaway' from the Nigerian Civil Service Union by men who were out of sympathy with the no-strike policy of the Civil Service Union. Agitation against the unjust treatment of African employees by certain of the European management and constant demands for the upgrading of technical and craft workers enabled the union to attract considerable support. In the same year as the Railway Workers' Union was established the Nigerian Union of Teachers was founded; this organization was registered in 1941.

The passing of the Trade Union Ordinance gave an immense fillip to trade union organization, and within the next two years 14 unions with a membership of 4,629 had been established. By 1944 the number had been increased to 91 unions with a membership of 30,000, and by 1958 to no less than 298 unions with a returned membership of 236,000.

The growth of the trade union movement in the West African colonies was by no means a smooth development. The newly created organizations had many problems to overcome, but they were helped considerably by labour departments and by

[5] Dr. Jagan also seems bent on trying again to bring the unions under the control of the government by legislation similar to that over which he was thwarted in 1953.

the labour officers from the United Kingdom who had been specially appointed to assist the unions.

In 1946 the Secretary of State for the Colonies sent a memorandum to all four territories stressing the importance attached by the British Government to the active promotion of good industrial relations by departments of labour. As a step towards this end, labour advisory boards made up of representatives of unions and employers were established in each territory.[6] Minimum wage boards were also set up and Whitley councils were eventually brought into being in the Civil Service. In Sierra Leone wages councils had been established in 1945.

These efforts to create a sound structure of industrial relations met with many difficulties, and the period following the second world war was marked by a considerable number of strikes and a number of serious disturbances. The troubles were threefold. In the first place the unions were immature, unstable and often badly led. In the second place employers showed little understanding of the significance of the development of unions, and they often resisted attempts to bargain instead of helping and encouraging them. The employers were, of course, almost as ignorant of modern industrial relations techniques as were the unions; there was, however, less excuse for their negative response. In the third place the unions were in one degree or another associated with rising independence movements. The combined influence of these factors stimulated the unions to make demands that could not be satisfied as quickly as their leaders had led members to believe.

The structure of the Nigerian trade union movement was as disorderly as that of the British. It included all types of unions —occupational, craft, industrial and general. Many of the unions were small and membership was confined to a single employer. Often new unions were established for only a few workers and the life of these organizations was quite frequently very short.

The need for some kind of central body to co-ordinate the activities of the multifarious organizations which had sprung up was recognized fairly early in Nigeria. After negotiations, propaganda and persuasion, 31 unions were persuaded to send

[6] The L.A.B.'s in Nigeria were really minimum wage boards, and no labour advisory board as such was established until about 1956.

delegates to a conference, held in July 1942, to found a Trades Union Congress. The Labour Department reported in the following year 'that this Trades Union Congress is already functioning satisfactorily and has rendered considerable assistance to the Department of Labour in the settlement of disputes and the general application of labour measures'.[7]

The promising start made by the Nigerian T.U.C. was not, however, consolidated. Personal rivalries and the strain created by an ill-advised general strike proved too much for the strength of the organization, and the T.U.C. collapsed five years after its foundation. During the next decade successive attempts were made to build up a central organization that would unify the politically divided unions, but each fresh start was quickly followed by a revival of old suspicions, which within a few months led again to internecine warfare and the formation of yet another central body by a breakaway group.

Before full independence was achieved in 1960, the two events which had the most powerful influence on the development of industrial relations in Nigeria were the General Strike of 1945 and the tragic shooting affray during the strike at Enugu in 1949.

The General Strike of 1945 brought to an end a period in which there had been close co-operation between trade unions and the government. 'Everyone seemed satisfied that the trade union movement had at least got off to a good start.'[8]   The General Strike, therefore, came as a great shock to the government, especially since it arose out of claims made by Civil Service unions.   The main point at issue was a promise made by the governor in 1942 to keep the cost-of-living allowance in step with any change in the level of prices.   The strike began when the government refused to grant an increase in wage rates and allowances on grounds of maintaining a stable economy.   Once the stoppage had commenced, it spread to other occupations fairly quickly and nationalist politicians were quick to grasp its value to their cause.

The General Strike of 1945 did not, however, rouse feelings as much as did the dispute at Enugu in 1949.   This dispute eventually led to a situation in which the police fired on de-

---

[7] Quoted by T. M. Yesufu, *An Introduction to Industrial Relations in Nigeria* (Oxford, 1962).

[8] T. M. Yesufu, *ibid.*

monstrating workers, killing and wounding over 50 persons. Widespread civil disturbances followed this unfortunate incident.   Although the judical inquiry into these events found the trade union leaders concerned to be culpable, having grossly misled their followers,[9] the breakdown in industrial relations was to no small extent provoked by the insensitive attitude of the colliery management and the behaviour of administrative officers, who appear to have been quite out of touch with many aspects of the situation.[10]   Blame for the shooting was found by the Commission of Enquiry to rest largely with the police, who had found themselves in a difficult situation, owing to errors of leadership, and had precipitately used their arms.

Since 1950 considerable progress has been made.   The trade union movement of Nigeria has many problems to overcome, but in spite of splits and divisions at the national level, largely brought about by the political struggle between the International Confederation of Free Trade Unions and the World Federation of Trade Unions, many gains have been made locally.   While the trade union movement is still beset by the problem of too many small units, influenced by the pulls and pushes of regional and national politics, and torn by personal animosities, some of the unions of government employees have overcome these difficulties.   The Teachers' Union is an especially notable example of a soundly organized union, well administered and constructively led.

In Sierra Leone, some 24 per cent. of the employed labour force were on the trade union books in 1959.   The actual figure for paid-up members would be much lower, but nevertheless the trade unions in this territory are generally stable organizations.   Most workers are covered by wage negotiations and wage rates settled by collective bargaining are enforceable by law.   Wage rates in Sierra Leone appear to be among the highest in West Africa;   how far this is due to the well-organized character of the unions it is difficult to say, but they have certainly exercised some influence.

[9] See *Report of Commission of Enquiry into the Disorders in the Eastern Provinces of Nigeria*, November 1949 (H.M.S.O., Colonial No. 256, 1950).   The findings of the Commission with regard to the individual chiefly concerned were that 'His behaviour at best showed a greater interest in his financial improvement than was consistent with his devotion to the cause of the miners, and at worst exposed him to the charge that he deliberately used his position to enrich himself'.

[10] *Op. cit.*

The origins of trade unions in Sierra Leone may be traced back to before the first world war, but it was not until after the trade union ordinance was passed in 1939 that any were registered. By 1942 there were 11 unions in existence with a membership of 5,000; in 1958 the number had increased to 23 and the membership to over 26,000.

The most interesting feature of trade union development in Sierra Leone has been the remarkable stability of the unions. Compared with adjacent territories, Sierra Leone has not suffered from a multiplicity of small overlapping unions. In the early stages of union development the labour department under the influence of Mr. Edgar Parry, a British trade union official who had gone out as a labour adviser, successfully persuaded labour leaders to combine their organizations into effective units, and this structure has been maintained by legislation forbidding the registration of competing unions. Thus the outlines of the present structure, which were already formed by 1946, were firmly consolidated by a deliberate policy imposed on the unions. Moreover, among the general secretaries of the Freetown unions in 1940, there were a few, notably H. W. Georgestone, M. C. Grant, S. P. Stevens and G. Thomas, who have remained among the leaders of Sierra Leone unionism throughout the years. All of them showed exceptional ability at combining effective union leadership with political activity.

The half-dozen larger unions are continually active in negotiating individual grievances with individual employers and departments, as well as pursuing major claims through a long-established machinery of collective bargaining based upon a system of joint industrial councils.

In 1955 there was an unfortunate breakdown of relations between the unions and employers in two of the most important joint industrial councils, culminating in a serious riot. A subsequent inquiry[11] strongly criticized both union leaders and employers for failing to show a better understanding of the requirements of collective bargaining; the government was also found to have been at fault in a number of respects, and proposals were made to improve the machinery of industrial relations. The effect of this incident was to impress on all con-

[11] *Commission of Inquiry into the Strike and Riots in Freetown in February, 1955* (G.P., Sierra Leone).

cerned the dangers of a breakdown of negotiations and the need
to improve relations all round.

One of the problems has been that in spite of the development
of a quite mature system of industrial relations the unions are
often poorly administered. Two of the most important organizations, the Railway Workers and the United Mineworkers,
have obtained the 'check-off', and it is the confident hope of all
concerned that this will enable them to improve their organizational arrangements. During the last decade there has been a
steady growth in union membership in the provinces, especially
in the Artisans' Union which is now the largest in the territory,
but this has given rise to problems of communication and administration which are far from being solved.

A Sierra Leone T.U.C. was established soon after the first
unions were registered, but a split occurred which was not
mended until 1946. The Sierra Leone Council of Labour, then
brought into existence, remains active today. Its objects are to
promote the interests of all affiliated organizations and generally
to seek to improve the economic and social conditions of the
workers. The Council lists its aims as the achievement of full
citizenship, extension of state and municipal enterprise,
workers' participation in the management of public services, a
legal minimum wage and working week, unemployment provisions, pension rights, better housing and education facilities.
The Council has not, however, been developed as a militant
political body, as has happened in a number of other territories.
It is frequently consulted by the government and it participates
in a quietly influential advisory 'Joint Consultative Committee'
with representatives of the employers. This committee considers all proposed labour legislation and most other matters of
labour policy; its recommendations seem to be generally
accepted.

A Labour Party was formed some years ago by Marcus Grant,
a former labour leader, who had been severely criticized for his
part in the 1955 riot. The party fought the 1957 elections, but
lost every seat and most of its deposits. In 1961, S. P. Stevens,
with support from a section of the unions, formed a new party.

Following the passing of a Trade Union Ordinance in 1941,
the first trade union was registered in the Gold Coast in 1942;
by 1952 there were 73 unions with a combined membership of

E

almost 50,000.[12]   All types of unions had been established, but many were small, weak, badly-led house unions that were not capable of protecting their members' interests properly.   As in Nigeria, and by contrast with Sierra Leone, the trade union movement in the Gold Coast was torn by personal rivalries and conflicting ideologies.

The trade unions played quite an important part in the fight waged by Dr. Nkrumah to achieve independence.   The leaders of the unions were rather suspicious of the nationalist movement, but they were compelled by the course of events and the rising tide of nationalist sentiment to identify themselves with the movement for independence.

When in January 1950 Nkrumah launched his Action Campaign it was with union support.   A few months earlier a situation had arisen which had led the Gold Coast T.U.C. to threaten to call a general strike.   This came about when the government dismissed a number of employees in the meteorological department who had gone on strike, in spite of a warning that they would be acting in breach of contract and therefore were liable to dismissal.   The government responded to the T.U.C.'s threat with a strong statement that a general strike would be illegal and that it would have to take appropriate measures to protect the public interest.   The strike of meteorological officers petered out, but the T.U.C. continued to attack the government.   It demanded the withdrawal of an official circular concerning the political activities of civil servants and called for the immediate granting of Dominion status to the Gold Coast.

Angry with the government and influenced by Nkrumah's nationalist movement, the T.U.C. issued notice of a general strike on 7th January 1950.   On the following day Nkrumah declared that the time had come to take positive action against the colonial government.   The response was great in Accra; shops were closed, railways and road transport ceased, but the Mines Employees' Union did not participate in this show of nationalist feeling.   The government declared a state of emergency and the army assumed control of Accra.   The strike lasted, however, until 19th January.   Some days later Nkru-

[12] For a discussion of the origins of trade unions in the Gold Coast, see the previous chapter.

mah, the T.U.C. leaders and others were arrested, charged with instigating an illegal strike and sentenced to a term of imprisonment.

The effect on the unions looked as if it might be disastrous. The T.U.C. became moribund, many active trade unionists lost their jobs and the unions declined in membership. At the end of 1950 the labour department helped to re-establish the T.U.C.; it encouraged the leaders of the unions—who were already distrustful of Nkrumah and were now none too happy at the consequences of industrial militancy—to concentrate on the non-political aspects of union organization.

The situation changed entirely when the Convention People's Party, in spite of the fact that its leader, Kwame Nkrumah, was in jail, swept in to victory at the 1951 elections. Within a few days the governor summoned Nkrumah from prison to form a government. Strikes, go-slow and sabotage, which had been a patriotic duty in the struggle for national independence, became activities that could not in future be tolerated. Nkrumah had neither strong attachment to the established trade unions nor belief in the value of an independent trade union movement, but he recognized the advantage to be gained from well-organized trade unions. It was essential, however, that they should be tied to Nkrumah's party and not free to cause industrial trouble or to be used by an opposition group.

The significance of Nkrumah's climb to fame and power was recognized and after 1951 the unions began to work more closely with the C.P.P. After their release from prison, the former trade union leaders who were strong supporters of the C.P.P. regained their influence and gradually achieved control. In 1953, John Tettegah, one of Nkrumah's strong supporters, was elected assistant general secretary of the T.U.C. and soon afterwards general secretary.

The 1954 Conference of the T.U.C., under the influence of Tettegah, decided to establish a committee to examine the structure of the trade union movement. The committee reported that the multiplicity of small unions was having an adverse effect on the development of a strong, well-co-ordinated trade union movement. It was decided to encourage amalgamation, but even with labour department support, little was

achieved; by 1956 only five national unions had been formed.
No doubt in time, with economic development, the concentration of unions into larger units would have gone further, just as
it had done in Britain and most other countries, but the new
leaders of the T.U.C. were impatient and not prepared to wait
on such a likely, but long-run course of events.

In 1956 the Annual Congress of the Ghana T.U.C. accepted
a recommendation calling for more speedy progress. The
resolution stated:

> We must now positively consider the feasibility of merging the
> various registered trade unions with the Trades Union Congress,
> so that Congress could become a negotiating body. Departments
> can be created and a centralized executive to direct our affairs
> throughout Ghana. This may take the form of the General
> Workers' Union of Malta. Our experience is that the present
> structure has become too complex to operate. We must turn to
> something like the General Federation of Jewish Labour in Israel
> (Histadruth). This is a new nation and we must build trade
> union machinery that can hasten the building of socialism and
> raise the living standards of the working people. The British
> system of trade unionism suits an industrialized capitalist state
> like Britain and America. In our view it is an impostor on Ghana
> and not suitable for us.

The leaders of the Ghana T.U.C. stated their desire quite
clearly:

> We wish to see built in Ghana a gigantic labour organization,
> co-ordinated and centralized, with a general staff capable of
> taking decisions and manoeuvering with monopoly capital in
> securing for the workers economic independence in an inde-
> pendent Ghana.

In pursuit of this aim it was decided to send the general
secretary to Israel and Germany to study the trade union
organizations of these countries. Following this tour, it was
eventually agreed between the leaders of the T.U.C. and the
government that new legislation should be introduced to bring
about the reorganization of the trade unions embodying
features borrowed from both the German and the Israeli labour
movements. The T.U.C. leaders did not intend to allow anything to interfere with their scheme to create a highly cen-

tralized trade union movement, and they were strongly supported by the government, which was ready to bring about the desired reorganization by legislation.

The Industrial Relations Act, 1958, compelled the existing unions to merge into 24 new industrial unions under the control of the T.U.C. (this number was reduced to 16 in 1960). Opposition to this exercise of legal *force majeure* came from the Mines Employees' Union, The Railway Locomotive Enginemen's Union and the United Africa Company Union, but their attempts to avoid being taken over were quickly and easily crushed. The trade union movement in Ghana thus had its structure reshaped and at the same time it was placed firmly under the control of the political party in power.

Northern and Southern Rhodesia

The development in Northern Rhodesia of the coppermining industry was made possible with the help of large numbers of white miners who were attracted to the mines and persuaded to endure the hardships and ugliness of the life on the 'copper belt' by extremely high rates of pay. These European miners saw that the best way to protect their interests was to do as workers had done elsewhere; that is, to form a trade union to resist any attempt to encroach upon the standards of pay which they had achieved.

The European Mineworkers' Union, founded in 1936, soon grew into the most powerful labour organization in Central Africa. It ruthlessly pursued a militant policy in the protection of the interests of European mining employees. Within a very few years of its establishment, it was seeking to negotiate a closed-shop agreement with the companies, and this it secured in 1941. The union's success owed something to the exigencies of war and the anxiety of the British Government to avoid any interruption in copper production. This agreement was confirmed in 1945, and it has been reaffirmed on a number of occasions since then. As loss of membership meant the loss of employment in the mines, the closed shop made it possible for the union to impose a rigid discipline on its members, including, for instance, compulsory attendance at union meetings. Branch committees have an absolute power to expel any member for committing any one of a large number of offences, including, in the committee's opinion, working or acting contrary to the interests of the union or its members. The independent power of the branches is thus very great, and union headquarters is only able to impose a limited control over them.[13]

Two other European trade unions established before 1950 were the large and important unions of salaried workers—the European Civil Servants' Association and the Mine Officials' and Salaried Staffs' Association. In 1950, after some activity by officials from Southern Rhodesia, a small branch of the Amalgamated Engineering Union was established in the territory, mainly among the employees of motor traders. Its membership has fluctuated, reaching 1,000 in 1954, then declining drastically. But it is now, after reorganization, an important union of engineering workers employed on the railways. The A.E.U. is one of the few British unions to develop direct links with the colonies; its first overseas branches were established in Australia and South Africa at the turn of the century, and it was from South Africa that the A.E.U. extended its organization into Rhodesia. Two small unions of European building trade workers and municipal employees were registered in 1952; the former was replaced in 1954 by an Industrial Workers' Union. In 1953, the now defunct Cement Workers' Union and the Distributive and Allied Trades' Union were formed; and in 1956 and 1957 two branches of unions with headquarters in South Africa were registered—the South African Typographical Union and the South African Society of Bank Officers. A branch of the Southern Rhodesian Guild of Journalists was also established at this time. Few of the unions of Europeans established since 1950 have as many as 200 members in Northern Rhodesia.

There is no trade union centre within Northern Rhodesia to which European trade unions are affiliated. When a number of African unions formed the Trades Union Congress in 1951, the European unions refused to join it. However, in 1955 three large European unions, together with some European trade unions in Southern Rhodesia, formed a Federal Trades Union Congress, which affiliated to the I.C.F.T.U. in 1957. It has

[13] *Report of the Commission . . . into the Stoppage in the Mining Industry in Northern Rhodesia in July 1957* (G.P., Lusaka, 1957), paragraph 19.

been active in many ways, and it has made strong representations to the governments concerned about such matters as the trade union legislation of 1958 in Northern Rhodesia and the amendment of the industrial conciliation legislation in Southern Rhodesia. In general, its policy has been in line with that of most European trade unions over the question of African participation in industry, and so far as Northern Rhodesia is concerned, it has tended to support the principle of equal pay for equal work as a means of protecting the interests of European artisans. For example, in May 1957 it actively supported the protest of the European Mineworkers' Union against proposals for 'job fragmentation' which it thought might be used to allow Africans to infiltrate into European-held positions in the mines. In 1959 and 1960 it was considering disaffiliation from the I.C.F.T.U. because it believed that the International was too pro-African in its policy. However, under the pressure of the 'wind of change' in 1961, the Federal Trades Union Congress amended its constitution to permit the affiliation of African organizations.

The first trade union of Africans was formed by the shop assistants in the Copperbelt towns in 1947. Initially, the Shop Assistants' Union had a membership of 200, but by 1949 this had grown to 1,300, organized in 8 or 9 branches throughout the country. Some months after the Shop Assistants' Union had been founded, the first trade union of African employees in the copper mines was formed. This step was the final stage in the evolution from a system of tribal representation introduced soon after the Roan Antelope Mine was started.

Recruitment to the mines had been of concern to the tribal chiefs, and in the early stages of this development an Elder of each tribe was nominated or approved by the chief at home to watch over the interests of members of the tribe employed in the mines. Thus tribal authority and its responsibility for the welfare of its members was maintained. Elders were expected to communicate grievances and complaints to the compound manager, the official responsible for the discipline and welfare of the African mine employees. The Elders were also frequently used as arbitrators in personal disputes between members of the same tribe. Occasionally the Council of Elders was consulted by management and the influence of the

Elders was used to make management decisions known to the employees.[14]

In the late 30's the Tribal Elder system was extended to the Mufulira Mine, which was under the effective control of the same group of companies, and to the other copper mines after the strikes in 1940. As a result of pressure from the labour department the system was changed to one in which the representatives of the men were elected on a tribal basis. The labour officers kept in touch with these representatives, giving them advice and guidance.

A number of authorities have commented on the effectiveness of the Tribal Elder system.[15] It would appear that the Council of Elders was fairly effective for matters of day-to-day consultation in the normal course of industrial relations; and it was certainly a considerable advance on the alternative method, employed in other mines before 1940, of using the private compound police force as a means of liaison between the management and the employees.[16] However, the loyalty of the workers in their industrial environment, to what were in effect nominees of the traditional tribal authorities, does not seem to have been very strong. At the time of the 1935 strikes and disturbances on the Copperbelt it is said that the Tribal Elders at Roan Antelope were unable to act as liaison between management and workers, and that they became either militant leaders of the strike, or, more often, were rejected by the men and sometimes even had to seek government protection. During the 1940 strike at Mufulira the Elders were ineffective, and after counsel by the District Commissioner the men elected a strike committee of 17, which acted for them throughout the strike. Nevertheless the Forster Commission, which inquired into the 1940 strike and disturbances which occurred, was strongly in favour of extending the Tribal Elder system, on the evidence it heard, to the Nkana and Nchanga. It should be

[14] F. Spearpoint, *The African Native and the Rhodesian Copper Mines*, Supplement to the *Journal of Royal African Society*, xxxvi, 144, 1937, pp. 19–20.
[15] Especially F. Spearpoint, *ibid.*, *Report of the Commission . . . into Disturbances in the Copperbelt of N. Rhodesia*, 1935 (H.M.S.O. 1935, Cmnd. 5009); *Report of Commission . . . into Disturbances in the Copperbelt, N. Rhodesia*, 1940 (G.P., Lusaka 1940); A. L. Epstein, *Politics in an Urban African Community* (Manchester, 1958); J. C. Mitchell, 'Africans in Industrial Towns in N. Rhodesia', Duke of Edinburgh's Study Conference Report, Vol. II (London, 1956).
[16] F. Spearpoint, *ibid.*, pp. 18–19. *Report of 1935 Commission*, para. 32.

added that there was no strike or trouble of any kind in 1940 at Roan Antelope, where the Elder system had been in operation longest.

The 1940 Forster Commission did, in fact, consider the alternative—trade unions for Africans. It concluded that

for trades unionism, as trades unionism is generally understood by the British workers, the African worker in Northern Rhodesia is clearly not yet ready. The reason for this unreadiness is not far to seek; in most instances it has not even begun. Further, his introduction to industrialism and industrial conditions is of a very recent date, too recent to admit of his intelligent participation in the more elaborate trades union system existing in Great Britain.[17]

This view had the agreement of the labour department. The Labour Commissioner, in evidence, stated that the government should aim at the 'eventual' establishment of African trades unions, though Africans were not then ripe for this development. The Inquiry Commission considered that the Elder system would probably develop, and would produce 'the seed from which will spring the African trade unions of the future'.[18]

However, with the extension of industrialism, and the steady rise of an elite which no longer felt itself primarily under tribal discipline, the system of tribal representation could not last. For about five or six years from 1942, and co-incidentally with the officially-encouraged extension of the system of tribal representation, considerable activity among various groups of workers, in the copper mines and elsewhere, were actively promoting the formation of other committees and associations. Among the first of these were the Boss Boys' committees in the mines, formed in 1942 by the more advanced supervisory grades. These met with the cautious approval of the labour department, which sought to guide them along sound lines of development. The co-operation of the mining companies to foster the progress of the committees was secured,[19] and tripartite discussions were introduced in 1943, in which the committees, the companies concerned and the labour department

[17] *Report of Commission . . . into Disturbances on the Copperbelt, N. Rhodesia*, 1940, para 175.   [18] *Ibid.*, para. 180.

[19] In fact, it had been the original intention of the companies at Nkana and Nchanga to associate the Boss Boys (who were probably thought to be loyal to the employers) with the work of the tribal representatives. It may have been this move which originally led to the formation of Boss Boys' associations, and hence indirectly to a decline in the influence of the representatives.

took part. The committees experienced some frustration, however; they are reported to have felt that little was accomplished in their consultative meetings, and, although the management and government regarded them as committees representing only their own grades (the African supervisory grades in the mines), they seem to have regarded themselves rather as the leaders of the miners as a whole. There was some conflict between the committees and the tribal representatives, and it was alleged that the committees were prone to discuss matters which lay within the province of the latter. There seems to have been little contact between the committees on different mines, though each committee kept in touch with those they represented, and general meetings of Boss Boys were held fairly frequently.

The mines Boss Boys' committees continued to act in this manner until 1947. Meanwhile, other developments were taking place both in the mines and in other parts of the economy. In 1943, again with the hesitant approval of the labour department, shop assistants' associations were formed in four different Copperbelt towns, and each drew up a list of grievances which they forwarded to the local chambers of commerce through the labour department. Shop assistants were among the more politically minded of the employed workers in Northern Rhodesia at that period, and these associations, at times at least, were more active in their own field than the mines Boss Boys' committees were in theirs. However, although contacts with the employers' organizations were facilitated by the labour department, they received little response or recognition from the traders for several years; the government appears to have feared at one stage that this lack of sympathy would be a cause of some unrest; but by 1946 or 1947 negotiations were being undertaken on a regular basis. A somewhat similar development was the formation of clerks' associations in the mines. The clerks had no representation on the Boss Boys' committees and yet felt themselves separate from the manual workers. However, they were no more successful than the shop assistants in making contact with the management.

There was little further progress towards organization by employees until 1946 or 1947. In 1944 the tribal representative system was extended to the railways at the Livingstone and

Broken Hill depots, and to a large sawmill at Livingstone, but this did not prevent a Southern Rhodesia railway strike in 1945 from spreading to the railway employees at Broken Hill.   Concurrently with the railway strike a stoppage of work occurred at the Broken Hill Mine in 1945.

The mining employees elected a strike committee at Broken Hill, as they had done at Mufulira Mine in 1940, and this committee demanded recognition by the employers as a permanent employees' committee, dealing with all complaints and grievances arising through work, and thus confining the tribal representatives to compound questions, housing, water, rations, etc.   Recognition was granted by the management, though the government seems to have had doubts about the wisdom of this decision, and meetings with the Broken Hill management continued through 1946 and 1947.

The only other developments of this period were, firstly, the formation in 1946 of a Contractors' Labour Association with an elected committee at the newly developing town of Chingola, in the Copperbelt; and secondly, the change-over in 1946 by the railways from tribal representation to a system of representatives elected departmentally.

Meanwhile, both government policy and unofficial European opinion were moving towards acceptance of the inevitable development of African trade unions.   Debates in the Legislative Council in 1945 and 1946 showed how rapidly this opinion was developing.   It would appear that Europeans—officials, trade unionists and others—were frequently being asked for advice on trade union principles in the years 1945–47.   In 1946 a British trade union official was appointed to the labour department to help develop collective bargaining in the territory.   Attempts were also being made to complete a satisfactory draft of trade union legislation[20] and to improve the standard of labour administration.

During this period the labour department seems to have been pressing for the development of the Boss Boys' committees into a more representative kind of organization.   This suggestion

[20] In fact, a rather illiberal Trade Union Bill had been introduced into the Legislative Council in 1942, and after a stormy debate, during which it received much criticism, it received a second reading. It was then referred to a Select Committee, where it was lost.   The revised Bill was first published in 1947, but not introduced into the Council until 1949.

was at first resisted by the mining companies, but by late 1947
the companies had withdrawn their opposition, and they stated
in October, before the Dalgleish Commission of Inquiry into the
advancement of Africans in industry, that 'if the Africans did
set up a trade union, the companies would be prepared to
recognize that trade union, provided they were satisfied that the
union was a representative one of the Africans'.[21]

Immediately before this, in September 1947, the European
Mineworkers' Union, influenced by the course of events, had
announced a very considerable change in policy—namely, that
in future it intended to organize the African mineworkers into
African branches which would be an integral part of the Mineworkers' Union.   The only apparent result of this announcement was that the Chamber of Mines, appearing before the
Dalgleish Commission, stated that although there was no agreement preventing Africans joining and becoming part of the
European Union, the companies would not recognize that
union as representing the Africans.   However, the companies
themselves seem to have envisaged a union of Africans 'under
government until they get enough experience to stand on their
own feet'.[22]

In 1947 the Boss Boys' committee at Nkana Mine was expanded into a committee of 17 members representative of all
workers and all departments at the mine, and this committee
took the lead in a movement to form a trade union of mineworkers.   A true trade union developed from this at Nkana and
by the end of 1948 it had a membership of 2,600.   Other unions
were formed about the same time at the other mines on the
Copperbelt.   Encouraged by the labour department, all these
unions began working towards amalgamation into a single
African Mineworkers' Union, having first rejected a reiterated
proposal from the European Mineworkers in the middle of 1948
that they should form a branch of that union.

At the beginning of 1949, with the fulfilment of the amalgamation plans, the Northern Rhodesia African Mineworkers'
Union was established, and it immediately entered into negotiations with the mining companies, who granted it recogni-

[21] *Report of the Commission appointed to inquire into the Advancement of Africans in
Industry* (G.P., Lusaka, 1948), para. 252.
[22] *Ibid.*

tion soon afterwards. By the end of 1949 the union claimed a membership of 19,000, and it continued to expand and increase its activities for the next three or four years. In 1950 it secured a comprehensive agreement with the employers, which included the right to have union dues deducted from wages; in the same year its first full-time general secretary was appointed and an efficient head-office administration was established. By 1951 the union was claiming a 90 per cent. paid-up membership of African mining employees. However, relations with the management began to deteriorate thereafter, and the union then received a number of set-backs. In 1953 the check-off was withdrawn and a drastic falling-off in financial support occurred in the following year.[23] The formation of a breakaway Mines African Staff Association, followed by a series of strikes (mainly in connection with the recognition of the African Staff Association), led to the arrest, detention and, later, the rustication of almost 60 persons, including all of its leaders and officials. Other leaders were lost to the Mines African Staff Association, which represented most of the 'advanced' posts to which Africans had been promoted by agreement with the European Union.

With the formation of the Mineworkers' Union, the Boss Boy's committees ceased to exist. As for the tribal representatives in the mines, they seem to have been rather unpopular for some time before 1948 with those whom they were designed to represent, although the mining companies thought highly of them. After 1949 there tended to be a considerable amount of rivalry between the trade union and the councils of tribal representatives, and the managements attempted to increase the prestige of the latter in opposition to the union. Eventually matters came to a head, and in 1953 a vote was held among the employees at which there was an overwhelming poll for the abolition of the tribal representative system and for the

[23] The check-off was withdrawn because union dues were raised from 6d. to 2s. 6d. by the union leaders without consulting the members. At that time the union leaders were under suspicion for having misused union funds for their personal gain. There was no legislation in force regarding the auditing of trade union accounts, and the employers felt that they could not take the responsibility of collecting a fivefold increase in trade union dues from about 35,000 employees without further evidence that this was desired by them and that proper provision had been made to prevent the substantial sums involved from being fraudulently converted to private use. The check-off was re-introduced in 1957, following a recommendation by the Honeyman Commission that the auditing of union accounts should be made a legal requirement.

representation of the employees by the trade union system. The fact was, African workers were no longer prepared to accept a system of authority rooted in their tribal connections and based upon their village homes. Their commitment to work in the mines had broken this attachment and they were ready to accept a new structure of collective organization that reflected their changed status and needs as mineworkers.

Other groups of workers had formed associations and had been seeking information on trade unionism during the formative period, and the trade union labour officer was advising some of these groups during 1947. As a result, a Drivers' Association was established in 1948, with branches in the Copperbelt and at Lusaka; it was transformed into a trade union in 1951, but went out of existence in 1956. The association of building contractors' employees which had been formed in 1946 became the General Workers' Trade Union in 1949, and this union was still on the Register at the end of 1957, although it had experienced considerable internal trouble and its returns were much in arrears. The African Civil Servants' Association was formed in the same year, as was an Association of Domestic Servants, which, however, never developed into a union; the Civil Servants' Organization has had over 1,000 members since 1952. In 1950 the railway workers and teachers formed trade unions, though the teachers' union had ceased to exist by the end of 1953.

The process of forming unions continued for some years, two unions having been established in each of the next four years, and three in 1956. However, no new union was registered between 1956 and 1959, owing mainly to a change in the law and a tightening up of the provision relating to the keeping of union accounts. The eight unions which were established between 1951 and 1954 included two municipal workers' unions, a rather small Government Workers' Trade Union, a hotel and catering workers' union, a factory workers' and a cement workers' union, a union of employees of the Central African Road Services and the important Mines African Staff Association. The unions formed in 1956 were two staff associations, one of the municipal salaried staff at Broken Hill, and the other of the African Mines Police; and one manual workers' union— the General Construction and Transport Workers' Union.

A number of these unions subsequently ceased to exist, in some cases because they were refused registration when the law was changed in 1956 making registration compulsory. In 1959 there were 21 unions in existence, of which 11 had European members and 10 had African members. The largest African union was the Northern Rhodesian African Mineworkers' Trade Union, with a claimed membership of 28,000 out of a total work force of about 35,000.[24]

Kenya

There were no African trade unions registered in Kenya at the end of the second world war, although there were some unregistered African staff associations. An Asian trade union, the East African Ramgazhia Artisans' Union, was registered in 1937 and remained on the register until 1948, though inactive for the last few years of its life. Also in 1937 the Labour Trade Union of East Africa was registered; and in 1941 a small East African Standard Asian Staff Union was formed. This last union is still in existence, with a membership of about 70. The Labour Trade Union, led by a militant Indian, Makhan Singh, set out to cater for both Africans and Asians, but its membership seems to have been almost entirely Asian.

In the first three years after the end of the war several unions, including the first wholly African unions, were established. There were three registrations in 1946. The Typographical Union of Kenya was a union of both African and Asian printers, which today is an entirely African organization. A Nairobi African Taxi-Drivers' Union formed in 1946 changed its name in 1947 to the Kenya African Road Transport and Mechanics' Union, and in 1948 to the Transport and Allied Workers' Union. This was at one time the largest union in Kenya, and in 1953 claimed a membership of over 10,000. However, by 1957 its paid-up membership was said to be only 750. The third union formed in 1946, the Thika Native Motor Drivers' Association, claimed a membership of about 200 in 1948, but went out of existence in 1949.

In 1947 one African and two Asian trade unions were registered. The African union, the African Workers' Federation, collapsed after its leader, Chege Kebachia, was deported

[24] Statement to Morrison Commission, May 1962.

to Northern Kenya for his part in the disturbances that accompanied a strike the union called in Mombasa. One of the Asian unions, the Railway Asian, is now the largest and most important Asian union in Kenya, with over 2,000 members.

A number of other unions were registered in the next few years, and a move was made to form an East African Trades Union Congress; this body did not succeed in securing registration as a society and its promoter, Makhan Singh, was deported for undesirable activities. In 1952 the Kenya Federation of Registered Trade Unions was established; later it was renamed the Kenya Federation of Labour. Under the exceptionally able leadership of Tom Mboya, and with the aid of large subsidies from the I.C.F.T.U. and the A.F.L.–C.I.O., the Kenya Federation of Labour has become an influential organization.

Trade union development was considerably affected by the appearance of the Mau Mau movement and the Emergency Regulations that had to be introduced to cope with it. Before the emergency some 60,000 workers were nominally members of unions, but arrests and detention of union leaders on suspicion and proof of connection with Mau Mau inevitably had an impact on the unions. Since the emergency some unions have made excellent progress, but others have rather lagged behind. With constitutional advance, trade union development in Kenya has inevitably been adversely affected by the involvement of leaders in the struggles of rival factions for political power. There has been a failure to organize effectively at the employment level, due in part to growing tribal differences; and an increasing African racial assertiveness has made cooperation with Asian workers in trade unions extremely difficult.

Tanganyika

Legislation relating to trade unions was adopted by Tanganyika and Nyasaland in 1932, and in Uganda in 1937. There was, however, little trade union activity in these territories until after the second world war.

The first trade union in Tanganyika of which there is any record was the Union of Shop Assistants, formed and registered in 1933 with its headquarters in Dar-es-Salaam. The union achieved little except to change its name in 1936 and eventually it ceased to exist. Another union was registered in 1939, but it soon became moribund. It was in 1944 that the labour department first became aware of a development of combinations to seek an improvement in working conditions. In that year, in several widely separated parts of the country, a number of associations were formed among domestic servants and motor drivers and later among tailors. These organizations had an initial success in recruiting members, but failed to hold them, and gradually they faded out. Only one important union was registered in this period and that was the Stevedores and Dockworkers' Union, which came into existence in 1947 following the serious stoppage of work at Dar-es-Salaam in September of that year. The union claimed 1,500 members on its formation and by 1949 it had increased this number to 2,200 and accumulated over £2,000 in funds. In 1948 a joint agreement had been signed between the union and the port industry covering wages and working conditions. Unfortunately the leaders of this union were tempted to use their position to benefit themselves from the funds of the organization and they found themselves under arrest. The final catastrophe occurred when a strike was called which ended with disturbances and the arrest of all the members of the union's executive council.

More unions were established in the next few years, but a real and rapid advance in trade unionism did not begin until 1955. In that year 14 new employees' organizations were registered and the Tanganyika Federation of Labour was established. Although by the end of 1957 none of the African unions on the register at the end of 1954 remained in existence, total trade union membership rose during this period from 500 to 35,000. This growth was achieved without any great proliferation in the number of trade unions—the number on the register at the end of 1957 was the same as at the end of 1955. Much of this development was due to the activities of the Tanganyika Federation of Labour, which, during its many discussions with the trade unions about the need to revise their constitutions to conform to the new trade union law enacted in 1956, encouraged the formation of a number of territory-wide unions to replace local and provincial organizations. Many of the small unions became branches of larger ones. In this period, too, large

F

groups of industrial and agricultural workers were organized
for the first time, and unions of railway workers, dock workers,
local government employees, transport, building and hotel and
catering workers were established, as well as, most significantly,
a national union of plantation workers in 1958.

The development of the Tanganyika Federation of Labour
was greatly assisted by the labour department, the I.C.F.T.U.
and the British T.U.C., but it was looked upon with suspicion
and distrust by many sections of the government and local
management.   Seeking to curb the rising power of the Federation, the government extended the list of essential services in
which strikes and lock-outs were illegal and arbitration compulsory (see Chapter 11, p. 321).   It was also decided, following a marked growth in the number and membership of the
trade unions, to introduce new and more restrictive legislation.
This was passed through the legislature against the opposition
of both the Tanganyika Federation of Labour and the British
T.U.C., and in spite of cautionary advice from the Secretary
of State for the Colonies.   The Act was severely condemned
by the unions as unnecessarily restrictive, but it required considerable pressure from Whitehall before the Government of
Tanganyika could be persuaded to make any amendment.

The desire of the government to curb the power of the
Federation of Labour was prompted not only by fear of the
economic strength of the unions, but also by their potential
political influence.   There seems to have been a fairly close
relationship between the Federation of Labour and the powerful
Tanganyika African National Union.   After this organization
had swept the board in the 1958 general elections, threats of a
general strike, unless certain political concessions were granted,
were made by groups connected with the Federation.   Allegations were made that union collectors were also collecting for
the African National Union.   Certainly one of the effects of
creating a powerful central federation before the affiliated
unions are well and truly established is that it tends to become a
highly politically-conscious body.

The political link between the T.F.L. and the T.A.N.U. has
been consolidated since independence by the introduction of
legislation similar to that adopted in Ghana.   Under it the
Minister of Labour has power to appoint a federation as the sole

'designated federation' to which all unions must belong. Henceforth the 'check-off' may be imposed by law if desired by not less than 10 members; and with the consent of the Minister the designated federation is to receive a specified share of revenues of the unions. To make certain that the unions do not embarrass the government in its efforts to promote the economic development of Tanganyika, strikes and lockouts have been made illegal unless all attempts at securing a settlement have failed and the Minister has not submitted the dispute to a tribunal for settlement.[25] The Trade Disputes Settlement Act is based upon the essential services procedures that were the subject of bitter criticism by the Tanganyika Federation of Labour when the territory was under British rule, and it is believed that this extension to all employment is not looked upon with favour by the Federation.

Nyasaland

In Nyasaland, economic development has been relatively slower than in some of the other places and there has long been a surplus of labour in the country. In fact, at one stage, about twice as many Nyasalanders were employed outside the country —principally on the farms, mines and industries of Southern Rhodesia, South Africa and Northern Rhodesia—as were employed within it. The small demand for labour, the dominance of agriculture and the fact that the more enterprising individuals emigrate to find work in other territories, the past low level of secondary and higher education and the lack of large towns or centres of industry have all inhibited the formation of unions.

In these circumstances it is not surprising that in spite of the existence of trade union legislation since 1932, there appears to have been no move towards the formation of a permanent trade union until 1948, when, with the approval of the employers who formed an association at the same time, the motor transport workers formed a trade union based on Blantyre. This union was registered in 1949, with 70 members. Several unions were established in 1950, but it was not until 1954 that the now largest and most important union in the country, the Railway African Workers' Trade Union, was established. By 1957 this union claimed 1,000 members. The Civil Service Staff

[25] Trade Disputes (Settlement) Act 1962.

Association, formed in 1950, which represents the more junior grades, did not register as a trade union. A European Civil Servants' Association, formed a year or two later, reconstituted itself in 1957 as an inter-racial association of senior civil servants. By 1958 there were four unions and employers' associations registered in Nyasaland, with a total trade union membership of not more than 1,500. In 1960, 5 new unions were registered, bringing the total number up to 9. Obviously a trade union movement of this size, even though it is growing, is not likely to exercise great power, although it cannot be ignored either economically or politically.

The great majority of employers in the territory reluctantly accepted trade unionism; they were not keen on any form of consultation with their employees as a group, preferring to negotiate with individuals and to decide terms of service on a personal basis. But in spite of reservations the employers showed goodwill towards the unions, and their recognition; and reasonably good relations have been built up based upon the successful development of collective bargaining. The government's attitude to the development of trade unionism was to encourage without too much positive enthusiasm, although at an early stage it was quite strongly in favour of the establishment of works committees.

Efforts to establish a national trade union centre have been made, but progress has been rather slow. The development of the trade union movement has inevitably been affected by the political crisis arising out of African opposition to the Central African Federation to which Nyasaland belongs. A number of leading trade unionists were arrested and detained in February 1959, during the state of emergency in the territory. Following the arrests a delegation from the I.C.F.T.U. visited Nyasaland in May 1959. It found that neither the Nyasaland T.U.C. nor any of its affiliates had been connected with the disturbances. The Nyasaland Government stated in reply that it had never maintained that the T.U.C. or the unions themselves were involved in the disturbances, but that many officials and trade union members 'have been found to warrant detention solely by reason of their activities on behalf of the Nyasaland African National Congress'.

Uganda

The first union to register under the 1937 trade union ordinance in Uganda was the Uganda African Motor Drivers' Association in 1939. This union was active in both the political and industrial fields, and was much involved in Buganda political intrigues. A report of a Commission of Inquiry in 1945 stated that 'its avowed objects are exemplary, but its activities seem to have been mostly in the political field'. The general secretary of the union was eventually deported for his part in the plot against the Buganda Government, which eventually culminated in the assassination of the *Katikiro* (Prime Minister) of the Buganda Court.

The development of unions continued, and in 1949 a trade union labour officer from the United Kingdom was appointed to Uganda. From this time the labour department was able to give more assistance and encouragement to employees seeking advice about trade unionism. However, the growth of the unions continued to be slow. By 1957 there were 13 unions registered with a total membership of 4,800. The most important of them was the Uganda Railway African Union with a membership of 3,000. Other unions established included the Uganda General Clerical Union, the General Transport and Allied Workers' Union, the Uganda Printing Trade Union and the Uganda Tobacco Workers' Union.

To some extent the slow development of trade unions was met by the establishment of works committees, of which there were about 70 in 1958. The growth of these committees was less due to spontaneous enthusiasm for joint consultation than to the efforts of the department of labour, which was also responsible for promoting several wages councils. These organizational developments did, however, help employers and workers to recognize the importance of the machinery through which problems of industrial relations could be resolved.

In addition to the registered trade unions in Uganda a number of employees' associations have notified their existence to the Registrar under the terms of the 1952 Trade Union Ordinance. The first of these, whose existence was reported in 1953, were the African, Asian and European Civil Servants' Associations. These associations have maintained or increased their membership since that date, the African Association now claiming 1,500 members and the others about 800 each. In 1954 a Government Indian School Teachers' Union was registered as an employees' association with a membership of 200. In 1956 a Dispensers' Association, a Medical Laboratory Assistants' Association and an Asian Printers' Association were on the Registrar's books, and in 1957 associations of African teachers, nursing orderlies and veterinary assistants were added. Only one of these associations, the Asian Printers' Association, has so far been converted into a trade union, combining with a nascent African staff association. It is noticeable that almost all of them are associations of public servants; there is provision in the legislation for associations to be formed in private employment as well, but none has yet appeared.

Up to 1959 the Uganda trade union movement was by no means fully representative of the employed workers of the country, but since then there has been a considerable expansion of trade union activity, and the number of unions has now reached 47, with a total membership of 45,000. This spurt in trade union activity was stimulated by the decision of the I.C.F.T.U. in 1958 to establish a Labour College at Kampala, for the purpose of training trade union leaders from the English-speaking territories of Africa. The College drew attention to the trade union movement in Uganda, which has benefited from the advice and financial assistance made available to it. The most important new unions to be established are the National Union of Plantation Workers (Uganda) with 7,000 members and the Uganda Public Employees' Union with 4,000 members. The largest union in the country is Uganda Vernacular, Primary and Junior Secondary Teachers' Union with over 10,000 members.

Following a visit from a delegation from the I.C.F.T.U. in 1955, a national centre was established. This is, however, a very weak body and there has been much dissension among its members. The Uganda Trades Union Congress was in danger of disintegration when the Railway African Union withdrew from membership, but with help and financial assistance from outside, it has managed to survive, although tribal jealousies and party politics remain a constant threat to its stability. In 1961 a rival Uganda Federation of Labour was inspired by the

All-African Trade Union Federation, but this collapsed when its leader left to take a job with management.

One of the main obstacles to union development in Uganda is the migrant character of labour. Most of the employed workers are migrants from Kenya and Ruanda Urundi, but the majority of indigenous labourers are engaged in the growing of cotton, coffee, tobacco and other agricultural crops.

Aden and Mauritius

The first union to register in Aden was the Harbour Pilots' Association, with a membership of 11 European pilots. This was in 1951. A Trade Unions and Trade Disputes Ordinance which legalized trade unions and made provision for their registration had been adopted in 1942. But ten years later, in 1952, the Annual Report of the Colony stated 'The work-people of the Colony have no conception of labour organization or of collective bargaining'. The report for the following year recorded the registration of three unions: the Aden Harbour Pilots' Association, the Aden Air Ministry Civilian Employees' Association and a Technical Workers' Trade Union, with a total membership of almost 4,000. The report still insisted, with a slight concession to this development, that 'the work-people of the colony have little conception of labour organization or of collective bargaining'.

It might be argued that the workers of Aden still have little conception of labour organization, but the idea of trade unionism rapidly caught on and at one point there were 45 unions in being; however, by 1957 this number had been reduced to 27 unions and 5 employees' associations. Most of these organizations were of the Gold-Coast–Nigerian house-union type. Before 1957 the unions registered were associated with particular employers, such as the Cory Brothers Employees' Union, Besse Local Employees' Union, B.P. Aden Employees' Union, Caltex Employees' Union and so on. Each government department also had its own union. Then in 1957 attention began to be paid to the question of reorganizing the unions on an industrial basis, and moves towards establishing a federation began. This development was suggested by visiting British trade union experts sent to the colony by the T.U.C. to help the development of unions on generally sounder lines.

The most important of the new groupings registered in 1959 was in the stevedoring, shipping and trading sector. The General and Port Workers' Union is a loose amalgamation or fairly close federation of the old house unions in the trading firms. A federation of petroleum workers is designed to combine all the petroleum unions; a Government Workers' Union to combine together all the departmental unions. This structural development has strengthened the power of the Aden Trades Union Council, which was formed in 1956 after a series of strikes. It has had a stormy history so far. In the few years since trade unionism began in Aden the colony has been convulsed by industrial stoppages. A political general strike was called in 1958, and the T.U.C. has shown little disposition to co-operate with the government ever since. The Aden T.U.C. has avowed political objects, and in 1960 was probably the most potent political force in the colony. The political parties have been weak and ineffective, and from time to time various 'fronts' have been formed, in which the T.U.C. has had by far the strongest voice.

Since 1956 the trade unions in Aden have been the subject of more examination and advice from official and unofficial visitors than the unions of any other territory. In spite of this attention the industrial relations situation deteriorated to such a degree in 1959 that the government decided to invite an independent British expert to advise the colony on how the situation could be improved. The outcome of this study was a recommendation that compulsory arbitration should be introduced. This was followed by legislation (discussed in Chapter 11) which make strikes illegal and arbitration compulsory, but permits the unions to escape from this restriction on certain conditions.

Events in the island of Mauritius have been rather different from Aden, but not entirely dissimilar to those that have occurred in the Caribbean. The opposition of the employees, and the procrastination of the authorities when faced by the fact of union organization in the inter-war period, produced the inevitable explosion. This took place in the summer of 1937, when for three weeks the island was convulsed by large-scale strikes and public disorder. The Industrial Associations Ordinance that was subsequently passed was based on South African legislation, and was very far from the kind of trade union law that had existed in Britain for more than half a century. It was enough, however, to encourage the formation of some 40 unions in the three years following the passing of the ordinance. Although there was an attempt to form a mass general union based upon the labourers employed on the island's sugar estates, this did not have the success that its politically-minded leaders hoped for. Unions of engineering and technical employees, government servants and employees, dock workers, clerical workers, shop assistants and teachers were among the organizations established in the early period of development. By 1957 there were some 70 unions in existence, boasting a total membership of 18,966, of which some 16,243 had paid their dues.

Malaya and Singapore

The occupation of Malaya and Singapore by the Japanese during the second world war inevitably interrupted the growth of trade unions. In 1939 there were a large number of organizations which had the characteristics of trade unions and were registered under the Societies Ordinance. Some catered for employers only, some for employees only, while others looked after the interests of both. The great majority of these societies were purely Chinese organizations; the Chinese were far better organized than either of the other racial groups, and most industries employing them had some kind of society to cater for their interests. There were about 70 racially-mixed organizations, of which the most important were the teachers' associations and the Singapore Traction Company Employees' Association. The Indians were less interested in forming unions than the Chinese; and the Malays who lived mainly in the more rural areas, were almost completely untouched by any urge to organize.

In 1940 a Trade Union Ordinance was passed in Malaya but no unions were registered under it before the Japanese captured the country in 1941. During the occupation many of the societies that had existed simply died. The economy of the country was disrupted and those workers who were interested in organization were either recruited for the guerilla armies formed by the communists or were encouraged by the Japanese to join the anti-British Indian National Army. In both of these organizations the young men who joined were indoctrinated with political ideologies that were antipathetic to the future development of a democratic system of society.

In the period immediately following the surrender of the Japanese, before a stable government could be restored, encouragement was given to the formation of 'responsible democratic trade unions, and as a special help in this connection a Trade Union Adviser's Department was established'.[26] The Malayan Communist Party was intent, however, on carrying out a revolution, and to this end it set up its own trade union organizations. The controlling body in this communist machine was a General Labour Union, which accepted other unions as affiliates, as well as individual members. A change had to be made when the General Labour Union was refused registration on the grounds that its constitution did not comply with the conditions laid down in the trade union ordinances of Malaya and Singapore. It was then decided by the communists to establish two organizations, the Singapore Federation of Trade Unions and the Pan-Malayan Federation of Trade Unions. These two organizations were federations only in name; in practice they were highly-centralized, well-disciplined, politically-dominated machines, developed so as to secure and maintain control of the mass of work-people in both countries. The methods employed by the federations were frequently far removed from normal trade unionism. Two British trade unionists, S. S. Awberry and F. W. Dalley, who were sent to report on the trade union situation in Malaya and Singapore, came to the conclusion, after careful investigation, that intimidation, violence and other illegitimate means of putting pressure on unwilling victims were frequently used by the federations to secure their ends.[27] Not all the unions were affiliated to the federations, but those that were independent were constantly under attack from the communist-inspired organizations.

Although a special trade union adviser was appointed and the governments of both territories (through the labour departments in Singapore and Kuala Lumpur) gave strong support to

[26] S. S. Awberry and F. W. Dalley, *Labour and Trade Union Organisation in the Federation of Malaya and Singapore* (H.M.S.O. Colonial No. 234, 1948), p. 24.

[27] Awberry and Dalley, *ibid.*, p. 27. See also V. Purcell, *Malaya Communist or Free* (London, 1954), p. 178. A. Josey, *Trade Unions in Malaya* (Singapore, 1958).

the development of independent trade unions, little progress was made in the first few years after the Japanese occupation. A number of independent unions were established, but subjected as they were to constant attacks from the communist unions and hostility from employers who detested unionism of any type, they remained weak and unstable. During this period, hundreds of strikes occurred and it became obvious that so long as a powerful communist-controlled trade union movement existed there was little chance of making progress towards a genuine development of industrial relations based upon the give and take of peaceful collective bargaining.

In an effort to change the climate of industrial relations by getting rid of the political leaders of the unions, the Government of Malaya introduced a new Trade Union Ordinance in 1948 which (1) limited federations of unions to unions catering for workers in similar occupations and industries; (2) required all union officials, with the exception of the secretary, to have had three years' employment in the industry in which their union existed. The effect of this legislation was to bring about the closing down of about one hundred unions. Since the Pan-Malayan Federation could not meet the conditions imposed by the new law, the Communist Party was faced with crisis. Its rapid progress towards capturing power through the trade union movement had been brought to a halt. Prevented from achieving its aim through industrial disorder and economic chaos, the Communist Party turned to armed rebellion. At the call of the Party many of the senior officers of the communist-controlled unions seized the funds of their organizations and disappeared into the jungle to join the guerilla army, through which the Communist Party hoped to overthrow the Malayan Government. Bereft of their leaders, without cash resources, the 129 unions previously dominated by the Communist Party simply collapsed. The membership of these unions, which was over 80,000, and many more in other unions that were under communist influence if not direct control, just evaporated. The significance of the Communist Party's decision for the trade union movement in Malaya can be judged by the fact that out of 302 unions it was officially believed that only some 63 were genuinely independent and they had only half as many members as the communist-dominated unions.

After the collapse the independent unions were given support and encouragement by the government. It was not easy, however, to rebuild the trade union movement under the conditions imposed by the Emergency Regulations. Moreover, the Chinese, who had been predominantly members of the communist-controlled unions, were now reluctant to belong to labour organizations. However, a labour group on the Legislative Council took steps to initiate a delegate conference of trade union representatives, and a working committee was set up to promote the establishment of a Malayan Trades Union Council. In March 1950 the T.U.C. was launched. With previous experience in mind it was agreed that the T.U.C. should have very limited objectives and should not be given far-reaching authority over its affiliated organizations. The elected president of the new body was P. P. Narayanan, general secretary of the mainly Indian Plantation Workers' Union. The P.W.U. had been founded in 1946 and developed by intelligent leadership and sound administration into the most successful union in South-East Asia; by 1958 it had a membership of 170,000. Narayanan, secretary of the P.W.U., is a man of exceptional talent and he has played a notable part in the rebuilding of the Malayan trade union movement.

The great weakness in Malayan trade unionism, after the 'emergency' was declared over, twelve years after it had been proclaimed, lay in its predominantly Indian membership. The Chinese remained reluctant to join unions. Since independence, the government has been dominated by Malays, and the Chinese, fearing to exacerbate Malayan hostility, have preferred to remain uncommitted. They have believed that many Malays would like to pursue an anti-Chinese policy—even to the extent of forcing them to return to China—similar to that carried out in Indonesia. The Malays themselves have not been union members in substantial numbers, mainly because, unlike the Chinese and Indians, they have not sought paid employment in the unionized occupations until recently. In the past the Malays were almost all farmers and fishermen, although some were employed as domestic servants and government employees. Now, however, they are leaving the rural kampongs for the cities and are entering industrial employment in increasing numbers. If the Malayan trade union movement

is to be truly representative it must in the future attract Chinese
and Malay members on a scale commensurate with their
economic status in the community.

As these developments were taking place in Malaya a similar
pattern of events occurred in Singapore. A Trades Union Congress was established in 1951 by 28 non-communist unions.
Most of these organizations were led by English-speaking
Chinese and Indians, and they claimed a total membership of
24,000. There were at that time some 107 unions registered
with a total membership of approximately 58,000. Many of
the unions that did not join the T.U.C. were extremely small,
but a number of large industrial unions also refused to affiliate.
Unions catering for government employees were not permitted
by a government decree to belong to the T.U.C. The British
authorities were afraid that the unions might once again be
captured by the communists and used for subversive purposes.
It was not until 1957, after important constitutional changes
had occurred, that a Labour Front Government, whose Chief
Minister, Lim Yew Hock, had been the first president of the
T.U.C., lifted this ban.

In spite of a considerable political advance, and a steady
improvement in Singapore's economic situation, the T.U.C.
leaders did not succeed in establishing clear control of the
labour movement. In 1957 only 59 unions (with a membership of 65,000) out of the 202 unions then registered in Singapore (with a total membership of 156,000) were affiliated to the
T.U.C. The problem which faced the T.U.C. was that it
lacked leaders with experience and ability to run its affairs
efficiently. It also had to face continuous attack from the
extreme left-wing unions, led by non-English speaking Chinese.
The great majority of the people of Singapore do not speak
English, and left-wing trade unionists and politicians have
fostered the belief that to speak English is a sign of subservience
to colonialism. To be successful, trade union leaders in
Singapore must be able to speak fluently several Chinese dialects,
Malay and Tamil, as well as English. Those educated in
English schools were often unable to do this.

In 1955 the left-wing unions established a rival organization
to the T.U.C.—the Singapore Trade Union Working Committee. This organization had within its ranks persons who

had been associated with the communist-led unions prior to the 'emergency'. Mounting evidence indicated that the leaders of the S.T.U.W.C. were following similar policies to those which had culminated in the armed rebellion in 1948.

Faced by these facts, the Labour Front Government of Lim Yew Hock decided to arrest and to place in detention some of the most extreme left-wing leaders of the so-called 'Middle-Road Unions'.[28] The Singapore Factory and Shop Workers' Union, which had a membership of 30,000, was dissolved and its certificate of registration was cancelled on the grounds that the union had been used for purposes inconsistent with its objects and rules.

Following the defeat of the Labour Front Government, in the first election held after self-government in domestic affairs had been granted, the victorious People's Action Party released the detained left-wing trade union leaders. They at once returned to 'Middle Road' and began to re-establish their old positions of power and influence within the unions. The socialist leaders of the P.A.P. tried hard to work with the left-wing Chinese union leaders, but they were not prepared to permit them to occupy positions from which they could dominate the party. To prevent the pro-communist union leaders from creating a series of massive industrial disturbances which would enable them to overthrow the government and seize power, a system of compulsory arbitration on the Australian model was introduced. The government also considered introducing a Bill, similar to the Ghana Industrial Relations Act, to reduce the over-large number of unions drastically and to reorganize them on an industrial union basis; general unions were to be made illegal. The unions were then, as in Ghana, to be brought under the control of the T.U.C., which would not have had any legal power to engage in industrial activities. This Bill was eventually withdrawn when it became apparent that it could be passed only at the cost of a fierce fight with the pro-communist union leaders whose strength lay with the general unions which were to be eliminated. In addition it was by no means certain that the T.U.C., with its enhanced power, could not be captured from within by the tough, effective communist trade union leaders.

[28] Middle Road is an address of the unions, not a political position.

The steps taken by the leaders of the P.A.P. Government to strengthen the unions against the employers, and, at the same time, to prevent the communists from gaining the ascendency, have been criticized both by the employers and the communists and their supporters. Many observers, however, share the view expressed by Lee Kuan Yew, P.A.P. Prime Minister of Singapore, soon after assuming office, 'If you try to run the undiluted British style of democracy in the context of South-East Asia, you will collapse.' [29] It remains to be seen whether the P.A.P. will succeed in promoting the development of stable, responsible trade unionism in the absence of legislation that brings the unions firmly under political control and which could be, in principle, in conflict with traditional British concepts of freedom of association.

Hong Kong

After the re-occupation of Hong Kong by British forces, efforts were made to encourage a system of industrial relations based on the development of collective agreements freely negotiated between responsible trade unions and forward-looking employers. In 1960 this aim was still a long way from being realized in Hong Kong. The principal reasons why it had not been achieved were to be found in the nature of the Hong Kong Trade Unions and the attitude of the Hong Kong employers.

Trade unionism exists in Hong Kong, but its main purpose is to provide certain social benefits and to support political objectives. Collective bargaining, grievance procedure and the widespread industrial activities engaged in by unions in Britain, Europe or America, are barely carried on at all by the unions in Hong Kong.

The most fundamental feature of the trade union movement in Hong Kong is that it is split into three major sections. One part, the Hong Kong and Kowloon Trades Union Council, is associated with the Government in Formosa and strongly supports the claims of Chiang Kai-shek as the legitimate leader of all the Chinese. Another section, the Hong Kong Federation of Trade Unions, is equally closely attached

[29] John Lowe, *The Malayan Experiment*, Fabian International and Commonwealth Bureau, Research Series 213, 1960.

to the Chinese Communist Party, and supports the People's Government in Peking. The third section of independent unions is so far a weak, and, with perhaps the exception of the teachers' union, an almost negligible force.

The largest of the three organizations is the communist-controlled Federation of Trade Unions. In 1959 the F.T.U. had an affiliated membership of 65 unions (with a total of 144,000 members) and the support of 25 other unions (with a membership of 12,000). In all, some 90 unions, with a total membership of over 150,000, were on the communist side.

The Hong Kong and Kowloon Trades Union Council, which supports the Kuomintang, had 68 unions affiliated, with a membership of 34,000, and the support of another 53 unions with a further 22,000 members; making altogether 121 unions with a membership of 56,000 in support of the Chinese Government in Formosa.

The independent unions number 33, and they had a combined membership of approximately 16,000.

These figures give only a rough idea of the comparative size of the main sections of the Hong Kong Trade Union Movement. No membership totals are given in the annual report for the colony, simply because it is well known that the figures supplied by the unions are most unreliable. There is no doubt that the communist bloc is the largest and that it has been growing at the expense of the other sections.

Although the unions are diametrically opposed on political policies, there is not much to choose between them when it comes to methods of organization and relations with employers. All the unions in Hong Kong tend to be more concerned with problems of welfare rather than with industrial negotiation. The two political trade union organizations run clinics and schools for their members. They regard schools as particularly important, because through them they are able to indoctrinate the young and subsequently to use them in political demonstrations.

The only section of employment in which there is anything like collective bargaining is in the docks.[30] Chinese employers, especially some of those who have settled in Hong Kong as

[30] A major effort has been made to keep the unions at bay in the tramways by the development of an intensive system of joint consultation.

refugees from Shanghai, are notoriously ruthless in their employment policies. They simply will not be bound by agreements, and the Department of Labour has the utmost difficulty in persuading them to obey the laws relating to the health, safety and welfare of their employees. Non-Chinese employers are almost as strongly opposed to recognizing unions for collective bargaining purposes, though they are generally more ready to obey the law and to act with consideration for their employees' interests.

The trade union problems of Hong Kong cannot be divorced from the unique economic and political circumstances which dominate this remarkable city. In the decade between 1950 and 1960 something like 1,000,000 refugees sought asylum within its boundaries. Capital, too, has flowed into the colony and an astonishing industrial revolution has occurred. In a dozen years Hong Kong has been changed from a great entrepôt city into a tremendous manufacturing centre. The attitude of employers and employees alike is to get rich as quickly as possible. No one knows how long Hong Kong will remain under British rule, and everyone is aware that under another régime the opportunity to make money may not be so easy.

The delicate position of Hong Kong is a factor recognized by the British authorities and the Chinese population alike. Since the communist leaders of China apparently have no desire at present to secure Hong Kong by forcible means, they have not encouraged their supporters to engage in outright subversive action. The communist unions rarely call strikes and their behaviour, on the whole, has been circumspect. How long this policy will continue, it is impossible to say, but so long as it does, Hong Kong industrial relations will be relatively peaceful. There is, of course, always the danger that there may be another clash similar to the one that occurred between Kuomintang supporters and communist supporters in 1956, when in several days of rioting many people were injured and much damage to property was done.

If the level of economic prosperity continues to rise and the external political situation does not deteriorate it is likely that a system of industrial relations based on collective bargaining will gradually develop. It will probably come first in the British and American owned firms that are familiar with the

G

techniques of negotiation. However, before substantial progress is made, there will have to be a thorough reorganization of
the trade unions. Their number will have to be reduced, their
administration improved and their policy of concentrating on
general projects of social welfare changed for one of concentration on industrial problems and the vocational interests of their
members. A more positive lead is required from the government, which preaches the virtues of collective bargaining, but
hesitates to give really active support to its development.

North Borneo, Brunei and Sarawak

Trade unions have been organized in each of the three
British territories on the island of Borneo. The first union to be
organized was the North Borneo Clerical Union, which catered
for clerks in the employment of the government. This union
later changed its name to the North Borneo Junior Civil Service
Association. Before this union was established guilds had
existed among the Chinese section of the population.

Pre-war legislation gave the government powers to regulate
'the performance of agreements to labour and include provisions
relating to notice and termination, hours of work, rest days and
holidays, tasks and piece-work, payment of wages, overtime,
employment of women and children, the truck system, health,
housing and sanitation, hospitals and medical care, food
supplies, keeping of check rolls and wage accounts, inspection
of place of employment, investigation of complaints and settlement of disputes'.[31] The first Trade Union Ordinance was
passed in 1947. In the same year a labour department was
established and a Joint Labour Adviser for the three Borneo
territories was appointed. By 1958 the scope of the department
had been considerably extended; six unions with a total
membership of almost 2,000 were registered.

The first trade unions appeared in Sarawak at about the same
time as in North Borneo. Four organizations were founded
soon after the passing of the first Trade Union Ordinance and
were registered in 1948. By 1958 their number had grown to
38. Some of the smaller organizations were more like guilds
than unions, and even the larger organizations, such as the
Kuching Wharf Labourers' Union, with members in 15 ports

[31] Colonial Annual Report, North Borneo, 1947, p. 11.

in Sarawak, has many characteristics that make it more like a guild than a trade union. This union, for example, acts as a labour contractor, supplying labour to the ports of Sarawak. It receives a considerable income for this activity, which it then ultimately shares out among its members as an annual bonus at the times of the principal communal religious festivals.

The Secretary of Chinese Affairs acted as 'Protector of Labour' until it was decided to appoint a joint Labour Commissioner for Sarawak and the State of Brunei in 1954. Under the agreement between the two territories the Commissioner's office was located just over the border in Brunei, at Kuala Belait, which is the centre of the Brunei oilfields and is fairly close to the oilfields and refinery at Miri in Sarawak. The disadvantage of this arrangement was that the Labour Commissioner was rarely able to get to Kuching, the capital of Sarawak, or to Sibu, its most thriving provincial town, because of the difficulty of communications in a territory virtually without roads. In 1956 it was decided that Sarawak should have its own separate Labour Commissioner, and an officer who had had experience in this work in other overseas territories was appointed.

Among the tropical territories of the Commonwealth having an oil industry, Brunei was unique, in 1959, in that not only were there no trade unions, but it had no ordinance specifically designed to give trade unions a legal status. There appeared to be nothing in the law to make trade unions illegal, but in the absence of specific legislation, there was an element of doubt. A labour ordinance based upon the Colonial Office Model Ordinance was under discussion in 1960, and during the year meetings were held among oilfield workers for the purpose of starting a trade union.

The Sultan of Brunei and the Legislative Council were rather reluctant to encourage the development of trade unions, fearing that they might become a vehicle through which radical elements would stir up unrest. The Shell Oil Company, which is the major employer in Brunei, has, in principle, adopted a neutral attitude. It would be unfair to suggest that the outstanding conditions of employment which it has provided— steady employment, good wages, excellent low-cost housing, free medical care, free transport, schools and clubs—were designed to keep trade unionism from developing for as long as possible, even though this, in fact, is what happened.

Labour relations in the oilfields are inevitably paternalistic, but considerable effort is made to encourage local initiative and there are no bars to promotion. Although there was no union in 1951, the company established a joint consultative committee elected on a communal basis, representative of all sections of the labour force. The company provides first-class trade school facilities and gives every encouragement to employees to improve their skill and knowledge. It was recognized by the company that with the constitutional development of Brunei, unions would almost certainly emerge, but there was a fear that the unions might be used as the basis of political organizations at the expense of hitherto peaceful and constructive industrial relations. This danger did not arise because of a failure to provide good conditions of employment, but because the formation of trade unions is related both to a desire for high wages and good working conditions and also to other fundamental political and social factors.

Fiji

The development of trade unionism in Fiji was stimulated by the disturbance to the traditional pattern of life made by the second world war. The building of an airport and other military installations brought soldiers, sailors and airmen to the island; new ideas were imported, and the conditions encouraged the formation of unions. The farmers had been, in fact, the first to organize in Fiji, but they were rapidly followed, in the first wave of trade unionism, by the sugar industry employees, firemen, seamen and teachers. In 1942 the workers employed in processing sugar, the territory's main crop, formed a trade union. This was registered in the following year under the trade union ordinance which had been passed in 1943. In 1947, when a new labour ordinance was adopted, repealing or consolidating much of the previous legislation as it affected labour, there were already 17 trade unions in existence. By 1958, 39 unions were registered, of which 4 had over 1,000 members each. Among the groups of employees organized were aerodrome workers, commercial employees, firemen, motor-drivers, Public Works Department employees, gold miners, seamen, stevedores, sugar-mill workers, teachers and self-employed dairy-farmers and sugar-cane farmers.

The development of trade unions in Fiji has been complicated by the acute racial division between Indians and Fijians. Most of the unions have been inter-racial, but following the riots which occurred during a strike against the oil companies in Fiji, in December, 1959, the Fijian workers have been encouraged by their chiefs to break away from the Indian-led unions, and a separate Trades Union Congress was set up in 1960.

Many of the larger enterprises in Fiji are managed by Australians, most of whom would like to see a central feature of the system of industrial relations in Australia—compulsory arbitration—introduced into Fiji. The unions, too, tend to favour the idea of having wages determined and enforced by a legal procedure rather than by a collective bargaining process. Until the passing of the Industrial Disputes (Arbitration and Inquiry) Ordinance in 1958, the governor had power to impose a settlement in the case of a dispute that threatened to hurt the economic and social interest of the people of the territory. Since 1958 the powers available to the government are roughly the same as those possessed by the British Government. That is to say the government cannot now impose penal sanctions on strikers, but it may establish arbitration tribunals and order inquiries into disputes. No award or recommendation is legally binding.

It was unfortunate that only one year after the adoption of the new ordinance, on the advice of the Colonial Office, a strike should have turned into an ugly display of delinquent violence, as a result of irresponsible union leadership and weak direction of the police. However, the fears aroused by this event have induced changes in attitudes and policies on the part of employers, the public authorities and the trade unions that could substantially improve industrial relations in Fiji.

As in other territories, the principal problems which confront the unions in Fiji are those of administration, finance and leadership. Some organizations have unfortunately been seriously hurt by the dishonest conduct of leaders who have corruptly used union funds for their own purposes.

Although by 1960 trade unionism had become well established in all the territories with which we are concerned, many problems of organization had still to be overcome.   In some cases there were too many small unions, weakly organized and badly led.   Membership was frequently unstable and the flow of finance meagre and unreliable.   Inadequate resources and inefficient administration were a general feature of unions in every territory, but these deficiencies had not prevented them from playing an important role in industry and society.   This role was inevitably influenced by the end of colonial status and the achievement of political independence.   In some territories the unions had become so closely attached to political parties they were in danger, through the encroachment of politicians, of losing their ability to protect their members' interest.   After independence was achieved the place of unions in the political structure in many territories became unsettled and ambiguous.   In the next chapter the influence of politics on the growth and development of the unions and the problems of determining their relationship to the state will be considered.

CHAPTER 3

TRADE UNIONS AND POLITICS

THE history of trade unionism in the colonies has been closely bound up with the political evolution of each territory. This was inevitable since the very existence of trade unions must always raise questions of great political significance in any society. Trade unions are thus necessarily involved in politics, but they are not political parties any more than churches or employers' associations, which are also involved in politics, are political parties. The primary purpose of a trade union is to protect and advance the vocational interest of its members. To do this successfully it must frequently use its organized strength to press political parties, whether in or out of power, to legislate in a way that will benefit its members. The extent to which unions will seek to achieve their ends by the exercise of political influence, rather than by the exertion of direct pressure on employers by the process of collective bargaining, will vary according to the prevailing circumstances.

If unions are not allowed by law to carry out their functions by means of collective bargaining, if they are not allowed to call out their members on strike, if they are restricted and hampered by the law in other respects, they will be compelled to exercise political pressure to bring about the legal changes necessary to permit the exercise of these rights. Thus British trade unions were involved in the struggle to reform Parliament in the nineteenth century, since this was a necessary prerequisite to securing the legislative changes the unions required in order to engage effectively in collective bargaining.

Even after the unions in Britain had firmly established themselves, they still found it necessary to act as a political pressure group. State regulation, they had found from experience, was the only effective way of protecting their members from dangerous conditions of employment leading to industrial accidents and disease, and from conditions of 'sweated labour' in certain trades; they also found it was the only way to safeguard the welfare of women and children, who were difficult to

unionize. The general economic and social environment
which basically determined the social status and standard of
living of their members was another factor that could not be
altered by negotiations with employers. The unions were thus
compelled to look to the government for action that would bring
about an employment situation that would favour their
members. But the interest of trade unionists in politics did not
derive solely from a narrow sectional interest in better conditions of employment in their trade. It also stemmed from the
natural radicalism of men who were keen trade unionists because they wished to see a root-and-branch reform of society.
British trade unionism has had its utopian, socialist idealism
since the days of Robert Owen, and its behaviour has been
conditioned as much by this influence as by the more prosaic
appeal to the sectional interest of its members.

When British unions reached the stage in their development
where they were convinced that they could hope for little from
the two established political parties, they were persuaded to
form their own party in co-operation with various socialist
societies. This was a matter of practical expediency, but it has
produced a continuing problem of balancing the obvious advantages of sectionalism with the pursuit of theoretical ideas
which, if attained, would be in direct conflict with many of the
basic features of British trade unionism.

In Europe unions were first organized in several countries by
socialist parties. Liberal and Catholic political organizations
quickly followed suit and organized trade unions among their
working-class supporters. Trade unions, therefore, were
originally offshoots of political parties which needed to build up
large followings in order to pursue their ideological aims. The
fostering of trade unions committed to the ideology of the party
was a simple and obvious way of obtaining mass support; it was
equally obvious to the established authorities that they would
hinder the growth of radical parties by making trade unions
illegal.

In Belgium, Holland, France and Italy trade unions are still
organized on the basis of political and religious ideology. This
does not mean, however, that the unions in those countries have
completely sacrificed their functions as trade unions and become mere appendages to the political parties whose ideology

they share. They are first and foremost trade unions, and their efforts are primarily directed towards improving the wages and working conditions of their members.

The significance of their different functions soon became apparent to the unions in Europe after the dictatorial systems of government had given way to democratic processes. Once political parties of liberals and socialists had gained the right to lawful existence, there was less need to organize under the pretext of forming a trade union or friendly society. The unions found that attachment to a political party could also be an embarrassment. Union leaders began to resent the expectation that they should subordinate their interests to those of the party. The functions of the trade unions were different from those of the political party, and the unions saw no reason why they should be called upon to jeopardize their future merely to advance the aims of the party. With the development of democracy the unions became a political force in their own right. Though bound by a common ideology and a desire to secure the attainment of common social objectives, Continental unions were not prepared to accept the position of an inferior body dominated by the parties that had brought them into being, with the exception of unions organized and dominated by communists and—to a lesser extent—by Catholics.[1]

The role of unions under communist control, as expounded by Lenin and developed in practice, is that of acting as a 'school for communism'. Unions exist to further the aims of the Communist Party, whose policy is determined by the leaders of the Soviet Union. Their duty is, therefore, first and always to support Soviet foreign policy and to carry out the orders of the party, even if this means acting in a manner that is contrary to the interest of their members and dangerous to the development of an effective trade union movement.

Catholic-dominated trade unions are also expected to shape their policies in the light of Catholic social philosophy. For the most part, however, the Catholic unions are free to press for objectives that are of direct trade union interest, and on such questions they may come into conflict with the political parties which are also strongly influenced by Catholic religious beliefs.

[1] See W. Pickles, 'Trade Unions in the Political Climate', in *Industrial Relations: Contemporary Problems and Perspectives*, ed. B. C. Roberts (London, 1962).

Catholic trade unions are not exploited to serve the interests of the Church with the same degree of ruthlessness as are the labour organizations controlled by the Communist Party; the difference is therefore substantial.

Today, with the exception of Norway and Britain, where trade unions preceded the formation of political parties, there are no Continental countries which have unions organically linked to a political labour party.   Unions in Europe and elsewhere still broadly support particular political ideologies and generally have a closer relation to one party than to another, but except for the communist unions their attachment does not extend to the point where they are controlled by the party and compelled to accept the dictates of party leaders.

There can be little doubt that the dominant influence of political ideologies on the European trade union movements in the early stages of their development has had an adverse effect on the role of the unions in industry.   Their relatively weak position in relation to employers has meant that collective bargaining in such countries as France, Italy, Germany and Belgium has been less well developed than in Britain or America. Nor have the unions been strong enough to protect the interests of their members by a system of shop stewards when a grievance arises.   Thus the unions in the countries where ideology and party politics have been predominant have been weakened and divided.   In these circumstances the unions have inevitably had to look to the state for the protection of their members, and legislation has come to play a much more important role in industrial relations than in Britain.

From the experience of trade union movements in Britain, Europe and elsewhere, it should come as no surprise to find that unions in the tropical territories of the Commonwealth have sought to achieve their objectives by political means; or that unions have been promoted by politicans for the purpose of advancing their interests.   It would indeed have been unusual if they had remained aloof from all political association.   The critics of colonial trade unions have, in effect, assumed that these *new* organizations should have started from a state of development that has only been reached elsewhere in the world after considerable experience and when certain social conditions have been fulfilled.   The interesting question is, will unions in most countries of the tropical commonwealth develop along broadly the same lines as unions have developed in the more advanced industrial countries of the world? Will they achieve a position in which they are organically independent of the employers and political parties? Or will they fail to assert a functional independence, become instead completely dominated by a political party, and on its achievement of power be absorbed in the administrative machinery of the state, as was the case in the Soviet Union? It will be possible to give a more positive answer to these questions after trends in the various territories have been surveyed.

British influence has been used to encourage non-political trade unionism. No attempt has been made to make support for a political party a legal offence, but labour officers and government officials have condemned political action as a dangerous form of union activity. This advice has been based on two objectives: firstly, a desire to promote stable responsible unions, and secondly, a wish to avoid encouraging political movements that might have adverse effects on the economic development and good government of the territories.

The basic objection to political activities on the part of trade unions at an early stage in their development was that the more exciting character of political agitation inevitably tended to draw trade union leadership away from the more humdrum but essential activities of building a viable organization. It was feared that if newly-established trade unions became political bodies, then they might never become effective trade unions. Experience tended to bear out this concern; for the effect of political activities on the development of the unions has almost always been adverse.

The distrust of political trade unionism was by no means merely the predictable reaction of established authority to a threat to its power. There was also in it the genuine fear that political trade unionism might turn out to be no more than mob terrorism—a vehicle for the aggrandizement of ambitious, self-seeking, local politicians and destructive of the orderly political and economic progress that was in the best interest of the people of the territories as a whole.

However strong the arguments advanced by colonial administrators, businessmen and indigenous leaders that the

attachment of trade unions to political movements might have
adverse consequences for the people of the territories, they were
hardly likely to have much effect, coming from critics who had a
vested interest in maintaining their superior position. The
link forged between trade unions and political movements was
inevitable, since it was believed that it was only by having a
union basis for party organization that rapid political progress
could be made. But little thought was given to the danger
that this link might have for the unions, or even concern when
its consequences became manifest.

Since the ruling British authorities had the power to legislate
to create a legal framework within which trade unions could
lawfully exist, it was on them that pressure had to be exerted.
The objective of nationalist movements was to rid their territories of colonial rule so as to raise the standards of the indigenous population; thus there was a natural identity of aim
between the unions and the nationalist political movements in
so far as both desired to promote the interests of the workers and
peasants. When, in addition to the political rulers of the
territories, the major employers were British or aliens who
had invested their money and talents with the support of the
British, it was inevitable that the unions should see the attainment of their economic objectives as closely bound up with the
political goals of the nationalist leaders.

The political activities of the unions in the colonial territories
have been as clearly the product of social circumstances as the
political activities of their predecessors in the older countries.
Denunciation of the unions as the tools of political agitators was
perhaps a natural response by exasperated colonial civil servants and expatriate businessmen, but this cry was rather like
that of Canute when he upbraided the waves for their temerity.
Until the leaders of the indigenous people had been given the
opportunity to participate in government and until the lot of
the mass of the workers had been vastly improved, it was idle
to consider that trade unionism could be divorced entirely from
politics. Even independence and a rapid advance in economic
growth would not bring a complete separation. The relationship of the unions to the government and their functional role
and responsibilities would, however, be affected by constitutional and economic developments.

Although it was impossible to divorce the development of trade unions from the influence of political factors, it was clear that apart from any desire to avoid political disturbance there were substantial reasons for attempting to persuade union leaders to concentrate on the task of building well-organized unions and developing non-political functions.

It has been the experience in other countries that the subordination of union activities to the achievement of political aims has generally had an adverse effect on union development. If union members are recruited on the basis of their vocational interests without regard to political, religious and other beliefs, there is a danger that an attachment to a political party will have a serious effect on the unity of the organization. It was the experience of being constantly involved in the conflicts between rival political theories and rival political leaders that convinced unions in Europe and America that they must become independent of the political parties with which they had been closely associated. Another reason why unions have been counselled against forming too close an attachment to political parties is that this has made their acceptance and recognition by employers more difficult. It is hard enough in any circumstances to persuade employers, who have been used to determining conditions of employment without interference, to accept willingly an obligation to bargain with a newly developed union. If the union is also engaged in making a political attack on the employer's position in the territory, the hostility it arouses is an additional handicap to its recognition.

When union leaders are more interested in politics than in the building of a sound system of industrial relations, experience has shown that not only do they neglect the organizational requirements of their unions, but unfortunately when advantageous political opportunities occur, they sometimes leave their union in the lurch. Even more disastrously, they may come to regard the unions as mere political conveniences, and when they attain political power they may be mainly concerned with seeing that the unions do their bidding rather than with helping them to develop as strong autonomous bodies.

The Influence of Political Factors in Different Territories

An examination of developments in the territories of the British tropical Commonwealth reveals a variety of situations. In all cases unions have been closely connected with the growth of indigenous political movements. Developments have not followed a uniform pattern, but it is possible to discern significant trends and to indicate the conditions necessary to achieve a system of trade unionism that is not completely subordinated to a political organization.

West Indies

In the West Indies, trade unionism was closely associated with the achievement of political and social reform. The unions were mainly developed by leaders who were politically ambitious, and labour organizations have formed the basis of, for example, the Labour Party and the People's National Party in Jamaica. In Antigua the Trades and Labour Union is both a trade union and a political party. In Trinidad there has been more of a separation between the unions and political organizations, though union leaders have been interested in politics and politicians have been active in the unions. Captain Cipriani's Trinidad Working Men's Association stressed that it was not a trade union, but it was profoundly interested in improving the conditions of labour. Trade unions formed later in Trinidad developed associations with various political parties, but they never became so closely involved as to lose their identity or forget their trade union purpose. When the People's National Movement was formed in 1956 it attracted support from most of the membership of the unions, but many of the leaders of the unions were reluctant to accept the domination of the P.N.M., and insisted on the Trades Union Council remaining an independent body. They were able to do this because many of the unions had been established for a long time; their leaders were already important and influential figures who did not need political support to gain recognition and make progress in collective bargaining. This has not, however, insulated the Trinidad trade unions from the influence of political factors, but the situation was one in which the unions had a better chance of developing on traditional British and American lines than was the case in some other territories.

In British Guiana the trade unions have also remained independent of both the main political parties. Some of the union leaders have shown a keen political interest in the opposition party led by Forbes Burnham, but the unions have not formally attached themselves to this party. Dr. Jagan, the leader of the governing People's Progressive Party, sought to promote the Guianese Industrial Workers' Union among sugar workers as a rival to the well-established Manpower Citizens' Association. This move failed because the leaders of the established union refused to bow to political pressure of this kind; they concentrated on improving the wages and working conditions of their members. With the aid of enlightened employers, who were afraid that politics might have a devastating effect on their industrial relations, considerable improvements in wages and working conditions were negotiated. The unusual situation then developed in which the Indian employees of the sugar estates were not only both active political supporters of Dr. Jagan and his party but were, at the same time, members of a trade union which bitterly criticized the party and its leaders.

The situation is as yet far from stable, and the latest development in British Guiana has been for the President of the Manpower Citizens' Association to join up with other prominent anti-Jagan political figures to form a new political party. The effect that this has had on the political behaviour of his union's members has been small; they have continued to vote for Dr. Jagan. What is more important, this activity of the President has provided Dr. Jagan with an opportunity of encouraging another rival union that may successfully enlist the allegiance of the employees of the sugar estates. If this move is effective, then political and economic decisions in British Guiana will be much more under the influence of Dr. Jagan's party than has been the case in the past.

The emergence of reasonably stable local governments in most of the West Indian territories has given the unions a good opportunity to concentrate on their specific problems. The political battle for self-government was won relatively easily, and the parties in power are generally pragmatic rather than dogmatic in their philosophy. Their sympathies are with the workers from whom they receive their support, but this is not carried to the point where it is construed as requiring either the liquidation of union independence or the liquidation of private enterprise. The spread of education and the growth of a solid block of middle-class citizens with a vested interest in a free society are powerful factors conducive to a system of industrial relations that is broadly similar to the western model.

Differences have arisen between the government and certain unions in Trinidad and the political leaders have sought to crush this opposition. They have not, however, attempted to place the unions in a position where they would be completely dominated and used for political ends—not perhaps because they would not have liked to do so, but because independent trade unionism has been strong enough to put up stiff resistance. And there was public opinion to be considered. There would have been a strong reaction to any direct attempt to destroy the unions by dictatorial means. It was, therefore, more expedient to seek to discredit difficult trade union leaders and to use other and more subtle forms of political pressure to persuade the unions to support rather than to oppose the policies of the government.

In Barbados the chance issue of personal conflict between the leader of the Barbados Workers' Union and the leader of the Barbados Labour Party led to a situation which prevented the union from becoming intimately tied to the government. This divorce between the union and the party has meant that the union has concentrated on organization and collective bargaining far more effectively than might have been the case if its senior officer had been made Minister of Labour at an early stage. The Barbados Workers' Union also happens to have a history of twenty years of steady development and it is one of the most efficiently organized trade unions in the tropical Commonwealth.

But even when unions have been intimately related to political parties, as they have been in Jamaica, when conditions allow they are likely to develop along independent lines. With the advent of stable self-government and a rapid rate of economic growth, the unions have found it necessary to direct their attention to the bread-and-butter issues of industrial relations. The unions remain greatly concerned with politics and the success of their parties; however, this is not an all-embracing Soviet-type relationship, but rather the kind of link that prevails in the free countries of the western world.

Many employers complain that the unions are able to call upon the government to exercise political pressure when they fail to achieve their objectives by collective bargaining. There can be no doubt that the governments of the West Indian territories have given some help to the unions, but they have been fairly careful not to press this too far. Most big employers had been in a very strong bargaining position for a long time, and it was hardly to be expected that they should continue to enjoy quite the same freedom from pressure to provide better wages and working conditions when political and social conditions changed. The necessity to come to terms with the realities of the situation has generally been accepted by governments, industry and unions.

In the small islands of the West Indies a particular problem is that ministers retain their trade union positions after they have attained public office. This is the situation in Antigua, where the Chief Minister is also President of the Antigua Workers' Union, and in several other islands. The argument used to justify the holding of a dual office is that there is a shortage of able men, but however valid this contention, it is also true that nothing grows in the shadow of a big tree. The retention of trade union posts by ministers on occasion inevitably leads to the exercise of political pressure that can have an adverse effect on the development of good industrial relations. Thus an employer was recently threatened with expulsion from the island of Antigua because of a trade dispute in which he was involved. It is difficult for the government to be impartial when its leaders are also senior officials of the union.

Malaya

Turning to South-East Asia, Malaya, Singapore and Hong Kong, we find three entirely different situations, ranging from the non-political unionism to entirely political unionism. The unions of Malay were, until the emergency in 1948, completely dominated by the Communist Party. The policy of the Communist Party was to use the unions to serve the ends of the party; it was not interested in the slightest in trade unionism for its own sake. The consequence of this complete

H

subordination of the unions to the interest of the party was the almost total destruction of the unions when the party decided that their leaders should take to the jungle in a violent attempt to secure power.

This experience was the vital factor that produced the prevailing situation in which the unions are content to stay out of party politics. The non-political character of the contemporary Malayan trade union movement is further consolidated by the racial situation in Malaya and the composition of the Malayan trade unions. The communist-dominated trade unions were largely made up of Chinese members and leaders. The Malayan trade unions of today have relatively few Chinese members and most of its officers are Indian. Although the largest element in the population is Malay and the government is dominated by Malays, the Malay membership of the unions is quite small, though growing in importance. In these circumstances the Indian union leaders are reluctant to involve the unions in political issues that might lead to the promotion of separatist Malay and perhaps Chinese trade unions.

Certain attempts have been made by socialists and supporters of the Peasant Party to secure influence in the unions, but in the prevailing conditions these have not been very successful. In the 1959 State Council elections the strong union areas returned a number of Socialist Front candidates; these results do not, however, reflect a major decision on the part of the unions to engage in political activities.

Singapore

The position of the unions in Singapore is quite different from that of Malaya. The development of unions was closely connected with the subsequent establishment of a political party pledged to secure self-government and to raise the standard of living of the workers. Mr. Lim Yew Hock, a moderate socialist who engineered the growth of the unions in Singapore, eventually became the Chief Minister and leader of the Labour Party. His rival is the present Prime Minister, Mr. Lee Kuan Yew, who rose to power with the support of an important section of the unions which had been captured by sympathizers with the Communist Government of China. The influence of left-wing extremists in the Singapore trade union movement has been facilitated by the fact that most union members are Chinese-speaking workers who are more ready to follow leaders educated in Chinese schools than English-speaking and English-educated Chinese. Membership of the left-wing unions is a form of protest against British rule and influence, rather than an interest in trade unionism as a collective bargaining institution.

The highly political character of the unions in Singapore has not prevented them from developing their industrial activities. Indeed, the leaders of the politically militant unions have skilfully used the threat of political action to press the British and the larger employers to make economic concessions. Determined not to be outflanked on the left, Lee Kuan Yew's Socialist Government gave conspicuous support to the unions to gain recognition, secure concessions and to build up the strength of their organization. At the same time, however, faced by the danger that his pro-communist supporters would use their growing influence in the trade unions to destroy him as he had destroyed his predecessor, Lee Kuan Yew and his cabinet colleagues decided to introduce legislation to prevent industrial disputes being used as a means of creating civil disorder, as recounted in Chapter 2.

The situation in Singapore has, therefore, been one in which the development of non-political trade unionism was almost impossible. Either the unions were allowed to develop freely and fully under the total domination of the extreme left-wing politically-inspired element, or efforts had to be made to bring them under the political control of the more moderate People's Action Party.

There are unions in Singapore which would prefer to concentrate on improving the wages and working conditions of their members and leave political agitation to the political parties, but they are in a minority and it is unlikely that they can survive the political pressures that are exerted upon them from one side or the other. These unions are composed of members who are employed for the most part in the public service. Their members have more stable jobs, they have better wages and working conditions and they have a higher standard of education than many other groups of workers. They, therefore, have more to lose from political adventures, and they are more keenly aware of the issues involved.

In the long run, the extent to which the unions in Singapore are able to develop a *modus vivendi* in which they are able to exercise their functions as agencies for protecting and promoting the occupational interests of their members by collective bargaining will depend on the successful establishment of stable political and economic conditions.   The Singapore Government faces a difficulty in this respect, since the attainment of a rate of economic development that will provide a solution for Singapore's growing unemployment problem is to a large extent dependent upon a closer integration with Malaya.   The price of bringing about the integration of Malay and Singapore may well involve the removal of the communists and their sympathizers from the leadership of Singapore's most powerful unions.   It is unlikely that this can be achieved without deliberate political action.

Hong Kong

The trade union movements of Hong Kong are almost totally politically orientated.   They have not so far developed beyond the stage of existing to support the rival political ideologies of the Kuomintang and the communists.   Their failure to develop industrial functions is due to a number of factors.   The history of Chinese trade unionism is almost entirely one of political agitation.   From their inception, the unions have been caught up in the struggle for political power that has been waged in China since the first world war.   The communists have triumphed on the mainland, and they have brought the unions under political control, as they have done in every other country where they have been successful.   In Hong Kong there is a stable colonial government, and in this situation the struggle between the Chinese supporters of the Kuomintang and the communists continues.

In spite of the government's policy of encouraging non-political trade unions, the social and economic climate of Hong Kong has been hostile to this development since the return of the British in 1945.   Although there has been a phenomenal growth of industry in the past decade, the great influx of refugees has provided a supply of labour that has exceeded demand.   In these circumstances employers in Hong Kong have been able to resist collective bargaining attempts. The uncertain position of the colony has not encouraged a constructive attitude to industrial relations: employers have been mainly concerned to maximize their short-run profits rather than to build up the goodwill of their employees. There are feeble signs that point in the direction of a collective bargaining system, but so long as the political future of the colony is uncertain, and the working population is faced by a difficult employment situation, it is unlikely that there will be a development of trade unionism that will make for the emergence of a western-type system of industrial relations. The unions will continue to concentrate on political demonstrations and social activities outside the place of work, because these give greater satisfaction than attempts to negotiate with their employers, who are not only stronger and cleverer but are also supported by the authorities who are more concerned with maintaining law and order than with promoting the development of a better system of industrial relations.

Aden

Great efforts have been made in Aden to promote a trade union movement and an industrial relations system that would encourage the growth of collective bargaining. The unions are, however, strongly motivated by political considerations and their tactics have been greatly influenced by this factor. Strikes in Aden were so numerous that the government, in desperation, introduced a system of compulsory arbitration. This step had the effect of quelling, temporarily at any rate, the almost continuous industrial unrest, but the unions refused to co-operate in the new procedure. It is unlikely that this can work well if the union's intransigence is continued. However, it is the hope of the authorities that compulsory arbitration may have the effect of pushing the unions into a more positive attitude to collective bargaining.

The problem of creating responsible unions and a stable system of industrial relations in Aden is complicated not only by the territory's colonial status but also by the racial composition of its working population. Most of the unskilled workers are Arabs, and a large proportion are temporary residents from the

Yemen.   It is this element that forms the most important part of the membership of the Aden T.U.C. and greatly influences its policy.

The major objective of the Aden T.U.C. is to advance the political and social interests of its Arab members by seeking 'the liberation of the occupied south'; that is, Aden Colony and Protectorates, and its unification with the Yemen.   This is to be followed by the overthrow of the present Yemeni régime and the establishment in its place of a socialist republic which would be linked up with the United Arab Republic.

The fact that the aims of the T.U.C. are quite impracticable in the context of Aden's strategic importance to Britain is a frustrating factor to the union leaders and a constant source of irritation to Aden's middle class and the British authorities.   The T.U.C. has become the most potent force in the politics of Aden, partly because of the weakness of the nationalist political parties.   The Aden T.U.C. is not organically tied to either of the two parties, except on specific issues; it has preferred to take its own stand on every political question.   It is, however, greatly influenced by Cairo and probably receives financial assistance from the U.A.R., as well as advice on tactics.

Immigration is one of the issues on which the T.U.C. feels most strongly.   Most of the jobs in the middle occupational strata are held by Indians.   Artisans, especially at the middle level, are solidly Indian, and so are nearly all the clerks. Moreover, Indians holding positions of foremen, senior clerks and other supervisory posts, resist the advancement of Arabs into these higher occupations, as they have resisted the advancement of indigenous workers to some degree in East Africa. Arab education was for long neglected and there were few suitably trained Aden-born workers available for technical and commercial jobs, but there has been a vast improvement in the provision of educational facilities and opportunities to enter skilled trades in recent years, and this will eventually overcome the shortage of trained and experienced Arabs.

In this situation the immigration of Indians, who in the past have been brought in by business firms whenever they desired to fill skilled-workers' posts, has become a highly-charged political issue.   Aden was administered by the Government of India from 1839 to 1937; during this period Indians entered Aden freely, but the policy of the Aden Government is now to admit only essential workers.

The Labour Commissioner is responsible for ensuring that no one receives a permit to enter if there is anyone locally who has the qualifications for the job. The Commissioner had the advice of a committee, consisting of a European and an Asian employer and two trade unionists, to help him and the immigration authorities to decide on applications for admission. Unfortunately, the trade union representatives soon left this committee, claiming that they had to take this step because their advice was disregarded. By automatically opposing every application irrespective of its merits the trade union representatives had made unanimity difficult; but, the unions alleged, they were compelled to adopt this attitude, as the employers tended always to favour admission. The official reply to the complaints of the union representatives was that the committee was only advisory and that it must be left to the Labour Commissioner and the immigration authorities to make the final decision. In fact, the Labour Commissioner was strongly against being saddled with the responsibility for making these decisions, as they tended to create friction between the labour department and the trade union movement. It was also admitted by the authorities that despite safeguards, employers sometimes abused the scheme and were able to get away with it.

The management of the British Petroleum Refinery has for some years recognized the need to discourage immigration and to give local inhabitants an opportunity to fill jobs previously occupied by Asians. The company does not allow any immigrant worker to stay longer than six years, and wherever practicable, a local man is trained to take over the job of an immigrant as soon as possible.

The Aden T.U.C. complains that the government, with its policy of Aden-ization rather than Arab-ization, is favouring the Indians. Indians can become citizens and obtain the right to vote after seven years. It is alleged by the T.U.C. that the Yemenis are treated by the administration as foreigners, and that they are in general denied the vote unless they can prove that they were born in the colony. The Aden T.U.C.

represents the unfranchised Yemenis, and a Yemeni franchise is a major plank in its platform.

In the circumstances which have prevailed in Aden it would have been odd had a trade union movement developed with little or no interest in politics. Yet in spite of the fact that the leaders of the unions, and especially the T.U.C., are strongly politically motivated, it is misleading to analyse their behaviour only in political terms. The Aden T.U.C. is well aware of its power to exploit the situation to the best advantage of its members. It has used the strike and threat of strike to considerable advantage. Employers providing the best wages and conditions complain that because they are Europeans they are singled out for unfair attention by the unions. It may seem unfair to an employer providing better wages and working conditions than the average that the union should not be grateful, but the union knows full well that higher wages are paid and better conditions are provided because the employer is vulnerable and that he can be squeezed for more.

The propensity of unions to strike in Aden is therefore not only a political phenomenon, it is also an industrial trade union activity. Employers themselves are not without responsibility for the readiness of unions to cease work. They have often reacted to union claims by standing out on the wrong issues, often refusing to budge until a strike has been called, and then instead of negotiating a settlement after a return to work they have simply given in and conceded the union's claims in full. Since strikes appear to have secured many gains, it is difficult to persuade union leaders that they would have been more successful if they had been less aggressive. Even if some union leaders would genuinely prefer to follow more conciliatory methods, they are prisoners of the situation they have, in part, created, and it is not easy for them to persuade their followers that they should change course.

Had there been a different political situation in Aden, the development of compulsory arbitration might have proved to be the means by which the unions could have broken free from the policy of striking first and talking afterwards. But making strikes illegal has not prevented them from happening for political reasons, and until the political factors are changed a better climate of industrial relations will not develop. Undoubtedly the unions have behaved irresponsibly and allowed political motives to override their industrial interests, but even so, a major share of the responsibility for bringing about improved relations rests with the employers, as many strikes have been provoked by their refusal to consult with the unions on such items as redundancy, the employment of immigrant artisans and other issues of importance.

West Africa

Trade unionism in most of the African territories has been influenced by political factors. There are, however, a number of different political situations to be considered. In almost all cases trade unions were started as independent bodies with the primary object of improving the wages and working conditions of people who joined them. Many of the leaders of the unions developed political ambitions and allied their organizations to nationalist parties, but there are few instances of political parties founding trade unions to promote their cause.

When the trade unions in Nigeria formed the first Trades Union Congress in that country, Obafemi Awolowo was elected secretary-editor of its publication; later, Awolowo became the leader of the Action Party. From its beginning the Congress took a great interest in political affairs, agitating for labour representation in the Legislative Council. From the outset the first Nigerian T.U.C. suffered from the personal rivalries and the political ambitions of its leaders, and finally a split occurred in 1949 on the issue of association with the new and rival political parties, the Action Group Party and the National Council of Nigeria and the Cameroons.

Following this breakdown a new body, the Nigerian National Federation of Labour, was established by elements dissatisfied with the political views of the leaders of the Nigerian T.U.C. In 1950 an attempt was made to bring the two rival central organizations together under the aegis of a third body, the Nigerian Labour Congress. Immediately following its first public meeting the Nigerian Labour Congress affiliated with the World Federation of Trade Unions. Some of the leaders of the N.L.C. were strong supporters of communism, and they sought to persuade the other union leaders to adopt a hostile attitude to the International Confederation of Free Trade Unions.

Torn by political discussion, the Nigerian Labour Congress collapsed, and little progress was made by the National Federation of Labour or the Nigerian Trade Union Congress during the next two years. In fact, the majority of registered unions refused to affiliate to either association. In August 1953 a conference of trade unions made a fresh start by establishing an all-Nigeria Trade Union Federation on a similar basis to the original T.U.C. One of its objects, however, was the establishment of a Labour Party for the purpose of realizing a socialist government.

The Federation was strongly influenced by men with left-wing ideas, and a rift soon occurred over the question of affiliation to the International Confederation of Free Trade Unions. Certain unions withdrew from what they alleged was a communist-influenced organization, and eventually, in 1957, set up another national centre, the National Council of Trade Unions of Nigeria. After two years of hostile exchanges the differences of opinion were patched up at a conference in 1959, when a merger was agreed on the basis 'that while recognizing the right of the individual to believe in any brand of political ideology, we nevertheless take cognizance of the events which led to disunity in the past, and agree therefore that in the interest of permanent unity, communism, fascism and national political partisanship shall not be projected in the Nigerian Labour Movement'. [2]

Within six months of the foundation of the new Trades Union Congress of Nigeria the rift had once more opened wide over the issue of affiliation with the I.C.F.T.U., and the acceptance of financial help from this body. In 1960 the political opponents of the supporters within the T.U.C. of the I.C.F.T.U. broke away to form a body calling itself the Nigerian T.U.C.

In spite of the fact that attempts to form a central organization have always foundered on the shoals of political ideology and ambition, there is a strong current of opinion in Nigeria that unions should be primarily concerned with the industrial interests of their members, 'and on the whole, trade union political action has been left to the central organizations which

[2] Quoted by T. M. Yesufu in *An Introduction to Industrial Relations in Nigeria* (an unpublished thesis in the University of London, 1960).

have existed from time to time'.[3] It is an important question, however, whether the advent of independence will lead to a more pronounced emphasis on the political functions of unions.

It is likely that political factors will continue to exert an influence on trade union behaviour, but since the great parties in Nigeria are organized broadly on a tribal basis it is unlikely that the unions, which cut across tribal and regional boundaries and therefore constitute the sole unifying organization in the country, will be subordinated to the interests of a single party as is the case in Ghana. The unions know that the tribal allegiance of the members is strong, and they are well aware that too close an identity with any of the parties would destroy organizational unity.

The fact that the country is a federation of three territories, each forming a powerful entity, makes the possibility of single party domination unlikely. Sentiment in the Department of Labour is in favour of a system of industrial relations that is in harmony with the principles embodied in I.L.O. conventions. So long as there is no political development that would drastically change the basis of Nigerian law affecting industrial relations, the approach to trade unionism is likely to continue along the lines established during the period of British rule. Although the political parties are certain to continue to attract support in the unions, events in Ghana, where the freedom of the unions has been drastically curtailed and a number of union leaders have had to seek refuge in adjacent countries, are a warning of the fate which might overtake Nigerian unions if they allowed themselves to become entirely subordinate to political interests.

The course of events in Ghana since that country became independent has completely changed the pattern of trade union organization and behaviour, and fundamentally changed the system of industrial relations. Since 1958, the unions have been reorganized by legislation and brought under the control of the T.U.C., which in turn has been made into an instrument of the ruling party. Collective bargaining has been made obligatory, but it may only be carried on by licensed trade unions. The right to strike has been virtually eliminated and compulsory arbitration has been introduced in its place.

[3] See T. M. Yesufu, *op. cit.*

Trade union membership is now compulsory for all workers whose conditions of employment are determined by the new system of collective bargaining and arbitration.

There were obvious weaknesses in the trade union movement and the system of industrial relations that had developed under British inspiration.   Most of the large number of unions that had sprung up were too small to be administered efficiently and too weak to bargain effectively.   There was need to reorganize the unions on more appropriate lines.   But fundamentally it was not for this reason that the Ghana Government deliberately broke with British policy—described as a 'capitalist-inspired system'.   The leaders of the triumphant Convention People's Party were concerned to create a trade union movement that would be completely under their control. They were not prepared to allow the trade unions to become the basis of an effective opposition.   The primary function of the unions in the new state was to be the same as that of unions in the Soviet Union.   They were to be an instrument of the party; a means through which the party could exercise influence and control.   Through a subordinate trade union movement the government would be able to bring pressure to bear upon employers or to damp down demands from workers for improvements in wages and working conditions to suit the political circumstances.

Dr. Nkrumah and his supporters are well aware of the need to promote economic growth and to maintain economic and political stability.   Control of the trade unions could be of some help in this respect.   However powerful the trade unions might become, the government felt that it could not afford to allow them to jeopardize its programme of attracting capital, raising productivity and preventing inflation by permitting free collective bargaining and the unrestrained exercise of the right to strike.

It is difficult to forecast what effect these measures will have on the future development of trade unions and industrial relations in Ghana.   If they bear too harshly on the members of the unions they may well provoke revolt.   This may simply take the form of a gradual degeneration of the unions, or it may take a more active and violent form.   Much will depend on the efficiency and subtlety of Ghana's political leadership.   Whatever happens in the long run, the trade union movement in Ghana has been subordinated completely to the political objectives of the C.P.P. Its functions are still to protect and promote the vocational interest of union members, but only within the context of a policy that is determined entirely outside the union. So far, however, the government has not sought to interfere with the bargaining process between unions and employers. It has been possible for negotiations to take place and for agreements to be freely reached.

The Ghana trade unions are being actively used by the C.P.P. to foster the dream of a Pan-African empire cherished by Dr. Nkrumah. In spite of the fact that the International Confederation of Free Trade Unions has given considerable help to African trade unions, the Ghana T.U.C. has denounced its activities and promoted a rival organization of African unions. Dr. Nkrumah's aim is to create an African nationalist movement that will oust white men and white influence from the entire continent, but whilst the policy of the Ghana T.U.C. has attracted the support of Guinea, Egypt and the North African states, it has met with opposition from union centres in Nigeria, Kenya and other countries in East and Central Africa.

Pan-Africanism is an attractive idea to many Africans, and it is possible at some future date that an African trade union federation will be established. Today there are many obstacles to the idea of a Pan-African federation and there is little chance that they will be overcome in the immediate future. The activities of the Ghana trade unions are calculated mainly to disrupt the work of the I.C.F.T.U., rather than to achieve a positive advance in trade union organization. The damage that is being done to the development of stable trade unionism in Africa by the demands of political nationalism is accounted of no consequence when set against the ambitions of the leaders of Ghana and its like-minded allies.

East and Central Africa

Tom Mboya, the leader of the Kenya Federation of Labour, is the most influential African supporter of the I.C.F.T.U. Many observers in Kenya, including employers, regard him as an extremely able and intelligent unionist. If in trade union affairs Mboya has conducted his activities with moderation, as a politician he has not always behaved with the same circum-spection. His political utterances have been as radical as those of any other African nationalist leader. But he has managed with remarkable skill to keep his trade union and political activities separate without tarnishing his image to his African followers and his European sympathizers. After be-coming Minister of Labour, Mboya showed considerable courage in stating the responsibilities of labour as well as em-ployers in a developing economy. His speeches displayed a balance and vision that marked him out as a man of exceptional talent and integrity who knew that the experience of the older countries could not be disregarded by Africa.

The Kenya Federation of Labour built up by Mboya is with-out question a highly significant factor in the political situation in Africa, and the I.C.F.T.U. and A.F.L.–C.I.O. have given it considerable financial assistance. Mboya has been severely attacked by the Ghanaian trade union leaders for associating with the I.C.F.T.U., and he is clearly seen as an obstacle to the claims of Dr. Nkrumah to be the natural leader of modern Africa. Between Mboya and Nkrumah there is a wide ideo-logical gulf. For Nkrumah, unions exist only to fulfil the pur-pose of the state. This is not Mboya's view of the status of the unions. Unlike Nkrumah, he is not prompted by a totalitarian philosophy to sacrifice the independence of the unions to the aims of a political party; he does believe, however, that in an under-developed country the unions must work closely with employers and governments, but at the same time the basic rights of the unions must be preserved.[4]

In the other East and Central African territories leaders of the unions are active supporters of the nationalist cause. As in Kenya, the political interests of union leaders have not pre-vented them from seeking to improve the wages and working conditions of their members. Whether the trade unions will be able to maintain their freedom from political domination after colonial rule is ended it is not yet possible to say. The existence of white settlers and large-scale enterprises owned by British, South African and other nationals created an entirely different situation from that in Ghana.

In Northern Rhodesia, in spite of the fact that political

[4] *The Times*, 18th August 1962.

conditions have encouraged African politicians to use the unions to promote their cause, the most outstanding trade union leader in Central Africa, the late Lawrence Katilingu, denounced political interference and sought to build a trade union as a collective bargaining organization. In this objective, the leader of the African Mineworkers' Union had the support of the labour department and other sections of responsible opinion, but, given the circumstances in which trade unionism developed in Northern Rhodesia, politics could not be kept out of the unions.

African trade union leaders in Northern Rhodesia have occupied a peculiar and almost unique position. In contrast to West Africa and even some parts of East Africa, for example Buganda and the Coast, there was no urban civilization in Northern Rhodesia before European enterprise brought the railways, mines, commerce and industry to the territory and encouraged the formation of large centres of population in what had been formerly very sparsely populated lands. Traditional tribal organization, adequate for the rural civilization of the African population, could not be transported to the new towns with their admixture of different tribes and more complex institutions. With the stablizing of populations in urban centres, new norms of behaviour were established and the population were less ready to accept the authority of distant tribal institutions.

Some attempts were made by the authorities in the 1930's and 1940's to extend native institutions to the Africans living in towns. Tribal Elders were appointed to act as liaison between the administration and the various sections of the population; native courts, whose members were appointed by the chiefs in the tribal areas, had jurisdiction in the towns; and proposals were made from time to time to establish urban native authorities analogous to the authorities in rural areas. Many of these institutions, however, have now been rejected by the African town dwellers, whose loyalty has been given to the new elites which have been created in the towns—these include educated men, teachers and those who occupy positions of prestige in the urban community as supervisors, clerks and executive employees, and in some cases, traders, shopkeepers and independent artisans. It is these men who are the natural leaders of the urban working-class populations, rather than the older and more conservative men of chiefly families, who had authority in the tribal community. It was largely they who, in the early stages, formed the urban 'welfare societies' which aimed at improving the lot of the African town dwellers through voluntary effort and through pressure applied (via the administration) on the town authorities. It was the same group of people who later founded the African National Congress, and who took positions on the few elected bodies which have been established to give the Africans some say in the management of their own urban affairs.

Moreover, in the earlier stages, when there were comparatively few men able and willing to take part in public activities, it fell to very much the same group of men (most of whom were in employment in one form or another) to take the lead in founding trade unions to represent the Africans as workers, and put their case to the employers. The ordinary, uneducated African town dweller tended, at least until five or six years ago, to look to one fairly small group of people for leadership, and not to distinguish very clearly between leadership in political and in industrial matters. Thus it was a very common feature in Northern Rhodesia in the period 1950–53 to see one man, probably a senior clerk or teacher by profession, holding office as a branch officer, or even general official of a trade union, as a leader of the local welfare society or of the local branch of Congress, as a member of the Urban Advisory Committee, and possibly as a member of the African Representative Council.

This state of affairs fairly soon began to cause some concern. The 1952 Report of the Labour Department notes that racial and political issues were already affecting industrial relations in the territory, and prophesied that their effect would increase. The Labour Department at that time was constantly advising the unions not to embroil themselves in politics. In 1953 the African National Congress called for a complete stoppage of work in the territory for two days, in protest against the proposals for federation. However, the union leaders, despite the fact that most of them were thought to be ardent Congress supporters, generally refused to allow the union machinery to be used in support of the strike on the grounds that it was purely political; and it was only a partial success. It would appear, then, that labour department counsel had been heeded.

In fact, at this time there was a small body of trade union leaders, who, although they were usually enthusiastic supporters of the African National Congress, and might even hold office in it, nevertheless were careful to distinguish between union affairs and national political affairs and tried not to let political issues affect the conduct of industrial relations. However, this reasonable approach did not appeal to the militant group of younger and more recently appointed officials who were primarily nationalist supporters of Congress, rather than industrial leaders, and in 1954 and 1955 several ill-advised strikes were called, which ended in failure and greatly weakened the whole trade union movement in the territory.

In fact, from about the time that the Central African Federation was imposed the National Congress itself began to make some policy changes. It developed a rather militant left wing composed largely of younger men who, with the rapid growth in Congress membership and organization, took on many of the minor but fairly influential branch offices, and as a result, the rather older, less radical leaders of the Congress movement have sometimes been in danger of losing influence and office.[5] The younger officials of the National Congress have, indeed, seen the movement as having a duty to take an interest in all aspects of African life—its aim is in part 'African advancement', which is as much concerned with social and economic as with political advance.

Hence nationalist politics have not stopped short of interfering in industrial matters. Congress itself, for example, has made efforts to withdraw all labour from firms offering poor conditions of work. It has planned to retract all African labour from Northern Rhodesian farms, on the grounds of the poor conditions and low wages paid. It organized numerous boycotts, and gave strong support to the African Mineworkers' Union during its 1956 dispute with the employers and the Staff Association; and so on. The more extremist officials and

---

[5] This conflict culminated, in late 1958, in the breaking away of the more extreme elements of the A.N.C., to form the Zambia African National Congress. This body was subsequently declared illegal and all its leaders were detained.

I

members of the National Congress have, probably on their own initiative rather than as a matter of Congress policy, 'infiltrated' at various times into the leadership of several trade unions, and have used their positions to try to change the policy of the unions so as to make them more militant, to challenge the authority of moderate leaders and, possibly, to use the unions as the industrial wing of a militant nationalist political party.

The effect of these policies, so far as the unions are concerned, has not been entirely beneficial. Union administration suffered seriously from the inexperience of the new officials. The unsuccessful strikes of 1954 and 1955 weakened the unions financially and economically, as well as arousing the anger of the powerful European unofficial opinion in the territory. The fairly general suspicion that extremist politicians were at the back of union policy in 1956 gave the government the excuse for mass arrests and detentions at the end of that year, and when the leaders of the Zambia National Congress were rounded up in March 1959, many leading trade unionists were among those arrested.

After the 1956 arrests, the crises in the affairs of several trade unions—in particular the Mineworkers' Union—gave some of the older and more moderate leaders an opportunity to reassert themselves and to try to bring back the former policies of moderation. In the Mineworkers' Union the President, L. C. Katilungu, successfully consolidated his position after a considerable period during 1957 and early 1958, in which he had to fight off attempts by left-wing Congress members to gain a foothold among the officials of the union.

It would appear then that for about three years, up to the end of 1956, the African trade unions in Northern Rhodesia were open to a good deal of political influence; after that, the danger of such influence was guarded against, and attempts were made to stave off attacks from those who were apparently more interested in politics than in industrial relations. In view of the success of the 'extremists' from 1953 to 1956, it is curious that the subsequent more moderate policies proved fairly successful. However, it may be explained by the fact that the more moderate leaders received support from the government, some co-operation from the employers, and, for the first time, enjoyed close and friendly contacts with the European trade unions in the territory.

Many of the Northern Rhodesian trade union leaders remained supporters of the African National Congress—and, of course, they were not all moderates, very far from it. A few of the most influential, however, left the Congress. One who did so in 1957 was L. C. Katilungu; at that time Congress members appeared to be attacking his position as president and secretary of the Mineworkers' Union. For a short time in 1957 he joined the liberal multi-racial Constitution Party, but he resigned when attacks were made on him for mixing politics and trade unionism. He stood as an Independent in 1959 for the Copperbelt African reserved seat in the elections for the territorial legislative council, but was defeated by the mainly European electorate. A somewhat similar case is that of G. Lewanika, who was one of the principal founders of the African National Congress in 1951, a founder member of the African Mineworkers' Union, and since 1953 President of the Mines African Staff Association. He also resigned from Congress in 1957, to join the ruling United Federal Party. Shortly afterwards he announced his intention to stand for election to the Federal Parliament, and this he did in 1958, being elected as a member of the Government Party.

These two leaders had a further interesting feature in common—that they were both members of chiefly families. Katilungu [6] was closely related to, and in close contact with, the Paramount Chief of the Bemba; Lewanika is a relative of the Lozi (Barotse) Paramount Chief. These ties might well have been a further source of strength to them as union leaders, in so far as tribal authority still meant something to the ordinary employees, who were possibly only temporarily away from home, and therefore still subject to home influences. [7]

The political factors influencing the African trade unions in Northern Rhodesia are made more complex by the existence of several powerful white employee trade unions. In the mines and on the railways, these unions have been the major obstacle to the advance of Africans to better-paid occupations.

[6] Katilungu was killed in a motor accident in 1961.

[7] There can also be elements of weakness in this position. Epstein notes that derogatory remarks were made about Katilungu in 1954 as the 'Paramount Chief of the Workers' Union'.

Concessions have been made, but the European unions are determined not to allow the promotion of Africans to destroy the employment opportunities of their members. The political influence of these unions has recently been thrown against any extension of the franchise to Africans that would threaten the maintenance of a European-dominated government.

The problems of East and Central Africa are complex and will not easily be resolved. But African political influence is bound to grow in every territory and it will be surprising if the unions are not affected by this development. So far a clear view of the future of the trade unions has not emerged. Most of the political leaders who have come to power have relatively little interest in the development of a vigorous trade union movement. They are mainly concerned to see that the unions do not impede economic progress, and do not become a cause of political instability. There is a reasonable possibility that as employers learn to welcome unions as collective bargaining agents, systems of industrial relations will develop that will permit unions to carry out their functions without the complete loss of their independence.

Mauritius

Trade unionism in Mauritius has, from its beginning, been much influenced by politicians and politics. The founders of the first unions were socialists who were greatly influenced by the links between trade unions and socialist parties in Britain and Europe. When they failed to persuade the Government of Mauritius to pass the legislation necessary for the development of trade unions and a modern system of industrial relations they turned their attention to founding a Labour Party, just as the British trade unions had done thirty-five years previously.

The Mauritius Labour Party, which was established in 1936, sought first to obtain the desired trade union legislation; then to achieve improvements in social welfare for the benefit of the working people. At the inaugural meeting of the Mauritius Labour Party, mentioned in the previous chapter, the following resolution was passed for transmission to the Secretary of State for the Colonies: 'That legislation be introduced in

Mauritius to secure the working classes the right of association by trade unions, old age pensions and other measures recommended by the International Labour Bureau.'[8]

The Secretary of State, in his reply to this resolution, informed the leaders of the Labour Party that there was no objection on the part of the British Government to the introduction of legislation on such matters as minimum wages, old-age pensions and trade unions and that any practicable proposals that might be put to him after proper consideration in the Colony would receive his sympathetic attention.

The failure of the British Government to push the Mauritius Government into taking active steps to introduce legislation that would provide a legal basis for trade unions was partly responsible for the serious unrest that occurred in 1937. Since the 1920's there had been agitation for a change in the law to permit the development of trade unions, but no action had been taken by the Legislative Council, in spite of repeated suggestions from the Secretary of State for the Colonies that appropriate legislation should be passed.

The effect of the intransigent attitude of the Legislative Council was to strengthen the link between trade unionism and politics. The Labour Party had no funds of its own; being an unincorporated body, it was not permitted to manage, deposit or invest funds, and created the *Société de Bienfaisance des Travailleurs d'Ile Maurice* as a benevolent society for workers. Through this society, which was registered under the Friendly Societies Act, the Labour Party was able to make complaints to the International Labour Organization which would not have been received from a purely political body. This situation changed in 1938 with the passing of an Industrial Associations' Ordinance, which permitted workers to form associations on certain restrictive conditions, so long as they were not called trade unions. This manifestly jejune ordinance was changed only after the second world war.

The attitude of the authorities to the development of trade unions ensured that the industrial associations would be politically-dominated bodies. When the Trade Union Council was eventually formed in 1946, it became possible to distinguish

---

[8] Quoted in a report on the development of unions in Mauritius prepared by Mr. K. A. Baker, first Trade Union Adviser to the Government of Mauritius.

the functions and administration of the trade unions from the functions and administration of the Labour Party. The connection between the party and the unions remained close, however, until after the death, in 1956, of M. G. Rozemont, who was leader of the Artisans' and General Workers' Union, Executive Committee member of the I.C.F.T.U. and leader of the Mauritius Labour Party.

In 1959, under a new constitution, the Labour Party was returned to power as the Government of Mauritius. There had already been conflict between the political leaders of the Labour Party and the leaders of some of the unions who, it was alleged, had been associated with the formation of a rival political organization, the Independent Forward Bloc.

The leaders of the Labour Party, especially the Minister of Labour, attacked the Mauritius T.U.C. and the leaders of its affiliated unions. In 1960, the Labour Government of Mauritius prepared a Bill under which it would have had power to create a new national trade union centre in opposition to the Trades Union Council. This Bill was only withdrawn after strong representations had been made from various quarters as to its undesirability.

Early in 1960 after fruitless efforts had been made by a representative of the British T.U.C. to achieve greater unity among the divided trade union movements in Mauritius, the Labour Adviser to the Secretary of State for the Colonies succeeded in bringing the Mauritius T.U.C. and the breakaway Confederation of Trade Unions together to establish a Central Joint Council. After a period in which the Council appeared to be making little headway, it was announced in July 1962 that the Confederation of Trade Unions had quit the W.F.T.U. and had been accepted into affiliation with the I.C.F.T.U., to which the Mauritius T.U.C. was already affiliated, on condition that it was willing to take steps towards creating a single national trade union centre on the island.

The stability and progress of the trade unions in Mauritius have unfortunately been constantly undermined by the conflicts and intrigues of union leaders and politicians more concerned with fostering their own ambitions than with reconciling differences and promoting a viable, well-organized and responsible trade union movement. For the first time in several years there now appears to be the promise of a genuine advance, which might lead to the elimination of the absurd rivalries that resulted in the creation of 73 unions with a total membership of 25,000, divided into no fewer than 6 trade union centres.

Unions and Political Activity after Independence

Trade unionism in the tropical territories of the Commonwealth has been closely connected with the emergence of political parties and the achievement of self-government and independence. But it is clear from our examination of the history of its evolution that trade unionism was not solely an expression of political desires. Unions were often founded by politicians, as indeed they were in Europe and other parts of the world, but they attracted members, as they did elsewhere, because work-people felt a need for the support of an organization to cushion them from the impact of managerial authority when they entered into paid employment.

The development of a system of industrial relations based on collective bargaining and agreed rules of employment, instead of submission to the unilateral decisions of an autocratic management, depends on the fulfilment of a number of important conditions. Unions must be viable and ready to enter into agreements which they are prepared to honour; however, this is only possible when they are protected by at least a framework of laws that establishes their right to exist, to bargain and to use the strike weapon. Until these circumstances have been achieved, a collective bargaining system is impossible and collective action is bound to concentrate on bringing about such changes in the law as are necessary for unions to develop.

In all countries the emergence of trade unions and the growth of a system of collective bargaining have been intimately related to advancement of democratic rights in general. Since the legal status of the unions in the dependent territories was determined by a colonial administration, it was inevitable that the achievement of the basic rights of union organization and bargaining became synonymous with the achievement of self-government and independence from colonial rule.

There was little chance that the unions would be prepared to concentrate on carrying out their industrial functions so long as the issues of self-government and independence remained to be solved. But even with these stumbling-blocks out of the way, there have been many factors influencing the unions and persuading them to play an active part in politics.

One of the difficulties of the unions in breaking clear from political activities stems from the simple fact that many of the founders and leaders of the unions have become important political figures. Though they may no longer personally lead a union, having moved entirely into politics and perhaps become members of a government, they maintain influence and sometimes control over the organization which they formerly led. Often there has been a shortage of men with the skill, experience and personal qualities required in both the union leader and the politician and it has been a natural development for one man to combine these functions.

Politics have been attractive to union leaders because many of them have been intellectuals who only became trade union leaders as a means of realizing their political ambitions. In a period when a country is developing rapidly and has a desperate need for the kind of talent that is capable of organizing unions, politics offers high rewards to union leaders. There is more glamour, more prestige, higher income and greater opportunities for travel if one is an important politician than if one is merely a trade union leader. It is, therefore, not difficult to understand why trade union leaders have been attracted by the lure of political office.

This situation is only changed when self-government has been achieved and there is a regular ladder of promotion to political leadership through the political parties. This does not mean that the unions then cease to provide an important pathway to political office, but that they have ceased to be the main route to the top of the political tree. As the parties settle into the task of government, problems inevitably arise because of their relationship with the unions, but eventually the facts of the situation serve to bring about a clarification of the respective roles. Difficulties are created by the reluctance of governments to trust the unions to act responsibly; and leaders who cling to union office after becoming ministers further confuse and blur the relationship. However, in the long run leaders begin to emerge whose main loyalty is to the unions rather than to the party to which the union might be attached or which is supported by the leaders.

The emergence of leaders from the body of the organization is a vitally important feature of the evolution of trade unions. This second phase of union development only occurs when the intellectuals and politicians, the outsiders who formed the unions have gone into politics permanently and have given up their union jobs. The new type of union leader tends to be more deeply rooted in the union, to be more concerned about the bread-and-butter problems of his members and the success of his organization. This phase is already evident in many unions in the tropical territories of the Commonwealth.

The need to recognize the change required in the role of the trade unions when a democratic system of government has been attained is not always obvious to union leaders and members who have become used to engaging in political agitation. It sometimes happens that the new set of union leaders are more politically radical than their predecessors, and they seek to emulate the successful transition that others made from union leadership to political office. This is the kind of situation that has existed in Singapore, where, after self-government had been achieved, many of the union leaders were concerned to overthrow the party elected in order to win political power.

The relationship of the unions to the process of government has been, and still is, one of the most difficult problems in advanced states. Unions have continued to play an important role in politics in Britain and in most other countries where they exist, but they have learned to keep their industrial and political activities separate. Although in Britain many unions affiliate to the Labour Party and their influence is an important factor in the making of the party's policy, they also constantly emphasize their independence. The freedom of the unions from party domination is especially evident when there is a Labour government; during these periods the unions have continued to exercise their functions with little regard for their effect on the fortunes of the government. When faced by the task of tailoring their policy to suit the needs of the government, they have insisted that they must place their members' interests first. In other words, although British unions are highly concerned about political questions, their behaviour is mainly influenced by their immediate functional responsibilities and not by the future achievement of the ideological goals to which they formally adhere.

In many of the newly independent tropical territories of the Commonwealth there is a danger that the dominant political party will insist on depriving the unions of their freedom of action, reducing them to subservient instruments of its will. Having used labour organizations to obtain power, many political leaders are unwilling to permit rivals to capture the unions and so repeat the process with themselves as victims.   A more legitimate reason for closely regulating the activities of the unions stems from the fact that the governments of most territories are anxious to achieve the maximum rate of economic growth, and they cannot afford to let the unions pursue their own interests to the point where they jeopardize this aim.   The temptation to bring the unions under the political control of the government is, therefore, quite strong, and this objective is often supported by union leaders who themselves aspire to positions of political importance.

The notion that independent voluntary associations pursuing their own interests—sometimes in the teeth of opposition by the government—are an essential feature of a democratic system of government, is not easily accepted by political leaders used to exercising a good deal of dictatorial authority.   There is a tendency in some of the territories to equate democracy with the mere act of voting.   The idea that it is necessary to have an 'opposition', and to permit independent organizations to pursue their own ends without political control, is rejected, for example, in Ghana as inappropriate to the country's need for a stable administration and need to make rapid economic progress. This was, of course, the view of the leaders of the Communist Party after the Russian Revolution, of Hitler and his National Socialist movement and Mussolini's system of Fascism.

It is interesting to note that in the Soviet Union, after forty years in which the trade unions have been agencies of the state with the primary duty of maintaining labour discipline and fostering the achievement of the government's policy, a big effort is now being made to galvanize the factory committees into action on behalf of their members instead of merely supporting the decisions of the directors of Soviet enterprises.   If independent trade unionism is totally eliminated it becomes impossible to protect the interests of union members effectively, since collective bargaining is undermined and the unions become a means by which the government achieves its ends. The aims of the dominant party and the methods employed by the government may be perfectly sound and in the best interests of the people, but this fact can never be properly tested unless there are independent bodies, such as trade unions, which can act as a check on those acting in the name of the state.

The relationship between trade unions and the state is throughout the world defined in many ways and it is not likely that all the developing countries will come to adopt the same pattern. In the nature of things it is not any easy task that lies before the leaders of the unions and the political parties in the newly independent territories of the Commonwealth. There is hope, however, that if the unions are allowed to develop freely within an appropriate framework of law they will succeed in defining the limits of legitimate behaviour as unions in the older political democracies have done. There is certainly no reason to assume that unions in the tropical Commonwealth territories are less capable of arriving at a satisfactory *modus vivendi* with the state than unions in other parts of the world.

CHAPTER 4

TRADE UNION ORGANIZATION

UNIONS of all types are to be found in the territories of the tropical Commonwealth. In some cases unions have been organized on the basis of the craft or occupation of the members; in others the unit of organization is the company or establishment employing the members; in some cases it is the industry or service in which the members work; in several territories the all-embracing general union is the predominant form.

The pattern of union organization that has developed has been influenced by ideas imported from the older industrial countries, but indigenous factors ultimately have been responsible for the shape that unions have taken. Although registration of unions is generally required as a condition of their lawful existence, in only a few instances have deliberate attempts been made to shape the structure of union organization by legal regulation. In most territories the law permits any handful of wage or salary earners to combine—to organize themselves as a trade union; and many territories have taken full advantage of this freedom. As the following table shows, a number of territories have a great many very small organizations. In certain territories efforts have been made, on the advice of British labour officers and labour commissioners, to discourage the indiscriminate establishment of unions, and in Sierra Leone and Northern Rhodesia registration of a new union is refused if a competent union has already been registered.[1] This policy is not looked upon with favour by the I.L.O., which takes the view that administrative limitations on the freedom to organize are always liable to abuse.[2] There is clearly a possible danger that the exercise of legal control over the establishment of new unions may be used to further interests other than those of the work-people who wish to join unions, but this must be set against the disadvantage to union members, employers and the public of having too many unions.

[1] See Chapter 10, p. 271.
[2] See *Report of Committee of Experts on the Application of Conventions and Recommendations*, Report 111, Part IV, 1955.

The authorities in British territories have generally been reluctant to limit the freedom of employees to form trade unions of their own choice; the reasons are the same as those given by the I.L.O. The lack of legal inhibition unfortunately has led, in a number of territories, to a situation where there are many more

NUMBER OF REGISTERED WORKERS' UNIONS AND ASSOCIATIONS WITH THEIR MEMBERSHIP*

	1938		1947		1958		1960	
	No. of Unions	Membership	No. of Unions	Membership	No. of Unions	Membership	No. of Unions	Membership
AFRICA								
The Gambia	—		3	60	4	1,300	5	2,300
Sierra Leone	2		8	n.a.	23	n.a.	9	11,600
Ghana	—		30	n.a.	69	n.a.	16	300,000
Nigeria	6		114	n.a.	268	231,287	347	259,072
Uganda	3		2	n.a.	19	4,784	47	26,300
Kenya	2		6	n.a.	42	18,357	45	45,700
Tanganyika	—		3	n.a.	30	33,895	27	80,500
Zanzibar			2	n.a.	19	3,053	13	4,900
Northern Rhodesia	1		3	n.a.	22	25,279	20	32,400
Nyasaland	—		—		4	1,470	5	4,900
WEST INDIES								
British Guiana	9		27	n.a.	36	20,766	36	38,300
British Honduras	—		3	280	6	3,408	5	2,200
Trinidad and Tobago	17		23	20,000	64	41,118	36	53,000
Grenada	—		2	n.a.	7	1,739	11	9,100
St. Vincent	2		3	706	4	1,439	6	3,100
Barbados	—		4	n.a.	3	12,494	3	13,200
St. Lucia	—		2	5,930	6	2,100	9	5,600
Dominica	—		2	4,640	3	6,697	3	4,300
St. Kitts/Nevis	—		1	n.a.	3	2,411	3	3,900
Jamaica	6		23	63,000	19	63,809	20	162,100
Antigua			1	n.a.	2	4,500	2	16,300
ATLANTIC, INDIAN AND PACIFIC OCEANS								
St. Helena	—		—	n.a.	1	n.a.	1	n.a.
Aden	—		—		28	12,024	34	18,800
Mauritius	25		27	n.a.	52	15,931	57	23,300
Seychelles	—		—		1	175	4	552
North Borneo	—		—		4	589	4	1,300
Brunei	—		—				—	
Sarawak	—		4	n.a.	25	5,404	33	7,800
Fiji	—		10	n.a.	21	10,420 †	30	12,100 †
ASIA								
Malaya	—		270	195,113	249	n.a.	250	183,876
Singapore	—		159	n.a.	216	139,838	130	144,770
Hong Kong	—		136	n.a.	232	205,692	245	231,500

* Unions of employers have been excluded wherever the information available has made this possible.
† Estimated.

unions than is desirable, whether looked at from the need to improve the efficiency of union organization or the need to promote good industrial relations.

The creation of large numbers of small trade unions, which has been the tendency in West Africa, Mauritius, Malaya, Singapore and Hong Kong, has been the result of a variety of

factors favourable to this development.   In differing degrees of
significance the structure of industry, geographical barriers,
poor communications, the political and social climate, the
attitude of employers, local patriotism, tribal associations and
the supply of men capable of organizing unions—all these
factors have had their influence on the pattern of trade unionism
and have tended to stimulate the emergency of a large number
of small organizations.

In most countries, trade unions have been small organizations
in the first period of their development.   In Britain in the early
part of the nineteenth century, when the units of employment
were small local establishments, the trade unions were also
small local organizations.   Before the railways provided a
swift and reliable means of travel and the 'penny post' a cheap
and rapid method of communication, unions were inevitably
limited by the difficulties of contact;   they did not become
nation-wide organizations until industry and social conditions
made this expansion possible.   In tropical territories, therefore,
we should expect to find unions organized on a local basis and
limited in size, because the units of employment have frequently
been small in scale and because, until recent times, communications have been at least as difficult as they were in Britain before
the railway age began.

In addition to the factors cited, perhaps the attitude of union
leaders has been the most important obstacle to the development of industry-wide and nationally organized trade unions.
Unions have very often been founded by individuals who have
seen in the running of a labour organization an opportunity to
advance their political aims or to make a living more or less in
the same way that a person may embark upon a business enterprise.   Having created a union as an instrument to further his
ambitions, a union leader is generally reluctant to see it merged
into a larger organization if this entails a loss of its control.

Even when union leaders have had a wider and deeper sense
of purpose than their own aggrandizement or the furtherance of
their political ambitions, they have been circumscribed by other
factors.   Unfortunately, in communities just emerging from a
state of relatively primitive economic development and political
dependence, personal opportunism is greatly fostered by circumstances and union leaders, and members have often been

the victims of personal jealousy. As yet, many workers in the developing territories do not see the union as a social institution capable of satisfying needs which have hitherto been met by the extended family, the tribe or the village. To workers who have not become permanently committed to employment in an urban community trade union membership has little binding significance, and the idea of loyalty to a trade union as a band of brothers combining their strength in a mutual endeavour to promote the welfare of all the members of the group, is lacking.

The idea of trade unionism as something for which each member should be willing to make some sacrifice is a difficult one to establish in societies which have been ruled by superstition, taboo, and the force and authority of chiefs and all-powerful alien rulers. Education and urbanization work fantastically quickly to change men and women from primitive creatures to modern industrial citizens, but they take some time to effect this transition and during this interim period trade unions suffer from the inability of their members to co-operate voluntarily.

Many trade unionists are impatient of the over-large number of small unions and would like to follow the example of Ghana and bring about a change by compulsion. This policy may be adopted in some African territories, but it would meet with resistance in others where unions are strongly established. It would certainly be an advantage in some territories if the rate of amalgamation were speeded up, but even in the absence of drastic measures the general trend is clearly towards larger unions, just as it has been in Britain and every other industrially developed country. The evidence shows quite clearly that in spite of the factors making for small unions, when the employment situation and social conditions have been favourable, large unions have tended to develop. There are some large organizations even in those territories, such as Nigeria, where the average trade union is very small. When the average trade union had a membership of only 750 the Nigerian Union of Teachers claimed to be over 30,000 strong. It is also worth noting that the distribution of membership in relation to the size and number of organizations is not entirely different from that of the industrially more-advanced countries. The largest trade unions in Nigeria had between them in 1957, 50 per cent. of total union membership; in the United Kingdom the seven largest unions had approximately one-third of total trade union membership. In other words, in Nigeria there is already a high degree of membership concentration in a small number of large unions as there is in Britain and many other countries.

In some territories, such as the West Indian islands of Antigua, Barbados, Jamaica, St. Kitt's and St. Vincent, the exact opposite to small fragmented unionism has emerged. In these places there is not a multiplicity of unions, but one large organization, with perhaps a few less important unions also registered. This 'general' or 'blanket' type of union covers every kind of worker, including some peasants, small craftsmen and traders working for themselves, and has resulted largely because trade unionism was fostered by politicians seeking political goals, rather than by workers seeking to establish a body to protect their vocational interests. Unionism of this type was made possible by the scale of the working population and its concentration in a relatively small area. Most of the working population in these West Indian islands were employed as manual labourers on the sugar estates, plantations, docks and other public services. It was a relatively homogeneous labour force, largely undifferentiated by craft skill. It was not strongly influenced by such factors as tribal association or other forms of parochial organization, and because they had no alternative group loyalties, West Indians (with the exception of Trinidad and British Guiana where racial differences have altered the situation) could be bonded together in a mass general union with the simple common aim of advancing the interests of the working man.

The general unions in the West Indies have tended to change their character, since internal self-government was conceded. Once they, or the party with which they are closely associated, come into power they are compelled to turn towards the task of improving their members' wages and working conditions. Political success, in effect, deprives them of their role as a political opposition. Since they are no longer engaged in a political crusade and have no political duty other than to give general support to the government, they would begin to lose the interest of their members if they did not find a new *raison d'être*. Thus, the blanket-unions in the West Indies are gradually becoming orthodox trade unions seeking to negotiate collective agreements instead of organizing mass demonstrations. This development has been followed by another. Concentration on the issues of wages and working conditions means, in effect, concentration upon sectional interests rather than on matters of interest to all members. It therefore becomes necessary to permit the different groups to express their opinions on their own problems, and this logically leads, if not to a break-up of the general union, to making provision for the consideration of the separate sectional points of view. This development can be seen in Barbados and Jamaica, which are industrially and socially the most advanced islands, and where general unions predominate.

Thus we see that as urbanization takes place, industry develops and the units of employment grow larger, communications are improved and the modern notions of group organization and function are understood, and political self-government is conceded, the social and economic factors making for small unions gradually disappear. Unions grow larger and they begin to attain the viability that has been lacking in their first stages of development.

The Recruitment of Union Members

In the early stages of trade union development in every country, membership has tended to fluctuate a good deal. This has also been the case in the territories with which we are concerned. The loyalty of those who are recruited by extravagant hopes will depend to a great extent on the organization's success. Their faith has to be supported by concrete results; if the achievements of the union are few and its gains negligible it will lose members.

Since few unions in the tropical countries have been able to regulate entry into jobs, or to provide substantial friendly benefits, they have had little power to compel workers to join and little to offer members who have come to the conclusion that the union has not done enough to protect and promote their interests. The minimum formality is required to join a union and none at all to leave it; it is, therefore, easy to enter and even easier to leave. Recruitment should be on the basis of signing an entry form, but it may involve no more than the collection of a name and a token contribution. Sometimes

K

even these tangible minimum requirements are dispensed with, and membership is reckoned merely in terms of the numbers supporting a strike, or of the number of employees in an industry who have shown some interest. In some territories the official statistics distinguish paid-up membership from the total claimed or estimated.

Under the conditions that exist in many of the tropical territories, union membership is bound to be difficult to maintain for a number of reasons. In the early stages of trade union development employers have generally vigorously resisted attempts to organize their employees. They often refused permission to union organizers to come on their land or to enter their premises; and they did not hesitate to intimidate their employees when they found signs of union organization. Because of government policy and the pressure of events, the attitude of employers has changed considerably; the extent of this change is examined more fully in later chapters. From outright opposition, they have, for the most part, now come round to acceptance and recognition and, in the case of many large British, Canadian and American companies, to giving encouragement and even assistance to unions. Small employers usually prove to be the most stubborn in their opposition, and many of their employees are still not organized. In these respects there is little that is basically different in the story of unions in the tropical territories of the Commonwealth from that of unions in any other part of the world. The opposition of employers is perhaps not so important a factor in the stability of union organization as illiteracy, lack of experience, racial and tribal differences, unstable employment, low wages, migratory labour, weak leadership, personal opportunism, political conflict and corruption.

Some of these factors are likely to exercise an adverse influence on the growth of trade unions for a long time. They will only be eliminated by industrial development and a rise in incomes, and the growth of urbanized communities with stable industrial populations. The trade unions can, of course, do something themselves to improve their present situation, especially if they are helped by governments and political parties. Their leaders could make greater efforts to learn how to do their job more effectively. Much more attention could

be given to the problems of union organization and to the provision of a better service to members. A much greater educational effort is required in most territories to bring about both
an improvement in the performance of union leaders and a
better understanding by the rank and file of the role that they
must play if their organizations are to be able to look after their
interests effectively.

Union Finance

One of the most important features of well-organized,
soundly-based trade unions is a steady income and a healthy
annual balance after all expenses have been met. It has been
the universal experience of trade unions that they have had to
become financially sound before they have been able to carry
out their main functions successfully. The assurance of a
regular flow of contributions from members is, therefore, one of
the essential priorities of many unions in the tropical territories.
Before this can be achieved members have to be recruited and
at least the rudiments of an organization to collect the contributions has to be created. When unions are, to all intents and
purposes, 'one man bands', this is not an easy task. One of the
great problems which faces trade union leaders in the tropical
territories is the difficulty of building any form of reliable
voluntary local leadership that is capable of systematically
collecting contributions and administering branch organizations efficiently and honestly. This has been achieved to some
extent in a few unions, for example in the Barbados Workers'
Union, but this is the exception rather than the rule.

The difficulty of maintaining a stable membership and a
regular collection of union contributions has given rise to a
demand for the check-off system. Under this type of arrangement, employers agree to collect the union contributions from
the pay packet of their workers and to pay over the total amount
to the union week by week.

The check-off has traditionally not been looked upon with
favour by the British trade unions, and it exists in only a few
areas of trade union activity in Britain. The attitude of British
trade unionists has been shaped by their fear that the check-off
would sap their independence and weaken their organizational
strength. Having succeeded in building a large and powerful

trade union movement without the aid of this kind of assistance, British unions have perhaps exaggerated the risks. American and Canadian trade unions, which have adopted the check-off system as a normal and desirable feature of effective organization, have certainly not succumbed to the dangers envisaged.

The British T.U.C., the Overseas Employers' Federation and the advisers to the Secretary of State for the Colonies are now in agreement that under the conditions of union organization in most of the tropical territories of the Commonwealth the check-off has more advantages than drawbacks. The check-off system is beginning to spread and a growing number of agreements have been made with employers, especially in the West Indies and Africa, that they will collect union dues and remit them directly to the secretary of the union. In Ghana and Tanganyika the check-off has been made a legal requirement and employers who may be reluctant to collect union contributions can be compelled by law to do so.

The problems faced by trade union organizers have often made sound leadership difficult and have encouraged unfortunate practices. In the absence of a regular flow of contributions, union leaders have been compelled to find alternative ways of financing their salaries. This has sometimes led to their founding a number of unions in the hope that they would obtain in total sufficient funds out of which they could compensate themselves. Thus, some unions have been created to suit the needs of their founder rather than their potential members. Another unfortunate consequence of inadequate finances has been the sheer weakness of administration that it has entailed. Lack of funds for salaries, office equipment, correspondence, travel and propaganda has not only kept unions weak, it has encouraged union leaders to resort to other devices to stimulate the interest of workers in the organization. One method developed in the West Indies, Africa and elsewhere has been to demand for union members a pay increase back-dated months prior to the claim. The successful pursuit of the demand then means that every worker obtains not only an increase in pay, but a lump sum in back payment as well. The lump sum is in many respects more important than the increase in the regular weekly pay packet, since it enables the union organizer to obtain a much larger contribution from grateful members than is possible if he attempts to gather weekly payments. The lump sum also enables the workers to pay off the debts they have contracted with money-lenders, or to pay the necessary costs of religious and social celebrations, or to make a capital payment for the assets of a small business, bicycle, radio or other piece of equipment. Back pay is, in other words, a method of saving—saving that would otherwise not be made. The good side of the back-pay system has, however, to be set against the disadvantages to workers, employers and the unions. It encourages indebtedness and enables parasitic money-lenders to make an enormous profit; it encourages irresponsible wage claims and makes the development of realistic wage negotiations more difficult; it places employers in a difficult position when calculating their labour costs, since they are never quite sure until after a settlement how much their labour supply has cost them for months past; and it prevents the development of a system of regular wage payments to the officials of the unions, thus encouraging an irresponsible attitude among members and leaders alike.

The instability of union income is, at bottom, a reflection of the instability of employment, the migrant character of labour, low wages and the weakness of the bonds of a form of organization that is new to most workers. This is not a situation that has occurred only in colonial territories. In every other country in the early days of union development, membership was highly unstable and the flow of income erratic. The consolidation of unions was achieved as industries and services offering regular employment at reasonable wages developed. Experience in the tropical territories also suggests that, as industrial employment expands and wage levels rise, membership of unions will become more stable, and with stable membership will come improved finances. This situation has, in fact, already been achieved by some unions in most of the territories.

With the rise in union incomes and the spread of the check-off it becomes increasingly necessary that unions develop a system which ensures that union funds are not pilfered or squandered through careless administration. The most contentious issues, apart from politics, have generally risen out of the administration of union funds. It is usually a statutory requirement that unions make proper provision in their rules for the accurate keeping of accounts, but book-keeping is often rudimentary and rules are frequently violated.

High standards of honesty are not promoted by low and irregular salaries, a membership which lacks experience of democratic control and which has a tolerant attitude towards peculation. Corruption is widespread in the trade unions in these tropical territories, and it is unlikely to disappear until there is a fundamental change in the social behaviour patterns that make it an endemic feature.

Efforts have been made by registrars to bring about an improvement in standards of book-keeping, but they have to face the problem that to take action against union leaders for misappropriating union funds often amounts to putting the union out of business. Frequently, therefore, they decided, with the support of labour officers and employers, that a severe warning was the strongest penalty that they should administer. Unions have been struck off the register, union officials have been prosecuted, but where these sterner policies have been pursued the authorities are distinctly unpopular; their actions are not always looked upon with favour by the members who are being robbed by the defaulting officials. Putting union officials in prison for fraudulent conversion looks to the members suspiciously like an attack on the union. Nevertheless, if union members are to be protected from the dishonest behaviour of union leaders some action has to be taken. It is very easy to slip into the attitude of condoning theft because corruption is a widespread feature of society. It is sometimes suggested that union leaders should not be expected to observe higher standards than are expected of other members of society, but there is this difference: the money to which union leaders help themselves belongs to workers who are very far from being rich; moreover, corruption discourages the development of the organizational systems that must be mastered by work-people in a modern developed industrial society.

It is difficult to avoid the conclusion that in most territories it would have been wise to make a standard form of simple book-keeping a legal requirement. Instead of merely stipulating general rules relating to the keeping of accounts, the law should have been precise and detailed; the actual books to be used ought to have been obtainable only from the labour department of the territory. It might have been a condition of registration that the secretary of the union should complete a course in the keeping of account books. Such a policy would have evoked criticism from within the territories, and perhaps from the I.L.O., but it would have been more constructive than the largely negative controls of the present laws. Adminstered properly, such legal requirements could have been a great help to the development of sound unions.

Labour departments, University extra-mural departments and the I.C.F.T.U. have tried to improve the situation by providing educational courses, but the scope of this work is too limited to arouse the enthusiasm of those who are not interested in learning. Standards are slowly improving, however, and it is important that after independence even greater efforts should be made to ensure that slipshod book-keeping and falsification of accounts do not grow worse instead of better. It is particularly important to maintain good standards of book-keeping and honesty in administration when the check-off system is used, since large sums of money may be passing into the coffers of the union. It might well be made mandatory that the check-off will be legally permitted only after the union has satisfied the registrar that its system of accounting meets required standards.

Union Leadership

Three types of trade union leader have emerged in the colonial territories. The first type is the man who has come from the ranks of the employees who form the membership of the union; the second type is the outsider, often a businessman or clerical employee possessing the gift of leadership who has seen the unions as a means of advancing his personal interests and ambitions; the third type is the well-educated, well-travelled professional man—usually a lawyer—who is concerned to build trade unions as a means of advancing a political cause.

Some of the earliest trade unions in the West Indies were started by men who were skilled artisans, but in the general absence of a numerically significant class of this type of worker there has been little spontaneous development of the classic kind of craft trade unionism. The leaders of unions of public service employees have to a large extent been drawn from the ranks of union members.   This is also true of unions of water-front workers, miners and railwaymen, who have found effective leaders among their own members.

In the colonies, however, there has been a great shortage of manual workers with the social skills necessary to form and lead unions.   This vacuum has been filled by leaders of the other two types.   Discontent among the mass of less-skilled workers provided an opportunity, for those who were ready to seize it, to create and lead powerful trade union organizations.

Perhaps the most important feature of the second type of trade union leader has been personal quality.   The leaders of the mass trade unions that were formed in the West Indies following the riots in the 1930's were men who exercised an appeal to the atavistic instincts of their supporters.   Their promises of better wages and working conditions evoked an immediate response in people who had long dreamed of a 'messiah' who would lead the 'black man' out of his miserable economic and political servitude.   These leaders and their followers were little concerned with the theory or practice of democracy.   They expected their followers to obey without question, to pay what contribution they could, and not to ask for any formal account to be rendered.   Union members were quite ready to accept this role so long as the leadership excited their enthusiasm.   They neither understood nor cared about the principles of democratic government.   However, when they lost interest or found union membership disadvantageous they showed their feelings by not responding to the call of the leaders.

Personal magnetism is an important feature of leadership everywhere and at all times, but it is of vital significance in the primary stages of the development of such an institution as trade unionism, before the patterns of organizational behaviour are consolidated in a firmly established structure.   The type of union leader who has the charismatic quality which inspires a large following generally has little interest in developing a structured organization, since this implies a limitation of his own power.   When faced by the legal rules laid down in trade union ordinances to protect the interests of union members and designed to foster the development of a democratic system of union government, this type of union leader has generally ignored their existence until compelled to do otherwise.

The third type of leader who has played an important role in the development of trade unions in the colonial territories has been the intellectual outsider who saw the organizing of labour as a means of achieving the wider political goals of self-government and national independence. Trade unionism offered an opportunity of employment and of achievement for men who had returned home after being educated in Britain, to find that there was little scope for their talent, or that, in spite of professional ability, they were excluded by social and political discrimination from playing a full part in the government of their country. Organizing a union gave them an opportunity to hit at the source of their frustration and the means to influence the social and political development of their homeland. The intellectual type of union leader has not been entirely immune from the temptations of personal aggrandizement, but he has generally been more concerned than union leaders of the second type, to create a structure of trade union organization in which the principles of democracy have been given some weight. Whatever their attitude towards the development of a democratic system of union government, the founders of trade unions in colonial territories have exercised considerable power over the membership.

It is not surprising that the first generation of union leaders should have been autocratic. There is a tendency in all countries for men who have created an institution to look upon themselves as proprietors, rather than as leaders owing their position to the votes of the members. In Britain and the United States, such men as Ernest Bevin and John L. Lewis, who had much to do with building the organizations which they led, were strongly inclined to behave in this way. In the light of the social and political background against which trade unions were established in the colonies, the readiness of their leaders to act as if they were hereditary chiefs or European government officials rather than as democratically elected leaders should not be difficult to understand.

The idea of democracy with its complex structure of representative government, its subtle conventions and behaviour patterns, is not deeply rooted in these territories. The notion of developing unions as democratic organizations was imported from the more advanced industrial countries; it did not grow out of the immediate circumstances which led to the emergence of trade unions in the colonies.

Unlike British unions, colonial trade unions have not gone through the stage of development described by the Webbs as primitive democracy.   In their earliest period of development founders of unions in Britain thought it desirable that all members should take part in the making of decisions so that they would be ready to assume the positions of leadership which were passed round by rotation.   The early British union was a community of equals in vocational skill, social experience and status, and the members, though perhaps not equally endowed with the qualities required of effective leaders, had in common a background of knowledge and experience which made it possible for each of them to assume the responsibility of leadership.

These conditions were only present to a limited extent in colonial territories; where they existed, and where there were sizeable groups of employees such as teachers who had the social skills necessary to form unions, the organizations quickly developed a self-generating system of leadership.   But where there was no rank and file membership with the capacity to made a democratic system of union government work effectively, leaders were inevitably encouraged to behave autocratically, since there was little check on their exercise of authority.

In some territories legal limitations have been imposed on outsiders acting as union leaders.   The law in Kenya, for example, has permitted only one officer of the union, the secretary, to be a non-employee of the industry from which the union members are recruited.[3]   The object of this legal restriction has been to force the emergence of leaders who have an interest in and knowledge of the affairs of the industry, and to prevent politicians from starting or taking over unions for their own use.   It is difficult to know whether this kind of law has achieved the desired result; it has not prevented unions from having political associations and it may have had the bad effect of encouraging a proliferation of small unions.

In many of the territories unions are now in a second phase of

[3] See Chapter 10.

development. Many of their original leaders have retired or are dead, and others have become professional politicians. The new leaders are less likely to be intellectuals drawn from outside; more often they are aspiring workers who not only have the intelligence, ambition and ability required of leaders—they also have had the experience of growing up with the unions and, therefore, are closely identified with the members as fellow workers. These second-stage union leaders generally still enjoy considerable power and prestige, but they tend to see the problems of union functions and government from a rather different point of view from their predecessors. Having grown up with the union, they have more concern for its organizational development than leaders from outside, and they are less likely to regard it as a stepping-stone to political ends.

There are, of course, other factors of great significance which affect the power of union leaders. In Africa, for example, tribal connections are still extremely important. Unions have generally cut across tribal boundaries, but a union leader with a majority of members from his own tribe will be in a stronger position than one with a majority of members from a different tribe. If the union leader has also been a chief or close relation of a chief, as has happened in a number of instances, he will carry the prestige of chiefly status into his new role of union leader. His hereditary advantages will not protect him from opposition and attack if he fails, as a union leader, to satisfy the demands of his members and the expectations of his fellow union leaders.

Racial and national differences are also important. Where various races and nationalities are living side by side, as they are in many territories, there has been a tendency for each racial group to show greater loyalty to leaders from its own group. In some places—for example in Northern Rhodesia, Kenya and Uganda—employees have organized on the basis of race; in these territories the separate unions of Europeans, Asians and Africans have tended to consolidate the distrust of each group for the others. Fortunately this division is breaking down and the trend is now towards unified organization, but this will not be completely achieved for some time. It is impossible to ignore the significance of the racial factors in any study of trade union organization and leadership, but in many unions the differences of race and colour have been successfully overcome. Although some unions have been organized on a racial basis, most unions in the territories tend to be inter-racial and are therefore helping to eliminate racial isolation and racial conflicts.

Language has been an extremely important factor in the making of union leaders. It is necessary to speak to union members in a tongue that they understand; therefore a thorough grasp of the vernacular is an essential feature of successful leadership. However, where the language of communication with government officials, employers and supervisors is English, it is also essential that union leaders should be fairly fluent in this language. The need for union leaders to have this command of different languages has not been an insuperable barrier to organization, but it has undoubtedly been a hindrance to organization and the development of good industrial relations.

The ability to appeal to a largely illiterate mass of workers in terms that they can understand was the secret of the success of E. M. Gairy, the leader of the Grenada Manual and Mental Workers' Union and the Grenada Labour Party. Gairy had no scruples; his object was to discredit the white and coloured businessmen and government officials who dominated Grenada before the rise of trade unionism. His method, which gave delight to his followers, was to accuse his opponents of every form of crime, to suggest that they were sexually depraved and to give lurid details of their imagined private lives.[4] By this means Gairy titillated his readers, impressed them with his daring and demonstrated that the island's 'establishment' was n no way morally superior to the 'barefoot blackman'. Those who were attacked were reluctant to seek legal redress, since the defence of the union leader would consist, they believed, in more mud-slinging.

[4] The contents of *The Thunder*, the weekly cyclostyled journal, are almost unbelievably crude and libellous. The aim of the paper was proclaimed on the front page to be 'to educate the masses, entertain the other classes, and to straighten up the social hypocrites in Grenada—Land of Spice and Hypocrisy'. The following is a typical example of the paper's style: 'A certain whiteheaded businessman with the instincts of a chief is the most vindictive businessman in the City. He sues his male customers if their wives or girl friends refuse to go riding with him at nights. His lovely elegant kept miss does not know all his tricks. Wow!'

As a union leader Gairy was able to do as he pleased; his followers were prepared to forgive any misdemeanour that he might commit. He was able openly to flaunt his taste for expensive clothes, flashy cars, girl friends and other indulgences without being called to account. This pattern of behaviour in fact helped to establish his authority over his followers.

Gairy was disfranchised for breaking up the election meetings of his opponents, but the loss of political rights did little more than temporarily to check his career; he subsequently became Chief Minister and political boss of the island.

In 1962 Gairy was found by a Commission of Inquiry to have seriously abused his authority with regard to the spending of public money. In the light of the report the constitution was suspended and Gairy was removed from office as Chief Minister.[5]

Democratic Control

The powers and duties of union officers in the colonial territories are constitutionally determined, as they are in most countries, by the rules of the organization. These rules are to some extent influenced by the need to satisfy the requirements of the law, but since the law had tended in this respect to follow the British principle of minimum interference, an extensive legal control has not been adopted.[6] However, in the drafting of their constitutions unions have often been given advice by labour departments and registrars, and by the British T.U.C., and they have been encouraged to follow the pattern of the model rules devised to meet the needs of the circumstances.

The basic principles embodied in the rules of the unions are those of representative government; provision is generally made for leaders at the local and national level to be elected, and members are entitled to an account of their stewardship. But in practice the status and power of union leaders have made the observance of rules a difficult problem. Moreover, we know from the conduct of elections in British unions that it is no easy matter to persuade members to take their responsibilities

[5] Gairy's subsequent defeat in a general election regrettably owed less to 'squandermania' and the misuse of public funds than to the desertion of some of his erstwhile political associates.
[6] See Chapter 10.

seriously.   There is a strong tendency in all voluntary organizations to leave the conduct of affairs to the established leaders.
In this respect there is only a relative difference between the
situation in the tropical territories and that which prevails in
Britain and America.

Some of the unions have reached the stage where they hold
regular conferences of their members to determine policy, but
many dispense with this procedure.   Difficulty of communications, the high cost of travel over long distances and the problem
of organizing a conference when members have little or no
experience of conference procedure make this method of union
government expensive and difficult to organize.

The unions with a membership drawn from such groups of
employees as teachers or civil servants are less subject to limitations imposed by a lack of social skills.   Even unions with a
general membership drawn from every type of worker, such as
the Barbados Workers' Union, have shown that a democratic
system of government can be given real meaning, although it
must be admitted that in some ways conditions are more
favourable than in some of the larger territories.   In particular,
there is a fairly high level of literacy in Barbados.   The island
is very small, and most workers may be said to be urbanized,
though many of them work on sugar estates.   The colony has
been under British rule since early in the seventeenth century
and it has long had a form of self-government which has undoubtedly helped to spread an understanding of principles
and procedures throughout the population.   The Barbados
Workers' Union has divided its membership into 42 trade
sections.   Each section is governed by a committee of elected
leaders who are responsible to the national leaders of the union.
Local leaders are responsible for conducting the affairs of the
union up to the point where it is necessary for them to call on
the services of an officer from headquarters.   Meetings of
members are held regularly, and before agreements are signed
they are explained at meetings and the support of members
obtained for the course proposed by the leaders.   This union
also maintains an admirable system of accounting, and it submits an annual report to its members.   Examples of unions in
other territories could also be cited as evidence to show that a
democratic system of union government and efficient, honest

administration are possible even under the trying conditions that exist in the tropical territories.

Although the formal machinery of democracy may often work in a creaky fashion and in some cases not at all, there is usually no lack of opposition to the leaders of the unions unless it has been eliminated by political action. Even when democracy is honoured more in the breach than in the observance there is the constant threat of rival factions leading a breakaway and forming a new union.

The senior office in an important trade union in the tropical territories is a very coveted position, and palace revolutions are quite common. In most organizations there are those who would like to obtain the fruits of office and who are ready to seize any opportunity of pushing an established leader out of his position. Jealousy, rivalry, intrigue and overweening personal ambition have been marked features of trade union leadership in many of the tropical territories. There are therefore significant limitations to the power that union leaders are able to wield unless they are sustained by political factors which entrench their position.

Thus the leadership of unions in the tropical territories has been characterized by dictatorial features and by an incessant and opportunistic struggle between rival contenders for office. Both types of leadership are produced by circumstances in which there is: (1) a limited supply of the social skills necessary to govern and administer unions democratically, and (2) considerable reward for office in terms of prestige, power and financial remuneration. Until democratic ideas take deeper root and the membership of the unions is able to exercise a more vigorous influence, it is unlikely that the extreme features of the pattern of union leadership will disappear.

One of the great rewards of union leadership is the opportunity it brings for aggrandizement. The leaders of the more important unions often live in a style that can only be sustained by a lavish use of union funds. It is taken for granted by some leaders that they are entitled to purchase a large American car at the expense of the union, to enjoy the comfort of a modern office and home, to be well dressed and to travel widely.

It is not infrequently argued that it is necessary for the union leader to compare favourably with employers and senior government officials, since it is only in this way that he can demonstrate his status to members and to the leaders of the society to which he belongs. There is some truth in this argument, but for the most part it is a rationalization of a simple desire to enjoy a high standard of living. In this respect the behaviour of union leaders who have exploited their positions in the tropical territories is not fundamentally different from that of many American union leaders.[7]

Foreign travel is certainly a valuable experience for union leaders, since visits to other countries enable them to see at first hand how unions are organized elsewhere. It brings them into personal contact with the trade union leaders in the more advanced countries who are in a position to give them advice and help, and it increases their prestige and influence. Unfortunately, the desire to travel abroad has sometimes been allowed to get out of hand and there have been instances of unions bankrupted by the excessive expenditures of union leaders visiting countries overseas. Leaving the home country can also be dangerous, and it has sometimes happened that union leaders have returned to find that in their absence their rivals have been able to establish an ascendancy.

A typical example of the dangers of making trips to far-off places occurred recently in Malaya when the president of a union went abroad and in his absence his office was declared vacant and a new president was elected.

In 1959 the president and secretary of an important union in British Guiana were charged with spending the union's money extravagantly on journeys, and support was given to the accusation when both officers subsequently decided that it was necessary to attend a conference in Jamaica and coolly spent a quarter of the union's funds on the trip. There were clearly no legitimate reasons for both officers to go to this conference, and their decision showed either a supreme contempt for the democratic processes in the union or culpable ignorance of the requirements of responsible union leadership. Both were determined to make this trip, because each felt that the other would gain some benefit of which he would be deprived if he stayed at home. Warnings of the danger to the union, to their position as leaders, were privately given by labour officers and

[7] See B. C. Roberts, *Trade Unions in a Free Society*, Chapter 4, Part Two.

by the management of the company with which the union had a check-off agreement, but to no avail. The outcome was exactly as predicted; the principal critics of the leadership organized a revolt and the union practically disintegrated.

It would be quite wrong to suggest that every union is incompetently administered and undemocratically governed in the tropical territories of the Commonwealth. Many unions are reasonably well administered, and some would bear comparison with the average British trade union. There is, however, a very great need to develop much further the interest and the skills that would enable the general standard of union administration to be raised. As they succeed in this respect the trade unions make a valuable contribution to society, since they enable an important body of citizens to acquire an understanding of the responsibilities they must shoulder to make democratic government possible. This function of trade unionism has been of considerable significance in the more advanced industrial countries of the world; it could be of equal importance in the territories that have just emerged as fully self-governing states.

Central Organizations

British trade unionism was at least a century old before an enduring central body, the Trades Union Congress, was established. In most of the territories of the tropical Commonwealth, steps have usually been taken at an early stage of trade union development to form a central council. The existence of a central organization can be a valuable aid to young trade unions that need help and guidance from mature union leaders; unfortunately most of the central bodies created have not given the kind of assistance that would have been most helpful to the affiliated organizations.

The advantage which a strong trade union centre should bring lies in the fact that available resources of money and men can be concentrated and marshalled in the most effective way instead of being spread thinly over a large number of separate unions. This advantage has more often than not been lost by a failure to organize efficiently and by a desire on the part of the leaders of the central body to engage in political activities.

It has been an experience common to almost all of the central

L

organizations that they have become arenas of political conflict. In some cases the leaders of the central body have become identified with a particular party; as a result splits have occurred several times in Nigeria, and in Hong Kong and Fiji. Personal rivalries, political quarrels, inadequate funds, poor administration and ineffective leadership have kept the central bodies weak in most of the territories. In the West Indies only Trinidad and British Guiana have developed even a modestly successful T.U.C. In Africa the Tanganyikan T.U.C. is perhaps the most highly developed, with the exception of the Ghana T.U.C. The central body in Ghana has become extremely important, since legislative enactment has invested it with special powers and responsibilities.

The experience of the trade union movements in France, Germany and Italy illustrates the danger of developing powerful trade union centres before an effective foundation of strong unions has been laid. In each of these countries impressive central bodies were established and their political role was considered to be highly important. However, the unions themselves remained weak, and failed to develop a firm grip on the loyalty of workers in the factories, mines and mills. This situation resulted in relatively weak trade union movements that almost completely collapsed under the political onslaught of anti-trade union movements of the 1930's.

The main problem that faces an independent trade union centre is that of building up the strength of the trade union movement without antagonizing the government or the affiliated unions. This is by no means easy, since experience indicates that a trade union centre which pursues a vigorous policy is likely to come into conflict with the government. There is a danger of general strikes and anti-government political alliances, and it is, therefore, not surprising that governments in many countries have looked upon trade union centres with suspicion. In some extreme cases legal restrictions have been imposed, as in the Bahamas, to prevent the development of a central body.

The opposite policy, which constitutes an equally important threat to the development of a healthy trade union movement, is the one pursued in Ghana. In this case the T.U.C. is an agent of the government, and through it the unions are controlled. Apart from the loss of independence that this policy entails, there is a danger that the movement may become bureaucratic and out of touch with the feeling of the rank and file membership. The strikes which occurred at Takoradi, following the introduction of an unpopular budget against which the T.U.C. was not free to protest, indicate that conflict can arise within the trade union movement when the central organization has lost its representative character. Nevertheless, it would be unfair not to recognize that in the industrial relations field the Ghana T.U.C. has acted with a considerable degree of responsibility; its relations with the Ghana Employers' Confederation have developed well, and together these two organizations have agreed on important advances in the scope of collective bargaining and joint consultation.

There is not likely to be any uniformity in the development of central trade union organizations in the future. Where there are well-established and strongly organized unions, the central bodies will probably remain relatively weak unless political circumstances lead to the deliberate enhancement of their power by a decision of the government, as happened in Ghana. On the other hand, where unions are relatively weak, as in the case of Tanganyika, there is a much greater chance that the central body will be strong, especially if substantial help is received from international sources. It may well happen, however, as it appears to have done in Kenya, that the building up of a strong central body discourages the development of the member unions. Leaders of the central organization are generally concerned to avoid taking any steps that might weaken their authority. Therefore in practice they tend to starve the unions of funds and to draw off the more talented leaders who are naturally attracted to the central organization. It is for these reasons that some experienced trade unionists consider that it may be a mistake to concentrate on building up a powerful central organization before the unions themselves have become strongly established. Others, however, feel that because it is so much easier to create a central organization, this course should be followed in spite of the disadvantages.

CHAPTER 5

THE INFLUENCE OF THE
BRITISH TRADES UNION CONGRESS

THE British Trades Union Congress has made a substantial contribution to the development of trade unionism in the territories of the Commonwealth with which we are concerned in this study, by providing direct advice and assistance to the unions and by exerting an influence on the development of the policy of the British Government and the policy of British firms which operate in these areas.

The interest of the T.U.C. in the problems of the colonial territories was first aroused by specific issues that affected British workers, such as the question of sugar bounties and free trade in the 1890's, and the importation of indentured Chinese labour into South Africa after the Boer War.[1] From time to time the attention of the T.U.C. was called to particular incidents in the colonies and occasionally someone interested in forming a trade union wrote or called upon the General Secretary of the T.U.C. in search of information on how this might best be done. In 1930, during the period of the second Labour Government, the T.U.C. supported the passing of an I.L.O. Convention on Forced Labour, but no special effort seems to have been made to associate the T.U.C. with the steps taken by Lord Passfield, the Colonial Secretary, to encourage the development of trade unions in the colonies.

The occurrence of the widespread riots in the West Indies persuaded the General Council that the T.U.C. should take a more positive interest in the problems of labour in the colonies, and arrangements were made in 1937 to keep the Council in constant touch with developments. On the recommendation of the General Secretary an advisory committee on colonial problems was set up. The committee was composed of four members of the General Council and nine outsiders who had

[1] See B. C. Roberts, *The Trade Union Congress, 1868-1921* (London, 1958).

146

expert knowledge and experience of colonial problems.[2] One member, Dr. Drummond Shiels, had been Under-Secretary at the Colonial Office during the second Labour Government and had exercised an important influence on the development of official policy in the field of labour affairs. Mr. A. Creech Jones, M.P., was to become Secretary of State for the Colonies in the third Labour Government. Another member of the committee was the distinguished academic authority on colonial questions, Professor W. M. MacMillan.

This committee met for the first time on 22nd December 1937. Its purpose, defined in a memorandum drawn up by the General Secretary, Sir Walter Citrine, was stated to be to make 'an investigation into the conditions of the principal races of the Colonial Empire, the principal object being to see how far the T.U.C. can contribute towards raising their standard of life and generally improving their conditions'.

The committee adopted the following programme of work:

1. To consider first the best means of remedying immediate grievances, such as exploitation by under-payment and excessive hours of work and repressive administration, etc.

2. To consider the best means of extending trade unionism among native workers, having regard to local conditions and difficulties; and with this object in view to formulate a simplified model system of trade union organization applicable to the colonies in general, or where, as in Africa, trade unionism was still largely unrealizable to safeguard the interests of indigenous workers, pending their transition to industrial organization, by the appointment of qualified labour commissioners.

3. To study the most effective means of bettering health, wages and hours, housing and working conditions and the enforcement of minimum wage legislation.

4. To approach the Colonial Office with the view of encouraging the idea of setting up labour departments, government inspectorates and the establishment of a scheme in the United Kingdom for training the personnel required.

5. To urge the Colonial Office to form within its headquarters a special department and advisory committee to attend exclusively to the problems of native labour.

[2] General Council Members: Sir Arthur Pugh; Ebby Edwards; Arthur Shaw; George Hicks. Other members: C. Roden Buxton; J. F. N. Green; Professor W. M. MacMillan; Roy McGregor; H. S. L. Polak; T. Reid; W. Macgregor Ross; Dr. Drummond Shiels; A. Creech Jones.

The General Council had already entered into an arrangement with a man who had some years before gone to South Africa to help the Industrial and Commercial Workers' Union, from whom it received a regular flow of information about labour problems in South Africa.   It was suggested that the T.U.C. should extend this idea to other territories if suitable correspondents could be found.   In this way the committee would have its own sources of information on events occurring in the colonies.

Citrine informed the Advisory Committee that the General Council was anxious for representatives from the colonies to participate in the annual discussions at the I.L.O. and that it might be possible to bring some of the colonial representatives to meet the committee in London.   Later on, the committee might want to send its own investigators to the colonies to gather information on the spot.

At its next meeting the committee was able to discuss a draft of the model trade union rules, the preparation of which had been suggested at its first gathering;   these were eventually approved and copies were sent to the Colonial Office, the I.L.O., the High Commissioner for India and to all trade unions known to exist in the colonies.

During the year the committee pressed the Colonial Office to establish a Labour Department and an Advisory Committee to reinforce the newly appointed Labour Adviser to the Colonial Secretary.   At the suggestion of the Colonial Secretary, the Advisory Committee of the T.U.C. met his Labour Adviser, Major Orde-Browne, before he left to investigate and report on labour conditions in the West Indies in August 1938.

This meeting was of great significance because it established a precedent of consultation with the T.U.C. on labour problems in the colonies.   The T.U.C. was delighted to learn from Major Orde-Browne that it would be part of his job to stimulate trade unions in the West Indies;   and also that it was proposed to appoint labour commissioners who would be trained by the United Kingdom's Ministry of Labour.   These commissioners in the colonies would act as his permanent liaison officers.

Early in 1939, the T.U.C. was advised by the Colonial Office that it was proposed to create a Social Services Department which would be given responsibility for questions relating to labour, education, medical services, housing and other social problems. The Colonial Advisory Committee of the T.U.C. was not satisfied that this new department would, among all its other tasks, be able to give enough attention to labour problems. Nor was the committee satisfied that adequate provision had been made for the new department to hear the views of the T.U.C. at regular intervals. It was therefore decided to seek an interview with the head of the new department and to continue to press for a permanent Labour Advisory Committee to the Colonial Secretary, but it was not until three years later that this proposal was accepted.

In the meantime the interest of the T.U.C. in colonial labour problems was greatly stimulated by the appointment of Sir Walter Citrine to the Royal Commission on the West Indies, which was charged with the task of investigating social and economic conditions and of making recommendations. During the work of this commission, Citrine was able to gain first-hand experience of colonial problems and to establish contact with the leaders of the labour movements in the various territories, and also to arrange for correspondents to send regular reports on the local situation to the T.U.C.

Citrine was impressed by the urgent need to develop union leaders from the ranks of the membership. Few workers had received more than a rudimentary education and there was a widespread ignorance of principles and methods of organizing and administering unions. On his return to London, Citrine proposed that one or two scholarships should be provided at Ruskin College for the training of West and East Indian trade unionists. He also suggested that consideration should be given to the possibility of sending an experienced trade union adviser to the West Indies for a minimum period of a year or eighteen months. Another idea put forward by the General Secretary was the preparation of an elementary practical course in trade unionism, covering such matters as how to organize, how to conduct negotiations, how to manage meetings and to administer the union. This type of course might be conducted by correspondence or by local teachers.

The recommendations of the General Secretary were all accepted, but before they could be put into effect the second world war started and attention inevitably shifted from colonial problems to other matters. The T.U.C. Colonial Advisory Committee did not meet so frequently, but important developments took place during the war period.

Following the Government's decision to establish a Colonial Development and Welfare Fund, it was decided to send a number of experienced British trade unionists to the colonies as advisers on trade union development. The T.U.C. was asked by the Colonial Office to select a list of candidates from which the most suitable could be chosen to attend a course of training by the Ministry of Labour in factory personnel management and welfare supervision. After the first two labour officers had been chosen and trained the T.U.C. criticized the courses on the grounds that the curriculum was already familiar to the officers concerned and was not sufficiently relevant to the conditions that they would meet in the colonies. The difficulty which faced the ministry was that there was nobody available who was familiar with colonial labour problems and there was little or no written material in existence that could be of use in this connection, although some help might have been given by anthropologists who had knowledge of native patterns of social organization and who had begun to study the effect of wage employment on traditional forms of organization and behaviour.

In 1942 the T.U.C. were advised that the Secretary of State had decided, three years after the proposal had first been made, to establish an advisory committee on labour problems. This committee was not a representative body, since members were invited to serve on an individual basis, but it largely met the desires of the General Council. A close liaison had already developed between the T.U.C. and the Colonial Office, but there were inevitable suspicions that the views of the T.U.C. did not always get through to the Secretary of State with the force that the General Council desired. The new committee, while not supposed to be a representative body, provided an opportunity for regular meetings between representatives of the T.U.C., the employers with overseas interests and those responsible for labour matters in the Colonial Office. At a later stage, in 1956, representatives of the T.U.C. and the Overseas Employers' Federation began to meet at regular intervals to discuss issues of common concern on an informal basis.

Following suggestions from the T.U.C., Ruskin College made its correspondence courses available first to West Indian trade unionists and then to union members in other colonies.   Immediately following the end of the second world war, two trade union officers took up the scholarships at Ruskin College that the T.U.C. had, in 1939, decided in principle to award.   Both men, R. A. Gittens of Trinidad and H. A. Glasspole of Jamaica, were later to play notable parts in the development of trade unionism in the West Indies.   During the next decade trade union officers from many territories were brought to Britain to spend a year at Ruskin College, as T.U.C. students.

In 1946 the T.U.C. appointed E. E. Esua of the Nigerian Union of Teachers as one of the advisers to its delegation to the International Labour Organization conference.   Some years later the T.U.C. was responsible for arranging the regular attendance of colonial trade unionists as observers at the I.L.O. annual conference.

Following the passing of a resolution at the 1946 Congress, calling on the T.U.C. to render further assistance to the trade unions in the colonies, the General Council decided to launch an appeal to all affiliated unions to contribute towards the institution of a Colonial Fund out of which financial assistance could be given to unions most urgently in need of such help. The fund's first grant of £500 was made to the Jamaican Trades Union Congress.   In the years that have since elapsed the British Trades Union Congress has provided financial assistance to the value of hundreds of thousands of pounds to colonial trade unions.

By 1950, the work of the British T.U.C. in assisting the development of trade unionism in the colonies had reached a stage when it was thought desirable to appoint an officer who would be specially responsible for this field of its activities. Following this appointment it was decided to undertake a systematic inquiry into the needs of colonial trade unions.   It was felt that the resources of the T.U.C. might be put to more effective use if a co-ordinated programme were to be carried out instead of treating each request for help as an individual item. Some of the assistance the T.U.C. had provided had produced very little result, and there was clearly a need to think out a method that would ensure that the money available was spent in a way that would produce most effect.

Experience showed that to make a financial grant was not always the best way of helping to develop an efficient and effective trade union. It was decided, therefore, to create a 'basic unit' of essential office equipment. This standard purchase included a typewriter, duplicator and accessories, stationery and a basic library of essential books. These items could be supplied with the minimum of fuss and the maximum speed, and the T.U.C. had the satisfaction of knowing that its money had been well spent. The T.U.C. did not confine its help to the provision of office equipment; in some cases it bought vehicles for the transport of union officers where this was essential for the effective organization of a union. It paid off debts, and met the cost of printing bills, rents for offices, salaries of organizers and the fares of officials who attended conferences and training schools overseas.

In addition to providing this type of material aid the T.U.C. has directly assisted the colonial trade unions by sending out British experts to help in the finding of a solution to particular problems. The first such mission of inquiry was carried out at the request of the Colonial Office in 1946 when F. W. Dalley, Assistant Secretary of the Railway Clerks' Association, visited Trinidad. Other missions have visited Singapore and Malaya, the African territories, Mauritius, Aden, the Bahamas, British Guiana, Fiji and Trinidad again. When the number of the T.U.C. staff engaged solely on work in the colonies was increased to three it became possible for members of the Commonwealth Department to spend considerable periods in the territories.

The T.U.C. has been an active watchdog on every issue concerning the welfare of workers in the colonies. It has been particularly anxious to see that each territory adopted legislation to promote healthy trade unionism, and it has constantly pressed its criticisms on the Colonial Secretary whenever it has found the territories lacking in this respect. For example, the T.U.C. was particularly concerned with events in Kenya when, following the appearance of the Mau Mau movement, emergency measures were introduced that threatened to destroy the trade union movement. The 'emergency powers' legislation which gave governments sweeping authority to declare almost any strike a public danger was vigorously condemned and pressure was brought to bear upon the Colonial Secretary to provide laws more in keeping with the liberal standards that had for a long time been established in Britain and in most of the colonies. In carrying out its work the T.U.C. was influenced by a belief that it was better to help to lay the foundations of unions in the colonies rather than to concentrate on the strengthening of the central bodies.

For a time the T.U.C. concentrated on helping the national centres, but it soon came to the conclusion that to build up a central organization on weak foundations was a waste of resources. There was then a shift in policy; henceforth help was given to specific unions. Instead of giving aid in small amounts, the T.U.C. decided to put a great deal of money into organizing the union it had decided to help so that it was really capable of standing on its own feet; attention could then be turned to building up another organization.

There is little point in developing trade unions which do not have the ability to negotiate on behalf of their members, either because they are unable to persuade employers to bargain with them or because they lack the interest to develop negotiating machinery. The T.U.C. has been much concerned during the last decade to help unions to secure recognition and to bargain effectively. The regular meetings with the officers of the Overseas Employers' Federation have been important in this regard. The mutual respect which the officers of the T.U.C. and the O.E.F. have for each other has greatly helped to encourage British companies operating in the colonial territories to accept the principles of collective bargaining and the need to promote better industrial relations by developing negotiating machinery.

The influence of the T.U.C. on employers and the British Government has been fruitful if it is judged in terms of the progress made in the territories in the past twenty-five years, but if judged by the standards of trade union development, wage levels and industrial relations in Britain, or most of the older industrialized countries, then it is apparent that there is still much to be achieved in the tropical territories of the Commonwealth. However, by comparison with the past, the rate at which trade unions and industrial relations have developed has been spectacular.

The approach of the T.U.C. to the problems of trade

unionism in these territories has been essentially cautious. In the early stages its activities were stimulated by events as they occurred; later they became more systematic and purposeful. Although anxious to encourage and help the growth of trade unions and a healthy system of industrial relations, the T.U.C. has always been careful to avoid thrusting its assistance forward, believing that any tendency to do this would have an undesirable effect. Such a policy would have exposed the T.U.C. to the charge of seeking to dominate the unions in the colonial territories. It would also have encouraged the unions to look to charitable aid instead of themselves building viable organizations that would not require outside help.

Although this discreet approach has been criticized as not doing enough to help, the T.U.C. has also been attacked for seeking to promote a system of industrial relations on the British pattern. The attitude of the trade unionists in the colonies to the activities of the T.U.C. has been one of gratitude tempered by a certain element of jealousy and distrust that arose from the association of the T.U.C. with colonialism and the policy of the British Government.

The reaction of the T.U.C. to the problems of trade union organization and industrial relations has inevitably been heavily influenced by British experience, beliefs and values. Since the labour policy of the Colonial Office has been influenced by the same factors, it is not surprising that the attitude of the T.U.C. has often coincided with that of the British Government. There is no evidence, however, to suggest that the T.U.C. has not arrived at its conclusions independently. When it has believed the British Government to be wrong, or local governments to be acting erroneously, it has attacked them vigorously, in private and in public.

Essential services legislation and its use in the territories is a good example of an issue on which the T.U.C. came into conflict with the British Government. The T.U.C. was not opposed to the existence of laws which gave the governments of the territories power to keep essential services going by restricting the right to strike. It was recognized that no government could stand aside if grave damage to the health, safety and economic interests of the people of the territory was threatened by the action of a trade union. But it protested vigorously against the extension of the law to include, as it did in Tanganyika, almost all major industries, as well as gas, electricity, water, health and sanitary services.

In the opinion of the T.U.C. such a broad interpretation of essential services was a serious abuse of the duty to protect the public welfare and indicated a reluctance on the part of the authorities to accept the principles of free collective bargaining and a failure to encourage the development of voluntary machinery through which industrial disputes could be settled without recourse to legal intervention.

The General Council of the T.U.C. has been well aware that the different conditions prevailing in the colonial territories would mean departures from British practice. What the T.U.C. has not been prepared to concede is that the broad principles of freedom of association and freedom of collective bargaining enjoyed in Britain are irrelevant to the workers and unions of colonial territories.   In practical terms this has meant that the T.U.C. has supported policies of persuasion rather than coercion.   For example, the T.U.C. has disapproved of the large number of small trade unions in some territories; it would like to see them amalgamate into larger and more effective organizations, but any attempt to deprive these unions of the right to exist by legal fiat has been condemned.

Unlike the French, the T.U.C. never thought in terms of creating colonial offshoots of its own organization. In the French colonies the structure and form of the trade union organization in the metropolitan country was duplicated exactly. To some extent this gave the trade unionists in the French colonies a greater sense of purpose and status than was the case with the unions which existed in the British territories. However, this policy has also had disadvantages, since it has meant that the unions in the territories have imported the weak as well as the strong points of French trade unionism.

The British T.U.C. became involved in a conflict over fundamental issues when Ghana became an independent territory, and it was decided to reorganize the trade unions by legislation and to bring them under the control of a political party.   The General Secretary of the British T.U.C. took exception to statements made by Dr. Nkrumah, the Prime Minister of Ghana, that the British T.U.C. had for many years been trying to reach the goal that the Ghana Government had made possible by legislation.   In order to make the view of the T.U.C. clear, Sir Vincent Tewson wrote to Dr. Nkrumah to inform him that 'the British T.U.C. would not support such legislation if it were introduced into this country, since it would be in conflict with the basic operation of the movement as a movement free and independent of the government'.[3]   Dr. Nkrumah denied that he had ever spoken the words ascribed to him by *The Ghanaian Worker*, the journal of the Ghana T.U.C., but John Tettegah, leader of the Ghana T.U.C., made no secret of his opinion of the British belief in a free and independent trade union movement. He categorically rejected the notion of free trade unionism as suitable for Ghana, and he severely criticized the British T.U.C. and International Confederation of Free Trade Unions for supporting this policy in Africa.

The future work of the T.U.C. in relation to the tropical territories of the Commonwealth is bound to be influenced by their change in status from colonies to independent members of the Commonwealth.   They will no longer be a responsibility of the Colonial Office and this will eventually bring the work of the Colonial Labour Advisory Committee, in which the representatives of the T.U.C. have played a prominent part, to an end.   The experience and influence of the T.U.C. will, however, continue to be of great importance to developing countries in connection with the new Department of Technical Cooperation.

With the end of the responsibility of the Colonial Office the links established by the T.U.C. with unions in the former British colonies will become even more important in the future than they have been in the past.   In most cases where the unions are affiliated to the I.C.F.T.U. it is possible that the T.U.C. will become less directly involved in giving advice and assistance, but there may well remain a strong desire on the part of the unions to retain the close relations that have been developed by past association, since there is often a high degree of mutual respect.   Thus while the emphasis of the work of the T.U.C. is bound to be changed by the emergence of the colonial territories into fully self-governing countries, it is not likely to cease suddenly and completely; it will be carried on as an important responsibility.

[3] T.U.C. Annual Report, 1959.

CHAPTER 6

INTERNATIONAL TRADE UNION ORGANIZATIONS AND TRADE UNION DEVELOPMENT

LITTLE attention was given by the international trade union movement to the problems of workers in the colonial territories until the second world war. There were several reasons why not much interest was shown prior to this time. The International Federation of Trade Unions was for the most part an association of European trade union movements, and it was natural in the light of events—the growth of fascism, the rise of Hitler, the Spanish Civil War and the development of Soviet-directed communism—that the I.F.T.U. should be mainly concerned with problems that immediately threatened the interests of its members.

This situation completely changed during the second world war. The common struggle which Soviet Russia had been compelled to share by Hitler's attack upon it, created a strong desire in the trade union movements of the democratic countries to achieve a unified world-wide trade union movement. The British T.U.C., which suggested the foundation of a new world trade union organization and proposed the establishment of a preparatory committee, hoped that the ideological differences which had divided the I.F.T.U. from the Soviet-sponsored 'Red' International of Labour Unions would be eliminated in a new era of goodwill and the common endeavour to rebuild a war-shattered world.

When the founding conference of the new World Federation of Trade Unions was eventually held in 1945, the trade union movements had developed sufficiently well in British territories for the T.U.C. to arrange for delegates and observers to be present from British Guiana, Nigeria, Sierra Leone, the Gambia, Gold Coast and Northern Rhodesia. The importance of industrially less-advanced parts of the world was recognized by the European and American labour movements, but the

157

main attention was inevitably focused upon the problems of post-war developments stemming from the relations of the great powers. In April 1947 a Trade Union Conference was organized at Dakar, French West Africa, for the purpose of collecting information on African trade unionism. All but two of the British territories sent delegates. The work of the W.F.T.U. was, however, soon largely vitiated by the development of the 'cold war'.

In 1948, after it had become increasingly apparent that the Russians were determined to use the W.F.T.U. as a vehicle for communist propaganda against the Western Powers, regardless of the effects that this might have on the influence of the organization and after all attempts to persuade the Russians to change their policy had failed, it was decided by the British, American and the non-communist West European trade union movements to withdraw to form a new world trade union organization free from the domination of any government. When the International Confederation of Free Trade Unions was founded in 1949 most of the trade union movements in the colonies joined, but a few of them were not keen to disaffiliate from the W.F.T.U., and it was some time before several organizations withdrew to join the new body.

After the foundation of the I.C.F.T.U. in 1949 special attention was given to assisting the trade unions in the tropical countries of the world. Offices were established in the Caribbean, West and East Africa and South-East Asia. Training schools were later set up in India and Africa, and courses in basic trade union organization have been run in a number of countries.

The I.C.F.T.U. has done much to help the development of unions in tropical territories through the provision of organizational assistance and financial subsidies. It has established field offices in a number of countries and training colleges in Kampala, Calcutta and Mexico City. From the headquarters of the I.C.F.T.U. a constant stream of helpful advice and practical aid flows to the territories but these efforts have been considerably weakened by a number of factors. There has been constant criticism by affiliates of the work of the I.C.F.T.U., and its directing body has frequently been divided on issues of policy; the American trade unions have not always been prepared to co-operate fully with the I.C.F.T.U., and other organizations have had reservations about the conduct of certain aspects of its policy. The administration of the I.C.F.T.U. and its operations in the field have often been inefficient, it has lacked an adequate staff and it has never had sufficient funds to carry out its programme fully.

The British T.U.C. has been critical of the I.C.F.T.U. on a number of grounds, and the differences of opinion have never been finally cleared up. A major factor in the relative weakness of the I.C.F.T.U. in the colonial field has been the difference of opinion between the British T.U.C. and European trade union movements and the A.F.L.–C.I.O. on the policy the International Confederation should follow with regard to the fight against communism and the abolition of colonialism.

Both the T.U.C. and the A.F.L.–C.I.O. have their own programmes of activity in the colonial territories. Although the British T.U.C. was helping the development of trade unions in British overseas territories long before the I.C.F.T.U. came into existence, it has channelled very large sums of money into the I.C.F.T.U. solidarity fund and supported the activities of the International organization in the territories.

The A.F.L.–C.I.O., in the years immediately following the war, appointed its own representatives in Europe, Latin America, South-East Asia and Japan. Since the mid-1950's, attention has also been given to Africa. The primary purpose of the American effort is to oppose communism and colonialism. In Britain it was strongly felt that the American unions did not appreciate the fact that it was British policy ultimately to give each colony its independence, but that it would be disastrous for the territories if the British Government simply walked out, before a viable system of government and a public administration competent to deal with the problems that arise after independence had been established. This is a task that takes time. The activities of the American unions have encouraged nationalist movements, but often, unfortunately, they have contributed little towards the speeding up of the necessary development of soundly organized trade unionism. And they have shown little knowledge and understanding of the work done to promote the growth of unions and effective labour

M

administration by British Governments and the British trade unions.

Many members of the European trade union organizations have felt that the American union leaders were too strongly motivated by ideological considerations. The self-righteous attitude often displayed by the representatives of the American unions has provoked distrust of their ability to understand the problems of either the European labour movements or those of the under-developed territories of Africa, Asia and the Caribbean.

The A.F.L.–C.I.O. have made it abundantly clear that they believe that the European unions have not waged war vigorously enough on communism and colonialism. The Americans have not, therefore, been prepared to reduce their independent activities, and they have shown at times a reluctance to increase their contributions to the I.C.F.T.U. funds until assured of changes in its policy.

Faced by this problem, the executive leadership of the I.C.F.T.U. has sought to persuade the British T.U.C. to give up its own programme of assistance to colonial trade unions in the hope of persuading the A.F.L.–C.I.O. that it, too, should hand over this work to the international body.

A case could be made out in favour of this course, but there were also powerful arguments against it. The T.U.C. had done and was still doing work which neither the I.C.F.T.U. nor the A.F.L.–C.I.O. could duplicate. Over the past thirty years the T.U.C. had established a close relationship with many of the unions in British colonies and its officers had gained far more experience of the problems of colonial trade unions than those of any other organization. The T.U.C. had also developed relations with the Overseas Employers' Federation in Britain and with the British Government, both of which were directly responsible for the employment and welfare of thousands of work-people in the tropical territories of the Commonwealth. Through this relationship, the T.U.C. was able to exercise an important influence that had greatly benefited the trade unions and had encouraged the growth of constructive industrial relations.

There are a number of trade union centres in British territories that have refused to join the I.C.F.T.U. or any other international organization. At different times, these have included such important bodies as the Antigua Trades and Labour Union, the Nigerian Teachers' Union, the Oil Workers' Union of Trinidad and the All Nigeria Trade Union Federation. The British T.U.C. has long had good relations with these organizations, and it has taken the view that it could not accept the suggestion of the I.C.F.T.U. that it should only give assistance to bodies affiliated to the International Confederation.

The attitude of the T.U.C. was sharply criticized on the grounds that organizations that refused to align themselves with the I.C.F.T.U. were motivated by a sympathy for communism. The T.U.C. believed that to label an uncommitted union as 'red' and to refuse to give it assistance, was to abandon any possibility of influencing its outlook and policy. Furthermore, this attitude might simply drive the unaffiliated unions into much closer relations with the communist countries and the World Federation of Trade Unions.

These problems were repeatedly discussed between the T.U.C., the I.C.F.T.U. and the A.F.L.–C.I.O., but no agreement was reached. After persistent pressure from the Americans, the General Secretary of the I.C.F.T.U., J. H. Oldenbrock, was compelled to resign, apparently because he did not pursue a sufficiently vigorous anti-communist and anti-colonial policy, allegedly under the influence of the T.U.C. His successor, Omer Becu, was the choice of the A.F.L.–C.I.O., but reports were soon to appear suggesting that the new leadership was not proving satisfactory to the American trade unions. A further aspect of the conflict over the aims and methods of the I.C.F.T.U. centred on the use of the International Solidarity Fund and the relation of this fund to the general finances of the I.C.F.T.U.

In the circumstances of trade union development in the tropical territories of the world, it is impossible to avoid taking political considerations into account when making decisions to provide assistance. But many European trade unionists are inclined to the view that the policies of the I.C.F.T.U., especially under the prompting of the Americans, have been weighted far too heavily by political rather than trade union objectives. They feel, for example, that while the decisions to supply central bodies with large sums of money might be justified on organizational grounds, they are, in fact, often decided upon for political reasons.

The difficulties which face the I.C.F.T.U. in Africa have certainly been greatly aggravated by the hostility of the Pan-African movement launched by Dr. Nkrumah. The I.C.F.T.U. is apparently regarded by the leaders of Ghanaian T.U.C. as a white, European-dominated organization.[1] Dr. Nkrumah's objective is to build a powerful African nationalist movement on the basis of an appeal to the racial emotions of black Africans. From the point of view of the development of political and economic stability and racial harmony in Africa and the rest of the world, the substitution of one kind of nationalist intolerance for another is no advance. When, in addition, the Pan-African movement is inclined to lean heavily towards the Soviet Union for assistance and advice the rest of the world has reason to suspect the benefits that might flow from its design for a future African state. It does not follow, however, that the policy of the I.C.F.T.U. has always been the best counter-move to these developments.

The fears of the leaders of the A.F.L.–C.I.O. and other members of the I.C.F.T.U. that Russia's influence in the under-developed countries might prevail have been stimulated by the activities of the World Federation of Trade Unions. This organization, which has had its headquarters in Prague since 1957, and which is an open instrument of Soviet foreign policy, has in recent years made considerable efforts to influence trade unions in the African, Asian and other less-developed territories.

The strength of the W.F.T.U. outside the Eastern European countries is not to be measured solely in terms of its affiliated membership, which is to be found mainly in the French-speaking African territories (where trade union movements have grown up under the influence of the communist-dominated C.G.T.), in Latin America and to some extent in Asia. The trade union movements of the Arab countries of the Middle East and North Africa are not affiliated, but they have close relations with the W.F.T.U., and they are prepared to take

[1] John Tettegah, General Secretary of the Ghana T.U.C., urged a total war on African trade unions that refused to join the All African Trade Union Federation, established in Casablanca in 1961. Since then, however, there have been signs of a less aggressive attitude to the I.C.F.T.U.

financial help and technical assistance from it. It is impossible to discover from the published reports of the W.F.T.U. Congress who were delegates and who were merely observers.

The propaganda carried on by the W.F.T.U. is incessant, and is always directed against the so-called 'imperialists'. British, European and American employers are condemned as 'monopoly capitalists', and the I.C.F.T.U. and the unions affiliated to it are described as the willing tools of these agents of imperialism.

While the W.F.T.U. denounces the I.C.F.T.U. and denigrates the work that is done by that organization, at the same time it preaches continuously the need for trade union unity and working-class solidarity. This is, of course, a classic communist propaganda technique; refusal to accept communist policy and communist leadership is violently attacked as a crime against the basic philosophy of trade unionism. The use of every means available to undermine and destroy the I.C.F.T.U. is always accompanied by the disingenuous claim that the objective is greater unity. What, in fact, the communists mean by unity is a process of co-operation, absorption and elimination, leaving only the communists in complete control of the unions.

It is difficult to assess the effect of the stream of propaganda put out from the Prague headquarters of the W.F.T.U. The constant iteration of anti-colonialism and anti-capitalism must have some influence on the minds of workers in the territories if they are exposed to it. Every incident affecting race relations in America and Britain is written up and proclaimed as evidence of the hostile attitude of the 'imperialists' towards the people of Africa, Asia and the other tropical areas of the world.

The W.F.T.U. has sought to influence trade union opinion by the provision of scholarships for those officials who would like to take a trip to Russia and Eastern Europe. Trade unionists from Africa and Asia have been sent to special courses held at the W.F.T.U. schools in Hungary and East Germany.

Substantial grants have been made to 'neutral' organizations such as the All-African Trade Union Federation established at Casablanca under the inspiration of the Ghana Government.

The extent to which the A.A.T.U.F. is dependent upon the W.F.T.U. for funds and its willingness to accept the political direction of the Russian-dominated World Federation was revealed when a confidential letter written by the Sudanese Secretary of the W.F.T.U. to the head of the International Department of the Ghana T.U.C. was 'obtained' and printed by the Nigerian press and the I.C.F.T.U.[2]

Most of the leaders of the unions in the less-developed countries of the world are well aware that both the W.F.T.U. and the I.C.F.T.U. are anxious to win their support. Some of them are influenced by a tactical desire to maximize their strategic position and have been motivated by this consideration rather than by a strong desire to enter the communist camp. The pressure exerted by the W.F.T.U. has been important in this respect, since it has constantly induced the Americans and the I.C.F.T.U. to seek to outbid the communists by attacking colonialism and by providing aid and assistance.

The difficulties which face an international trade union movement, even when the policy issues are set aside, are inevitably great. It is not easy to find the huge sums of money that are required to finance an international trade union assistance scheme, and if more money were available there is still the problem of finding the right kind of experienced trade unionists who are willing and able to spend substantial periods of time working in the territories with the local trade union movements. A good deal of suspicion and hostility will have to be overcome; it takes quite a time to earn the confidence of the local trade unions, and it often takes longer to make an impression on businessmen and government officials, who do not always take kindly to outside interference, especially when they feel, sometimes with justification, that the advice given is not always responsible.

In the long run the success of the I.C.F.T.U. will depend upon its ability to help in the building of well-organized and well-run trade union movements. The political conflict between communism and democracy cannot be won by labour organization; the major battle has to be fought at other levels. Labour organizations certainly have a part to play, but the role of the I.C.F.T.U. should be to promote sound trade union-

[2] See *Free Labour World*, May 1962.

ism and good industrial relations, since it is these things that will finally determine the success or failure of the I.C.F.T.U. The difficulty which confronts the I.C.F.T.U. is to provide effective assistance when constantly challenged by political situations which threaten to make the achievement of a genuine trade unionism impossible.

Perhaps the most effective help that is being given by international trade union organizations in the tropical territories is that provided by the international trade secretariats. There are more than 20 of these bodies, organized on the basis of common industrial interests. They have an independent existence, but they are ideologically linked with the I.C.F.T.U. and have a close working relationship with it.[3]

The work of the I.T.S. has received much less publicity, and it has been much less hindered by policy questions than the I.C.F.T.U. This is because the I.T.S. are primarily concerned with the organizational, economic and industrial factors affecting member unions. They are thus able to by-pass many of the ideological and political obstacles that confront the I.C.F.T.U. and have been able to retain the support of unions that look with suspicion on the I.C.F.T.U.

The International Transport Workers' Federation, the Plantation Workers' International Federation, the Public Services International, the International Federation of Mineworkers and Post, Telegraph and Telephone International have all, in recent years, shown a growing interest in the problems of their affiliates in tropical territories. Representatives of the trade secretariats have been quietly and effectively helping the local unions in the territories to build up their organizations. They have helped to establish sound methods of administration, assisted unions to prepare for negotiations and they have often helped to bring rival bodies together and develop a more satisfactory trade union structure.

The efforts made by the international trade secretariats have so far been on a limited scale, but they have been a most important complement to the work of the I.C.F.T.U. Consideration is being given to ways and means of extending the work of the I.T.S., and a recommendation that there should be co-

[3] The W.F.T.U. has created duplicate organizations, but these have little or no standing in international trade union affairs.

operation with the I.C.F.T.U. to establish a pool of field representatives is being examined.

In this and other ways, increasing effort is being made by the I.T.S. to bring the experience of the trade unions in the more advanced countries to the aid of the unions in the less-developed regions of the world.

Part Two

The Development of Labour Policy and Administration

THE EVOLUTION OF
COLONIAL OFFICE LABOUR POLICY

IN British colonial policy much weight has always been given to the opinions of the local administration of the various colonial territories, and to the local knowledge and experience on which these opinions are based. The administration of a dependent territory is the responsibility of the local government, and particularly of the governor, whose powers may be constrained constitutionally to a greater or lesser degree by responsibility given to local legislatures, or to unofficial members of his executive council.

In purely legal and constitutional terms the Secretary of State for the Colonies is responsible to the British Parliament for the administration and good government of all the territories; and where the British Government has declared itself on a specific issue of policy, the Colonial Office holds itself responsible for seeing that that policy is put into effect in the territories concerned. Nevertheless, it is usual to leave much to the discretion of the territorial governments, and the judgment of the governor is often allowed to override the advice given by the Colonial Office, so long as the explicit terms of the latter's policy are not obviously ignored or defied. If a given matter becomes an important issue affecting public opinion in Britain, or becomes important to the British Government, then the strength of that opinion will be reflected in the degree of pressure exerted to get local law or practice changed. Otherwise the Colonial Office tends to accept arguments to the effect that local conditions make the suggested changes inapplicable or unacceptable. In the last resort the Colonial Secretary does have the ultimate authority to put his own wishes into practice, and he may dismiss the governor, or may transfer an official whose presence is an embarrassment which impedes the acceptance of the policy concerned. Even where constitutional advance has gone so far as to introduce a measure of

169

responsible government, the governor may, in the last resort, suspend the constitution.

In any case, the policy decisions made in the Colonial Office, and the opinions it expresses have a great deal of influence on what happens in the colonial territories, and Colonial Office advice is often the strongest of the many pressures to which a colonial government is subject. Conversely, however, knowledge of what will be acceptable in the territories concerned usually affects the way in which a new Colonial Office policy is formulated. Exchanges of information and of ideas between the dependent territories and the metropolitan government are of considerable significance, both in formulating policy and in agreeing changes within the territories themselves.

The general picture of British colonial administration, then, is one of flexibility and diversity, reflecting the range of different social and economic conditions in different territories, the different views and personalities of governors and their advisers, the different historical developments and stages of constitutional advancement reached. There is, however, a certain unity of constitutional principle, of basic policy on such matters as human rights and social policy, and also to some extent of legal framework—a unity which shows the influence of the Colonial Office. It is the diversity and the flexibility which makes a simple treatment of any question of colonial policy impossible.

In this chapter the labour policies, and especially the policies which are concerned with trade unions and industrial relations generally, are dealt with from the Colonial Office standpoint, and from the point of view of the effectiveness of their transmission from London to the dependencies. The history of Colonial Office labour policies since the 1920's is outlined briefly, and the organization which has been developed within the Colonial Office to deal with labour matters is described. The nature of the relations between the Colonial Office departments and the dependencies is analysed, as well as the influences which affect the formulation of policy in London. Developments in the territories themselves, which have been greatly influenced by the policies of the Colonial Office, are examined in Chapter 9.

Before the first world war the Colonial Office had no general labour policy. This was not because labour problems were unimportant, but rather that the office was not in the habit of laying down general policy on any question at this time. A considerable discretion in these and other matters was left to the governor and the administration on the spot. Particular problems did, of course, call for special consideration. The supply of contract labour from India and China was a case in point. Indentured labour had been recruited and shipped to such places as Natal, Malaya, Mauritius, Fiji, British Guiana and Trinidad, and this practice had provoked conflicting pressures for and against its continuance. As territories have progressed towards independence the broad purpose of constitutional development has been to increase the measure of local representation so as finally to achieve full suffrage and self-government. In the early stages of this evolution the unofficial members of the executive council or legislature were almost inevitably appointed and there was perhaps an unavoidable inclination to select well-known businessmen or other prominent local figures. The legislature did not, therefore, in this period of constitutional development reflect a full balance of opinion; it often displayed a tendency to be reactionary and against social progress. During this phase of constitutional development a Colonial Secretary was very reluctant to override a strong local expression of opinion, since this would have tended to retard development. It was factors such as these that were largely responsible for the slow-gathering momentum of labour policy.

In the African territories official policy favoured indirect rule and the preservation of tribal authority as far as this was possible. In Malaya a similar bias towards the Sultans and their entourage prevailed; in Fiji it was towards the Chiefs. None of these sources of local influence and authority encouraged the growth of trade unions, which were looked upon as misguided and possibly subversive organizations. Only recently, after losing most of their power to political parties and elected bodies, have the traditional local leaders begun to change their attitude towards the activities of unions. Mine owners, plantation managers and settlers, who were anxious to obtain a steady supply of co-operative workers, were strong supporters of chiefly authority and much against any manifestation of trade unionism. Labour was, however, not always easy to obtain, and the problem of securing the labour required by the plantations and settlers and by government for public works and the need to improve and to control the systems of recruitment, contract, discipline and forced labour were issues that were becoming increasingly important when the first world war broke out.

The first world war stimulated interest in the colonies and brought a new responsibility to the Colonial Office; it also stimulated interest in labour problems. With the creation of the International Labour Organization in 1919, international attention began to be paid to labour standards, including standards in the non-self-governing territories for which members of the I.L.O. were responsible.

The Emergence of a Labour Policy

Throughout the 20's labour matters assumed a growing importance for the Colonial Office. In the early years of the decade labour conditions in East Africa, especially in Kenya, were the subject of discussion in Parliament, and petitions were presented to the government from missions and other sources. Forced labour and the measures permissible by the government to 'encourage' labourers to enter employment led to the sending of several despatches to the Governor of Kenya. With the passing of the Indian Emigration Act in 1922, the Colonial Office was pressed by the Indian Government and the India Office to encourage the colonies to enter into agreements to regulate the employment of contract labour, and considerable progress was made.[1] During this period labour departments were established in a number of colonies, and the standards they were expected to promote became a subject of active consideration in the Colonial Office.

Events in India during the 1920's had a significant influence on labour developments in Ceylon and on British politics. During these years there was a rapid growth of trade unions in India, and this was accompanied by a considerable increase in the number of strikes. An important element in this upsurge of militancy was the activity of Indian and British communists, who saw in the development of trade unions in India an opportunity for the promotion of revolutionary political doctrines.

[1] See Chapter 9.

The Government of India responded to this situation in 1924 by arresting five leading Indian communists and charging them with seeking to promote a violent revolution. At this time there were no laws applying specially to trade unions in India, as legal regulation had not been considered necessary. Faced by a rapid development of trade unions and rising militancy, the government decided to introduce a Trade Union Act that embodied the general principles of British trade union law, and in addition provided for the compulsory registration of unions.[2]

In spite of the Trade Union Act, communist influence in the Indian unions continued to grow, accompanied by industrial unrest. After the appointment in 1929 of a Royal Commission under the leadership of J. H. Whitley (Chairman of the famous committee that had been responsible for one of the most celebrated reports ever made on British industrial relations) to consider how industrial relations in India might be improved, the communists succeeded in splitting the trade union movement by persuading an important section not to give evidence.

The Commission considered the problems affecting the growth of the unions and asked whether the organization of labour was really appropriate in circumstances that were entirely different in so many respects from those that had existed in Britain and Europe. Were there not other and more suitable methods of protecting and advancing the interests of workers? The Commission concluded that:

> It may be urged that this movement (trade unionism) which suffers from so many handicaps, which demands qualities at present so rare among Indian workmen and which is admittedly exotic in origin, is ill-suited to Indian needs and the whole development of trade unions is a move in the wrong direction. As regards the foreign character of the movement we would observe that modern industrialism is itself a western importation. The difficulties which it creates for labour in India are similar to the difficulties which it has created elsewhere, and there is no evidence of any alternative remedy that is likely to prove effective. Everything that we have seen in India has forced upon us the conviction that the need for organization among Indian workmen is great and that, unless industry and the State develop along entirely different lines from those at present followed, nothing but a strong

[2] See A. Prakash, *The State in Relation to Trade Unions and Trade Disputes in India* (an unpublished thesis, University of London, 1953).

trade union movement will give the Indian workman adequate protection. Legislation can act as a palliative and prevent graver abuses, but there are strict limitations to the power of Government and the public to protect workmen who are unable to protect themselves. Labour laws, indeed, find one of their most effective sanctions in the support of organized unions. Nor is labour the only party that will benefit from a sound development of the trade union movement. Employers and the public generally should welcome its growth.[3]

In the event, the Indian Government did not wait for the report of the Commission, but passed a Trade Disputes Act in 1929. This Act borrowed heavily from the British Trade Unions and Trade Disputes Act of 1927. The Act prohibited all strikes that had an objective other than the furtherance of a trade dispute within the trade or industry in which the strikers were employed; and strikes designed or calculated to inflict severe general and prolonged hardship upon the community.[4] It made strikes and lockouts in public utilities illegal unless 14 days' notice had been given of the intention to strike. This legislation, though bitterly attacked in India and in Britain, was not strong enough to curb the activities of the communists in the Indian trade unions, and they continued to foment strikes for political reasons.

The extreme 'left wing' of the British trade union movement and Labour Party paid a great deal of attention to events in India. The Government of India's decision to arrest a number of active communist members of the trade unions for seditious activity, and their subsequent trial at Meerut evoked a storm of protest from left-wing labour leaders everywhere and caused a sharp division of opinion within the British Labour movement.[5]

Much exercised by events in India and other parts of the colonial empire, it was natural that the Labour Party, on its return to power in 1924 and 1929, decided to pay more attention to labour matters than previous administrations and to make some changes in policy. Hence, when the East African

---

[3] *Royal Commission on Labour In India (1929-31)*, Cmnd. 3883, p. 322.
[4] See A. Prakash, *The State in Relation to Trade Unions and Trade Disputes in India* (an unpublished thesis, University of London, 1953).
[5] See S. D. Punekar, *Trade Unionism in India*, Bombay 1948; H. Pelling, *The British Communist Party*, London 1958; M. R. Massin, *Communist Party of India*, New Delhi, 1954.

Royal Commission, consisting of one Conservative M.P., one Labour M.P., and one Liberal M.P., was appointed to visit Northern Rhodesia, Nyasaland, Kenya, Uganda and Tanganyika, in July 1924, it was asked, among other things, to report on:

(a) the action necessary to ameliorate the social conditions of the natives of East Africa, including improvement of health and economic development; and

(b) the economic relations between natives and non-natives with special reference to labour contracts, care of labourers, certificates of identification, employment of women and children.

It was, however, on constitutional matters rather than labour and social matters that the Commission's report had its impact.

In 1926 the leader of the Labour Party, Ramsay MacDonald, visited Ceylon, and in the following year two members of the General Council of the T.U.C., A. A. Purcell and J. Hallsworth, visited India to attend the meeting of the Indian National Congress. One of them also visited Ceylon. In the same year a constitutional commission arrived in Ceylon and one of its members was a Labour M.P., Dr. T. Drummond Shiels, who soon afterwards played an important part in the development of colonial labour policy when the Labour Party formed a government in 1929. Shortly before the Labour Party's return to office the party had held a Commonwealth conference which was attended by representatives from Australia, Canada, South Africa, India, Ceylon, Trinidad, Palestine and Ireland. Problems of the labour movements and social and economic development were discussed at this conference.

The importance which the Labour Government of 1929 attached to Colonial problems was emphasized by the appointment of Lord Passfield (Sidney Webb) to the post of Secretary of State for the Colonies, and Dr. Drummond Shiels as Parliamentary Under-Secretary. Almost the first task that confronted the new Secretary of State was a request from Ceylon that approval should be given to a statute similar to the Trade Disputes Act adopted later in the same year in India. Lord Passfield refused to agree to the Ceylon Government's proposed Bill, since it was based on the British Trade Unions and Trade

N

Disputes Act of 1927, which the Labour Party was pledged to repeal at the earliest opportunity—an opportunity which it was not able to take until 1945.[6] However, approval was given to a Trade Disputes Act based on the principles of the British Industrial Courts Act of 1919.

The leaders of the Labour Party and the British T.U.C. were in full sympathy with the efforts to form trade unions that had been made in several colonies, and they were anxious to support these developments. In 1930 a Colonial Office Labour Committee, consisting at this time entirely of officials from the Colonial Office and Ministry of Labour, was established, which was to deal over the next twelve years or so with such matters as the basic formulation of Colonial Office labour policy, the drafting of model laws and the effects on dependencies of some of the international labour conventions of the period. The lengthy discussions at Geneva, which were concerned with the drafting of the Forced Labour Convention of 1930, compelled the Colonial Office to examine the difficult question of labour standards appropriate to non-metropolitan[7] territories. The modifications to the laws in the colonies that were made necessary by the ratification of this and other conventions involved the Colonial Office in extensive negotiations with the governments of the territories, and the question of policy on labour matters began to take on a new significance. In the same year as the Forced Labour Convention was adopted, an important conference of Colonial governors and administrators took place, during which there was considerable discussion of labour matters. This discussion was under the chairmanship of the Parliamentary Under-Secretary Dr. Drummond Shiels, who more than once mentioned the understandable change of emphasis in Colonial Office policy which the advent of the Labour Government had brought about. There were prolonged discussions on the application of the recently adopted Forced Labour Convention, and later the Under-Secretary introduced many questions concerning labour legislation and administration. The absence of adequate labour and social

---

[6] For full details of this incident see K. V. Jayawardena, *The Labour Movement in Ceylon with reference to Political Factors, 1893–1947* (an unpublished thesis in the University of London, 1964).

[7] Non-metropolitan territories are those for which a member of the I.L.O. accepts responsibility.

legislation in some colonies had for some time been a concern to him personally, and he made special reference to the obsolescence of some existing legislation, such as the Master and Servants Laws, under which penal sanctions for breaches of contract, including verbal contracts, could be imposed. Laws regulating the employment of women and children were necessary if the United Kingdom Government was to stand by its obligations to apply international labour conventions to the colonies. The Government wished for the wider adoption and improvement of Workmen's Compensation Ordinances and were working out schemes whereby insurance facilities could be made available. They were also concerned about the absence of factory legislation. Dr. Shiels even suggested for consideration the possibility of widening the franchise in colonies with unofficial representatives in their legislatures, in order to make the unofficial members dependent for election on the votes of those whose social conditions most needed improvement. He forecast that colonial governments would be increasingly pressed to make their machinery of government more representative by extending the right to vote to a wider section of the community. In accordance with a recent White Paper on Native Taxation, he reiterated the policy that taxation must no longer be used to oblige people to go out from their own holdings to work for an employer; any taxes they were called upon to pay ought not to exceed an amount that could be met from the capacity of a man's holding.

Two questions in particular which had relevance to the adoption of a labour policy that was appropriate to the developments taking place in the colonies were brought up and discussed at this conference. Firstly, the chairman drew attention to the danger of a low wage policy, and to its adverse effects. He recognized that in some territories which imported labour much had been done recently to improve conditions, but that this had been due to pressure from the governments of the labourers' country of origin. The economic interests of labourers should be the concern of the colonial government, and action should not be forced by outside pressure. Secondly, he hoped that colonial governments would show sympathy with the increasing tendency for workers' organizations to be formed. The wisest policy was to guide the colonial peoples' increasing restlessness and discontent, whether economic or political, into constitutional channels, and to provide some safety valves and some opportunities for progress. It was easier for a government to deal with an organized body such as a trade union than with a number of irresponsible individuals. The success of co-operative societies in some places was an augury for the potential success of trade unions.

This was a fairly clear statement of policy by the new government, and a considerable departure from the previous relative unconcern with labour matters in the dependencies. It was now apparent that the Colonial Office had arrived at a stage where it was prepared to give a lead in formulating a policy for the improvement of labour and social conditions. The need for this lead was recognized in various degrees by the participants in the conference, and some agreement with the Under-Secretary's remarks was cautiously expressed, but there were considerable doubts as to the readiness of the colonies to accept such institutional developments as trade unions. The Secretary of State was convinced of the need for more positive action, and the Colonial Office Conference was followed, in September 1930, by a circular despatch to all colonial governments, advocating the passage of trade union legislation. The despatch maintained that trade unions would be a natural and legitimate development in the colonial territories as social and industrial progress took place, and it suggested that simple legislation, where no unions had yet become established, should be passed incorporating the principles of Sections 2 and 3 of the 1871 British Trade Union Act, which exempt trade unions from liability to prosecution and to civil action on the grounds that their objects or activities are in restraint of trade. Where a trade union movement was already in evidence, however, the existing legislation should be reviewed to see if it was still adequate. More comprehensive provisions might then become necessary.

The despatch recommended, in addition, the compulsory registration of all trade unions. The reason given for this was that the idea of combining together for economic purposes was so novel to the workers in most territories that 'sympathetic supervision and guidance' would be needed. Otherwise the unions might 'fall under the dominance of disaffected persons, by whom their activities may be diverted to improper and mischievous ends'. This despatch has often been referred to in the post-war period as being the first significant milestone in the development of trade unions in the dependencies; it represented a new departure in Colonial Office policy and at the same time initiated a series of new measures in legislation and administration by colonial governments.

In fact, from the point of view of Colonial Office policy the despatch, as has been seen, reflected and formalized a change which had been impending since the end of the first world war and had already been put to the representatives of colonial governments at the conference and discussed with them. Nevertheless, from the point of view of at least the majority of colonial governments to whom the despatch was addressed, its effect seems to have been slight. There was undoubtedly much resistance to the ideas it expressed, as they applied to each territory individually, and little or no action was taken for, in some cases, ten years or more.

Special significance is sometimes seen in the fact that the despatch was signed by the then Colonial Secretary, Lord Passfield, whose work on trade unionism might have been expected to have led him to be particularly interested in this kind of development.[8] However, there is no evidence that the Secretary of State himself paid any unusually great attention to labour questions during his term of office; and the great enthusiast and mover, as was apparent in the Colonial Office Conference, was almost certainly his Parliamentary Under-Secretary, Dr. Drummond Shiels. The frequent correspondence over this period between Lord Passfield and his wife makes no mention of any colonial labour matter, and there is no reference to the subject in Beatrice Webb's diaries of the period. It may be only a coincidence that on 15th September 1930, just two days before the date of the circular despatch, Lord Passfield in a letter to his wife, made the following comment on Graham Wallas: 'I can't imagine what he would do in my place, where I have to authorize daily by initialling innumerable decisions one after another, on endless matters on which I can form only the roughest kind of judgment, on the

[8] See, for instance, *Labour in the U.K. Dependencies*, Colonial Office Reference Pamphlet (H.M.S.O., 1957), p. 8.

advice of others. But there *have to be* decisions, irrespective of
what the philosophers say about them.'

It would perhaps be unfair to suggest that, however much it
may have accorded with the inclinations of Labour ministers,
as far as the Secretary of State was concerned the 1930
despatch was just one more decision to be initialled, but it is
likely that Lord Passfield played a less important part in
pressing for changes in Colonial Office labour policy than his
Parliamentary Under-Secretary.

The principles set out in the 1930 despatch set the course of
the official policy of the Colonial Office. However, owing
partly to the onset of the world depression, and partly to the
natural reluctance of colonial government officials to encourage
the creation of popular protest movements in the form of trade
unions, the despatch had little effect. After the death of the
Labour Government in 1931 the policy of the Colonial Office
remained unchanged, but relatively little thought was given to
colonial trade unionism by Colonial Secretaries in the National
Government of the early 1930's. A few territories—notably
Trinidad, Tanganyika, Nyasaland and the Gambia—did enact
some form of trade union legislation in 1932, but they were
exceptional, and in the early years of that decade the pressing
problems were financial and administrative. Unfortunately
for the colonies the depression brought drastic falls in revenue
and a consequent reduction in the public services.

Further despatches were, however, issued during the 30's.
In April 1931 a despatch, again from the Labour Government's
Secretary of State, pointed out that relatively little attention
had been paid in the colonies to international labour conventions. Metropolitan governments had an obligation to ensure
that effect was given by legislation to the provisions of these
conventions, so long as they were applicable, even though they
might not refer specifically to dependent territories. Colonial
governments were advised to consider this matter. One of
the conventions already adopted and ratified by the United
Kingdom was the Minimum Wage Fixing Convention of 1928,
and after consideration in the Colonial Office another circular
despatch was sent in 1932 to all colonial governments, suggesting that simple legislation be passed to empower governors to
fix minimum wages where there was a danger of rates being too

low; and for this purpose to provide for the appointment of wages advisory boards on which the interests of wage-earners would be adequately represented.

Two years later, in a further despatch, model workmen's compensation provisions were circulated to African colonies with a request that their application be considered. But again little immediate action resulted from these representations from London.

During this period the supervision of social and labour conditions in many territories had suffered because of the financial difficulties through which the territories were passing. Labour departments, where they already existed, had been closed down or reduced in staff, and shortages of staff everywhere resulted in labour conditions being given insufficient attention. This led to increasing concern among the small but growing number of people in Great Britain who were interested in colonial problems, and the question of supervision of labour conditions and of adequate labour legislation was raised in Parliament by Labour members in 1934 and 1935. In 1935 a strike in the Northern Rhodesian copper mines resulted in some deaths when the police opened fire, and this again drew attention to labour conditions and to the inadequacy of government machinery for labour supervision. It was at about the same time that a new Secretary of State for the Colonies, Mr. Malcolm MacDonald, was appointed. Mr. MacDonald immediately showed an interest in colonial labour questions, especially in matters such as the conditions in the Rhodesian mines. Studies of labour problems were initiated in the Colonial Office, and, as a result, in November 1935 a despatch was sent to all colonial governments asking for a revision of their arrangements for the supervision of employment conditions; it pointed out the importance of labour department functions, and asked that information should be sent back to the Colonial Secretary indicating to what extent machinery had been established to carry them out. The despatch set out the duties of a labour department, emphasizing particularly the function of enforcing legislation, thus forestalling complaints, rather than waiting for them to come to light before action was taken.

The Impact of Industrial Unrest

Concern over labour conditions continued to be expressed over the next few years, especially as all these communications from the Colonial Office had little apparent effect on the actions of colonial governments. Matters were to some extent brought to a head as a result of the series of strikes and disturbances in the Caribbean territories during 1935, and again at the beginning of 1937, and in the same year in Mauritius. The reports of the various inquiries into the 1937 troubles showed clearly that the very poor social conditions in which employees in the West Indies and Mauritius lived were an important factor, and drew attention to the inadequacy of government machinery for supervising conditions of employment, and the continuing lack of any of the 'safety valves' referred to in the 1930 despatch.

The unrest during 1937 led to a certain degree of concentration on labour matters in Parliamentary colonial debates, in which these factors were emphasized again. Following these discussions, the Colonial Secretary sent a further circular despatch in August 1937. This despatch, couched in rather more urgent terms than before, reminded colonial governments of the terms of Mr. MacDonald's despatch of 1935, and of the anxiety about labour conditions which continued to be expressed in Parliament. It reiterated that the establishment of labour departments should be the 'ultimate aim' in the larger dependencies, though care was taken to state that the Colonial Secretary was not insisting on uniformity or on the imposition of labour departments against the will of individual governments. However, in cases where a definite financial improvement had taken place, those governments should ensure that some of the benefits were now passed on to the workers. It was stressed that neither secretariats, nor native affairs departments, nor district administrations could cope adequately with labour matters in colonial dependencies. Furthermore, the despatch suggested that it was equally as important that the relations between employers and workers should not be ignored in agricultural colonies, as it was in those places where industries had become established. The setting up of specialist labour inspectorates should be seriously considered in all dependencies where there was a substantial wage-earning community, together with the duties already outlined in the previous despatch, and including the duty of giving advice on labour matters to the government.

This same despatch also asked for special surveys to be undertaken by colonial governments, preferably through their labour departments, of the regulations of contracts of employment, the abolition of penal sanctions for breach of contract by employees, and of workmen's compensation legislation. It expressed concern about the position of the lowest-paid workers in every territory, and the despatch requested again that steps should be taken everywhere to enable enquiries to be made into this kind of labour, and that effective use should be made of the legislation when enacted. Housing conditions, the transport of employees and the education of children of plantation workers were also suggested as being the concern of labour departments.

Finally, the Secretary of State asked for a review of the question of recognizing trade unions in the colonies. The prohibition of trade unions or their subjection to harassing controls would almost certainly encourage illegal bodies, which might develop into secret societies and become politically active. Thus, the restriction of trade unions might well give rise to 'extremist' organizations. It was a function of labour departments to report to the government on trade union developments, on the conduct of the unions and on the state of industrial relations.

This despatch had a greater impact than earlier communications, and it was followed by a series of moves in a number of colonies to put into effect many of the suggestions outlined. The more favourable response evoked from the governments of the colonies by this despatch was due to a growing realization, brought about by events, that labour unrest could not be prevented without the changes which the Colonial Office was advocating.

1937–1942: A Period of Vigorous Advance

The 1937 despatch also seems to have marked the beginning of a new and bolder phase in Colonial Office policy. From this time onwards labour matters were the subject of continuous attention within the Colonial Office instead of being considered *ad hoc* as issues arose in each territory. This change was part of a broader revision in Colonial Office thinking which affected a great many other spheres of activity besides labour; for example, general economic development, education, health, agriculture and scientific research. All began to receive systematic consideration and were made the subject of a general policy. In the following year, 1938, Major (later Sir Granville) Orde Browne, a former Provincial Commissioner of the Tanganyika Administration, founder of the first Tanganyika Labour Department and its head from 1925 to 1931, was sent to Northern Rhodesia to report to the United Kingdom Government on labour conditions in the protectorate, to recommend the administrative machinery which would be necessary and the legislation required to improve these conditions. On his return, Major Orde Browne was appointed to a new permanent post, created within the Colonial Office, of Labour Adviser to the Secretary of State.

In the next few years the newly appointed Labour Adviser paid extended visits to the West Indies, West Africa, Ceylon, Mauritius and Malaya. These visits were followed by the submission of detailed reports and recommendations which were published as Command Papers. The careful analysis of the problems and the practical suggestions made by Major Orde Browne had a considerable impact on the governments of the territories concerned.

A further important reorganization of the internal administration of the Colonial Office was made at the beginning of 1939. The pressure of events convinced the senior officials that more specialized knowledge should be made available on social and labour problems, and it was decided that a new technical department should be established. The Social Services Department was set up to deal with all questions of social and labour policy in the dependencies, to watch over the execution of policy and to provide a specialist staff who would be available to carry out the researches necessary for policy making and planning in these fields.

With the establishment of the new department the Colonial Office created within its own walls the facilities necessary for the providing of advice and administration that were essential if the rather inexperienced individual territorial governments were to be helped to pay more attention to labour conditions and to enact and enforce legislation to deal with the many problems which were facing them. The work of the Colonial Office had grown considerably when, after 1937, more and more labour legislation, including trade union ordinances, trade-disputes ordinances, arbitration and inquiry ordinances, began to be passed. With these developments in the territories the provision of technical information, circulation of model laws, criticism and approval of draft legislation and so on, became an important part of Colonial Office activities. Thus, in 1937, after prolonged study by a sub-committee of the Colonial Office Labour Committee, a draft Workmen's Compensation Ordinance was sent for consideration and subsequent enactment to the African colonies, most of which had hitherto not attempted to enact such laws. In 1938 details of legislation for conciliation and arbitration in industrial disputes was circulated with a model ordinance based on a recently enacted Trinidad law.

Following the establishment of the Social Services Department, a number of circular despatches were issued on the more detailed aspects of labour policy, including the need for the setting up of industrial conciliation and arbitration machinery, minimum wage-fixing machinery, legislation regulating the employment of children and young persons. In 1939 the recent Factories Acts of the United Kingdom and the administrative measures taken in connection with them were circulated to colonial territories with a request that local legislation should be examined in the light of the principles they embodied.

Not only draft legislation but also information, advice and requests on a whole range of labour topics were the subjects of the considerable number of communications from the Colonial Office in the years immediately before and during the war. The subject of statutory minimum wages continued to be referred to. In 1937 the various governments had been asked to inquire into the use which had been made of the minimum-wage machinery established in their territories. The following year another despatch pointed out the need to take movements in the cost of living into account when fixing wages, and, both then and in 1941, information on the construction and use of cost-of-living indices was provided. In 1938 another despatch referred to the various minimum age conventions of the I.L.O., and asked for the statutory minimum age for employment in industry to be raised everywhere to 14, and in other occupations to 12. In 1941 an important despatch, inspired by some recommendations made by Major Orde Browne in his report on labour in the West Indies, strongly recommended the establishment in all dependencies of labour advisory boards consisting, where possible, of representatives of employers and work-people. The functions of these boards would be to advise the local government on labour matters generally, to examine draft legislation before it was published and to make recommendations on any matters specifically referred to them.

In 1938, at about the same time as the Colonial Office was reshaping its internal organization so as to give closer and more continuous attention to labour matters, the Government came to the conclusion that the social and constitutional problems of the West Indies had reached a state when they ought to be fully investigated by a Royal Commission with power to make recommendations on the future course of action the British Government should pursue. Earlier in the year the government had established a Royal Commission to inquire into the possibility of closer association between the Rhodesias and Nyasaland. Both of these commissions gave a good deal of attention to labour problems. The Rhodesia–Nyasaland Commission, in its report, strongly emphasized the need to establish labour departments in each territory, and stressed the importance of developing a consistent and effective labour policy.

The West Indies Commission voiced strong criticism of the failure to implement Colonial Office policy so as to foster the development of trade unions.[9] It recommended the more

---

[9] 'Successive Secretaries of State for the Colonies have spoken publicly of the need for the encouragement of trade unions in the Colonial Empire, and from time to time over the last decade they have made representations to Colonial Governments in the West Indies drawing their attention to the desirability of facilitating the developments of trade unions. Despite this and the repeated statements of the present Secretary of State that Your Majesty's Government would welcome the establishment of trade unions, we were unable to discover that any real effort had been made until quite recent times to assist their formation and development.'
Further criticisms were made of the absence of laws permitting 'peaceful picketing' in most of the territories with the exception of Jamaica. The commission urged the need for the adoption of uniform principles and stressed that the law in each territory should provide 'in addition to the protection of the funds of trade unions against actions for tort and the legalization of peaceful picketing, for the compulsory registration of trade unions and the auditing of their funds; we believe that all of these conditions are essential to the proper development of trade unionism in the West Indies.'

(*West India Royal Commission, 1938–39*).

vigorous pursuit of policies already advocated by the Colonial Office, namely the passing of laws, if these did not already exist, to protect the unions from legal actions; and the development of labour administration, including the establishment of labour advisory boards, wages boards and an industrial court, Whitley councils for government employees, factory inspection and workmen's compensation. Most important with respect to the development of Colonial Office policy, it recommended that labour department and labour advisory committees, composed of persons with expert knowledge of labour and colonial questions, should be set up within the Colonial Office.

The United Kingdom Government accepted the findings of the Royal Commission on the West Indies, which were presented to Parliament in 1940,[10] and it immediately took steps to implement some of the recommendations. The outbreak of the second world war had underlined the urgency of meeting the problems which had been so clearly analysed by the various inquiries that had been set on foot in the previous few years. As a result of the war, many new problems arose with regard to the employment of labour, disruption of parts of the economy of some of the territories and the rapid development of employment in others through military works and production essential for the war effort. A circular despatch issued by the Colonial Office in December 1939 emphasized the difficult conditions likely to arise from the advent of war and the need to ensure that conditions of employment were adequately supervised.

The second world war, like the first world war, gave a further impetus to the development of colonial labour policy. A landmark in this respect was the passing of the Colonial Development and Welfare Act. This Act was passed in 1940, and it is worthy of special note that men were prepared to turn their minds to the task of building a better future for colonies at one of the blackest moments in British history. The purpose of the Act was to make available to the colonies, over a period of years, subventions from the United Kingdom for approved schemes of economic and social development.[11] On the insistence of a

[10] The Report was presented to the Colonial Secretary in 1939 and its recommendations to Parliament in 1940, but because of the war, it was not published until 1945.

[11] The West India Royal Commission, 1938–39, had recommended the setting up of a West Indian Welfare Fund, to be borne by the Imperial Exchequer, for

group of Labour M.P.s, who had the close co-operation of the then Parliamentary Under-Secretary of State for the Colonies, the Act included clauses stipulating that no territory might receive aid under its provisions unless it had in force legislation protecting the rights of trade unions, and unless the works for which the aid was to be used were carried out under a contract which embodied a fair wages clause, and which forbade the employment of children under the age of 14.   The inclusion of these conditions in the Act gave the Colonial Office almost its first real power to coerce colonial governments into carrying out the labour policies it was recommending, since almost every territory was anxious to receive financial assistance from the United Kingdom.   These provisions persuaded a number of colonial governments, which had been reluctant to comply with the wishes of the Colonial Office, to change their minds.   There was only one conspicuous exception—the Bahamas, which has never applied for aid under the Act, since it has never been willing to pass the legislation that would have made it eligible.

It appears, then, that during the four or five years from 1937 to 1941 and especially in the three or four years after the first appointment of a labour adviser, the British Government was putting a considerable amount of sustained pressure on the colonial territories in one way or another.   The representations made during this period were, moreover, far more effective than any which had been made in previous periods.   There were a number of reasons for this.   In some of the territories employment for wages was becoming noticeably more important, and the problems connected with it were becoming much more evident to the governments concerned.   The experiences of labour unrest in the West Indies, Mauritius, Northern Rhodesia, Kenya and elsewhere had shown up the effects of poor labour and social conditions, inadequate legislation and insufficient attention to labour administration.   The reports of the various visiting missions and commissions of inquiry (notably the visits of the labour adviser himself) and the detailed recommendations they had made, provided governments with some concrete proposals based on detailed assessment of the

---

the purpose of financing 'schemes for the general improvement of education, the health services, housing and slum clearance, the creation of labour departments, the provision of social welfare facilities and land settlement'.

particular situation in each place, which could not therefore be dismissed as inapplicable to the circumstances of that territory.

Some of the recommendations of this time were backed up by the authority of international labour conventions and by the United Kingdom's ratification of these conventions. There was necessarily frequent correspondence between the Colonial Office and colonial governments, so as to ensure that those conventions which had been ratified by the United Kingdom and which were applicable to the territory were in fact applied.

The next important step in the development of policy-making in the Colonial territories occurred when it was decided in 1942 to replace the Departmental Labour Committee, which had been set up in 1930, with a larger body. Membership of the old committee had been confined to officials of the Colonial Office, assisted from time to time by the attendance of officials from the Ministry of Labour and other departments. The majority of members of the new Colonial Labour Advisory Committee were independent persons; some were appointed for their wide knowledge of colonial problems and others because they were representative of the British T.U.C. and British employers' organizations. The function of this committee was to advise the Secretary of State, and it has continued to give valuable assistance in the formulation of policy, in the detailed criticism of legislation and in analysing situations as they have arisen in the different territories.

The Maturing of Labour Policy

By about 1942 or 1943, therefore, it could be said that a further stage of Colonial Office labour policy had been more or less completed. There were more than 300 trade unions in existence. Labour departments, or at least some form of specialist labour administration, had been established in most of the dependencies of any size, staffed by more than 150 labour advisers, labour officers and inspectors; and a whole corpus of labour legislation had been enacted in these territories, including fairly comprehensive trade union and trade disputes statutes, arbitration and conciliation laws, and legislation covering minimum wages, workmen's compensation, employment of women and children, and, to some extent, factories and shops.

There was, however, a general disquiet brought about by the continuing gap between the idealistic aims which had given rise to the enabling legislation on which the trade unions in colonies had been founded and the generally slow progress that was being made towards achieving stable and responsible workers' organizations. 'So far there has been practically no development of real trade unionism in the West Indies. There has been development in the formation of trade unions, but the degree of conversion of the workers to trade union principles has been small.'[12]   Thus concluded a group of labour officers in Trinidad in 1942. Similar situations were also being reported from other territories.   An interested observer wrote in May 1942, from Sierra Leone:

> Each union draws up a magnificent set of rules providing for sick pay, strike pay, grants to widows and countless other most desirable objects but all the funds go in paying the officers so that there is nothing left. When it comes to negotiating wages or other conditions of service there is a complete absence of a sense of responsibility; frequently the recognised, duly appointed officials of the unions will agree to certain terms either in settlement of a strike or to prevent a strike and will go back on the terms themselves almost as soon as they have signed them.   There is a good deal of jealousy between rival unions and each will outbid the other in trying to gain support from the unfortunate rank and file.[13]

It was this situation that prompted the newly established Colonial Labour Advisory Committee to recommend that experienced British trade unionists should be sent out to the colonies to join the staffs of labour departments for the purpose of advising on the growth of unions. The committee also recommended that leading British trade unionists should visit those territories where trade unions were already established to give them advice and encouragement   It was also proposed that unions in the colonies should be helped to send suitable representatives to Britain so as to enable them to obtain an insight into the way in which British trade unions were organized and how they functioned.   Through these means it was hoped that the lack of experience, which was one of the principal

[12] Report of a Conference of Labour Officers held in Trinidad, 1942.
[13] From a letter written by a local manager of an important British company.

weaknesses of colonial trade union leaders, might be remedied to some extent.

It was also realized in Whitehall that once the initial strong resistance to major innovations in the field of labour law and administration had been overcome, the main task of the Colonial Office was to build on the foundations. It inevitably became concerned with ways of obtaining more adequate labour administration and getting acceptance of more comprehensive or more up-to-date forms of legislation. Since that time the territories' needs for technical help and advice on the practical applications of policy have increased, especially as the complexity of both legislation and administration has grown considerably. Training facilities have been provided for labour department staffs; recruitment of specialist personnel for new labour departments, including men seconded from the Ministry of Labour, was undertaken during and just after the war; technical advice has been made available, especially on such subjects as employment services, cost-of-living indices and on Whitley councils, and other types of industrial relations machinery. Colonial governments were encouraged to take the initiative in formulating new pieces of legislation to suit special conditions; these then had to be carefully examined by the Colonial Office, which could make available its knowledge of the detailed variations in legislation necessitated by real differences in conditions in different areas of the world. The Colonial Office had always to keep itself fully informed of all developments in the individual territories, of strikes and industrial disputes, of new aspects of policy and administration, as well as of proposed changes in legislation. Visits by the labour advisory staff have also been of importance, in that they have provided means of personal contact between the Colonial Office and the local administration, especially those in charge of labour matters, which have helped to increase the degree of confidence between the two. Personal discussions have made the labour advisers directly aware of the particular problems of individual territories, and they have been able to give in return informal advice and practical help based on a wider background of information and experience than is available to the man on the spot. No doubt also the experience gained by the labour advisory staff has been of great value within the

o

Colonial Office; their advice to the Secretary of State on matters of policy will have been influenced considerably by their knowledge of the conditions to be faced in the territories, and the difficulties of application.

Information and requests from the Colonial Office have continued to be transmitted to the colonies by means of circular despatches, on much the same subjects. Except for significant changes in policy, circular despatches have become mainly concerned with such practical matters as the application of the provisions of international labour conventions and recommendations, with providing information about changes in British labour law and practice, or about detailed matters such as employment services, the establishment of negotiating and consultative machinery, technical training, apprenticeship and training within industry schemes. However, once the colonial territories had established specialist labour departments, staffed by qualified and experienced officers, the need for the circulation of basic information and advice in this way diminished somewhat, and in its place there have been more and more informal exchanges of views and more *ad hoc* advice on the application of particular policies in specific places.

The efficiency of colonial labour administration has also been advanced by the training facilities made available for labour officers. Training courses were, in fact, started in 1939, but were curtailed during the war. Since the war, arrangements with the British Ministry of Labour have allowed a considerable number of labour officers to undertake training in the metropolitan country, and these courses have included a period of practical experience in labour administration in the United Kingdom. Altogether more than 500 officers from the colonial and ex-colonial territories have been trained in Britain under these schemes.

These training facilities were supplemented in the larger dependencies, Nigeria in particular, by training schemes for men recruited locally prior to their appointment as labour officers. Apart from general training courses, opportunity has been given to labour officers to train in the United Kingdom for specialized work, such as factory inspection, employment exchange administration or as instructors for Training Within Industry courses.

Labour policy has been exhaustively discussed and to some extent co-ordinated at regional labour officers' conferences which have been held periodically in West Africa, East and Central Africa, and the Caribbean area. These conferences have helped to give the senior officers of the labour departments a sense of perspective and, through the regular participation of a member of the labour advisory staff, a better understanding of policy developments in the Colonial Office. Two important official conferences were held in London during the post-war period. The first, held in 1951, was a conference of the heads of all labour departments; the main theme on this occasion was on ways of achieving industrial harmony during the years ahead. The second conference, held in 1956, lasted longer and was known as the Conference on Labour Administration. It was attended by officials from most of the dependencies, and, towards the end, by some elected ministers of labour. Numerous papers concerned with various aspects of labour administration were studied and discussed, and the conclusions were made the basis of detailed recommendations which were later circulated to the governments of the dependencies for consideration as a basis for their future labour policies. The most important topics on the agenda at this 1956 conference had a direct bearing on trade unionism and industrial relations. The way in which the development of democratic trade unions could be stimulated was discussed at length, and the need for closer guidance from British trade unionists was emphasized. Conciliation and arbitration procedures were analysed, and there was prolonged consideration of the regulation of trade disputes in essential industries, including the question of how far compulsory arbitration might be imposed in industries essential to the economy.

Colonial Office policy on the general matter of trade union development has evolved slowly during the post-war period. To begin with, there continued to be a certain amount of concern about the legislative framework within which the trade unions would develop. It had been agreed in explicit terms during the war—in a statement which continued to have importance for some years—that '. . . experience has shown that in many colonies the development of the trade union movement has not reached a stage at which it would be advisable to have legislation based entirely upon that of the United Kingdom'.[14] Nevertheless, during the period up to 1950 a number of moves were made to persuade the dependencies to bring their legislation more closely into line with the British Acts, especially in such matters as the protection given to pickets, the concept of conspiracy in trade disputes and the prevention of intimidation and violence.   After the repeal of the 1927 Trade Disputes and Trade Unions Act in 1946 those territories which had provisions based on this Act were asked to consider removing them, but only a few did so.   At a later period considerable attention was paid to legislative or other means of improving standards of internal administration within trade unions, improving organization and making union leaders more effectively responsible to their members.   Around 1950, attention began to be paid to the question of preventing strikes in essential industries, and for some seven or eight years after this a number of territories were encouraged to enact legislation based on the British regulations of 1940, forbidding strikes in certain scheduled industries and services, and providing for compulsory arbitration in all disputes arising in these industries.   The application of this policy aroused a considerable amount of international criticism, especially in the case of Tanganyika, and it has since been dropped by the Colonial Office.   As British policy shifted against compulsion there were important moves by Ghana and Singapore to impose drastic limits on the right to strike.

Attention has also been paid to ways of influencing the development of trade unions other than by legislation.   The policy of giving official guidance and assistance to the unions through labour department channels has already been mentioned.   The provision of training facilities for trade unionists has been encouraged, and some territories, of which Nigeria is again an outstanding example, did a great deal in the late 40's and early 50's by providing lecturers, running short courses in the evenings and at week-ends, and stimulating the formation of autonomous trade union education committees.   As political nationalism has risen in the various territories in Africa it has

---

[14] See Nyasaland: *Report of the Committee . . . to consider Existing and Draft Labour Legislation* (G.P., Zomba, 1943), Chapter III, para. 2.   Also *Labour Legislation in the Colonial Territories* (H.M.S.O. No. 275, 1951), para. 10.

been the policy of the Colonial Office to try to keep the trade unions and their leaders as far as possible independent of the political parties. One of the aims of trade union education has been to emphasize the industrial role of the unions and to point out the disadvantages of concentrating on wider national issues, or in allying themselves with political parties on purely political issues. Considerable thought has been given, as specific circumstances have arisen, to the effect, on both political developments and industrial relations, of the general policy of encouraging strong industrially-based trade unions. This is illustrated by the difficulties which arose in East Africa on many occasions during the early 50's, when industrial disturbances, occurring in one territory after another, caused the local governments to become very suspicious of trade union activity, and to be reluctant to continue a policy of encouragement. Their view was endorsed by the conclusion reached by the East African Royal Commission of 1953–55 that 'the attempt to encourage the growth of trade unions on the British model is likely for some time to come to represent an expenditure of effort which might be employed more effectively in other directions'. This conclusion was widely deprecated by trade union circles, and was never accepted by the Colonial Office, but nevertheless it had a considerable influence on the governments of the territories concerned, who were themselves already more than half convinced of its truth.

Although it was not accepted by the Colonial Office that its policy over trade unions had in any sense failed or been found to be premature, it became increasingly concerned at the extent to which unions were adopting a political role. It sought to counter this development in the years after 1950 by paying more attention to ways of improving the system of industrial relations. Where trade unions were especially weak or non-existent, governments were encouraged to look into the advisability of establishing wage councils. In other cases the establishment of works committees or of joint consultative machinery was urged as a matter to be pressed upon public services and private employers alike. Regular meetings between employers and trade unions, within established negotiating machinery, were, at a later stage, emphasized as the best method of avoiding irresponsible strikes.

The Development of Colonial Office Organization

These are some of the many ways in which the Colonial Office has, over the recent decades, endeavoured to influence the labour policies of colonial governments. The internal machinery of the Colonial Office, by which labour policy was formulated and administered, has already been outlined, to some extent, in the foregoing description. There have been, in fact, three different groups of officials who have influenced the formulation of labour policy in any one area. It should be emphasized that the staff of the first two groups has been recruited on the same basis and moved freely from one department to the other. There has been, however, an important difference in background between these first two groups and the third, which has generally been selected from people who have had considerable experience in the labour field and who have actually handled labour problems in a colony.

The first and oldest of these groups was the 'geographical' department whose task was to keep in touch with all aspects of policy and government in the areas for which it was responsible (West Africa, East Africa, West Indies, etc.). This department has been, perhaps, the most important channel for liaison between the Secretary of State and the territories concerned. In general, the geographical department brought to the discussion of a new policy a close knowledge of local conditions and of what is likely to be acceptable to the government concerned.

The second of these groups was the Social Services Department, which has been responsible within the Colonial Office for the subjects of labour administration, trade unions and industrial relations, wage policy, relations with I.L.O. and I.C.F.T.U. and so on, as well as for housing, health and other matters. As the executive department specializing in the subject of labour, and with its specialized knowledge of such matters as I.L.O. policy, this department has sought to maintain uniformity of principle in the kind of policy adopted in different regions. It has kept watch on the way in which the various territories are complying with international labour conventions and adopted recommendations, and on any departures from the declared policy of the British Government.

The third group, and perhaps the most active, consists of the officials of the Labour Adviser's Department; their role has been quite different from the other two. The Labour Adviser has no administrative or executive functions. His duty is simply to keep himself as fully informed as possible about all aspects of labour in the dependencies and to make available the advice which his qualifications and experience can provide. Informally and unofficially this advice may be given readily to labour departments and governments in the dependencies, and his personal opinions may be welcomed in discussion within any one territory, without any feeling that the freedom of action is being prejudiced. Formally, however, the Adviser's duty is to the Colonial Office, and to this extent his advice and official opinion has always been given great weight in the formulation of policy within the office. Only after the fullest discussion, and after final agreement between the three departments concerned, has a policy proposal gone forward for approval through the under-secretaries to the Secretary of State. After this stage is reached any communication of the policy to the colonial governments concerned becomes official, and is a direct expression of the views of the Secretary of State.

Changes of policy must go through all the stages of examination, discussion, compromise and approval before they become official. They may, however, be initiated from many different sources, both inside and outside the Colonial Office, both official and unofficial. As for the external sources, there are, of course, all kinds of influences brought to bear on ministers which lead to the introduction of new aspects of policy. One of these which has already been mentioned earlier in this chapter is the general outlook of the political party which forms the government of the day, and of any particular groups associated with that party which will be likely to influence directly the ministers responsible for Colonial affairs. The Fabian Society and the Fabian Colonial Bureau, for instance, had a considerable impact on the colonial policy, including the colonial labour policy, of the wartime Coalition Government, and of the 1945 Labour Government. Public opinion in one of its forms may also be exercised in such a way as to influence ministers and officials, as, for instance, in the activities of the Churches and of some influential liberals over the question of

forced labour in Kenya, and some other issues during the 20's.
More recently, representations of this kind have been undertaken by more organized groups, such as the Anti-Slavery
Society, the African Bureau and the Movement for Colonial
Freedom, which have all been set up largely for the express
purpose of influencing policy. Pressure from the opposite side
towards maintaining the *status quo* is, of course, also strong,
though its sources are less easily identifiable.

Of more importance than these when labour policy is under
consideration are the representations of the Trades Union
Congress, organizations of employers, especially the Overseas
Employers' Federation, and, on the international level, the
International Confederation of Free Trade Unions. Representations by these organizations, based as they usually are on
detailed study of the problem concerned, are carefully considered, and they have a marked influence.

The Colonial Office may also be open on specific issues to unofficial representations made directly to the Colonial Office
from organizations—trade unions, political parties or other
interests—within the dependencies, especially when these are
putting forward views somewhat in opposition to those of the
local government. On the official level, one of the most
important ways in which policy changes may be initiated is by
the colonial governments themselves, and any proposed new
legislation or any new features of administration will cause considerable discussion of its implications in the Colonial Office.
In other cases a commission of inquiry or other official committee may make recommendations which may have to be
considered in the light of the knowledge available in the
Colonial Office. Or contacts with the British Ministry of
Labour and knowledge of domestic policy or domestic legislation may be a factor in formulating policy. In the same way,
of course, the work of the International Labour Organization
has had an important effect on Colonial Office policy, which
reflects the influence of conventions and recommendations
already ratified as well as the discussion and negotiations which
lead up to the formulation of new conventions or recommendations. Some of these influences, especially those of the employers and the Trade Union Congress, have made themselves
felt in the Colonial Labour Advisory Committee, where both

the interests and the experience and expert knowledge of these outside interests have been used to advantage in working out an agreed policy and in examining its application to the peculiar conditions of one territory or another. This committee has aided the officials concerned by bringing wider consideration to bear upon a proposal before advice has been tendered, and by ensuring that there would be no undue hostility to the new policy from any of the interests represented on the committee.

Thus, there are many influences which may help to determine Colonial Office policy, and it is only after consideration of all the likely points of view, from a variety of sources, that a new initiative on policy is likely to be taken officially. Once taken, of course, the process of getting the policy applied in the dependencies begins to operate. This, as has been seen, is by no means a straightforward matter, but depends almost entirely on the formal and informal channels of advice and consultation already described. It may, however, be fortunate that relations between the Colonial Office and the dependencies have grown in such a way that as territories have advanced further towards self-government and eventual independence their governments, and especially their civil servants, have retained their confidence in, and respect for, the officials of the Colonial Office. In fact, informal advice and informal consultations have probably been more in evidence as colonial governments have attained greater responsibility and as the services provided by the Colonial Office itself have become more highly developed. These informal contacts may well be considerably more influential—and certainly less unwelcome—than the formal advice tendered in official despatches from the Colonial Secretary in earlier stages of constitutional development, an answer to which would commit the colonial government concerned to an action or a point of view which it might later find embarrassing. Paradoxically, Colonial Office officials may have thought that it was much easier to influence the labour policies of the Nigerian or the Jamaican Governments in 1957, when these countries were virtually self-governing, than they did in 1937, when both governments were dominated by officials of the Colonial Service.

After independence has been achieved relations with the Colonial Office are inevitably broken. The Commonwealth

Relations Office, through which relations with the independent Commonwealth territories are handled, has not been concerned with the advisory functions which were one of the main responsibilities of the Colonial Office. In order to make British experience and technical expertise in every field available to any independent territories that might wish to make use of them, the Department of Technical Co-operation has been established. This department will henceforth take over many of the advisory and technical services previously supplied through the Colonial Office. It will, of course, provide assistance only when it is requested; unlike the Colonial Office in the past, it will not be concerned with initiating changes in policy and practice in the independent territories. British influence in the future will, therefore, be less direct and less continuous.

CHAPTER 8

THE DEVELOPMENT OF
LABOUR ADMINISTRATION

IN every country, no matter how small, there has inevitably to
be some process, when wage employment has become at all
important, by which the labour policy of the government is
formulated and administered, and through which labour
legislation is enforced. This chapter attempts to trace what
this process has been in British dependencies; to discover how
labour policies have been formulated by territorial governments
and what influences have caused them to decide on these
policies; and to trace the development of the specialized institutions which have been established to undertake the functions of
labour supervision, advise governments on their labour policies
and help to maintain industrial peace.

With the first establishment of colonial administrations, some
wage labour was inevitably taken into employment—in public
works, transport, administrative services, domestic service, etc.,
and usually also in trade and commerce, which began to expand
after stable administration had become assured. In some
territories also, important employers from outside the country—
plantation cultivators, mining companies or settler farmers—
soon entered the economy and began to employ labour.
Labour laws, usually in the form of master and servant ordinances, were passed, often within the first few years of colonial
administration, and these were later developed, made more
comprehensive and supplemented by further measures, sometimes protective, sometimes rather repressive. For the most
part, the enactment and enforcement of this early labour
legislation was not the special concern of any one department of
government. Day-to-day labour matters might be dealt with
by administrative officers in the course of their other duties;
and the outlines of labour policy were decided on in the secretariat of each territory, after consultation with various government departments concerned and with other interests, as part of
the general administrative functions of government. While

201

labour legislation remained fairly simple, the volume of employment small and the problems of labour in the territory not yet very complicated or very pressing, these arrangements probably appeared adequate.

However, there were some places where labour problems took on a more urgent and more complex aspect as early as the first world war. In particular, this was so in the West Indies, Malaya and Mauritius, where there was a high and continuing demand for labour on plantations of various kinds; and in Kenya, where the European settlers who arrived in the early 1900's found difficulty in inducing local inhabitants to enter employment. It was not easy to persuade men to leave their villages to work for a cash reward. Gradually, however, they began to see an advantage in working for a white man who was prepared to give them food and lodging as well as a cash payment. They were not prepared to commit themselves permanently to this way of life, but as a temporary means of raising their income above the subsistence level, paid employment had attractions. Young men began to look upon working for wages as an advantage and were prepared to travel great distances to find jobs. The supply of labour from neighbouring territories became important to the developing economies of the Rhodesias, and from India for sugar-cane cultivation in Fiji and for the development of commerce in Aden.

Labour from South India and China was recruited on a large scale for work in South-East Asia, and the population of Malaya and Singapore today consists largely of settled immigrants from these countries. The traffic in labour was originally started in the early nineteenth century by individual employers who imported workers at their own expense on the basis of a written contract to work. In order to protect the interests of the labourers, Sir Stamford Raffles issued an ordinance as early as 1823 which laid down conditions that employers were to observe when bringing workers from China and India. There was, however, considerable abuse of the rights of the imported labourers, and following disturbances among the Chinese labourers who had been imported into the Straits Settlement in the nineteenth century, public concern, aroused by the bad conditions of labour, led to a commission of inquiry in 1876. The outcome was an ordinance which established a Chinese

Protectorate.   The officers of the Protectorate were able to stop many of the worst abuses, such as the kidnapping of Chinese labourers for work on estates.   They were also able to bring about an improvement in the conditions of transit and to ensure that the immigrants were informed of their legal rights.

The Government of India sought to protect the interests of its emigrants by a series of Acts passed in 1883, 1897 and 1908, to regulate the recruitment in India, control conditions at the ports and to define the conditions under which unskilled labour might emigrate.   An Indian Immigration Agent was appointed by the Straits Settlement Government.   Abuses still occurred, and in order to bring the recruitment of labour and its transport from India under more satisfactory control, an Indian Immigration Fund was established in 1907.   This was accompanied by regulations which ensured that Indian immigrants were provided with proper transport facilities, food and medical attention *en route*, and eventual repatriation to India when this was desired.   These changes proved so successful that it was decided in 1910 to abolish by law the indenture system of recruitment of Indian labour.   Four years later it was made illegal to import Chinese labour under indenture into Malaya, but employers were allowed to continue to bring in Javanese from Sumatra under contract until 1932.

The Establishment of the Early Labour Departments

The abolition of indentured labour following the recommendation of a government committee was accompanied by the establishment of a department of labour, the earliest in the Colonial empire, which took over the functions of the Indian Immigration Department and the administration of the Indian Immigration Fund.

At first this department covered only the Straits Settlements and Federated Malay States, and for about twenty-five years its duties did not extend to Chinese labourers, who were still catered for by the Chinese Protectorate.   It was reorganized to some extent following the enactment of the 1923 Labour Ordinance and the signature of agreements with the Indian Government consequent on the passing of the Indian Emigration Act of 1922.

From the Indian side there had also long been concern over the conditions of employment of unskilled labourers who had been recruited for work as indentured labour, sometimes under unsatisfactory conditions, in the West Indies, Natal, Mauritius, Fiji and Ceylon, as well as in Malaya. Pressure had been put on receiving countries to improve conditions. In 1911 emigration to Natal had been prohibited, and in 1918, under wartime emergency regulations, indentured emigration was prohibited altogether. Finally, to put the prohibition on a permanent basis, and to ensure better protection in future, the Indian Emigration Act of 1922, which went considerably further than any of its predecessors, was passed.[1] Not only did this Act enable the Indian Government to supervise recruitment and conditions at the Indian ports, but it entirely prohibited subsidized emigration, or any emigration under an agreement to work as unskilled labourers except under conditions, both in India and in the receiving countries, which had been agreed by the Central Government of India and approved by the central legislature.

Under this Act of 1922 informal agreements were made in 1923 with the Governments of Ceylon, the Straits Settlements and the Federated and Unfederated States of Malaya.[2] Ceylon was to appoint an Emigration Commissioner to be stationed in India, who was to be subject to approval by the Government of India. He was to be responsible for disseminating correct information about conditions in Ceylon, was to appoint approved inspectors and to license and supervise the activities of recruiters, subject to the approval of district magistrates,[3] and, if required by the Indian Government, was to provide adequate accommodation for recruited men.

The Ceylon Government agreed to enact legislation making contracts of service for more than one month void, and to prevent certain abuses during recruitment.[4] The object was to

---

[1] For a statement of objects of this Act see *Gazette of India*, 1921, Part V, p. 109.
[2] See Notifications Nos. 136 Emi and 137 Emi, dated 17th February 1923, and Notifications Nos. 212 and 213 dated 10th March 1923 (*Gazette of India*, 1923, Part I).
[3] For these countries (Ceylon and Malaya) native recruiters (Kanganies) despatched by the employers themselves were to be allowed. See Notification No. 213 of 1923, *Gazette of India*, 1923, Part I.
[4] *Twenty-five Years of Labour Progress in Ceylon* (Ceylon Printers Ltd., 1948), p. 1, and *Indian Immigrant Labour Ordinance*, 1923, Ceylon Ordinance No. 1 of 1923.

ensure that no recruit was made liable for any part of the cost of recruitment or transport to work, which was to be met from a common fund raised in Ceylon. Any labourer wishing to return home for any sufficient reason was to be repatriated at the expense of Ceylon. The interests of the Indian workers in Ceylon were to be looked after by a specially appointed official. It was also agreed that periodic reports should be made to the Government of India on the welfare of Indian workers.[5]

In consequence of these requirements, the Department of Indian Immigrant Labour was formed in Ceylon in 1923, to carry out the various functions required by the Indian Act. The department was placed under the direction of a controller of Indian immigrant labour, with a staff of two inspectors who were empowered to enter property and examine conditions. At the same time an Advisory Board for Indian Immigrant Labour was established under the chairmanship of the Controller with the duty of advising on matters connected with recruitment, conditions of work, housing and medical care, and the administration of the Indian Immigration Fund, which was created to finance recruitment, transport and repatriation of Indian recruits. The Emigration Commissioner, who was to work in India, was given powers and duties conforming to those required by India.

Somewhat similar arrangements were made at the same time with the governments of the Malayan Peninsula, and new labour ordinances or enactments were passed in 1923 in both the Straits Settlements and the Federated Malay States. Further enactments followed in the next few years in the Unfederated States, and it was then that the Malayan Labour Department was extended to cover these areas. When the Malayan labour organization was finally complete the controller, whose headquarters were at Kuala Lumpur, had deputies and full-time staff both in Kuala Lumpur itself, for duties in the Federated Malay States and Malacca, and at Penang, for control over the other Straits Settlements. As for the Unfederated States, Johore employed a full-time officer, Kedah and Perlis shared a full-time officer, and in the other

---

[5] India exacted somewhat similar requirements from Mauritius in 1923, when, for one year only, the migration of up to 1,500 Indians was permitted. However, no organized immigration to Mauritius has taken place since 1924, and the agreement did not lead to the establishment of a permanent full-time labour department.

three States labour duties were carried on as part-time functions of administrative officers.[6]

Two or three labour departments were created in other colonial territories in the next few years. In 1924 Major Orde Browne, then a Senior Commissioner in the Tanganyika Administration, was charged with the task of investigating labour conditions in that territory and submitting recommendations to serve as a basis for considering the appointment of a labour commissioner 'for the organization and better control of labour affairs generally'. Following Orde Browne's report, a Tanganyika Labour Department was established, whose functions were 'to investigate all questions connected with labour economy, such as waste of labour, the method of reward, feeding, medical treatment, housing, etc.; to inspect the labour conditions on public undertakings such as railway and road constructions and on private plantations, and to supervise the erection and control of camps for labour on its way from and to the place of recruitment.'[7] The department was established with Major Orde Browne as its commissioner, and with a staff of three or four labour officers, who were charged with the inspection and control of labour, and who also had magisterial powers for the enforcement of some of the penal provisions of the labour legislation.

Uganda's Labour Department was established in the same year as the result of an administrative decision taken in 1924. Its object, as stated in the Colonial Report for that year, was 'the provision of labour for Government Departments and the care of labourers throughout the Protectorate'. In 1925 Kenya too had set up a labour inspectorate, though this remained within the Native Affairs Department.

Within the next three or four years small labour departments had also been formed in Malta and the British Solomon Islands Protectorate in the Western Pacific. In the Caribbean, however, despite chronic labour problems in this area, and despite the reliance some territories had placed for a fairly long time on East Indian labour, there was relatively little action. In British Guiana the Immigration Department was theoretically

[6] Annual Reports of the Labour Department, Malaya (Kuala Lumpur, F.M.S. Government Press).
[7] Despatch by Sir Donald Cameron accompanying *Report upon Labour in Tanganyika Territory* (H.M.S.O., Colonial No. 19, 1926).

responsible for the protection of Indian labourers until it was abolished during the retrenchments of 1932. After this 'the compilation of wage statistics, investigation of complaints, etc.' in British Guiana became a duty of the district commissioners.[8] In Jamaica also the Immigration Department was charged with certain labour functions concerning Indian labourers, while in Trinidad the Warden of the County of St. George had the title of Protector of Immigrants and Director of the Labour Bureau, which was an organization for placing labourers. In Mauritius, another territory which had relied on Indian workers, a certain number of full-time staff had worked under the Protector of Immigrants from at least 1842 until 1924, when immigration finally ceased. Although the title of Protector of Immigrants was retained in Mauritius after 1924, and the officer bearing this title was available to take complaints from labourers, there was then no full-time staff, and no department with the functions of inspection and regulation of working conditions.

The Impact of the Depression

The advent of the depression in 1931 came as a serious setback to progress in labour administration. Government expenditure in all three of the East African dependencies was cut drastically, and the labour departments were among the most seriously affected. In Tanganyika the department was disbanded altogether, and responsibility for labour matters was handed over to the Provincial Administration.[9] The department in Uganda was reduced to an inspectorate within the Administration, and the inspectorate in Kenya suffered from a severe reduction in staff. For a number of years these two inspectorates remained in operation with very few staff, and were only able to undertake work within a very restricted area

[8] H.C. Deb., 1934–35, Vol. 303, Cols. 1083–6.

[9] It was stated, perhaps not very convincingly, in the Tanganyika Mandate report for 1931, that the abolition of the department was not made principally on economic grounds. Its work was handed over to the Provincial Administration in accordance with the principle that the administrative officers should be responsible for the welfare of all the people in their own areas. The chief functions of the department, it was contended, could not be divorced from matters which were the direct concern of the Administration. Even more curiously, this report states that the labour department had been formed in 1925 to deal with an emergency situation. The report considered that conditions were now (in 1931, in the middle of the depression, when many thousands had lost their jobs and money wages had been cut by upwards of 20 per cent.) more normal.

P

of the territory concerned. In the Solomon Islands, too, the labour department of two officers was reduced to one. In other territories staffs were reduced and administrative expenses severely trimmed; in some cases there was a tendency to regard money spent on the protection of labour as a luxury that could be dispensed with in the circumstances.

The depression and its effects had unfortunate results not only on labour administration in the territories, but on the hopes of the Colonial Office for better labour conditions, more up-to-date protective legislation and the extension of effective labour administration in the dependencies. In July 1930 the second Colonial Office Conference, called during the Labour Party's second term of office, had discussed labour matters at some length. The Parliamentary Under-Secretary of State, Dr. (later Sir) Drummond Shiels, in the course of a long paper read to the conference, had said 'that in certain territories which relied largely on imported labour much had been done to improve conditions of labour, but this had been due to some extent to pressure by the government of the country from which labourers were imported. He would like to see the economic interests of labourers and others catered for on the initiative of Colonial Governments rather than as a result of pressure from outside, and he was glad to know that steps to this end were now being taken.'[10]

The stringent economies imposed in nearly all territories as the world depression set in reinforced the almost universal reluctance of the colonial governments to establish any of this new and expensive machinery for the supervision of labour conditions, and nothing further was done for a period. As the worst of the depression passed, however, a certain amount of pressure was exerted by the Labour opposition in the British Parliament for the re-establishment and expansion of labour departments in the dependencies. In particular, in the Colonial Debate of July 1935, the chief opposition spokesman, Mr. Lunn,[11] pressed, as he had done rather less urgently the previous year,[12] for the 'provision of labour inspectors or crea-

[10] Cmnd. 3628, p. 99.
[11] 304 H.C. Deb., 1934–35, Vol. 304, Cols. 2059–60.
[12] 292 H.C. Deb., 1933–34, Vol. 292, Col. 580. See also his Parliamentary question in 303 H.C. Deb., 1934–35, Vol. 303, Cols. 1081–6, the answer to which gives details of labour administration in various territories in 1930 and 1934.

tion of labour departments' which would supervise the welfare and working conditions of labourers. The recent industrial disturbances in the Northern Rhodesian copper mines, in which lives had been lost when the police opened fire, gave force to his arguments and to those of another opposition speaker.[13] The Secretary of State of that period, Mr. Malcolm MacDonald, appears himself to have been concerned about the need for better labour supervision. Replying to the Debate[14] he stated that he had already given instructions in the Colonial Office for the whole position to be reviewed, and said that he himself would like to be satisfied that especially where mining was going on, administration was adequate to protect the interests of 'native workers'.

In November 1935 the same Secretary of State addressed a circular despatch, referred to in Chapter 7, mentioning parliamentary interest in the subject, and pointing out the existence of labour departments in a number of dependencies, and the importance of their functions. He did not think the establishment of a separate labour department in every territory was necessary, but where there was no properly constituted department there should be adequate, properly co-ordinated arrangements for supervision of all labour conditions, including enforcement of laws relating to labour contracts, housing, sanitation and hospital facilities and of mining and factory inspection. Machinery which simply limited itself to investigating complaints would not be satisfactory: the aim should be to ensure that complaints did not arise.[15]

The effect of this despatch was almost negligible, but the demand for the establishment of labour departments continued in the United Kingdom. Further questions were asked in the Commons in December 1935. Two members, Morgan Jones and Creech Jones, stressed the subject's importance from the Opposition front bench in the Colonial Debate of July 1936, the

[13] Viz. Mr. Banfield. See H.C. Deb., 1934–35, Vol. 304, Col. 2119.

[14] H.C. Deb., 1934–35, Vol. 304, Col. 2133. Mr. MacDonald was Colonial Secretary only from June 1935 until the General Election in November 1935. In this period he seems to have given a good deal of attention to labour questions.

[15] An extract from this despatch appears in *Trinidad and Tobago Disturbances 1937, Report of Commission*, Cmnd. 5641, para. 171. In common with most other colonies, Trinidad virtually ignored its recommendations 'and sent no reply until after the recent disturbances, when, on 5th July, 1937, the present Governor telegraphed . . . saying that he had had in mind for a long time past the creation of a post of Secretary for Social Services' (*ibid.*, para. 172).

latter specifically mentioning the need to establish machinery in Northern Rhodesia to deal with trade disputes; and several speakers brought up the same subject during the 1937 colonial debate.

The last of these debates took place after the labour disturbances and riots in Trinidad, Barbados and elsewhere in the West Indies, and in Mauritius, had greatly increased public concern over labour conditions. Following the 1937 debate, a further circular despatch was sent by the Secretary of State (Mr. W. Ormsby Gore) enclosing a copy of the report of the debate, commenting on those replies which had so far been received to the 1935 despatch, and, among other matters, setting out in apparently much stronger terms than the despatch the desire of the British Government to have separate labour departments established in all the larger and more important dependencies, and for the rest to have full-time labour officers 'in all territories where there is a substantial wage-earning community, whether industrialized or not'. He noted also that one of the functions of labour departments would be to report to governments on any developments taking place towards trade union organization, as well as on the matters mentioned in the 1935 despatch.[16]

The Resurgence of Labour Administration

This fairly strongly worded despatch seems to have been effective in getting action from the colonial governments, and it was in the years 1938–40 that most labour departments, as they are known today, really began. There were various other reasons for this. The unrest during 1937 and the subsequent reports of inquiries, had caused concern within the territories themselves about the lack of contact between governments and the working population. In the United Kingdom Major Orde Browne had just been appointed to the post of Labour Adviser to the Secretary of State; and in the last half of 1938 and beginning of 1939 he had toured the Caribbean territories and had stressed the need in most places for the appointment of qualified full-time staff either to man labour departments or to give full-time attention to labour problems from within the ad-

[16] This despatch is reproduced as Appendix II to *The Colonial Empire in 1937–38,* Cmnd. 5760, pp. 78–9.

ministrations.[17]   The outbreak of war in 1939 meant that more attention had to be paid to labour in most territories, and a further circular despatch from the Colonial Office in December 1939 emphasized the need for colonial governments to do all in their power to ensure that labour conditions were properly supervised during the war and the critical post-war period.

So it was that in 1938 the Gold Coast established a labour department under a Chief Inspector of Labour, and in the same year Barbados, British Guiana, Grenada, Mauritius, Nyasaland, St. Vincent and Trinidad each appointed a full-time labour officer, and in some cases put him in charge of a nascent department.   A labour inspectorate with an establishment of three was set up within the secretariat in Nigeria in 1939, and converted into a separate labour department in 1942; in the same year a labour adviser was appointed to Jamaica and a labour officer sent to British Honduras.   In the first year or so of the war Sierra Leone, Northern Rhodesia, Hong Kong, Fiji and some other small West Indian islands appointed full-time officers or established departments.

The three East African territories which had first set up labour organizations in the 20's also reconstituted them.   In Kenya the labour section of the Provincial Administration was made into a separate department under a labour commissioner, in 1940.   Tanganyika had re-established in 1937 a small labour inspectorate as part of the Administration, to relieve the administrative staff of some responsibility for labour matters. The inspectorate is said not to have been wholly successful, and in 1940 it was converted into a new labour department with an executive head.   In Uganda, on the other hand, the inspectorate was not converted into a new labour department until the beginning of 1943.

Thus, by the middle of the war full-time staff was working in all the more important dependencies, and in many of the smaller ones too.   Aden and the Seychelles were among the exceptions.

During and immediately after the war all of these departments were working under very considerable difficulties.   In the larger territories the departments were all seriously short of

[17] The recommendations of Major Orde Browne were strongly supported by the West India Royal Commission, which reported soon afterwards. See Chapter 7.

senior staff; labour officers were called up for military service, or detached for duty in defence construction units and so on. Relatively few expatriate officers were available to staff the departments, and occasionally more experienced and more senior officers were taken away from labour departments for duties in the Administration or in other territories; secondments from the administration and from the U.K. Ministry of Labour were frequent, but tended to be temporary and of uncertain duration, and in at least one dependency applications from public servants for transfer to the labour department had had to be refused because of extreme shortage of staff elsewhere.

In addition to this, labour problems in wartime and immediately after were more complex and more acute than any that had been met before. In every dependency in Africa the volume of employment rose greatly at some stage of the war, and it was the responsibility of the provincial administrations and labour departments to secure an adequate supply of labour, especially for activities which were considered essential to the war effort. This category covered different activities in different places: labour in the tin mines and the rubber and oil-palm plantations in Nigeria; railway and port construction in Ghana; military constructions in Sierra Leone; sisal and rubber production and 'essential foodstuffs' (European agriculture) in Tanganyika; agriculture and building work in Kenya; the copper mines and the European-owned farms in Northern Rhodesia. The problems of the departments of labour lay in encouraging enough labour to come forward for these activities, while attempting to prevent the abuses which private and professional recruiters were apt to practise in their attempts to secure labour. Conscription for civil employment was introduced for a period in Nigeria, Tanganyika, Kenya and Northern Rhodesia, and this entailed considerably more work for the labour departments in supervising conditions under which the conscripts worked and lived. Conditions of employment in other occupations were also given attention, so far as the staff was available to do so, and in some places the opportunity was taken to encourage the raising of standards of housing, welfare and rations as a means of persuading men to come forward for work, and of making the existing labour force more stable.

Another serious wartime problem in Africa was the rapidly rising cost of living, especially the cost of and shortage of imported consumer goods which caused serious local food shortages to occur, and food prices to rise rapidly. Food shortages were especially serious in East Africa.

In the West Indies also, wartime labour problems were serious, though for somewhat different reasons. Military construction, comprising largely the construction of American military bases, considerably increased the demand for labour for a short period up to 1942, but when this was complete the cessation of shipping and of the export to Europe of some of the more important products of the islands, caused widespread unemployment and distress in agriculture and the ports, especially in Jamaica. The shortage of imported food required the redeployment of agricultural effort to grow local foodstuffs, and the cost of living rose rapidly. Stresses were caused by the presence of, and the high rates of pay offered by, the American forces in some West Indian islands. Unemployment was to some extent offset by opportunities to work in the Southern United States and, in the early stages, in the Canal Zone, but this migration absorbed only a small proportion of the surplus labour, and unemployment caused even more concern in both Jamaica and Barbados than was normal in peacetime.

Finally, the territories of South-East Asia and the Western Pacific were affected rather more seriously by the Japanese occupation in 1942, and the consequent disruption of both the economy and the existing administrative machine was inevitably considerable.

One beneficial effect of wartime conditions in Africa and the Caribbean was the fact that the importance of labour supervision became evident in all the dependencies: the labour departments, especially in Africa, became more securely established and their staffs were strengthened whenever personnel were available. A considerable volume of labour legislation was passed and the subject was given more serious attention by all colonial governments. Additionally, towards the end of the war and in the period immediately following it, the problems of transition received much attention. In almost every territory in Africa and in Jamaica, Trinidad, Mauritius and elsewhere, special resettlement or reabsorption units were

created, within or parallel to labour departments, to deal with
the re-employment and resettlement of ex-service men into
civil employment; and in some cases to provide technical training for them. In West Africa the volume of employment
declined markedly after the war had ended, and this created
further problems where considerable numbers of craftsmen
trained during the war, especially trained ex-service men, were
unwilling to revert to peasant agriculture and tended to form
groups of discontented urban unemployed.

Thus, the effect of the war was generally to enhance the
position of the labour departments and demonstrate the need
for and the effectiveness of their functions. In the few years
after the war ended there followed a fairly rapid increase in the
establishment of the departments, especially of those in African
countries with a considerable volume of employment.

Staffing

The staff of labour departments has been drawn from three
main sources. In the years before 1945 especially, and also
during the 'resettlement' period at the end of the war, many
members of labour departments were former members of the
provincial administration of the territories concerned, who had
been transferred, or, occasionally, seconded, to the labour
department, sometimes through their own wishes, sometimes
not. A number of the early labour commissioners in Africa were
former provincial commissioners, and in some territories there
has always been some movement back and forth between the
labour departments and the provincial administration. Some
departments, notably in East and Central Africa, have continued to be recruited in part from members of the provincial
administrations, and in Northern Rhodesia even now, a special
arrangement exists whereby labour officers, on recruitment to
the local civil service, are required to spend a considerable
period as assistant district officers in rural areas before reverting
to their work as labour officers.[18]

---

[18] This identification of labour department personnel with the policies of the
rural administrators is open to criticism on the grounds that administration in
urban industrial society is different from, and should be viewed from a different
standpoint from, rural administration in tribal communities. For an expression
of these criticisms see M. Gluckman, 'Tribalism in Modern British Central Africa"
in *Cahiers d'Études Africaines*, 1, 1960.

A second major source of labour department staff, especially among specialists or potential specialists in the larger departments, has been the United Kingdom Ministry of Labour. Ministry of Labour officers have been seconded or transferred to colonial labour departments ever since the earliest days, and they have become an important part of the staffs of many departments, and are often among the more stable elements of the departments.

From 1942, a third rather interesting source of labour officers was introduced by the Colonial Office as an experiment. This was the appointment of experienced officials of British trade unions, principally for the purpose of guiding the development of trade unionism and advising on and supervising industrial relations machinery in the territories concerned. Appointments of trade unionists continued for the next ten years or so, until at one stage there were about 20 of them serving in various territories, usually either on industrial relations work or specifically in advising trade unions on their organization, administration and policy. During one period there were 4 such officers working simultaneously in Nigeria on trade union work.

The policy of recruiting experienced British trade union officials proved to be of mixed value. In some cases these officers rapidly established their worth and made an effective contribution, but in others they had little or no impact either on the development of the unions or on the work of the labour department. Their task was by no means an easy one. They had, in the first place, to gain the confidence of the unions they were expected to help and guide; in the second, they had to maintain the confidence of the head of the labour department, and of the other senior officials of the territory in which they were working. It was not always possible to reconcile these two objectives, and conflicts sometimes occurred which finally led to resignation or the abandonment of any attempt to push the local government into radical positions.

These British labour officers knew a great deal about trade unionism, but they had no experience and little knowledge of the territories to which they were sent, and this inevitably placed them in a weak position in relation to the senior government officials who had behind them many years of colonial service. There was also a social gulf which was not easily bridged by every trade union official, especially by those who felt a strong emotional link with the local trade unions and their leaders. Inevitably mistakes were made, and sometimes these officers found that they were not greatly trusted by either the unions or their superiors. However, there were trade union advisers who achieved a remarkable degree of success and some who had a powerful influence on the development of the industrial relations system in the countries in which they worked; one such was Edgar Parry in Sierra Leone.

Another important source of labour department personnel, which has been of rapidly growing importance in most places, is through the recruitment of locally born officers. This source has been used least in some parts of East and Central Africa, and in some of the very small dependencies where opportunities for training as labour officers may be less. In West Africa and the West Indies, however, it has for some time been the most important source of recruitment. Nigeria was the territory which first began recruiting local people into the department. In 1942, as soon as the labour department was established, two Nigerian assistant labour officers in training were appointed, one of whom, after an academic course in the United Kingdom, rose rapidly within the department, had become an Assistant Commissioner of Labour by 1954, and by 1959 was Permanent Secretary to the Federal Ministry of Labour and Welfare. By the end of 1943, Nigeria had as many as 10 locally recruited assistant labour officers and assistant labour officers in training, several of whom remain in the highest posts in the department today. This policy was continued throughout the period of colonial government, so that by the middle 50's Nigeria was fortunate enough to have a considerable number of experienced local men in fairly senior positions, who were able to take over much of the administration and control of the department to replace the many expatriates who were withdrawn as independence approached. Although other territories, including some in West Africa and the West Indies, began this process of local recruitment rather later, most of them had a considerable proportion of experienced locally born officers in senior positions by the end of the 50's, and today most of the departments in these territories are entirely staffed by locally recruited officers. The most important exceptions have been the territories of East and Central Africa and Hong Kong. In Kenya and Northern Rhodesia, certainly, a number of locally born[19] recruits of European extraction have entered the labour departments on an equal footing with expatriates, but it was not until later that members of other local races were promoted to senior rank. Kenya appointed its first two African labour officers in 1956, and Uganda promoted one in 1957. Tanganyika appointed an assistant labour officer in 1957. No other Africans in these territories had, up to 1960, risen above the rank of labour inspectors in the labour departments, but since then further promotions to higher posts have been made. In Northern Rhodesia some African 'labour assistants' have been appointed since 1956, somewhat on the analogy of African 'district assistants' in the Administration of that territory, but the avenues of promotion from this grade to the senior staff are by no means clear. The rather smaller labour department in Nyasaland employs a considerable number of African labour assistants and inspectors, but here, too, the more senior staff was wholly expatriate until shortly before independence. There are a number of Chinese labour officers employed in the department of labour in Hong Kong, but the heads of departments are British. It is, of course, likely to be only a relatively short period before expatriate officers are replaced entirely by locally recruited personnel in every territory.[20]

Some kinds of post are more likely to remain occupied by European expatriates for some time than others. For the posts requiring high technical qualifications, such as inspectors of factories, and trade testing or training officers, it has been difficult to recruit qualified local personnel, and the posts of trade union labour officer, or trade union adviser, which were filled as a matter of policy by experienced British trade unionists, were for that reason not generally open to local officers. There have, however, been exceptions in this field. As early as 1946 a former general secretary of the first Nigerian Trades Union Congress was appointed to the Nigerian Department of Labour, and helped to establish the trade union section of that department. He later became the labour officer in

[19] Including white Southern Rhodesians serving in the Northern Rhodesian Government civil service.
[20] Considerable efforts are being made to train local personnel to fill the posts that will in due course become vacant.

charge of the industrial relations section of the department. In 1956 another former Nigerian trade unionist was appointed to the department as a Labour Officer (Trade Unions), with the same duties as the European trade unionists then employed in the department. One of the African labour officers appointed in Kenya in 1956 was also a former trade union official; he has subsequently become Industrial Relations Adviser. Promotion has in general throughout the territories been swift; in fact the speed at which it has taken place has created serious problems, since the necessary experience has not always been readily available.

Organization and Control

The organization of labour departments has, of course, varied with the size of the territory concerned, and the complexity of its labour problems; it has varied, too, with the stage of constitutional advance reached. In the larger territories under the typical colonial form of government, labour departments have generally been in charge of a commissioner of labour (known as the labour adviser in Jamaica). Under him there have usually been a deputy commissioner and perhaps one or more assistant commissioners, to whom responsibility for certain functions, or possibly for certain areas of the country, has been delegated. A staff of labour officers and senior labour officers have carried on the day-to-day work of the department in field stations situated in the main centres of employment, and in the various specialist sections of the department at headquarters. A labour officer stationed at an out-station in a small country town will normally have a small executive, clerical and inspectorate staff to help him, and will be responsible for all aspects of the department's work in his area, other than factory inspection. This may include the supervision of an employment exchange and youth employment service; inspection of industrial, commercial and agricultural undertakings and labour camps, and general enforcement of the provisions of protective labour legislation; collection of statistics from employers; advice to individual employers and workers, and consideration and representation of their grievances; supervising the operation of workmen's compensation provisions, keeping in touch with the progress of industrial relations in the district and being ready with advice and help to local trade unions on their organization and administration.   In some places it may include the supervision of recruiting activities, and attesting the contracts of recruited men.   Elsewhere the compulsory registration of labour may be an important activity.   These activities are co-ordinated throughout the territory by the labour commissioner, acting through the specialist sections of the department to which labour officers in the field are required to make regular detailed reports.

In smaller dependencies labour department organization is much simpler, and in such places as Aden, British Honduras or Grenada, the labour commissioner, assisted perhaps by one, two or three officers, and a small group of inspectors, may carry on most of the functions of the department himself.   In the Gambia and a few of the smallest territories there was, even up to the end of 1959, still no properly constituted labour department, but a qualified labour officer, responsible to the secretariat, carried out the appropriate duties.

Constitutional advance changes somewhat the organization of government departments, and the duties of the civil servants who head them.   In the stages before responsible government has been secured, the labour commissioner as well as being responsible for the functioning of the department, has usually been the government's chief adviser on labour matters, and has generally had a seat in the legislative council, where he has been the government's chief spokesman on labour policy, and has had the responsibility for introducing labour legislation into, and guiding it through, the council, and for answering questions which arise on labour matters, on behalf of the government. The labour commissioner has not usually been a member of the executive council, but he may often have been called in to the council for consultation and advice on matters which are the concern of his department.   Thus, although he has been the government's adviser and spokesman on labour policy, he has not officially been a maker of policy.

A further aspect of the labour commissioner's powers in this stage of constitutional development is that in the larger territories certain statutory powers and duties have been laid on him, either directly by statute or through regulations which have delegated the governor's powers to him.   He is, of course, responsible everywhere for the execution of labour legislation, and labour officers have the powers of entry and inspection essential for its enforcement.

The position of the commissioner as an official member of the legislative council was sometimes said to cause difficulties. There are cases where the labour commissioner may be glad of the platform which membership of the legislature gives, from which he can make clear the fundamentals of the department's policy.   This can be of advantage during periods of friction or misunderstanding.   Membership of the council may also in some circumstances allow the labour commissioner and the various unofficial interests represented in the council to keep in closer touch with each other, and it may have allowed the department more directly to influence the content of legislation passed through the council, though it must be said that once they are introduced, the debates on labour measures in most officially dominated legislatures have been desultory in the extreme.

Against these advantages, however, the argument is made that his position as official spokesman for the government exposes the commissioner—and by association the department—more openly to the suspicion that they are not and cannot be completely impartial in their duties as advisers or as conciliators.   The government is often the largest employer of labour in the territory, and is also the authority responsible for security—a function to which colonial governments give high priority, sometimes at the sacrifice of other rights and freedoms. Hence government policies may appear to be biased against the interests of employees, and against freedom of action by mass employees' organizations.   Moreover, at this early stage in constitutional development, popular leaders, including those leaders of the employees who are politically committed, are likely to be outspokenly opposed to the policies of the government as a whole.   Hence, if the head of the labour department is identified as the chief advocate of government labour policy when it has been formulated, as well as being known as chief adviser to the government in the formative stages of policy, the impartiality of the department may be called in question, and the confidence and trust which it has attempted to build up may be jeopardized.   There may even be times when the labour commissioner has to speak in support of a new government policy, imposed, say, after a breakdown in industrial relations, or serious labour disturbances, which his department has been advising against in private conclave or in the confidence of the executive council.   In all these respects his position in the legislature is very different from that of a minister of labour, especially an unofficial minister.   If a minister disagrees with government policy on labour matters he may resign, and would probably be expected to resign, whereas a career civil servant is in a more awkward situation.   If a civil servant disagrees with the executive council of which he is a member he must nevertheless carry out that policy impartially, though it will have been his responsibility to advise the executive council that it should follow a different course.

As constitutional advance takes place in the more important dependencies, the responsibilities of the labour commissioner in the legislative council, and some of his responsibility for formulating policy, gradually diminish.[21]   Once a majority of the legislative council consists of elected members, it is the rule for a few representatives of the elected majority, the 'unofficials', to be appointed as members of the executive council; and they, usually together with a number of 'officials', may be given responsibility for certain subjects or groups of subjects, corresponding to different government departments.   Thus, the member of the executive council responsible, *inter alia*, for labour will take over in the legislature the functions which used to be performed by the labour commissioner, who loses his seat there.   At this stage, however, the commissioner retains much of his power.   Responsibility for policy remains that of the executive council as a whole, not that of individual members, and the commissioner remains as chief adviser to the government.   He may still be called in to the executive council for advice, and he may still have direct access to the governor. He retains the statutory powers given to him under a number of ordinances, as well as full executive responsibility and responsibility for the administration of the department.

The transition from this position to full ministerial responsibility is generally gradual.   The members of the executive council may first be termed 'ministers', and given fuller

[21] The process of constitutional advance varies, of course, from territory to territory, and one or more of the stages noted here may be omitted.

responsibility for formulating the general lines of labour policy and presenting it for decision by the executive council. This position may last for some years before ministers are given any executive powers or responsibilities. The new 'ministry' with a very small staff, often simply a ministerial secretary with clerical assistance, may at this stage be separated from the department, although necessarily is kept in very close touch with it. The minister is able to call on the department for information, advice and technical help needed in the formation of policy. He can call for any information necessary to keep himself informed about labour matters, to enable him to answer parliamentary questions, and to be able to judge the impact on his own department's affairs of the various policies advocated by other ministers, and so on. At this stage of development, too, the minister himself may be given some statutory powers, the use of which will require even closer consultation between the department and the ministry.

This stage of constitutional development is obviously a rather delicate one from the point of view of personal relations, and it is essential for the proper running of the administrative machine that mutual trust be built up between the department and its minister. Major policy changes are a matter for decision by the executive council, but the initiative towards setting such changes in motion may come in the first place from the minister, or from the executive council as a whole. The dominant party may have had a particular item of labour policy as an important plank in its platform. Initiative may also come from the department, whose officers may wish to correct some abuse or anomaly which has come to their notice in the course of administration, or may desire the introduction of some measure making for more efficient labour administration. The scope for disagreement, and even ill-feeling, between minister and department over policy matters is thus considerable. The civil servants of the department have been accustomed, in practice, to making their own policy and to having their views seriously considered by the governor and other senior officials responsible for policy decisions. If the minister acts contrary to the department's advice, or without sufficient reference to it, officials may feel that he is pushing a measure through the legislature for short-term and not wholly praiseworthy political motives, or that he is disregarding for the same motives their urgent advice to introduce some politically unpopular measure. Conversely, the minister may feel occasionally that the departmental officials are being unnecessarily obstructive and apparently unwilling to accept and to co-operate with the new régime which he represents. Apart from any differences over policy, the minister has the delicate task of keeping a firm control of policy, while avoiding any appearance of interfering in the detailed administration of the department, which is the prerogative of the commissioner.

In the majority of cases where this stage has been reached friction has been kept well within practical bounds. In many instances, indeed, civil servants have developed a high regard for and confidence in the new minister. Isolated cases could, however, be cited where conflict has been caused by ministers, who are too politically minded, or simply inexperienced, to understand the implications of their decisions for their departmental staff. There have also been problems of adjustment by civil servants who have been hostile to the intrusion of political considerations into administration, and resented their own loss of status.

It is only in the final stage of responsible government—a stage reached for instance by Jamaica in 1955, Malaya in 1957 and Nigeria in 1959 [22]—that full ministerial responsibility is attained. The labour department and the 'ministry' may then

---

[22] In Ghana this pattern was not followed right up to its final stage, and although a Ministry of Labour was in existence from 1950 to 1959, and a certain amount of integration took place in 1953, the commissioner of labour still remained in office, and the department remained to some extent autonomous of the minister. In 1959, two years after Ghana's independence, the ministry was abolished and a labour department was re-created, physically separated from any ministry, though responsibility for labour affairs was included in the portfolio of the Minister for Economic Affairs. In Nigeria, although integration of the Federal Ministry of Labour and Welfare took place in 1959, and a complete reorganization of the whole Labour Department was made on the lines of the British Ministry of Labour, being reconstituted as a ministry under a permanent secretary, this still left the three regional ministers who are responsible for labour in the regional governments and legislatures in a somewhat anomalous position. As an example, the Western Regional Minister of Lands and Labour has under his charge a regional Ministry of Lands, but for the administration of labour policy he has to work, through the Permanent Secretary of the Ministry of Lands, in co-operation with the Federal Ministry of Labour's Principal Labour Officer in the Western Region. Principal labour officers thus have a dual function, as the chief executive officers of the federal ministry in each region, and as the chief adviser on labour, and to some extent head of a labour department, for the regional government concerned.

Q

be integrated, the post of labour commissioner disappear and constitutional responsibility for all executive and policy matters in the field of labour be transferred to the minister. The permanent secretary of the ministry would in that case become head of the department and the minister's chief adviser and chief executive—a position very similar to that in a ministry or department of state in the United Kingdom. In a number of cases the labour commissioner has become the permanent secretary. Trinidad and British Guiana retained the post of labour commissioner after the establishment of a ministry of labour. In both of these cases some difficulty was experienced in adjusting the functions of minister to those of the commissioner; there was a suspicion that the independent position of the commissioner was to some extent an embarrassment to the minister. A similar situation developed in Singapore, where a vigorous minister of labour was not inclined to permit the labour commissioner's role to stand in the way of a solution to a problem that seemed politically desirable.

The Formulation of Labour Policy

It is interesting to analyse the processes by which labour policy is formulated in colonial territories, and the influences which determine the content of these policies. In the early stages of colonial administration it is a fair generalization to say that labour matters were dealt with by colonial governments mainly on a pragmatic basis. The legislation which was enacted by official-dominated legislatures, and the administrative measures which were taken, were those which seemed best fitted for the economic or administrative purposes of the time. Thus, in the West Indies and in Mauritius, after slavery was abolished, and at a later stage in Malaya and Ceylon, government labour policy was directed to securing and retaining an adequate supply of labour, both for the government's own use and for the needs of the European employers, and to protect employees from some of the abuses of over-enthusiastic employers. In East and Central Africa a somewhat similar process took place, though since labour was even more difficult to obtain and the influence of employers considerably greater, in addition to measures for the protection of the workers emphasis was placed on measures to increase the supply of labour; these included the manipulation of native tax rates, strong administrative 'encouragement' of peasant farmers into employment, and penalties for breaking a contract by employees, which in practice were hardly ever enforced. In West Africa, on the other hand, where the economy and government revenue were not so dependent on enterprises employing large numbers of labourers, the emphasis in early labour legislation was almost entirely on regulation of contracts, on protective provisions and on the abolition of native forms of domestic slavery.

This situation changed during the 20's and 30's of the present century, as the Colonial Office began to pay more attention to social policies, and especially as a definite Colonial Office labour policy came into being. The change was accelerated when the influence of the International Labour Organization began to make itself felt, and international labour standards began to be laid down. The development of labour legislation throughout the British dependencies then began to move towards greater uniformity of principle, usually in accordance with internationally agreed standards, and modelled on the principles of United Kingdom legislation, although numerous variations and modifications, which had come about for peculiar historical, economic or social reasons were frequently retained. Since the 30's the trend towards greater uniformity has been accompanied by increasingly complex and comprehensive labour legislation.

Where there is no legislative council it is difficult to follow closely the nature of the processes by which colonial governments decide upon their policies, or by which legislation is formulated. Up to a certain stage, at least, of development, much of the process takes place in private, and usually takes the form of private discussions among officials; there are also consultations in confidence, with other interested parties. It is usual, for example, for government officials to discuss labour questions with important employers, and possibly, where these are available, with trade union centres. It is only in later stages of political and economic development that such bodies as labour advisory boards and committees offer the opportunity for more open discussion of labour policy, or for the consideration of proposals for new labour legislation. Only rarely in typical colonial conditions has the government had to take into account powerful and well-informed unofficial opinion inside the central legislature of the territory; the official presentation of trade union legislation before a colonial legislative council and the second reading debate on it have, for example, generally been most perfunctory, and the committee stage of a trade union Bill, as of most legislation, amounts to little more than a formality unless the Bill has gone before a select committee which might consider the amendments. Hence an analysis of the influences at work in the formulation of policy by colonial governments must rely to some extent on inference.

Some of the forces which have influenced the labour policy of colonial governments can however be described fairly confidently. New labour policies in a dependent territory may be initiated from a variety of sources. Requests may come from the Colonial Office and be supported by evidence of the obligations of the Secretary of State under international labour conventions or adopted recommendations, or by analogies found in British labour legislation which the Colonial Office considers it appropriate for the territory concerned to consider, by advice tendered by the Colonial Labour Advisory Committee, and so on. The Secretary of State may also be subject to pressure by members of the United Kingdom Parliament, or by bodies such as the British trade unions. Alternatively, in the post-war period the initiative for a change in policy or legislation may have come from the territory's own labour department, or from another department, for instance, the district administration, or the public works department. In taking the initiative for a change in policy the labour department itself may have been influenced by a number of factors, including the pressure of events such as an outbreak of labour unrest, pressure from employers or trade unions or from a sector of local public opinion. The knowledge of what has taken place in other countries in similar situations, perhaps through a study of legislation, perhaps through informal contacts with other labour departments, perhaps through the supply of information from the Colonial Office labour advisers, may have stimulated a decision to follow a similar course. In other cases action may have been taken after discussions between the labour commissioners of several different territories at labour commissioners' conferences such as those held fairly regularly since the war in East Africa.   Or a change in labour policy may be the result of recommendations by a board or commission of inquiry.   And, finally, at a stage where representative government has led to the appointment of unofficial ministers to the executive council, the policy of these ministers, perhaps as a result of pledges given at elections, may have caused changes to be made.

From whatever source the initiative for a change in policy has come, implementation has generally been preceded by prolonged discussions and exchanges of views between the different departments of government; in the case of labour policy the views of the departments most intimately concerned with the employment of labour have probably been given particular attention.   In official-dominated governments the matter would probably have been finally agreed in the governor's executive council by consultation between the most senior of these civil servants concerned.   In countries such as Kenya, where in the early years of the century there were already influential unofficial members of the executive council, more weight would certainly have been given to unofficial views of one or more sections of the community in deciding a government policy.   The same would be true in any territory where there was one powerful and economically dominant group of non-officials, such as the planters in Malaya and the West Indies.   In most cases, however, the prejudices and natural caution of senior government officials have tended to retard changes in policy.   In general, only after labour departments have been established in the various territories has change become easier.   It has made a good deal of difference whether a strong department with a confident and respected Commissioner at its head has become established.   In such cases the labour department, by putting forward independent advice (generally in accordance with Colonial Office views), has often persuaded the administration as a whole to agree to an advance in policy despite resistance by one or two important departmental heads or by an important unofficial pressure group.

One important development which helped this process was the creation during the 40's and 50's of labour advisory boards or committees within many of the territories themselves.

Earlier, more limited examples of such bodies were the Indian Immigration Committee established in Malaya in 1907, and the Board of Indian Immigrant Labour set up in Ceylon in 1923; both groups consisted mainly of representatives of employers and of governments, and they made recommendations concerning the supply, welfare and conditions of employment of Indian labourers in those two territories.   In Tanganyika also, a labour board had been established in 1924 to deal with all questions of government wage rates, but until 1940 this body had no responsibility for private employment or other labour legislation.   Most of the boards, however, were set up during or soon after the second world war, and many of them were established as a result of recommendations made by Major Orde Browne in his report on labour conditions in the West Indies— recommendations which were later passed on in despatches to governments in other parts of the world.   Major Orde Browne had said that the labour commissioner of a territory should not have to take sole responsibility for decisions of great importance, but should be able to ask an advisory board for guidance on especially difficult or important questions.   He would thus have access to the best available advice, and, if needed, would have the support of an important body of opinion in putting the decision through.   The boards, in Major Orde Browne's view, should have an impartial chairman and a membership as well balanced as possible between employers and labour, with power to co-opt additional professional or technical members.

These recommendations did, in fact, determine the form in which some labour advisory boards and committees were established, but there have been variations in the practice adopted; often the chairman has been the labour commissioner rather than an independent person, and there have been differences in the use which has been made of the boards.   The functions of the boards have generally been rather limited, and they usually have met only at the request of the government, to discuss specific questions which the government has submitted to them.   These might have included, for example, the content of important labour legislation, the possible application of international labour conventions, the possibility of taking measures to increase the supply of labour, appropriate means of improving industrial relations or the formulation of recommendations to employers on housing standards or other welfare amenities. In a few instances these boards took over from, or incorporated, committees which were already in existence for specific purposes, and where this happened the boards may have been more effective than their predecessors. The Central Labour Advisory Board of Nyasaland, for instance, was formed in 1941 as a successor to a committee on the engagement of labour for service abroad, and it has been closely consulted by the government on its policy for emigrant labour.

Where use has been made of these organizations and committees, the advantages to labour departments have usually been those specified by Major Orde Browne. Changes in policy and also the passage of legislation have been facilitated by prior discussion in these bodies. But in a few cases the committees have been unbalanced and the workers' side unrepresentative or non-existent. For example, in Tanganyika between 1941 and 1952 the labour board consisted of 6 officials and 6 unofficial representatives of employers. In 1952 it was reconstituted as the result of the recommendations of a local committee on manpower and it then included 3 officials, 8 employers' representatives and only 2 members (one of whom was a European) nominated by the government to represent African employees. The composition was not changed again until 1955. In Kenya the position was only slightly better, and the British T.U.C. expressed strong concern in 1953 and 1954 at the fact that workers' representatives on both the Labour Advisory Board and the Kenya Wages Advisory Board were nominated by the Kenya Government, and included no representatives of the trade union movement there.

It is natural that workers' organizations are reluctant to associate themselves with recommendations made by boards such as these. A number of measures passed by East African governments at this period were strongly opposed by the trade union movements concerned, on the grounds that their interests had not been consulted.

The Work of Labour Departments

The following examples illustrate the way some of the influences on policy and legislation have worked in particular instances. One example comes from Tanganyika, which enacted its first comprehensive Workmen's Compensation Ordinance in 1948. Tanganyika can fairly be described as having, at that time, an official-dominated legislature; its labour legislation was also co-ordinated with the other two East African territories. The Labour Commissioner's speech introducing the second reading debate on this Bill is therefore illuminating, giving as it does his version of the events leading up to the Bill's introduction. He began by assuring members that 'the matter had not been introduced without the fullest consultation having been made in the matter both by the Labour Department and the Labour Board of the Government and also by the corresponding Department and Board in Kenya'. He said later: 'Now this subject has been under periodic review and consideration for about the past twenty years, and in 1937 the Secretary of State submitted to all Colonial Governments in East and West Africa a draft Model Workmen's Compensation Act with a request that consideration should be given to its application to this and other territories. This Bill was referred to a number of bodies in the Territory, including employers, employers' associations, labour advisory boards, insurance companies, but no agreed conclusion had been reached upon it by the time the late war broke out.' The Commissioner then explained that the matter had been shelved until 1944, in which year it was again considered and brought up before the labour board. Northern Rhodesia had by then passed a Workmen's Compensation Ordinance which was thought to be a considerable advance on the model ordinance, and the labour board decided to follow this ordinance, but to extend it so as to include African workmen, who were excluded from the Northern Rhodesian provisions. After about two years' further consideration concrete proposals were put before the insurance companies with a request for premiums to be quoted. The Labour Commissioner said that there was no reply to this request, but later a despatch was received from the 'Secretary of State enclosing a memorandum from the Insurance companies asking why we were proceeding on different lines to Kenya and Uganda when they appeared to have an assurance that uniform legislation would be applied throughout East Africa. The matter rested there, and we did not quite know what to do.'

The Commissioner went on to say that during 1947 certain other factors came into play. The Convention on the Application of International Labour Standards to Non-Metropolitan Territories was passed at Geneva, as a result of which the Tanganyika Government considered itself pledged to apply the 1925 Workmen's Compensation Convention. Secondly, the Colonial Labour Advisory Board at the Colonial Office had been considering workmen's compensation legislation, and had come to the conclusion that the existing colonial legislation was in general satisfactory. 'That was all very well,' said the Labour Commissioner, 'but it did not help us very much as we had no legislation.' It was then found that in the absence of actuarial data insurance companies would not agree to make periodic payments to disabled Africans, one attractive feature of the Northern Rhodesian law. It was known, too, that it was necessary to have uniformity between the East African territories, especially in view of the importance of the joint services operated by the High Commission; but there were still many shortcomings in the model Act which had been approved by the Colonial Labour Advisory Committee and already passed in Kenya and Uganda.

Early in 1948 the Labour Commissioner said he 'received a direction that I must consider the enactment of Workmen's Compensation legislation'. He therefore took the opportunity afforded by the Inter-African Labour Conference at Jos, in Northern Nigeria, to have informal talks with officials of the Kenya Government, and to discuss the question with the labour commissioners of the British West African territories and of Northern Rhodesia. As a result he got an idea of the difficulties each of these territories was experiencing in administering their ordinances, and he also got informal agreement from Kenya that they would consider amendments to their ordinance to bring it into line with what Tanganyika considered should be provided. A conference of the East African labour commissioners was therefore held in April of the same year, and complete agreement was reached on the amendments necessary to improve the existing Kenya legislation. A new Bill was drafted and circulated to Kenya and Uganda. It was examined by the Tanganyika Labour Board in July and introduced into the Legislative Council in November, where it was passed with virtually no debate. The Bill was based on the original Kenya Ordinance, which was in turn based on the Colonial Office's model Bill, but it incorporated a number of important provisions derived from Northern Rhodesian legislation, some recommendations made informally by the Nigerian Labour Department on the basis of their administrative experience and some further requests from the Secretary of State to increase the compensation payable.

This is perhaps an extreme example, but it illustrates the factors considered, the type of pressures which would be applied and the kind of discussions that would be undertaken by a government which had a fairly active labour department, but not under pressure from any very strong unofficial bodies whose views it had to take into account. The same kind of procedure was later followed in Tanganyika, but more discussions seem to have taken place, both in London and in East Africa, with representatives of the Labour Adviser's Department at the Colonial Office. In territories where the unofficial interests had greater influence, no doubt there would have been more evidence of strong unofficial representations on issues which concerned them. As it was, the employers of Tanganyika were consulted in the course of reference to the labour boards, whose composition at that period has already been mentioned. The labour movement in Tanganyika was then so weak that it could be ignored, and there were no elected members of the legislature who were acting as spokesmen for either employers or workers.

A contrasting situation was found in Northern Rhodesia, where there are a number of strongly entrenched interest groups, and where there have usually been prolonged and well-informed debates on labour matters, both in the press and in the legislature. Examples from Northern Rhodesia may therefore serve to illustrate some of the other influences which have been brought to bear on the form of legislation introduced by colonial governments.

In 1942 the Northern Rhodesian Government decided to pass local legislation to replace and consolidate the British Trade Union Acts of 1871–1927, which had hitherto applied in that territory. A Bill was drafted and was published, after being approved by the Colonial Office. The Bill then received a considerable amount of local criticism and comment, especially from the European trade unions and the larger employers in the territory. After discussions with all these bodies, some modifications were made in the Bill before it was introduced into the Legislative Council. The Bill was in some respects rather restrictive. It provided for compulsory registration, and it applied the provisions of the 1927 Trade Disputes and Trade Unions Act establishing the principle of contracting-in when political funds were set up by unions. It also made all strikes and lockouts illegal if they took place before an attempt at conciliation had been made; and it gave protection to any-one refusing to take part in an illegal strike or lockout. The Bill met with a hostile reception in the legislature from a number of unofficial members, a majority of whom were at that time grouped together in the Northern Rhodesia Labour Party and who were themselves trade unionists. The Attorney-General thereupon assured the council that 'Government is not com-mitted to any one of the particular principles on which this Bill is based', and after being referred to a select committee the legislation was abandoned. No other trade union Bill was introduced into the Northern Rhodesian legislature until 1949, and that measure included none of the controversial points mentioned above.

A further example of the influence of unofficial opinion in Northern Rhodesia occurred in 1958, with an amendment which the government wished to make to the then existing trade union legislation. In 1957 a commission of inquiry had been appointed to investigate some strikes which had occurred among European mineworkers, and, *inter alia*, 'the suitability or otherwise of the provisions contained in the Laws of Northern Rhodesia . . . for the avoidance and prompt settlement of trade disputes'.

The commission had made a number of recommendations, in particular that the holding of secret ballots on the question of a strike should be mandatory for every trade union as one of the statutory provisions it is required to have in its rules; and that a 'closed shop' clause in an agreement between employers and a trade union should by law be made conditional on four things: that anyone declaring, instigating, counselling or abetting a strike before all the provisions for settlement of a dispute had

been exhausted should be liable to a penalty; that there should
be provision for an appeal to an independent person or a
judicial officer against suspension or expulsion from the union;
that strikes or lockouts should require secret ballots under
labour department supervision with a two-thirds majority to
make them lawful; and that within a month of the signing of
an agreement containing a closed-shop clause there should be
secret ballots under labour department supervision, again requiring a two-thirds majority to make it lawful.

The commission's report was published in October 1957, and
received a considerable amount of favourable publicity, and
demands for quick action on its recommendations. The
following month, after consultations with both sides of industry,
the government announced its general agreement with the conclusions and recommendations of the report, and initiated a
debate on it in the legislative council where the recommendations met with general approval; the main criticisms made
were that it did not go far enough in opposition to the closed-
shop system.[23]   The government thereupon drafted amending
legislation to put the commission's recommendations into effect,
and a Bill was published in February 1958, which was to be
introduced into the legislature in March. The unions had
accepted, in principle, the commission's report, but they were
not satisfied with the published Bill. Their opposition was
communicated to the trade union movement in the United
Kingdom, and to a delegation of the International Confederation of Free Trade Unions which was visiting the Rhodesias at
that time.   A trip to London was made by a joint delegation of
the general secretaries of the European and African Mineworkers' Unions (the first joint action ever taken by these two
unions), and representations were made by the Federal T.U.C.
of Rhodesia and Nyasaland—at that time a wholly European
body.

The British T.U.C., the British National Union of Mineworkers and the Mineworkers' International Federation all
studied the proposed legislation and subsequently formed a joint
delegation which had two meetings with the Parliamentary

[23] The bargaining strength and the political influence of the European trade
unions were very much less in 1958 than they had been in 1942. There were
fewer trade unionists in the legislature and there was no labour party as such to
consolidate their interests.

Under-Secretary of State for the Colonies before the Northern Rhodesian delegation arrived. After its arrival, several meetings were held, and a further joint delegation held discussions with Colonial Office officials. The intervention of the British and international bodies seems to have been of considerable advantage to the Northern Rhodesian Unions. The T.U.C. and the M.I.F. freely criticized the commission's recommendations; they considered that many of the aims could be better settled by agreement than by legislation, and they believed that some provisions were unenforceable or confusing. It seems that as a consequence of these representations the Northern Rhodesian Government was persuaded by the Colonial Office not to proceed with the Bill as drafted, but to prepare a revised measure to meet some of the criticisms. This it did. The introduction of the legislation was postponed for about six weeks, and a special meeting of the council had to be called for its enactment.

The announcement of this change of plan caused a great deal of embarrassment to the Northern Rhodesian Government, who were subjected to outspoken criticism in the press and in the legislative council, over a considerable period. In announcing the change in plans the government's spokesmen seem to have relied throughout on the rather weak argument that the government wished to implement the recommendations of the inquiry commission—'no more and no less', and that as the commission's report was an intricate document, and some of the recommendations were by no means clear, their intentions might possibly have been misunderstood when the original Bill was drafted. This excuse led one unofficial European member to ask sarcastically what exactly was the function of the government and of the legislative council? What was the function of a commission? Who was responsible for interpreting its findings and with whom should any objections to a Bill be lodged—to the government or to some outside source? He referred to the Bill having been 'hawked around London by Messrs. Purvis and Katilungu' and considered that subsequent events had been a 'smack in the face' and a 'deliberate insult' to the legislative council members. Other members spoke in sympathy with the criticisms and there seems to have been a strong feeling among unofficial members, at a time when new constitutional proposals were in the air, that the legislature and possibly the government were being made to lose face by the interference from London. The government had denied that the withdrawal of the Bill was in response to a 'direct instruction' from the Colonial Office, but as one member put it, 'they never instruct, my dear fellow, they advise'. It was only in the closing stages of the Bill's passage that a government spokesman made the point that the government had received much advice from many sources, including the Colonial Office, that they had rejected some and accepted that which they considered to be in the interests of the Territory.

The government officials' embarrassment may have been shared by the three unofficial Federal Party members, who by that time had been appointed to the executive council and who were therefore collectively responsible for its decisions. The severity of the unofficial members' attacks on the government was due to their desire to arouse European public opinion to the need for constitutional advance towards responsible government, and so to bring to an end having to submit to pressure from 'outside sources'. Such a clear-cut example of Colonial Office interference may have come at a most opportune moment, and good use was made of it. The government nevertheless persisted in its resolve to introduce the revised Bill, and it was duly passed.

Conclusions

As with their submission to the labour advisory boards, so with general labour policy, governments in different territories, and especially in different regions of the world, have given different stress to different aspects of policy. In Nigeria, the largest dependency of all, during the last twenty years of its colonial status, the trend was towards the gradual establishment of a social and legal framework based largely on that of the United Kingdom; on securing enforcement of the laws protecting wages, and on securing statutory minimum wages for certain under-privileged occupations. Up to about 1955 the government tried to act as a model employer and to set a reasonable standard of wages and working conditions and also of good relations with organizations of work-people. Other employers were urged to follow its example. It gave a good deal of help and encouragement to the trade unions; for a long period it carried out much educational work among unionists and stimulated self-education.   In Sierra Leone the government sought the same objectives, but adopted a rather different approach; and in some of the Caribbean territories much the same could be said, though in the Caribbean much more attention has usually had to be paid to unemployment problems than in West Africa.

In Malaya, on the other hand, the government tended to intervene more directly, in regulating the supply of immigrant labour, in controlling and supervising the welfare of labourers, in the general process of wage-fixing, and, especially after 1946, in the regulation of trade unions, their administration and their insulation from political influences.   The East and Central African territories also to a greater or lesser extent concentrated primarily on securing an adequate labour supply, on inspection and control of housing standards and ration allowances, and on watching over the welfare of recruited labourers, including their welfare on the journey to work.   These territories as a whole certainly gave less encouragement and less help to the emergent trade unions than their counterparts in West Africa, and one or two of them, until the late 1950's, were strictly neutral in their attitude to the formation of unions and to their recognition by employers, so long as there was industrial peace, but when disturbances occurred, definite hostility was shown.   During the last decade, however, there was some emphasis in the three East African territories on encouragement of joint consultation, on the formation of works committees, on wage policy, on minimum-wage legislation of various kinds and on the enforcement of such legislation.   However, after about 1950, the Government of Kenya did much to promote the establishment of a sound and comprehensive industrial relations system.   In Aden the government was compelled, by the attitude of the unions, to break with tradition and introduce a system of compulsory arbitration on the advice of experts from the Colonial Office.   The Government in Fiji has moved in the other direction, also on the advice of the Colonial Office, taking away from the governor the power to settle industrial disputes and legislating in favour of the traditional British voluntary approach to the settlement of conflict between unions and employers.

It is apparent from this survey of the growth of labour administration in colonies that one of the most dynamic factors has been the influence of the Colonial Office on local developments. Policy decisions made in Whitehall and their implementation were greatly influenced by social developments in Britain as well as in the colonies. The rise in the status of the British trade union movement, the development of modern methods of personnel administration and the extension of the interest of the International Labour Organization to non-metropolitan territories, stimulated Secretaries of State for the Colonies and their advisers to urge the adoption of policies inspired by British experience.

The need for positive policies was at first more apparent to policy-makers in London than in the colonies, but the growth of an employed working population gave rise to problems that demanded the active intervention of the governments of the territories for their solution. The adoption of protective legislation and the building up of labour departments with positive functions were resisted by employers who feared that their authority would be undermined and by administrations in colonies who were also afraid that orderly progress might be jeopardized by the development of trade unions—actively committed by their leaders to the achievement of self-government and the overthrow of 'white' domination. Thus, the pattern of development of labour administration in the tropical Commonwealth, while bearing the hall-mark of British influence, has been shaped in each territory by an interaction of various forces. The war, with its demand for labour, its disturbance of established ideas and methods of administration, and its impact on British policy was a potent element in speeding up the rate at which labour policies and administration were adopted. After the war the rapid growth of industrial investment and, in particular, the establishment of British, American and foreign enterprises, stimulated the development of modern ideas of labour administration.

The newer industrialists differed from the older economically powerful groups, such as planters and mine-owners, who were the first Europeans to invest a great deal of capital in most of the territories, and on whom the governments had relied for a good part of their revenue, and for the further economic development of the country. The economic importance and the social status enjoyed by the old-established colonial employers ensured that their views were given full consideration in the formulation of policy; and measures to secure an adequate supply of labour often tended to be given more prominence than the encouragement of strong, independent unions.

The establishment of the Overseas Employers' Federation and local associations of employers brought a new approach to labour problems by employers. Instead of the old negative opposition to innovation in labour administration, a more constructive policy of co-operation was developed. Many employers believed, as some may still do today, that labour departments would always tend to be on the side of the employees, but most of them have come to recognize that labour officers have a vital role to play in the development of a sound system of industrial relations.

In summarizing the factors that have been most significant in the development of labour administration, attention must obviously be focused upon the growth of the trade unions. Although labour departments and the laws which they administered were adopted before trade unionism emerged, the problems created by the organization of workers stimulated their further development. The close connection between unions and the political movements which have achieved the goals of internal self-government or complete independence has given rise to special problems.

So long as the territories were ruled by colonial governments the broad principles of policy in the field of labour administration were designed to favour the development of independent trade unions and to promote a system of industrial relations in which employers and workers would settle the conditions of employment with the minimum of government intervention. There were, of course, significant departures from the British model, as we have indicated in other chapters, but these did not amount to a fundamental break with the basic principles. With the advent of self-government relations between government and unions have changed in some territories and labour administration has taken on a new aspect.

The future role of labour departments will inevitably be determined by the road which the territories choose to follow

R

after self-government. Their functions and powers will be considerably changed if the totalitarian concept of the state is adopted. In this case the departments will be given the legal power to determine conditions of employment. How they exercise this authority will depend upon many factors. The new trend in Ghana, for example, has not yet been carried to the point where, as in the Soviet Union, the trade unions are merely a subordinate branch of the labour department, though the domination of the unions by the government has brought this perilously close.

If, after independence, territories continue to follow the British model the responsibilities of the labour departments will continue to develop, but they will have to achieve their objectives by persuasion and co-operation with unions and employers rather than by coercion. There is nothing in the history of labour administration in the territories to suggest that they will not be able to achieve effective results if they continue to observe the principles developed under British rule and conform to the International Labour Code.

CHAPTER 9

THE INFLUENCE OF THE
INTERNATIONAL LABOUR ORGANIZATION

THE influence of the standards established by the International Labour Code on the development of the law and government policy in the tropical territories of the British Commonwealth has been of significance. The existence of this code has given the British Government, employers and trade unions, a yardstick by which to measure the standards attained in the colonies; it has brought pressure to bear upon all concerned with labour problems, and stimulated the development of a progressive approach to their solution.

Under the constitution of the I.L.O., conventions adopted by the International Labour Conference apply only when they are specifically ratified by member states. If a member country fails to ratify a convention it must report on its current pattern of law and practice when it is called upon to do so by the International Labour Office. In the case of non-metropolitan territories, e.g. colonies and trust territories, the ratification of conventions applying to them is a matter for the metropolitan territory. Before 1946 it was up to the metropolitan territory to declare whether a convention would be applied in full or in part to any or all of its colonial territories. Since 1946, however, when the constitution of the I.L.O. was amended, members have been bound by Article 35 to apply all conventions which they have ratified to any non-metropolitan territories for whose international relations they are responsible, except where the subject matter of the convention is within the competence of the government of the territory, or where it would not be applicable owing to local conditions. As soon as possible after a member state has ratified a convention, it must make a declaration stating to what extent the convention is to be applied and giving whatever information is called for by the convention. When the subject matter of the convention is within the self-governing powers of the non-metropolitan territory the member state responsible for the international relations of that territory must bring the convention to the notice of the government of the territory, and they may then make a joint declaration on behalf of the territory accepting the obligations of the convention. If these obligations are not accepted on behalf of a territory the member state responsible must report to the Director General of the I.L.O. on the law and practice of the territory regarding the provisions of the convention, the extent to which they apply and the reasons which prevent or delay their acceptance.

Since the adoption in 1947 of the Labour Standards (Non-Metropolitan Territories) Convention the procedure for reporting on the application of conventions in non-metropolitan territories has been more stringent than for member states. The information received by the I.L.O. about the non-metropolitan territories is in fact as comprehensive as that obtained for the metropolitan countries.[1]

The first convention adopted by the I.L.O. which was of special significance for the non-metropolitan territories was the Forced Labour Convention of 1930. This convention obliged member countries to suppress immediately any form of compulsory labour except in certain closely defined circumstances. In cases where chiefs had administrative authority to recruit workers for the purpose of carrying out work of immediate necessity for the well-being of the community they would be allowed to continue subject to the code of protection laid down in the convention. Since 1957, when a new convention on forced labour was adopted by the International Labour Conference, the limited permission to use forced labour, sanctioned by the 1930 convention, has been withdrawn.[2]

In 1936 the I.L.O. moved a stage further in developing a code of protection for workers in the non-metropolitan territories, with the adoption of a convention on the recruiting of indigenous workers. This convention sought (1) to avoid the risk of pressure being brought to bear on populations by employers who required labour; (2) to ensure as far as possible that the political and social organization of the populations concerned would not be endangered by the demand for labour; (3) to see

---

[1] Report to the Governing Body of the I.L.O. from the Director General on the *Influence of Article 35 of the Constitution of the I.L.O. on the Application of Conventions in Non-Metropolitan Territories.*
[2] Abolition of Forced Labour Convention, 1957.

that as far as possible steps should be taken to deal with any adverse effects labour recruitment might have on indigenous populations.

Two more conventions designed to protect workers in non-metropolitan areas from exploitation by employers were adopted in 1939.[3] One was aimed at protecting the interests of the indigenous worker when he entered into a contract of employment. The second was concerned with the question of penal sanctions to which a worker might be subject under law if he was found to be in breach of a contract of employment.

The four conventions adopted by the I.L.O. prior to the second world war which were of special concern to workers in the non-metropolitan territories, were all ratified by the United Kingdom Government. The Forced Labour Convention of 1930 was applied in all the territories; and the Recruiting of Indigenous Workers Convention was given effect in all but those territories where recruiting of the kind envisaged did not exist and was not likely to be adopted.[4] The Contracts of Employment and Penal Sanctions Conventions were widely applied, but the governments of certain territories resisted their full application and, because these matters fell within their competence, they were allowed by the United Kingdom to refrain from putting the conventions completely into effect. Penal sanctions which could be imposed on juveniles for breaches of contract were generally abolished, but some territories insisted on maintaining desertion by adult male workers, recruited on contract, as an offence subject to penal sanctions.[5]

The war that was being fought against the tyranny of the Nazis stirred men's consciences about colonialism. It was difficult to fight for freedom and justice and not be concerned about the progress of colonial territories towards self-government and independence. The Americans, with their strong feelings against colonialism sought to have all non-self-governing territories placed under the trusteeship of the United Nations. When the I.L.O. met at Philadelphia after the war to consider its future role it was inevitably influenced by the

---

[3] Contracts of Employment (Indigenous Workers) Convention, 1939; Penal Sanctions (Indigenous Workers) Convention, 1939.
[4] *Labour in the United Kingdom Dependencies* (H.M.S.O., 1957).
[5] *Op. cit.*, p. 29.

upsurge of this sentiment in favour of advancing the development of the colonial territories. The Declaration of Philadelphia adopted by the I.L.O. as a statement of its fundamental aims emphasized the importance of measures to speed social and economic progress in the under-developed territories. Thus, with this declaration to spur them on, the I.L.O. set out to lay down what has been described as 'a social and economic charter for the dependent territories'.[6]

After the war government representatives and employers' and workers' delegates from the metropolitan countries were all prepared to agree that the influence of the I.L.O. on developments in colonial and mandated territories should be extended, and the 1947 meeting of the International Labour Conference devoted most of its time to the problems of the non-metropolitan territories. At the conference five new conventions were adopted and many others were extended to cover non-metropolitan territories. These new adoptions, together with the four conventions passed before the war, constituted a fairly comprehensive labour code. There now existed for colonial territories international standards relating to minimum wages, collective bargaining, deductions from wages, weekly rest-periods, annual holidays with pay, education and vocational training, minimum age of employment, medical examination of young persons, prohibition of night work for young persons, women's maternity protection, prohibition of employment of female employees underground, workmen's compensation for accidents, the establishment of labour inspectorates and protection of the right to organize in trade unions.

Since 1947 several other conventions have been passed, tightening up and extending older conventions. In addition, there have been a large number of recommendations which are less binding than conventions, since they do not require specific action by governments as a matter of obligation. They are in effect declarations of desirable policy that might be pursued in member countries in ways that are most appropriate to the prevailing system of industrial relations. In addition to conventions and recommendations the International Labour Conference, Regional Conferences and the Industrial Committees

[6] Overseas Employers' Federation, Occasional Papers, *The International Labour Organization.*

of the I.L.O. have passed resolutions and adopted reports which 'without having any formal legal authority, represent a wide consensus of opinion and can to this extent be regarded as a body of international standards supplementing the existing formal instruments'.[7]

The general policy of the I.L.O. on the development of industrial relations in the non-metropolitan territories was comprehensively formulated by the Committee of Experts on Social Policy in Non-Metropolitan Territories at a conference held in Dakar, French West Africa, in December 1955.

The Committee declared that to be fundamentally sound a system of industrial relations must rest on the right of workers and employers to establish and to join associations without interference from any other agency.[8] The object of governments should be to promote the growth of free, independent and stable trade unions, without regard to race, national origin or political affiliations. It was recognized that trade unions and employers' associations would inevitably be influenced by political factors, but the committee emphasized that the primary function of trade unions was to seek the improvement of the social and economic conditions of their members through the advancement of their vocational interests by industrial activities. To secure these essential objectives every territory should be subject to the Right of Association (Non-Metropolitan Territories) Convention, 1947, the Freedom of Association and Protection of the Right to Organize Convention, 1948, and the Right to Organize Convention and Collective Bargaining Convention, 1948.

The committee was firmly of the opinion that from the point of view of promoting good industrial relations, collective bargaining between free trade unions and employers was the most desirable system of determining wages and conditions of employment. Every effort should therefore be made to facilitate the development of independent trade unions and employers' associations. In particular, it was important that the conditions of registration should not be so onerous as to discourage the formation of unions. Labour departments should exist in

[7] C. Wilfred Jenks, *The International Protection of Trade Union Freedom* (London, 1957).
[8] Committee of Experts on Social Policy in non-Metropolitan Territories, 1955 Report.

each territory and they should be charged, *inter alia*, with the responsibility of advising and assisting workers and employers to form appropriate organizations and to run them efficiently. Where necessary, governments should legislate to protect workpeople from anti-unionism.[9]

Governments should also help to provide facilities for the education of workers and the training of trade union members in the principles of trade unionism; management and trade union officials should be assisted to study labour–management problems and human relations in industry. Steps should be taken to see that union officials had an opportunity to become acquainted with the best methods of trade union administration, keeping of proper accounts, holding of meetings and organizing of recruiting drives. Employers and unions ought to be encouraged by the governments to establish permanent machinery for the purpose of collective bargaining and the discussion of other important issues that might affect industrial relations.

In order to encourage the development of harmonious relations, provision should be made in every territory for the establishment of arrangements for helping the unions and employers to arrive at agreements. A conciliation service ought to be available and the governments should have power to investigate the causes of disputes; and arbitration facilities to suit the circumstances of the parties should be available. Governments themselves should observe good industrial relations practice and, wherever possible, should consult trade unions and employers before introducing legislation affecting their interests.

In effect, the attitude of the I.L.O. to the labour problems of the non-metropolitan territories has been that in principle they are no different from the problems which have existed in most other countries. Allowances have to be made for the state of economic and social development of the territories, but what has been tested by experience elsewhere as the most appropriate way of achieving the basic objectives of advancing and protecting the interests of labour is equally valid for the less industrialized, less well-developed parts of the world. The British Government and employers and trade unions have been entirely in accord with this policy.

[9] Committee of Experts on Social Policy, 1955 Report.

The Application of I.L.O. Standards by the British Government

When considering the extent to which the I.L.O. has exerted pressure on governments of British territories, it must be borne in mind that the British representatives to the I.L.O. have played an important part in shaping its policy. Since the substance of the International Labour Code has been in accord with prevailing British ideas, there has been an identity of viewpoint that has been satisfactory to the British Government. Such differences as have occurred have sometimes been on matters of principle, but more often the issues have been either the appropriateness of the timing or the suitability of a particular method for achieving an agreed goal.

The British Government ratified all the nine conventions passed with special reference to non-metropolitan territories up to the end of 1947. It has not yet ratified three of the four conventions passed since 1955. The reasons for not ratifying a convention are not only that current standards fall short of the convention and it is feared that it would be a difficult task to bring them up to the level required, but also that standards have already been achieved in different ways from those envisaged in the convention. There may also be other reasons why a convention is not ratified; for example, that the industry with which it is concerned does not exist in the territory.

Unfortunately, it does not always follow that once a convention is ratified steps will at once be taken to ensure that it is translated into effect. There have been very considerable differences in the application of conventions and other standards suggested by the International Labour Code.[10] In this respect the record of the British Government, by comparison with most other countries, is good, but it is difficult to understand why some conventions, for example the Freedom of Association and Protection of the Right to Organize Convention (1948), and the Right to Organize and Collective Bargaining Convention (1949) have not been applied in every British non-metropolitan territory when they have been applied in most of them.[11]

Failure to ratify a convention does not necessarily mean that

[10] In the case of Hong Kong only one declaration has been made since 1946, whereas nine have been made for Mauritius.

[11] In this respect there have been some surprising exceptions. For example, these two conventions have been the subject of declarations for all the West Indian territories with the exception of Antigua, Barbados, Monserrat and St. Kitts.

the ends it exists to promote are not regarded as good, nor does it mean that they have not been achieved. In both of the cases cited trade unions and collective bargaining have been actively encouraged and developed in all the territories irrespective of the I.L.O.'s conventions.

The British Government was one of the first to ratify the Forced Labour Convention of 1930, and in 1931, following a declaration applying it to every British dependency, a circular despatch was sent to all governments in the Colonies drawing their attention to its significance. Legislation in most territories followed soon afterwards; by 1943 the British Government was able to report 'in only eight territories is forced or compulsory labour, as defined by the convention, still permitted by law and each of these territories renders a special report each year on the subject which is transmitted to the International Labour Officer'. The attention of colonial governments was also drawn in 1931 to other international labour conventions and the 'obligation placed upon His Majesty's Government and Colonial Governments to ensure that effect was given by legislation to their requirements'.[12]   These conventions, which it was reported in 1943, had led 'to the enactment of a wide range of colonial legislation are the Minimum Wage-fixing Convention; the important group regulating the employment of women, young persons and children in industrial undertakings and the employment of young persons and children at sea; the group of maritime conventions concerning (a) indemnity for unemployment caused by the loss or foundering of a ship, (b) minimum age for young persons employed as trimmers and stokers, and (c) medical examination of young persons employed at sea; and the convention dealing with the protection against accidents of dock workers.'[13]

The legislative action that soon followed this despatch in Nigeria has been pointed out in a study made by the I.L.O. of the influence of international labour conventions on Nigerian Labour legislation.[14] 'Ordinance No. 17 of 1932 amended the Labour Ordinance of 1929 with a view to imple-

---

[12] *Labour Supervision in the Colonial Empire 1937–1943* (H.M.S.O. Colonial No. 185, 1943).
[13] *Op. cit.*
[14] 'Influence of I.L.O. Conventions on Nigerian Legislation', *International Labour Review*, Vol. LXXXII, No. 1, July 1960.

menting the Night Work (Women) Convention, 1919, and the Night Work of Young Persons (Industry) Convention, 1919. . . . The following year effect was given to the Minimum Age (Sea) Convention, 1920, by Ordinance No. 12 of 1955, which again followed closely the wording of the Convention.'

The I.L.O. survey gives many other examples of the influence of I.L.O. conventions on the development of the law in Nigeria relating to the employment of women, children and young persons, maritime employment, wages, safety, workmen's compensation and labour inspection.

There have, of course, been deviations from the standards laid down by the I.L.O. It is recognized in Article 35 of the I.L.O. constitution that it may not be possible for a convention to be applied in full owing to special factors and the local conditions in each territory. The immediate reaction of most colonial governments to a new convention has been that they are not ready for this legislation, and they have often sought to have its application modified. It has frequently been necessary to concede that a convention would not work in the circumstances of this colony or that, but equally often when colonial governments have had to yield to pressure from Whitehall they have found that they could, in fact, carry out the legislation. It is true that enforcement has not always reached the ideally desirable standard, usually owing to genuine difficulties of administration. Nevertheless, the evidence is overwhelming that the standards set have materially assisted local labour departments in their work and advanced the protection of workers against the more gross forms of exploitation.

It is sometimes suggested that the I.L.O. method of setting standards which are only applicable after they have been ratified leaves an easy escape route for any country that wishes to avoid accepting the obligation to observe such standards. This is quite true; it is also true that even when a convention has been ratified it may not be applied in full, since the I.L.O. has been compelled to leave room for some flexibility in the administration of the convention. However, the *Report of the Committee of Experts on the Influence of Article 35 of the Constitution of the I.L.O. on the Application of Conventions in Non-Metropolitan Territories*, made to the Governing Body in 1959, shows convincingly that the conventions have been of considerable importance.   The report states that 'the legislation on labour matters in the large majority of non-metropolitan territories is full of evidence of conscious effort to ensure correspondence between the terms of the territorial law and those of the relevant international labour instrument.   Sometimes this goes to the extent of quoting in full the terms of the Convention concerned which itself becomes the law of the territory.   In other cases the terms are scrupulously followed except on points on which it has been necessary to take account of local conditions.   Official publications, despatches to and from Governors, speeches in the legislature, all indicate a consciousness of obligations contracted and a desire to try as far as possible to meet international labour standards.'[15]

The Report of the Committee of Experts of the I.L.O. confirms that the British Government has treated its obligations under Article 35 seriously.[16]   Apart from fulfilling its obligations to communicate the texts of conventions which it has ratified to its self-governing territories, the report cites three factors which have tended to stimulate the adoption of legislation in United Kingdom non-metropolitan territories conforming to the international labour standards accepted by the British Government.   The first of these has been the practice of addressing circular despatches to colonial governors, drawing their attention to international labour conventions and suggesting measures to give them effect;   the second has been that of sending model labour laws, prepared by the Colonial Office, which take into account developments in international labour standards;   and the third has been the constant contact between the Colonial Office and the labour departments of the territories, including especially the visits of the Labour Adviser to the Colonial Secretary and his assistants, to advise on legislation and administration.

The conventions and recommendations of the I.L.O. have, in effect, been used by the Colonial Office as a means of bringing pressure on colonial governments to advance labour standards. However, in some cases where particular colonies have showed resistance to making the changes called for by the I.L.O. conventions, the British Government has, perhaps, allowed their arguments to carry too much weight.   This attitude has re-

[15] Geneva: March 1959.   [16] *Op. cit.*

flected the desire not to override strongly-held local views, but it might have been a wiser course to insist that they should bring their law into line with these international standards.

Thus, while it cannot be said that the I.L.O. has set the pace of social advance in the British colonies, since examples in most fields of development in trade unionism and industrial relations already existed long before the I.L.O. laid them down as standards that ought to be applied, its work has complemented British and local forces pushing in the same direction.

The Application of I.L.O. Standards after Independence

Some of the evils which the I.L.O. set out to eradicate and which British policy had abolished in the colonies, such as forced labour, restrictions on the right of work-people to form and join unions of their own choosing and severe limitations on the right to strike, have appeared again since various territories have been given their full independence.

Practices denounced as outrageous invasions of human liberty by ardent nationalists during the time that a territory was under colonial rule are now sometimes justified as being perfectly reasonable in an under-developed country. It has even been suggested that I.L.O. conventions designed to protect the interests of work-people in under-developed territories are insulting if applied after independence has been achieved. The Abolition of Forced Labour Convention of 1957 is regarded by the political leaders of some newly independent territories as a nuisance. Under this convention every member of the I.L.O. undertakes to suppress and not to make use of any form of compulsory labour:

  a. as a means of political coercion or education or as a punishment for holding or expressing political views or views ideologically opposed to the established political, social or economic system;
  b. as a method of mobilizing and using labour for purposes of economic development;
  c. as a means of labour discipline;
  d. as a punishment for having participated in strikes;
  e. as a means of racial, social, national or religious discrimination.

In order to speed up the rate of economic growth certain under-developed tropical territories feel that it is necessary to compel workers to join 'labour brigades' to carry out urgently required public works.   The arguments in favour of this policy are plausible, as plausible as they were when put forward by colonial governments, since it must be conceded that it is sometimes difficult to obtain an adequate supply of labour, at a price the government can afford, to ensure that building projects are completed.   Nevertheless, it may well be that the workers conscripted suffer hardship, and it may further be questioned whether it is just that a section of the community should lose a fundamental liberty in the interests of economic advance.   The answer to this question will depend on the relative value put on liberty and the achievement of an economic aim.   This is a classic conflict and one that is not easily resolved.

It is possible that it is desirable to make some concessions to the views of those who put material progress before freedom, but there can be no doubt that if men could have both freedom and a high rate of economic growth this is what they would most desire.   Any concession to those who would sacrifice liberty in the interest of economic growth must, therefore, be a retreat from the ideal of having both objectives realized.   It may be necessary to make some retreat, but in spite of suggestions that the principles adopted after decades of struggles in Europe and the colonial territories themselves should be abandoned, the I.L.O. has not yet been persuaded that it should condone violations of its fundamental principles.   Time might well have to be given to a country which violates the International Labour Code to re-establish the status of its laws and behaviour, but during any period when a country has deliberately set aside standards prescribed and accepted under the International Labour Code, it is surely right that it should be obliged to report at regular intervals on its progress towards the establishment of standards that have been approved by free societies all over the world.

At the first African Regional Conference of the I.L.O. held in Lagos in December 1960, the question of the application of the Freedom of Association and Protection of the Right to Organize Convention, 1948 (No. 87), and the Right to Organize and Collective Bargaining Convention, 1949 (No. 98), was discussed. Reference was made to the importance of protecting the right to strike, the desirability of safeguarding the right of association, and of the problems arising out of a multiplicity of trade unions, the circumstances when it was appropriate to introduce the 'check-off' system and the need to prevent racial discrimination. There was a reluctance on the part of many delegates to condemn compulsion, and evidence of a readiness to apply different standards to similar actions in countries under colonial government and countries enjoying independence. However, the resolution finally adopted by the conference called upon the Governing Body of the I.L.O. to make a solemn appeal to all African states to ratify and keep under review the conventions dealing in particular with forced labour, penal sanctions, freedom of association and right to organize, collective bargaining and discrimination.

An important change in the emphasis of the work of the I.L.O. has been going on steadily since the end of the second world war. The main work of the I.L.O. prior to 1947 lay in establishing the standards to which good governments and employers should conform. With the increased interest in the problems of the under-developed territories and the emphasis in Europe on economic recovery following the second world war, attention shifted from the setting of standards to the means of implementing them. Technical assistance has always been one of the functions of the I.L.O., but with the inauguration of the Marshall Plan for assisting European economic recovery and the Expanded Programme of Technical Assistance designed to help the under-developed territories, the work of the I.L.O. in this field became much more important. With the establishment of special United Nations funds for the provision of technical assistance and the promotion of economic development, the I.L.O. was able to draw on far greater resources than it could provide from its own budget.

The object of the technical assistance programme is to make available to the less-developed territories the skills and expertise of the more advanced countries. In order to avoid any fear of neo-colonialism, technical assistance is only provided when a territory asks for it. To avoid any suggestion of charity or that a country is being forced to accept advice against its will, the I.L.O. requires a recipient government to meet a substantial part of the cost of a project, and the government concerned is free to decide how the advice it receives can be best used.

The usual procedure when the I.L.O. receives a request for technical assistance is to send particulars of qualified persons to the government seeking assistance; the government is then free to make its own selection. In the decade from 1950 to 1960, 930 experts were recruited from 56 countries for this work. During this period these experts were sent on 1,364 missions in 82 countries. Advice through the missions has been given on a very wide range of problems, such as how to raise productivity, improve social conditions, revise laws affecting labour and trade unions, establish social insurance, provident and sickness schemes, employment bureaux and statistical services.

There has been some criticism that the recipient governments have not supported the work of these technical experts adequately with their own efforts and that there has been a tendency to look upon the I.L.O. and the other international agencies as reserves of aid to be drawn upon continuously. On the other hand, permanent gains can be claimed, and it is likely that this work of the I.L.O. will continue to be of the highest importance for a long time to come, if for no other reason than the fact that help received through the I.L.O. is politically often more acceptable than it would be if received directly from the country supplying the technical expert.

The I.L.O. has also done a great deal of educational work. In addition to the opportunity of attending the annual labour conference, the I.L.O. annually provides a number of fellowships and study grants which enable trade unionists and government officials to study in Britain, Europe, America and elsewhere. A number of worker trainee scholarships have also been awarded. A recent development in the educational work of the I.L.O. has been the establishment of an International Institute of Labour Studies at Geneva, which was opened in 1962.

The influence which the I.L.O. exerts on the course of industrial relations in the countries of the tropical Commonwealth has been real and important in the past, and through its educational and regional activities its importance is likely to continue in the future. The annual conference of the I.L.O. provides an opportunity for trade union, employer and government representatives to meet together and in committee to come to grips with problems of common interest. In the last decade the member states have followed the practice of inviting to the conference observers from the non-metropolitan territories for which they are responsible. These observers have exactly the same rights as full members to take part in the debates and committee sessions, apart from the right to vote. The British Government has made extensive use of this facility; it has invited representatives from all the more important territories of the tropical Commonwealth, thus enabling them to become familiar with the work of the I.L.O. at first hand. The bringing to Geneva of leaders of unions, representatives of employers' organizations and governments of colonial territories has resulted in personal contacts and friendships that have been an important factor in the development of labour policy and practice in London and the colonies.

With the evolution of colonial territories into independent nations, the membership of the I.L.O. has markedly changed. No longer is the I.L.O. primarily composed of the more advanced industrial countries, as it was before the second world war. Like the United Nations, the I.L.O. is numerically dominated by the under-developed territories, and this has led to a growing emphasis on their problems. This shift in the orientation of the I.L.O. is having an important influence, not only on the work of the organization, but also on its basic philosophy. There is a growing pressure from representatives of the less-developed territories, supported by a number of British, European and American intellectuals, that is being exerted against the traditional policies and principles of the I.L.O. It is suggested that the basic features of the International Labour Code were developed to meet the needs of the advanced industrial countries of the world and that they are not applicable to the problems that face the less-developed countries. This conflict of fundamental values is bound to become of greater significance and will have a profound influence on the future of the I.L.O.

A further development that has important implications for the future of the I.L.O. was the decision of the U.S.S.R. to become a member of the Organization. This development has inevitably brought the 'cold war' into the I.L.O. Fortunately

s

it has not so far influenced the character of the practical work of the Organization, but it has influenced the character of the discussions at the annual conference and led to a constant conflict between the Western employers' representatives and those from communist states.   From the point of view of the character of the I.L.O. this development is important, since the communist bloc has deliberately sought to exacerbate relations between the Western states and the under-developed territories.   Although representatives of under-developed territories tend to support Soviet-inspired proposals that are calculated to embarrass the free countries, they are well aware of the political motives of the sponsors.   The Overseas Employers' Federation, faced by this problem, has counselled its members not to follow the view of those who would have the employers withdraw in protest, but to take the positive line of participating fully in the work of the Organization and combating the twisted image of the West presented by the communist spokesmen.[17]

The contribution of the I.L.O. to the future development of the systems of industrial relations and the advancement of the welfare of workers in the newly independent territories of Africa, Asia and other parts of the world, will depend to a great extent on how these challenges are met.   The work of the I.L.O. in this respect will be not less important to those countries which were previously responsible for the non-metropolitan territories and which inevitably retain a considerable interest in the attainment by their one-time colonies of advanced standards in conditions of employment.

[17] Overseas Employers' Confederation, *op. cit.*

Part Three

The Development of Labour Law

CHAPTER 10

THE LEGAL REGULATION OF TRADE UNIONS

TRADE union enactments in the colonies have generally been based on metropolitan legislation, though with some minor modifications to meet the special conditions of the colonies, and with the major difference that registration has been made compulsory. However, colonial legislation has not always followed the British pattern closely and there have been other significant influences.

There are two recognizable strains in colonial trade union legislation; the first is exemplified by most of the Caribbean territories, West Africa and some of the smaller colonies, whose legislation stems more or less directly from the British Acts of 1871 to 1917, and in most cases, parts of the 1927 Act. The second strain, affecting mainly the territories of South-East Asia and—within the last decade—East Africa, has its origin in the British Acts, but it has been influenced by an ordinance passed in Ceylon in 1935 which owed something to the India Trade Union Act of 1926 and Trade Disputes Act of 1929, and by other ideas that may be traced to South Africa, Australia and the United States.

This second strain has developed much more freely than the first, and the laws in this group, while retaining the basic principles of protection contained in British and Indian legislation, have been much more detailed and explicit, and also generally more restrictive in content than those of the West Indies or West Africa. There are one or two other territories, such as the Bahamas, which do not fit into either of these patterns, and trade disputes legislation, as distinct from laws regulating trade unions, departs considerably from British precedents in many territories.

The historical development of trade union legislation in the colonial territories is far from straightforward. The first modern trade union acts were introduced by Jamaica in 1919 and by British Guiana in 1921. Previously a few rather outdated acts relating to trade disputes and combinations of workmen, had been passed in the West Indies. A notable example of this was in the Bahamas, which, in 1839, had enacted the operative parts of the British Combination Laws Repeal Act, and the Amendment Act of 1825, followed, in 1860, by the Molestation of Workmen Act of 1859. The latter act was repealed in the Bahamas in 1943 when the first trade union act was passed,[1] but the former continued to exist until 1958. In a few other West Indian territories sections of the criminal or penal code had been based more or less recognizably on Section 7 of the British Conspiracy and Protection of Property Act of 1875, protecting individuals and property against threats, intimidation and certain other nuisances. In some places, e.g. Barbados and British Guiana, the Criminal Code had created the special offence of assault by members of an unlawful conspiracy to raise wages, which carried high penalties.

On the whole, then, before 1930, legislation affecting trade unions was either rather antiquated, by British standards, or else it was non-existent. The only exceptions in the whole Colonial Empire were Jamaica and British Guiana. However, in most African territories which were annexed or whose status was changed in some way after 1871, it was provided that the jurisdiction of the courts should, so far as the circumstances of the territory permitted and until modified by subsequent local legislation, be in accordance with the common law, doctrines of equity and statutes of general application in England. The exact provisions differed from territory to territory, and in East Africa in particular the courts were left with very wide discretion as to the applicability of any aspect of the law. However, it seems to have been established that any trade unions formed in Northern Rhodesia, where the English statute law as it stood in 1911 was applicable, automatically had the protection given by the British acts of 1871, 1875, 1876 and 1906. It is possible that British trade union law, as it stood in 1900 and 1902 respectively, might also have been applied in Nigeria and Nyasaland, but as it happens, Northern Rhodesia was the only one of these territories in which really strong and active trade

---

[1] This repeal may have had the effect of withdrawing some protection from combinations of agricultural workers and domestic and hotel workers in the Bahamas, since these were excluded from the provisions of the 1943 Act.

unions had appeared before local legislation had superseded these provisions. After the European Mineworkers' Union had been established in Northern Rhodesia in 1937, the territorial government took steps to remove some of the existing anomalies. An Imperial Acts Extension Ordinance was passed in that year, which applied, in addition to the previous acts mentioned—the British Acts of 1913, 1917 and 1927 and the Industrial Courts Act of 1919—to Northern Rhodesia and provided for the appointment of local officials to carry out the functions of the Chief Registrar of Friendly Societies and of the Minister of Labour under those Acts.[2]

Following the recommendations in the circular despatch in 1930 from the Secretary of State for the Colonies, legislation began to be passed in other territories. In 1932, Trinidad and Tanganyika each enacted their first trade union statute. Ceylon followed in 1935 with an ordinance based mainly on the India Trade Union Act of 1926; Kenya and Uganda enacted legislation in 1937, Nigeria in 1938, Barbados and Sierra Leone in 1939, the Federated Malay States, the Straits Settlements and the Gambia in 1940, and Ghana in 1941. In most other territories trade union legislation was in force by 1943. Stimulation to this development had been given, in the first few years of the war, by the requirements of the Colonial Development and Welfare Act of 1940. In 1941, a model Trade Union Ordinance, based upon British legislation and practice, was adopted, and sent out to all colonies in a circular despatch from the Secretary of State. The model provided for the compulsory registration of trade unions; it declared that they were not unlawful because their objects were in restraint of trade, and it gave them immunity from actions in tort. Protection was provided against actions on grounds of conspiracy or inducement of breach of contract and the model also legalized peaceful picketing and removed any liability for interfering with the business of another person.

None of this first series of measures has remained unamended. Many laws have been completely re-enacted, some of them several times. As will become apparent, the general course of

[2] The registration facilities under this Ordinance were never used, however, and no trade union was registered in Northern Rhodesia until 1950 following the passing of the Trade Union Ordinance in 1949. See also Northern Rhodesia Hansard, No. 63, Col. 140.

events has been to make the legislation more comprehensive; for instance, the provisions of protection for pickets, or the protection of unions against actions for tort, which might not have been included in the original statutes. The tendency has been to make the legislation more complicated, more explicit, and sometimes to attempt to control more vigorously the constitutional forms and internal administration of trade unions and also their industrial and political activities. This is particularly noticeable in the legislation in the Bahamas, and in some of those statutes whose original inspiration departed from the spirit and intention of British legislation.

Nevertheless, almost all trade union statutes in these dependencies contain in recognizable form the more important protective features of British trade union legislation since 1871, though in some instances modified and reduced. The one outstanding difference in principle is in the case of registration. In the British Acts of 1871 and 1876, voluntary registration was introduced for the benefit of such trade unions as wished to avail themselves of it, and it gave to these unions additional privileges such as the ability to transfer property to new trustees without the need for conveyance, deed or assignment, etc.; the ability to dispose of the funds of deceased members on the basis of nominations; the provision of specific legal sanctions against defaulting officers, and special procedure in cases of fraud; the ability to sue and be sued in their own names, and the conclusive evidence given by the fact of registration that a trade union is a trade union as defined by statute, and has the privileges of a trade union. In return for these privileges, certain additional obligations were put upon registered unions, in that restrictions were placed on the form of their constitutions, they were required to make certain returns, and some restrictions were placed upon the way in which they should amalgamate and the way in which they might change their names.[3] The choice of whether or not to accept these additional privileges and obligations was, however, left entirely to the unions.

In the dependent territories since 1930, on the other hand, registration has usually been compulsory.[4] It is no longer a

---

[3] See N. A. Citrine, *Trade Union Law* (London, 1950).
[4] In Jamaica registration was voluntary until 1938 and in British Guiana until 1943. Up to 1944 Nyasaland's ordinance simply empowered the governor to

means to obtain additional rights and privileges as in Britain, but is a condition that must be fulfilled before a trade union may exist legally. Compulsory registration has been generally thought desirable as an additional protection to ordinary union members, as for example, against unscrupulous fly-by-night labour leaders, who are interested only in agitation, or in inducing employees to part with their money for the leader's own benefit. There have been other reasons besides this for compulsory registration, particularly the fact that with compulsory registration more would be known of protest movements, and colonial governments would be better able to keep a finger on the pulse of industrial organization and industrial feeling, so that they would know when and where industrial trouble was likely to break out, and which organizations and leaders they must watch. Thus, responsible organizations might be encouraged and the public interest protected. The extent to which it has been thought necessary to take legal powers to regulate the internal affairs of the unions has varied considerably from territory to territory. The obligations associated with registration are generally wider and more positive than those under voluntary registration in Great Britain; in some cases there is an obligation to open books, accounts and cash for inspection by the registrar whenever he wishes; elsewhere there are restrictions on trade union membership, and on the type of person who may become an officer of a registered union; in a few places restrictions have been imposed on the use of trade union funds, and so on.

There are other differences between the legal position of trade unions in the United Kingdom and in dependent territories, which do not emerge clearly simply from an analysis of the content of specific trade union and industrial relations legislation. The provisions of criminal law may differ from British criminal law in some territories in such a way as to affect the activities of trade unions and trade unionists. The law relating to sedition, assault and unlawful assembly may, for instance, be more widely known in the dependencies. Police

---

make provision for registration of trade unions. In Northern Rhodesia registration was voluntary until 1956, but after 1949 all trade unions were bound to notify the registrar of their existence, and after 1953 they were required to make annual returns to him.

powers, especially in the last decade in some territories in East and Central Africa, have been increased far beyond those in the metropolitan country. Territories such as Malaya, Kenya, and to a lesser extent Northern Rhodesia, Nyasaland and Uganda, have found it necessary to make extensive use in recent years of emergency powers, which in some cases have hindered what would otherwise have been the lawful activities of trade unions, and made organization difficult.

Legal obstacles have, however, been a relatively minor obstruction to trade union development in most territories. Social, economic and political factors have played a far larger part in determining the rate of trade union growth. The fact that the authorities have been given more powers to regulate the activities of the unions than has been the case in Britain, does not mean that there has been a complete departure from the principle that the law should permit the unions to develop with as little legal hindrance as possible.

Certain territories, of which perhaps Mauritius, Fiji and the Bahamas have been the most notable, were so strongly opposed to the development of trade unions that they refused to pass the legislation called for by the Colonial Office. Mauritius adopted instead an Industrial Associations Ordinance modelled on the South African Conciliation Act of 1937. The Commission of Inquiry which had been appointed in 1937, after disturbances on the sugar estates, had recommended, with some reservations, that the law should be changed to permit the development of trade unions. Mauritius employers were utterly opposed to the step, and when introducing the Industrial Associations Ordinance the governor stated that we have 'decided to avoid such terms as "Trade Union" which have behind them a legacy of interruption of work, strike and dislocation of industry. It is true that this practice in civilized countries is more or less a thing of the past and has been superseded by conciliation. Nevertheless, in the minds of many people a stigma is attached to the term trade union.' The ordinance permitted only scheduled classes of workers to form associations; agricultural workers, domestic service employees, teachers, and government servants were excluded, strikes were forbidden and a system of compulsory conciliation and arbitration was established. The Director of Labour and Registrar of

Industrial Associations was given wide powers to regulate the activities and administration of the Associations.

This ordinance was gradually amended during the next few years as events demonstrated the failure of the government's policy of discouraging the development of trade unions; also the colony might have found itself excluded from benefiting under the Colonial Development and Welfare Act had a change in the law not been made.[5]

In 1953, the Government of Mauritius announced that after consultation with the Colonial Office it had been decided to introduce new legislation. The government declared that it had come to this decision in the light of the following facts. 'Trade Unionism has developed to an appreciable extent in this Colony since the enactment of that Ordinance and, on the other hand, important changes have recently been brought about in Trade Union legislation in the U.K. It has consequently been found desirable that our own legislation in this respect should be amended to meet the present situation and also to correspond more adequately with modern ideas of Trade Unionism.'[6] The new Act was far more liberal than the old legislation; it brought the law more or less into line with that of the United Kingdom, with the exception that it provided for compulsory registration, prevented anyone convicted of fraud or dishonesty from holding office for ten years and required that a candidate for union office must have been normally and regularly engaged for a period of eighteen months in one of the industries represented.[7]

The Definition and Legal Status of Trade Unions

In most colonial legislation a trade union is defined in terms very similar to those used in the British Trade Union Acts of 1876 and 1913.[8] Indeed, in British Guiana and Trinidad the definitions are virtually the same in both form and word-

[5] See Chapter 7.
[6] White Paper on the Trade Unions and Trade Disputes Bill, Mauritius, February 1953.
[7] The Trade Union Ordinance, 1954.
[8] Jamaica, Ordinance No. 35 of 1938; Gambia, No. 5 of 1940; Aden, No. 34 of 1942; Nyasaland, No. 5 of 1944 (repealed 1958); Uganda, No. 6 of 1941 and No. 9 of 1943 (repealed 1952); Kenya, No. 1 of 1943 (repealed 1952); Tanganyika, No. 30 of 1941 (repealed 1956); Barbados, No. 5 of 1950; Sarawak, No. 10 of 1947; Hong Kong, No. 8 of 1948; Mauritius, No. 36 of 1954.

ing.[9] Variations in the definitions are relatively minor for the most part, but there was a major departure from the British pattern in the Bahamas, when in its Trade Union Act of 1943, this colony excluded domestic servants and agricultural workers. This Act was repealed in 1958, and in the new Act the term 'Trade Union' refers to 'any combination or association of workmen', thus removing any legal limitation on the right of any class of workers to organize. The definitions of a trade union made in the legislation of South-East Asia and East Africa also differed quite considerably from the position in Britain.

The first ordinance in this series, introduced by Ceylon in 1935, defined a trade union as any association or combination of workmen or employers, whether temporary or permanent, having among its objects one or more of the following:

(a) the regulation of relations between workmen and employers, or between workmen and workmen or between employers and employers; or

(b) the imposing of restrictive conditions on the conduct of any trade or industry; or

(c) the representation of either workmen or employers in trade disputes; or

(d) the promotion or organization or financing of strikes or lockouts in any trade or industry or the provision of pay or other benefits for its members during a strike or lockout.

Any federation of trade unions was also covered by the ordinance. The definition of a trade union was thus made both wider and more explicit than that in British legislation. The objects referred to did not necessarily have to be the principal objects of the association, and it would appear that any

[9] *Section 16, Trade Union Act, 1876*

'The term trade union means any combination, whether temporary or permanent, for regulating the relations between workmen and masters, or between workmen and workmen, or between masters and masters, or for imposing restrictive conditions on the conduct of any trade or business, whether such combination would or would not, if the principal Act had not been passed, have been deemed to have been an unlawful combination by reason of some one or more of its purposes being in restraint of trade.'

Section 2, Trade Union Act, 1913

'The expression "trade union" for the purpose of the Trade Union Acts . . . means any combination, whether temporary or permanent, the principal objects of which are under its constitution statutory objects.'

association which was involved incidentally in providing benefits for its members during a strike would be covered, although
such an association might well not fall within the British
definition of a trade union.   On the other hand, a trade union
in Ceylon does have to be an association of workmen or of
employers (this is not actually specified in British legislation).

The Ceylon definition was adopted by the legislation of the
Straits Settlements and the Federated Malay States in 1940,
although the latter did not include among its statutory objects
the imposing of restrictive conditions on a trade or industry.
In Ceylon and in Singapore, which as a successor state of the
Straits Settlements has inherited its legislation, the definition
has never been changed.   In the Federation of Malaya, however, where the 1940 Federated Malay Straits Ordinance has
been applied, federations of trade unions were excluded from
the definition, when, in 1948, special provisions were introduced, following the communist uprising.   When the trade
union legislation of Malaya was re-enacted in 1959, after
independence, the definition of a trade union was limited to
associations or combinations of workmen or employers whose
place of work is in the Federation; and the membership of a
union is confined to those who work in similar[10] trades,
occupations or industries.   The objects are those specified in
the 1940 Ordinance.   The aim of the Malayan Government,
which had the full support of the Malayan T.U.C., was to prevent the establishment of omnibus unions which would again
become mainly political organizations.   By restricting membership to workers employed in Malaya, unions under communist
control in Singapore were prevented from organizing in the
Federation.

Legislation in the three East African territories has been
different from that adopted elsewhere in several respects.
Under the 1952 Ordinances of Kenya and Uganda, and the
1958 legislation of Nyasaland, certain types of combination
other than trade unions were given legal recognition.   Under
the 1958 Nyasaland legislation a trade union was defined in
much the same terms as in Britain, but in a later section of the
ordinance it was provided that an employee's association, by

---

[10] 'Similar' is defined as 'similar in the opinion of the registrar', but an
appeal may be made to the minister against this opinion.

which, as in Uganda and Kenya, is meant a subsidiary organization, 'shall not, by reason only of its having as its principal object or one of its principal objects the regulation of relations . . . be deemed to be a trade union'.

In the territories influenced by the Indian Trade Union Act there is a provision that goes beyond British practice, in that a trade union may not only sue and be sued, but it may also be prosecuted in its own name.[11]   Damages may be exacted and fines may be recovered by distraint against any property of the trade union other than the benevolent funds.[12]   It is also made explicit in all these territories that 'every trade union shall be liable on any contract entered into by it or by any agent acting on its behalf' provided that the contract is not void or unenforceable at law, and provided also that it is not one of the agreements between unions and their members or between one union and another, which are unenforceable in Great Britain under the 1871 Act.

The Legal Regulation of Union Membership

There are very few legal restrictions in Great Britain on any employee or employer joining or forming a trade union. Almost the only limitations of this sort have been those on members of the police force, and those under the 1927 Trades Disputes and Trade Unions Act (repealed in 1946), which placed restrictions on the type of trade union which established civil servants might join.   In many territories, however, more extensive restrictions have been placed on the classes of persons who may become trade union members.   This greater legal interference with the right to form and join any type of union is to be explained by a desire to prevent outsiders using unions for their own ends and, in particular, a wish to confine unions' activities to industrial affairs, so as to prevent them from being used for mainly political purposes.   These objectives have not been desired solely by colonial governments—they have also been seen as desirable by the elected governments of territories after they have attained independence.

In Nigeria, for example, since 1943 it has been unlawful for

---

[11] In Ceylon, Malaya and Singapore an unregistered trade union may not sue.
[12] In Kenya the benevolent funds are not exempt.

any members of the Nigeria police force, or any native authority police force, and for employees of the prisons department of any native authority prison, to be members of a trade union, and the rules of every trade union must contain provisions stating the qualifications of membership 'which shall require *inter alia* that no person shall be eligible for membership of the trade union unless he is, or has been, regularly and normally engaged in the industry which the trade union represents'.

For three years after the 1958 Bahamas Act came into force no union could include hotel and building employees unless membership was confined solely to these categories of workers. The object of this limitation was to discourage the establishment of a large general union under the banner of the Bahamian Federation of Labour. This unusual provision was designed to give the workers in the two most important industries of the islands an opportunity to develop their own forms of organization on an industrial basis. Had they failed to take advantage of this protection, the restriction would automatically have lapsed at the end of the three-year period, and left them free to belong to an omnibus organization. There is now no other legal prohibition on membership, but the duty is laid on the Chief Industrial Officer, who also has the function of registrar, to encourage the formation of trade unions each representing a particular industry, or alternatively, a particular craft.

In Malaya and Singapore, the law, going a step further, stipulates that no government officer or servant may be a member of a trade union, or may be accepted by a trade union into membership, but the Head of State can exempt specified sections of government officers from these provisions, to such extent and under such conditions as he may decide. In the Federation of Malaya no one receiving state education may be a trade union member unless he is over 18 years old and a *bona fide* workman. This provision is directed against the attempts which have been made by Chinese communists to recruit schoolchildren into unions for political purposes.

In East Africa an attempt has been made to prevent the growth of inter-territorial organizations by limiting union membership to residents within each territory. It was feared that a union with headquarters outside the boundaries of a particular territory would be in a position to evade its legal responsibilities. The limitation imposed has meant that services common to all the territories, such as railways, post and telecommunications, have had to contend with separate unions. This situation has met with criticism from outside bodies which have given strong support to inter-territorial organizations. Should the East African territories eventually form a political federation this would invite the development of parallel trade union organizations.

In Kenya and Tanganyika (though not in Uganda) there has been an additional restriction, similar in effect to that in Nigeria and the Gold Coast, that members must be actually engaged in an industry or occupation with which the union is directly concerned. Since 1959 this has applied in Tanganyika only on first joining or forming the trade union.

Nyasaland was free of these restrictions on membership until 1958, since when, under new legislation, members of unions have actually to be engaged in the industry or occupation concerned, and must be employed or resident in the protectorate; and persons in established pensionable posts under the Crown may not, unless exempted by an order of the Governor in Council, belong to a trade union which has members who are not employed by the Crown.

In Hong Kong anyone is free to join a union, but, except with the consent of the Governor in Council, no registered union shall be affiliated or connected with any organization established outside the colony. This does not, in practice, prevent the unions from having close links with the Communist and Nationalist Chinese movements, as has been shown in previous chapters.

Freedom of Association and Protection of the Right to Organize

Clearly in British legislation there is very real freedom for almost all employees to organize in trade unions, and legal actions cannot be brought against them solely on the grounds that they are so organizing. There is also almost complete freedom under the law to associate as they wish—in large groups or small—or not to associate at all. The territories overseas, while following the British tradition, have departed from it in a number of respects. In the first place, there is compulsory registration, which can itself be said to limit freedom of association to some extent, in so far as it imposes constitutional and other restrictions on the form of all trade unions, and prevents any activities being carried on during the delays (which on some occasions have been considerable) prior to registration. However, after careful consideration the I.L.O. came to the conclusion that compulsory registration did not in itself constitute a violation of the principle of freedom of association, so long as the refusal to register was not based 'on anything other than failure to observe certain formalities which are not substantive in character'. The United Kingdom non-metropolitan territories were placed in this category.[13] In the early days of trade union legislation, for instance, in East Africa in the 30's and early 40's, and originally in Sierra Leone and Nigeria, the registrar had quite arbitrary powers to refuse registration, which might have seriously limited the right to organize at all.

Such arbitrary provisions now no longer exist, but in some territories, particularly in East Africa and South-East Asia, the grounds on which the registrar may refuse to register a trade union are quite extensive—extensive enough in some cases to restrict freedom of association. In Sierra Leone the registrar must refuse, and in Kenya, Uganda, Nyasaland, Mauritius, Hong Kong, North Borneo and Sarawak, he may refuse to register a union if he is satisfied that another union already registered is sufficiently representative of the whole of the interests which the applicant union seeks to serve. Such a union, therefore, no longer has the right to exist. With much the same effect, in the Bahamas since 1958, permission may not be given for the formation of a trade union, nor may the trade union be registered, if the Chief Industrial Officer 'is satisfied that the whole or a substantial proportion of the interests . . . are sufficiently represented by any other trade union or trade unions registered under this Act and duly functioning'. The aim of the legislation is clear; it is to try to prevent the creation of large numbers of small competing unions, none of which are likely to be capable of effective representation and many of which will not be viable. Sensible as the object may be, the

[13] I.L.O. Committee of Experts (Report III, Part IV), 43rd Session, Geneva, 1939.

T

method of attaining it is in conflict with British practice, and
the I.L.O. Committee of Experts have taken the view that it is
violation of the Freedom of Association Convention. The
Colonial Office has urged the I.L.O. to recognize that in this
question there is a real difficulty. The trade union movements
of Sierra Leone, Uganda and Kenya are by no means eager to
see the law amended, since it has been effective in preventing
the formation of splinter unions, and they regard it as a valuable
protection for existing organizations.

The matter was discussed at the first African Regional Conference of the I.L.O. held in Lagos, in December 1960, and it
has been remitted to the I.L.O. for further examination.[14]
What is being sought is a means of providing a safeguard against
an arbitrary decision, by some procedure which would perhaps
transfer final power from the registrar to some quite independent body on which employers and trade unions might be
represented, which could make a final decision that would be in
the interests of the workers, the trade unions and the development of good industrial relations. Whether an appropriate
formula which is not in conflict with essential principles can be
found remains to be seen.

Ghana, since independence, has gone much further than this
in restricting the right to organize as members wish. Under
the Industrial Relations Act of 1958, the Trades Union Congress
was established and the unions constituting the Congress were
set out by name. These specified unions were given many
rights and privileges which were denied to other unions, but at
that stage there was no prohibition of the right of unions which
were not members of the T.U.C. to exist, though they had little
power to do anything effective. However, in 1959 an amendment to the Industrial Relations Act forced all unions which
were not statutory members of the T.U.C. either to amalgamate
with the T.U.C. affiliates or to dissolve themselves. No new
union can be registered in Ghana unless it has the written consent of the minister of labour. Since 1960 only 16 named trade
unions may exist in Ghana, and as will be shown below, there is
now legally enforced compulsory trade union membership for

[14] In order to comply with the I.L.O. Convention 87, article 2, Sierra Leone
has agreed to a request to amend its legislation which entitles the registrar to refuse
to register a union 'if he is satisfied that another union already registered is sufficiently representative of the interests concerned'.

some employees in Ghana, while certain groups are not permitted to organize at all.

The converse of these statutory limitations on freedom of association is shown in the provisions designed to secure and protect the right of employees in practice to join or not to join the trade union of their choice.   This protection has various aspects.   There may be provisions to prevent employers from forbidding their workmen to join a trade union or from discriminating against them because of their trade union activities; or there may be restrictions on the right of employers and trade unions to impose a closed shop, forcing the workmen to join trade unions if they are to continue to be employed.   There may be defined 'unfair labour practices' which are forbidden by law.

In Great Britain there has been no provision in modern statutes declaring that the freedom of employers or workers to associate together as they wish is protected in any way.   There is, for example, nothing in law to prevent any employer from deciding that he will not give employment to trade union members,[15] and no statute is concerned to define or limit the right to negotiate a closed-shop agreement.   Although the courts have made certain rulings on the extent of the admissibility in Common Law of a closed-shop agreement, the scope for such arrangements is fairly wide.   It has been suggested, however, that the 'closed shop' is a violation of the basic concept of freedom of association and ought to be prohibited by law.[16]

A number of territories have sought to protect the unions against discrimination, in this respect following American and European practice rather than British.

In Northern Rhodesia from 1949 and in Uganda from 1952, employers were forbidden to 'make it a condition of employment of any employee that [he] . . . become a member of a trade union or other organization representing employees in any industry'.[17]   Any such conditions were void, and any employer

[15] Except in the case of certain nationalized industries which have a statutory duty to enter into relations with their trade unions.

[16] John A. Lincoln, 'Human Rights in Industry' in *Agenda for a Free Society* (London, 1961).

[17] This provision was copied by Northern Rhodesia in the first place from a similar provision in the Industrial Conciliation Act of Southern Rhodesia, which

imposing such a condition after the ordinance had come into force, was liable to a penalty of £50 or a year's imprisonment, or both. The same section provided that no employee should be prohibited by law from being or becoming a trade union member, or subjected to any penalty by reason of his membership. The object of these provisions was to protect the individual trade unionist against discrimination by employers who were hostile to union membership. In Britain unions have preferred to rely upon their own strength rather than on the law for protection against anti-union employers, but overseas, where the unions were in their infancy, their ability to defend their members against discrimination could not be presumed.

In 1958 Northern Rhodesia changed the law concerning the right to negotiate a closed-shop agreement in any undertaking.[18] Under these new provisions a closed-shop agreement is defined as 'an agreement between an employer and a trade union whereby the employer agrees not to employ or not to continue to employ either generally or in certain classes of employment, persons who are not members of such a trade union'.

To be legally valid, a closed-shop agreement must secure the support of the membership in a secret ballot. At least three-quarters of the paid-up members must record a vote at the ballot, and at least two-thirds of those voting must vote in favour. If these conditions are not fulfilled, or if a ballot is not held within one month of the agreement being signed, it becomes null and void. A new ballot must be held at least once every three years during the life of the agreement.

Every ballot under these provisions is to be supervised by the labour commissioner, or a person appointed by him, and he may make rules for the conduct of the ballots. At least 48 hours before each ballot the union must submit a statement to the labour commissioner of the number of paid-up members of the

in turn had been taken over from the 1937 Industrial Conciliation Act of South Africa. In the two latter statutes, however, the provisions did not apply to Africans.

[18] These provisions, and certain others, were passed in 1958, following the recommendations of the Honeyman Commission, which had inquired in 1957 into industrial unrest in the Northern Rhodesian mining industry. They were fairly obviously aimed at the Northern Rhodesian Mineworkers' Union, which was the only union in the territory both strong enough to have imposed a closed shop and willing to do so.

union at the end of the preceding month; this is to be taken as the basis for calculation of the proportion of members voting.

In the same amending ordinance there are two further provisions relating to closed-shop agreements. Firstly, anyone, except a trade union member at a properly convened trade union meeting held in a building, who is guilty of 'declaring, instigating or counselling a strike or lockout or instigating or advocating the continuance' of a strike or lockout, involving employees working under a closed-shop agreement, before 'all the provisions for the settlement of disputes . . . have been exhausted' is liable to a fine of £100, or six months' imprisonment or both. The provisions for settlement mentioned in this section are (a) that notification of a dispute must have been made to the chief secretary, (b) either 14 days must have elapsed without action having been taken, or else a conciliator must have been appointed, (c) either the conciliation proceedings must have been terminated by him for at least 14 days, or one or both parties must have withdrawn from the conciliation proceedings.

The second new provision is directed towards the protection of union members against unreasonable suspension or expulsion from a trade union which works under a closed-shop agreement. Any suspended or expelled member of such a trade union, as an alternative to any other legal remedy which he may have, may appeal within 30 days against his suspension or expulsion, either to an independent person to be agreed on between the member and his union, or failing that, to a magistrate of the district in which he is employed. The suspension or expulsion is then not to have effect until the appeal is determined. The person hearing the appeal has full discretion to inquire into all relevant matters; he may require the attendance of witnesses or the production of documents, take evidence on oath and award costs against either party. He is not to uphold any suspension or expulsion unless he is satisfied that the action taken by the trade union concerned was in accordance with its rules, and just and equitable having regard to all the circumstances of the case. His decision is final and binding on both parties, except that there may be an appeal to the High Court on a question of law only.

The Nyasaland Ordinance of 1958 deals much more simply

with the closed shop, while retaining the general form of the Northern Rhodesian provisions regarding freedom of association. In Nyasaland an employer may not make it a condition of employment that an employee shall neither be nor become a member 'of any or of a particular trade union', and the penalty may be imposed, not only on an employer but also on 'every person who attempts to compel, persuade or induce any employer' to impose such a condition.[19] Although similar in wording to the Northern Rhodesian law, this provision can, in fact—and this was admitted by a government spokesman in the second reading debate on the Bill[20]—be used to prevent the formation of a closed shop. Its main purpose was, however, not to prevent the closed shop, but to prevent employers from discriminating against union members.

The corresponding Bahamas legislation prohibits any agreement which seeks to make union membership a condition of employment. No employer, under the 1958 Act, may make it a term or condition of employment that a workman shall be or shall not be a member of any trade union. Any such term or condition is void, and the employer is liable to a penalty of £50.

The Bahamas Act, influenced by United States labour law, also has provisions protecting employees from certain unfair labour practices. No employer may dismiss any workman, or reduce his remuneration or alter the terms or conditions of employment to less favourable ones, or alter his position relative to other workmen to his disadvantage, because of the fact, or because he suspects or believes *either*: (a) that the workman has given information which he is required to give about terms and conditions of employment to the labour board, a labour officer or wages council, a conciliator or arbitration tribunal, or to his trade union or a trade union officer, or has given evidence in a court of law; *or* (b) that he is a member or has been a member of a trade union or has taken part outside working

[19] A virtually identical provision was taken over by the Colony of Aden in 1960.
[20] Nyasaland—Proceedings of 2nd Meeting of 73rd Session of the Legislative Council, p. 231. The Acting Solicitor General summed up his explanation of this clause as follows: 'Therefore the clause can be said to be designed to achieve two main objects. It attempts to preserve the right of the worker to belong to any trade union of his choice, or to belong to no trade union at all if he so prefers. It also protects the employer against having closed shops imposed upon him by workers or by union officials.' He earlier stated that the clause would cover 'recognition disputes between unions', but this is only true in so far as such disputes are connected with attempts to establish a closed shop.

hours, or, with the consent of the employer, in working hours, in lawful trade union activities. Any employer victimizing a employee in one of these ways may be fined £100, and the court may order the employee's reinstatement or award him damages or both.

The same Act also seeks to prevent employers from influencing trade unions by paying them money, and in the course of this attempt it prohibits the check-off entirely. No employer may 'pay any sum to any trade union', and it is illegal to make it a term or condition of employment that the employer shall deduct from wages any sum for payment to any trade union, or that the employer shall pay any sum himself. Any such term or condition is void. This provision runs counter to American practice and to the general trend in colonial legislation from about 1957, since when the policy has generally been to modify any provision in labour legislation, particularly the protection of wages clauses, likely to make voluntary check-off facilities illegal.

A more comprehensive example of legislation against unfair labour practices by employers is the Industrial Relations Ordinance of Singapore, passed in 1960. Here, anyone who induces or tries to induce another person not to become a trade union member or officer, or to leave a trade union, by offering, procuring or conferring an advantage on him, is liable to a fine of $2,000 or a year's imprisonment, or both. An exception is made for men who have been promoted to managerial positions on condition that they should not continue to be members or officers of a trade union. Similar penalties are provided for an employer who discriminates against any prospective employee because that person is, or proposes to become, a trade union officer or member, or that he will be entitled to the benefit of some legally binding collective agreement or award, or that he has appeared as a witness in some proceedings under the Industrial Relations Ordinance. Further, if an employer dismisses an employee, injures him in employment, alters his position to his prejudice, or threatens to do any of these things because the employee:

(a) is or proposes to become a trade union member or officer;

(b) is entitled to the benefit of a legally enforceable collective agreement or award;

(c) has appeared or proposes to appear to give evidence in some proceedings under the Industrial Relations Ordinance;

(d) is, as a trade unionist, openly dissatisfied with working conditions;

(e) is a member of a trade union which has served a notice proposing a new collective agreement, or has registered a trade dispute or is a party to statutory negotiation;

(f) has absented himself from work on trade union duties after having applied for leave and had it unreasonably withheld or deferred, or

(g) has absented himself, after informing the employer, in order to carry out duties as a member of the Industrial Arbitration Court;

then the employer is liable to the penalty of $2,000 or 12 months' imprisonment, and may be ordered by the Court to pay the employee the amount of wages lost, and to reinstate him in his former position.   If the facts are proved the onus is put on the employer to prove that his motive was not the one alleged.

In Singapore, and in certain other territories also, trade union members have some legal protection against unfair actions being taken against them by their trade unions or by trade union officials.

In Ghana, since independence was achieved in 1957, there have been very rapid developments in these matters based on the inter-related principles of compulsory negotiation, definition of and statutory remedies for unfair labour practices, provisions for compulsory check-off facilities and, since 1960, compulsory trade union membership for many categories of employees.   On the whole, the trend here has been to restrict rather than protect freedom to associate.

Certain trade unions in Ghana since 1958 have been able to obtain certificates giving them the right to force the employers concerned to negotiate with them over defined 'industrial matters', including, from 1958–60, the practice of the union shop.   These rights to certification and compulsory negotiation are described in more detail later.   They do not apply to public servants, municipal or local-government employers, or teachers, and they are hedged about with restrictions on the right to strike and with provisions for compulsory arbitration in certain circumstances. Since 1960 negotiations on the principle of the closed shop have become redundant, since it has been made compulsory for all employees covered by a certificate to negotiate to be members of the certificated trade union. No one who is not a member of that trade union may be kept in the employment concerned for more than a month.

The new Ghana legislation also gives the minister power to force employers to grant check-off facilities to a trade union, or in practice, to the T.U.C. Under the labour ordinance of pre-independence days, a clause stipulating that all wages must be paid in cash without any deduction can be varied by the commissioner of labour, who may authorize specific deductions. This device had been used in a few cases after 1956 to permit employers and trade unions to enter into check-off agreements. The 1958 Industrial Relations Act made more definite provision. The minister for labour might, after application by the Trades Union Congress, make an order permitting a trade union to request an employer to deduct specified sums from the wages of his employees, as listed in the notice given by the trade union, and to pay over specified proportions of the sums to the T.U.C. and to the union concerned, and, after 1959, a proportion of the union's allocation could be paid directly to a given branch as well.[21] The employer could not refuse such a request when approved by the minister, but any employee could, at least in theory, contract out of the deductions if he wished. Under the 1959 amendment a request to contract out had to be in writing, and a copy of the request had to be sent to the trade union. It is interesting to note that even at this stage the union was not required to prove that the employees listed in the request for check-off facilities were members of the trade union or were willing to allow the deductions to be made, and there was no protection against the manifest danger of

[21] Originally these provisions applied only to unions to which a certificate to negotiate had been issued. By the 1959 amendment, however, they were made to apply to any trade union, and hence unions of public servants, teachers and local-government employees could also get compulsory check-off facilities, if the Minister approved. There are, however, some inconsistencies between this amendment and the 1960 provisions for check-off, and the present situation seems again to prevent these unions from participation in compulsory check-off.

victimization by union members and officials of anyone known to have contracted out of the check-off arrangements.

In 1960 certain changes were made and some loopholes closed. The T.U.C. was given more control over the funds to be collected. Now the union can only require the employer to deduct sums, specified by the T.U.C., and not by the union, from the wages of employees who are covered by a certificate to negotiate. Other employees seem to be excluded altogether. All the money is now to be paid direct to the T.U.C.[22] The trade union no longer has to list the names of the employees from whom dues are to be deducted, since all employees covered by a certificate are *ipso facto* members. The statutory provision for contracting out has been repealed, but the statutory form of request to the employer still includes the proviso that it shall not apply to an employee who gives notice that he does not wish it to apply.[23]

Unfair labour practices were also defined in the 1958 Industrial Relations Act. Since the latest amendment in 1960 an unfair labour practice consists of:

(*a*) continuing to employ someone who is not a trade union member, if he is in a class covered by a certificate to negotiate and would share in the benefits of a statutorily enforceable collective agreement;

(*b*) discrimination against a person in respect of his employment or conditions of employment because he is a trade union member or officer;

(*c*) seeking to induce an employee to refrain from being or becoming a trade union member or officer by intimidation, dismissal or threats or penalties or by the inducement of a wage increase or other favourable alteration in conditions;

(*d*) taking part as an employer in the formation of a trade union, or making a contribution to a trade union with the intention of influencing it;

(*e*) failure by an employer to permit a full-time trade

---

[22] However, the 1959 provision that the union may direct that a proportion be paid to a branch of the trade union has not been deleted. It may be that this was an oversight.

[23] Such an employee might well be forced to leave his employment under the provisions for compulsory union membership, particularly if the rules of his union made no other provision for collecting dues from him.

union officer with members among his employees reasonable facilities for conferring with him or with the employees on matters affecting the members concerned;

(f) activities by an employee which are intended to cause a serious interference with the business of his employer;

(g) attempts by a trade union officer or other person to recruit members on the employer's premises without his consent;

(h) attempts by a trade union officer or other persons to confer with an employee on trade union matters on the employer's premises during working hours without his consent.

An Unfair Labour Practices Tribunal is set up to determine cases of alleged unfair labour practices. If the tribunal finds a person has been engaged in such a practice it may forbid him to continue or repeat the specified activities constituting the practice; it may require an employer to restore a victimized worker to his position and pay him compensation; or it may order a trade union which has received a contribution from an employer to refund it. The tribunal's decisions are subject to appeal to the High Court on the grounds that the evidence did not justify the findings, or that its order was unjustified.

Registration Procedure

There was originally a good deal of uniformity in the provisions for compulsory registration, but the different territories have tended to diverge as time has passed.

The present-day provisions in the Asian and East African territories are rather more detailed than elsewhere. In Ceylon and Kenya, for instance, every new trade union must apply to be registered within three months of its formation and in Malaya and Singapore within one month, but the registrar may grant an extension of various periods not exceeding an aggregate of six months. The legislation defines the date on which a trade union is deemed to be formed as 'the first date on which more than six employees or employers, as the case may be, agree in writing to become or to form' a trade union.

The way in which the members of a trade union must set about getting it registered varies comparatively little from place to place, and the procedure is generally based on that of the

United Kingdom. Usually any 7 members of a trade union may register or apply for registration on a prescribed form, provided certain other provisions are complied with. But in Nigeria, Ghana and Sierra Leone this can be done by any 5 members; in Nyasaland 15 signatures are required; in Tanganyika an application must be signed by at least 4 members if it is a trade union of employers and at least 20 if it is an employees' union; and in the Bahamas by not less than 3 members of an employers' organization and 7 of a trade union of employees. Application must invariably be accompanied by one or more copies of the rules, and by other particulars which vary somewhat from territory to territory, but which usually include the titles and names of the officers and the addresses of the head office of the union.

In the West Indies, much as in Great Britain, the registrar, subject to such powers as he possesses to refuse registration, is bound to register the trade union [24] if he is satisfied that the regulations have been complied with. This was originally the case in West Africa also, but now all four West African countries provide that on receipt of an application the registrar will publish a notice in the Gazette, and after six months' delay will consider any objections that have been brought to his notice. On being satisfied that no proper objection has been raised, that the union has complied with the regulations and, in Nigeria and Sierra Leone, that the provisions of its rules have been carried out 'so far as may be', and subject to his powers to refuse registration, he must register the union. In the Gambia he must consider the observations and objections of the labour officer, as well as any other objections, and in Ghana there is a list of specified persons, including the labour commissioner, whose observations are to be considered. Since 1959, however, no union may be registered in Ghana without the specific written consent of the minister.

Of the South-East Asian and East African territories, those in Africa have changed their provisions a large number of times. A feature common to almost all of them throughout has, however, been the power of the registrar to call for further information to satisfy himself that the application complies with the

---

[24] But in Trinidad, and formerly in Barbados, he has first to give permission to an applicant to take steps to form a trade union.

regulations or that the union is entitled to be registered.[25]   The fact of registration or of a refusal to register must also be notified in the official Gazette in all these territories.   In Kenya and Uganda the registrar may, at his discretion, defer registration, in which case the union becomes a 'Probationary Trade Union'.[26]   Between three and twelve months later, either on the application of the union, or of his own motion, he must further consider registration of the union, and if he is then satisfied he may register it.   On registration, the registrar must in every case issue to the trade union a certificate of registration.   The certificate, unless proved to have been withdrawn or cancelled, is conclusive evidence that the regulations with respect to registration had been fulfilled.

Provision is now made everywhere for some form of appeal against a refusal to register a trade union, and the development has generally been in the direction of making the registrar's powers rather less arbitrary.   Nevertheless, in some places the grounds on which he now can refuse registration are extensive, and the grounds for refusal are, of course, very important when registration is a pre-condition of existence of a trade union.

One rule common to Britain and all the territories is that no union may be registered under a name identical with that of any other existing trade union, or so closely resembling it that it is likely to mislead.   As for the other grounds of refusal, most West Indian territories follow British precedent fairly closely.

The conditions of registration imposed in Ceylon are more restrictive than in most of the other territories.   The registrar may not register a trade union, membership of which is open to public servants, (a) unless the rules restrict eligibility for membership, or for any office, to public servants employed in one specified government service, or of one specified class; (b) unless there is a rule that the union may not amalgamate or federate with any other trade union; and (c) unless there is a rule that there is to be no political fund.   In Sierra Leone there is also the important provision that the registrar must not register a union if he is satisfied that any other union already registered is sufficiently representative of the whole of the

[25] The exceptions were Kenya from 1943 to 1952 and Nyasaland up to 1958. This provision is based on s. 7 of the India Trade Union Act.

[26] Probationary trade unions have all the rights and privileges of registered trade unions, except that they may not amalgamate.

interests which the applicant union seeks to serve. Similar provisions have been adopted in Northern Rhodesia, Mauritius, Kenya, Hong Kong, North Borneo and Sarawak.[27]

The laws in East Africa and Nyasaland have given the registrar the widest powers of all. The 1952 Kenya legislation stipulated that he may refuse to register a trade union for any of the following nine reasons:

(a) the union has not complied with the provisions of the ordinance or of any regulations;

(b) any one of the principal objects of the union is unlawful or conflicts with a provision of the ordinance (in 1956 this was amended in Kenya to 'any one of the objects');

(c) the union is used for unlawful purposes;

(d) any other trade union already registered is sufficiently representative of the whole or a substantial proportion of the interests in respect of which the applicants seek representation (a procedure being provided for notifying other unions appearing to serve the same interests, and inviting objections);

(e) the principal purposes of the union are not in accord with those set out in the definition of 'trade unions';

(f) the union consists of persons engaged in more than one calling and its constitution does not contain suitable provision for the protection and promotion of their respective sectional industrial interests;

(g) the funds are being applied in an unlawful manner, or on an unlawful object, or any object not authorized by the ordinance or any regulations;

(h) the accounts of the unions are not being properly kept;

(i) the secretary or treasurer of the union is, in the registrar's opinion, incapable by reason of not being sufficiently literate in English or Swahili, of carrying out adequately the duties of his office.

The Uganda Ordinance of 1952 provided that the registrar may refuse registration for any of the first eight causes listed above. The 1956 Tanganyika legislation allowed a refusal on

[27] In Kenya the registrar is only to register a trade union 'if he is satisfied that none of the grounds on which . . . registration may be refused exists'; elsewhere in East Africa he *must* register the union, subject to discretionary powers to refuse.

all but the fourth and ninth of these causes; and also for the additional reason that the union seeking registration was a branch of an unregistered trade union.[28] In 1959 Tanganyika added yet another cause—namely that anyone on the executive of the union was not qualified to be an officer or executive member, or had not been properly appointed or elected. In Nyasaland all the grounds which are valid in Kenya apply,[29] and also two others: that the body applying is a branch of a trade union (not, as in Tanganyika, an unregistered trade union), or that its rules contravene any provisions of the ordinance, or do not provide for, or are inconsistent with, any matter for which provision must be made in the rules.

Since the early 1950's it has been the aim of Colonial Office policy to limit the discretionary powers of registrars of trade unions and to ensure as far as possible that their quasi-judicial functions are confined to the straightforward implementation of specific provisions laid down in the law—in other words, to remove any fear that the registrar's opinions of the purposes of any group coming to register a trade union, or of the personalities concerned, might be a factor affecting the right to be registered. So long as the law had been complied with, the application to be registered as a union had to be accepted as valid. Also, pressure was constantly exerted from the Colonial Office to ensure that in all territories there was the right of an appeal from the registrar to the courts and not to the administration.

Appeals from a Refusal to Register

The provisions for permitting an appeal from a refusal to register are obviously of great importance when registration is compulsory. Provision is now generally made for an appeal to the courts from the registrar's refusal to register.[30]

Originally in Nigeria, Sierra Leone and Hong Kong an appeal could be made only to the governor,[31] but since 1943 in

[28] This is meant to prevent branches of inter-territorial unions from being formed inside Tanganyika.

[29] But in Nyasaland it is not specified in which language the secretary and treasurer must be literate.

[30] However, there was no provision at all for an appeal in Jamaica from 1919 to 1959, in Tanganyika from 1932 to 1939, nor in Sierra Leone from 1939 to 1944. In the Gambia, from 1932 to 1940, there was no provision that the registrar might refuse registration, and therefore the question of appeal could not arise.

[31] This was also the case in Uganda from 1937 to 1939, in Kenya from 1937 to 1943 and Malaya from 1940 to 1948.

Nigeria an appeal may be made to the Supreme Court (now the High Court) and a further appeal against this court's order to the Nigerian Federal Supreme Court, formerly the West African Court of Appeal. This does not apply, however, when there is a refusal to register on the grounds that the union's name contains certain words which are not allowed. In this one case, in both Nigeria and Sierra Leone, the aggrieved union may have the matter referred to the governor, whose decision is final. Hong Kong has provided for appeals to the courts since 1961.[32]
. Elsewhere, the appeal is generally directly to the High Court, or Supreme Court, whose order is to be final. Generally, the court is empowered to make whatever order it thinks proper, including an order as to the costs of the appeal, and the registrar is entitled to be heard on the appeal. In Northern Rhodesia an appeal may also be made (presumably by a rival union or an aggrieved employer) from a decision by the registrar to register a trade union. Under the Industrial Associations Ordinance of Fiji the registrar's decision is final; there is no right of appeal except when a registration certificate is cancelled.

Powers to Cancel or Suspend Registration

Registrars of trade unions in Britain may cancel or with-draw the certificate of registration of a registered trade union on certain grounds laid down in the Trade Union Act Amendment Act of 1876, where the registrar's decision is final; an additional cause is stipulated in Section 2 of the 1913 Trade Union Act, from which an appeal is allowed to the High Court. Apart from a group of Asian and East African territories, the statutes do not depart very significantly from the British provisions, although, with the exception of Singapore, an appeal to the courts is now always provided against cancellation of a certificate.

The grounds for cancellation laid down in the 1876 Act are repeated without substantial change in most West Indies territories, West Africa and Northern Rhodesia. In effect, no certificate may be withdrawn or cancelled except by the registrar in the following cases:

[32] Trade Union Registration Ordinance, No. 52, 1961.

(a) at the request of the trade union;

(b) on proof to his satisfaction that—

    (i) the certificate has been obtained by fraud or mistake;

   (ii) the registration is void because one or more of the purposes of the trade union is unlawful;

  (iii) the union has wilfully and after notice from the registrar violated the provisions of the ordinance; or

  (iv) it has ceased to exist.

A further reason for cancellation in Ghana, Ceylon, Malaya and Singapore is that the union is being conducted for unlawful purposes. In Northern Rhodesia and many West Indies territories, but not in Jamaica, the certificate may be cancelled for the additional reason introduced into British legislation in 1913, namely: 'if the constitution of the union has been altered in such a manner that in his opinion the principal objects of the union are no longer statutory objects, or if in his opinion the principal objects for which the union is actually carried on are not statutory objects'. In the East African territories of Kenya, Uganda and Nyasaland a certificate may be withdrawn if a union whose constitution provides for the protection and promotion of sectional interests has failed to carry out these provisions. In Uganda, Tanganyika and Nyasaland registration may be cancelled if the accounts are not being kept in accordance with the provision of the ordinance. In Kenya and Tanganyika registration may be cancelled if it is discovered that the objects for which the union is actually carried on are such that had they been declared before registration, the registrar could properly have refused registration. In Tanganyika and Nyasaland it is a cause for cancellation if the trade union is a branch of an unregistered trade union, i.e. one whose headquarters is outside the territory concerned. In Tanganyika the registrar may cancel the certificate if he is satisfied that anyone on the executive is not qualified for office or for committee membership or has not been properly elected or appointed; or that the union has failed to revoke any rule he has previously refused to register. The registrar has power to suspend, as well as to cancel the registration of a trade union in Kenya and Uganda.

U

The procedure to be followed on cancellation of a registration has not varied very much from territory to territory. Generally, not less than two months' notice in writing, specifying briefly the ground for the proposed cancellation, must be given by the registrar before it can take effect.[33]

In the territories of Asia and East Africa, at any time within the period of the notice, the trade union may show cause in writing against the proposed cancellation or suspension, and if this is done the registrar 'may hold such enquiry as he may consider necessary in the circumstances'. If the union fails to show cause, or, having shown cause, does not satisfy the registrar, he may cancel or suspend the registration as the case may be, and make an order specifying briefly the grounds for the cancellation or suspension. After the order has been served the union has the right to appeal to the courts. In Malaya, since 1959, after the registrar has served a trade union with a notice that he proposes to cancel the registration, the minister may order that the union be prohibited from carrying on such activities as he may specify. The order must be published in the official Gazette and a copy must be served on the union, or posted up at any building it occupies as well as at the nearest police station. An appeal against the minister's order lies to the High Court.

The foregoing account of the conditions a trade union must observe to satisfy the registrar may give the impression of a far greater degree of regulation than is the case in practice. In many territories the registrar has in fact exercised little more authority than the registrar in Britain, and it is apparent from the very large number of trade unions that have been registered in many of the territories that the legal obstacles are not so formidable as they might appear.

In most territories the registrar has often been reluctant to cancel the registration of a union that has been in breach of the law. There are a number of explanations for this apparent leniency. A technical breach of the law is easily committed, and most unions in the territories have probably been in violation at some stage of their experience. Had registrars invoked their powers rigorously, it would have been necessary to close

---

[33] In Kenya and Uganda if the registration is to be suspended only one month's notice is required.

down a very large number of unions, and such a course would
have been in direct conflict with the general policy of encouraging and helping the development of trade unions urged
on the territories by the Colonial Office.   Quite often, when a
registrar has considered cancelling the registration of a union,
he has been counselled by the department of labour to give it
time to conform.   The aim has usually been to warn, to persuade and to help a union to meet the requirements of the law
rather than to impose the harsh penalty of cancelling a union's
right to exist.

Another reason why registrars have often been slow to de-
register unions arises out of the fact that very frequently trade
unions are the least important of their responsibilities.   Registrars have often had to accept the registration of unions as an
additional job which has turned out to have features that involve them in the political and social pressures associated with
the rise of trade unionism.   Moreover, the British tradition, in
which the registrar has probably been brought up, is one in
which the functions are almost purely formal.   This tradition
does not harmonize with the rigorous enforcement of what
could be rather onerous and restrictive rules.

Although moderation has been the general practice of registrars in most territories, there have been instances where a
tougher policy has been pursued.   The problem of enforcement
has probably been most acute in relation to the law regulating
the administration of trade unions, especially the administration
of their finances.

*Legal Regulation of the Constitution and Administration of Trade
Unions*

In Great Britain the rules of every registered trade union
must state: the name of the organization and its place of
business; its objects and the purposes for which its funds may
be used; the way in which members may qualify for benefit,
and the way in which fines and forfeitures may be imposed;
the manner of making, altering, amending and rescinding
rules; the means of appointment and removal of its committee, trustees and other officers; the way in which funds
are to be invested, and the audit of accounts; the right of all
persons having an interest in the funds to inspect the books and

the names of members; and the manner of dissolving the trade union.[34]

The object of these requirements is the encouragement of good administration, and the protection of the interests of union members from abuse or simply from the possible inefficiency of those responsible for the conduct of the union. Similarly, colonial territories have tried to achieve these objectives by legal requirements designed to promote sound administration and good government. These requirements, set forth in the British Acts, must be provided for in the rules of all registered trade unions in most of the territories, but there have been differences in approach to the various regulations; for example, some territories specify that the rules must state the subscriptions and dues to be paid, and there must be provision that full and accurate accounts be kept by the treasurer. In Nigeria and the Bahamas the rules must state the qualifications for membership, which require that only those who are or have been regularly engaged in the industry (or craft) concerned may be members; they must limit membership of the committee and qualifications for office to those who are members of the union, except that the chairman or secretary need not have been regularly employed in the industry; and they must provide for the keeping of a nominal roll showing the occupations and, where possible, the employers of all members. Trade union rules in Jamaica must state the duties of the committee, trustees, treasurer and other officers. In the Bahamas they must, in addition to the other provisions, provide for the circumstances and manner in which membership may be terminated and they must also provide for the holding of meetings and the keeping of minutes of the proceedings of all meetings. In Northern Rhodesia the rules must provide for 'the right of every member to a reasonable opportunity to vote'

---

[34] Furthermore, in Great Britain any trade union, registered or unregistered, whose funds are to be applied for political purposes must have rules, approved by the registrar, stating that payments in furtherance of political objects must be paid out of a separate political fund, that any member may be exempt from contributing to such a fund, that such a member shall not be placed under any disability by reason of his exemption and that contributions to the political fund shall not be a condition for admission to the union. Only in the territories which permit the establishment of political funds (Ghana, Northern Rhodesia, Trinidad and Barbados) do the same provisions apply. Elsewhere, either there are no provisions at all or, as in Asia and East Africa, political objects are completely forbidden.

and for the disqualification of a member from voting and from receiving benefits if his subscription is in arrears. These last two territories also require provisions regarding secret ballots. Originally, Northern Rhodesia required trade union rules to provide for 'secrecy of any ballot regarding the taking of a decision to call a strike or lockout', although the ballot was not then mandatory. In 1958 this was deleted and it was made necessary for the rules to provide for 'the holding of a secret ballot requiring the assent of a two-thirds majority of those voting, before a strike or lockout is called'.[35] The Bahamas law goes somewhat further. Since 1958 the constitution of every trade union and employers' organization must provide for the taking of a secret ballot for the election or removal of officers and committee members, the amendment of the constitution and the taking of strike or lockout action. Before a constitution is approved, the chief industrial officer must be satisfied that it gives every member an equal right and a reasonable opportunity under it to vote, and that the secrecy of the ballot is properly secured.[36]

All of the territories of Asia and East Africa follow the British law, but they also require that the designation of the officer or officers responsible for the custody and investment of funds shall be stated, and also the manner of the disposal of the funds available at the time of dissolution. The four East African territories require, in addition, provisions for 'the re-election of officers at intervals of not more than three years'; for the appointment or election of trustees; for the right of any member to a reasonable opportunity to vote; and for the disqualification of a member from voting and receiving benefits if his subscription is in arrears. In Kenya, Uganda and Nyasaland the rules must state the amount of subscription and fees payable by members. In Tanganyika, Uganda and Nyasaland, if union members are engaged in more than one trade or calling, there must be provision in the rules for the protection and promotion of the respective industrial interests of each section. In Uganda and Nyasaland provision must be made

---

[35] Elsewhere in the ordinance it is provided that all such ballots shall be supervised by the labour department, which may make rules governing their conduct.
[36] A ballot taken on the question of strike action must, in fact, be supervised by an officer of the department of labour, and the chief industrial officer may declare void a ballot taken for either of the other purposes mentioned.

for any contributory provident or pension funds to be kept separately. Only Nyasaland insists that the procedure to be followed when imposing any fine or forfeiture, or when proposing to expel a member, must be laid down. Kenya demands that the secretary and treasurer must be sufficiently literate in English or Swahili to be able to perform their duties adequately. Unions in Tanganyika are obliged to state in their rules that the treasurer must keep full and accurate accounts; and in Uganda the conditions under which honorary members may be appointed must be stated.

Malaya, since 1949, has required a statement of the manner of establishing and dissolving any branch of the trade union, and the way in which a branch and its accounts shall be administered. Since 1959, provision must be made for the election of an executive committee, and, subject to this, for the nomination, appointment or election not only of officers but also of trustees and employees. There must also be a provision prohibiting the employment of the secretary by any other trade union. Further interesting requirements in the latest Malayan legislation are that the rules must contain provisions for the deciding of disputes (a) between a member of the union or aggrieved former member, and the union, or a branch, or an officer; (b) between the union and one of its branches; (c) between a branch officer and his union; and (d) between any two or more branches.

All of these Asian and African territories except Ceylon and Hong Kong also have requirements for the holding of secret ballots. Singapore and the East African territories require unions to have rules that make a secret ballot necessary in the election of officers, amendment of rules, strikes, dissolutions and any other matter affecting members generally. In Malaya a secret ballot is now required only for the amendment of any rules that would increase the members' liability to contribute, or that would reduce the benefits to which they are entitled; for the election of delegates to a general meeting before the imposition of a levy; before amalgamation with or transference of engagements to another union, and before joining a trade union federation. It is now required that there be rules on the procedure for holding ballots, securing the secrecy of ballots and preserving the ballot papers.

Qualifications and Statutory Duties of Trade Union Officers

British legislation does not lay down the qualifications that trade union officers must have. The rules of a registered trade union simply have to provide for 'the appointment and removal of a general committee of management, of a trustee or trustees, treasurer and other officers', but apart from that there is no control at all over a trade union's activities in appointing its leaders. The West Indies and Gambia follow the English provisions with no great change, except that in British Guiana officers may not be trustees. Elsewhere, however, the restrictions go further. In the African territories generally no one may be a secretary or treasurer who, in the registrar's opinion, is incapable, through illiteracy, of carrying out his duties.[37] The law often insists that all, or a specific proportion, of the officers must actually be engaged in the industry or occupation with which the union is connected. In all cases the registrar, the minister or governor in council has discretionary power to allow exceptions.

In Kenya no one who has ever been convicted of any crime involving fraud or dishonesty may be a trade union officer. This was also the case in Tanganyika until 1959, but the disqualification is now limited to a period of three years after conviction, payment of fine or completion of sentence, whichever is the later. In Northern Rhodesia and Nyasaland the same prohibition applies for five years after conviction. In Uganda there is a life disqualification for offences involving fraud or dishonesty in connection with trade union funds. In Malaya no one may be an officer who has previously been an executive committee member of a trade union whose registration was cancelled on the grounds that the funds had been expended unlawfully or on an unauthorized object; or who has ever been convicted of criminal breach of trust, or extortion or intimidation, or of any offence which, in the minister's opinion, renders him unfit to hold office.

In the four East African territories no officer may at the same time be an officer of another trade union; and in Malaya no one who is not a Malayan citizen may be a trade union officer,

---

[37] In Kenya illiteracy of one of these officers justifies refusal to register a trade union.

unless the minister is satisfied (*a*) that the union concerned has no political objects, and (*b*) that it is needed to represent non-residents.

Some qualifications for trustees are laid down in the legislation of the Asian and East African territories. Usually, every trustee must be a member of the union, but in Uganda any bank may act as trustee, and in Nyasaland a non-member approved by the registrar may do so. In Kenya and Tanganyika no one who has ever been convicted of fraud or dishonesty may be a trustee, and in Nyasaland no one who has been convicted within the last five years may hold this office.

Few duties of trade union officers are explicitly detailed in the legislation, though a considerable number of the duties of the secretary—in particular in relation to the requirements of the registrar—may be inferred from the legislation. Where the legislation is more complicated, as it is in the Asian and East African territories, the number of these implied duties tends to increase. In a few cases certain duties are explicitly delegated to the secretary, or the committee of management—for instance, the obligation to apply for registration, or to render an annual statement of account to the registrar.

The duties of the treasurer in relation to trade union accounts are set out in every ordinance, and in Uganda, Tanganyika and Nyasaland there is a further provision requiring the officers to see that proper books of account are kept.

Regulations devised to protect union members from the election of officers who are almost totally unfitted by experience and education to become union leaders would seem to be a reasonable safeguard, but there is a danger, when the registrar is given discretionary powers to debar particular persons from holding office, that this power might be misapplied even when used in good faith. The right to appeal against the decision of a registrar is especially important in these circumstances.

Restrictions on the Use of Trade Union Funds

In British legislation very few restrictions are placed on the use of trade union funds. The objects of a registered trade union must be stated in its rules, and also the purpose for which the funds are applicable; but so long as the principal objects are those defined as statutory objects,[38] and none of the purposes of the trade union are unlawful, the funds may presumably be used in furtherance of any of the objects.   The one exception is the use of funds for certain political objects.   Under the provisions of the 1913 Act, the political objects have to be approved by the members, by a special balloting procedure; a separate political fund is then created, out of which expenditure on the political objects must be financed.   Any member may be exempted from contributing to this fund.

In Jamaica, British Guiana, Nigeria, Sierra Leone and the Gambia the restrictions are as slight as they are in Great Britain, and, moreover, there is no restriction on the use of funds for political purposes.   In Ghana, Malaya, Singapore and the Bahamas, it is illegal to use money, whether trade union funds or not, in support of an illegal strike or lockout.   Restrictions on the use of political funds, based on the provisions of the British Act of 1913, or, more usually, the more restrictive provisions of 1927, are in force in Ceylon, Malaya, Hong Kong, Ghana, Northern Rhodesia, Trinidad and Barbados.   Until 1958 they also applied in the Bahamas; this last territory, however, now entirely forbids the use of funds for political purposes.

With the exception of Ceylon, the territories of Asia and East Africa have limited the spending of trade union funds to a certain range of items.   Singapore, Hong Kong, Kenya and Uganda provide that the funds of a trade union may, subject to its rules and to the provisions of the ordinance, be expended only on the following seven objects:

(*a*) the payment of salaries and allowances to officers of the trade union;

(*b*) the payment of expenses for the administration of the trade union, including audit of the accounts of the funds of the trade union;

(*c*) the prosecution or defence of any legal proceedings to which the trade union or any member thereof is a party, when such prosecution or defence is undertaken for the purpose of securing or protecting any rights of the trade union as such, or any rights arising out of the relations

---

[38] Trade Union Act, 1871.   See N. A. Citrine, *Trade Union Law* (London, 1950), p. 204.

of any member with his employer, or with a person whom the member employs;

(d) the conduct of trade disputes on behalf of the trade union or any member thereof;

(e) the compensation of members for loss arising out of trade disputes;

(f) allowances to members or their dependents on account of death, old age, sickness, accidents or unemployment of such members; and

(g) any other object which by notification in the Gazette the governor [39] may, on the application of any trade union, declare to be an object for which such funds may be expended.

In Malaya, since 1959, and in Tanganyika and Nyasaland, the range of matters permitted is much wider and, indeed, the restrictiveness of the above list becomes more obvious in comparison. In all three of these territories, for instance, federation or affiliation fees are permitted, though under certain restricted conditions in Malaya and Nyasaland, as are (a) the editing, printing and publishing of journals, newsheets and publications for certain purposes; (b) contributions and fees to certain educational or cultural societies; (c) a number of educational, cultural, recreational and social provisions for members; (d) the erection, or the purchase or lease of a building for the union's business. In Malaya, in addition to provisions for political funds, the payment of train fares and maintenance expenses (supported by vouchers) and of wages lost through attending meetings is allowable. In Nyasaland and Tanganyika allowances may be made to members in distress. Social-insurance schemes and the supply of medicine and drugs to members are permitted; expenses may be paid, not only to officers but also to elected representatives of employees on union business; and contributions may be made to any other registered trade union which is in financial difficulties. In Tanganyika alone, legal advice may be obtained for the union, or for a member, over any matter arising out of the relations between a member and his employers or out of any civil cause.

[39] The references are to the governor in Uganda, but to the minister in Kenya. The corresponding section in Tanganyika refers to the registrar and to the governor in council in Hong Kong.

However, in none of these territories may union funds be used to pay a fine imposed on any individual.

The courts may grant an injunction restraining any unauthorized or unlawful use of funds in any of these territories on the application of five or more persons having a sufficient interest in the relief sought,[40] or at the request of the registrar or attorney general. In Malaya the registrar has the additional power, if he believes the officers of a trade union have ceased to function properly and that there is consequently a danger that the funds may be used unlawfully or for an unauthorized purpose, to direct that payment from the union's bank account be suspended. If any further payment is then made, the bank, or the Post Office in the case of Savings Bank deposits, is liable to reimburse the union for the amount of the payment.

Trade Union Accounts and Annual Statements to the Registrar

The long sections in the 1871 Trade Union Act concern the accounts of a trade union. Under Section 11, every treasurer of a registered trade union must render to the trustees or the members a true account of monies received and paid by him, and of the balance of money or securities he holds, whenever the rules of the union require him to do so, or whenever it is required by the members or the trustees. The trustees must appoint some fit and proper person to audit the accounts; and if required, the treasurer must hand over to the trustees the balance due from him, and all securities, effects, books, papers and property of the union which he holds. If he fails he may be sued by the trustees, who may be entitled to recover costs.

Section 16 of the 1871 Act requires 'a general statement of the receipts, funds, effects and expenditure' of every registered trade union to be sent to the registrar before 1st June each year. The form in which the return is made is prescribed by regulation, and it must include a full statement of assets and liabilities, receipts and expenditure; and the expenditure on each of the union's objects must be shown separately. Every member and depositor is entitled to receive a copy of the statement on application, without payment. The statement must be accompanied by a copy of all new rules, alterations of rules and changes of officers which have taken place during the year

[40] In Nyasaland by any officer or member of the trade union.

in question. Every union and every responsible officer of a union which fails to comply is liable to a penalty (of £25), and a larger penalty may be imposed for false statements in the returns.

The legislation in Barbados and the Gambia follows these British provisions, virtually without change. In all the other territories, however, although the legislation is based on the British statute, there are modifications and additional provisions.

In most of these territories it is laid down in the statute that the treasurer must keep full and accurate accounts. In Uganda, Tanganyika and Nyasaland the books must be sufficiently detailed to explain the transactions and financial position of the union, and must include a cash day-book. The law in almost all African and Asian territories insists that the registrar must approve auditors appointed by the union to audit both its own accounts and the annual returns; and in Ghana if the union fails to appoint an approved auditor the registrar himself may appoint one, and his expenses must be borne by the union. In Trinidad the auditor is always appointed by the registrar, but in the Bahamas he is appointed by the labour board. In British Guiana the union's accounts must be submitted for audit to the government Director of Audit. In the Bahamas the cost of the audit is borne by the labour board, which pays the audit fees; in British Guiana the government pays half, but in Trinidad the trade union is liable for the whole cost.

In Ghana, Nigeria and Sierra Leone all accounts submitted to the union by the treasurer must be sent to the registrar within one month; and in addition, the registrar may at any time call on the treasurer, committee or other officers to render detailed accounts of the funds of the union in respect of any particular period, showing in detail such information as he may require. It is an offence not to assist in the rendering of this account. In Nigeria if either the annual statement or the audited accounts transmitted to the registrar are in his opinion unsatisfactory, he may call for the books, records or other documents to be audited by himself or by an auditor of his choice. Failure to furnish any books or to hinder an auditor in the exercise of these powers is an offence. The cost of an audit of this kind falls on the union concerned, and if as a result of an examination of the books the registrar thinks that any criminal offence has been committed or that any sum (other than subscriptions due from members) was outstanding to the trade union, he can either institute criminal proceedings on behalf of and in the name of the trade union, or institute civil proceedings for the recovery of the money.

No other territory goes quite as far as this, but in most of them the registrar may require the treasurer or other officer to deliver detailed accounts to him in respect of any period he may specify,[41] and the accounts must be supported by such documents as the registrar may require. In Trinidad he may order the account books, vouchers, documents, etc., of a trade union to be inspected or audited at any time by a person appointed by the registrar, and the officers concerned must see that the books are accessible. Accounts must, in most cases, be available to all persons having an interest in the funds of the union. In Northern Rhodesia the registrar is also empowered, where misappropriation has been established, to sue the treasurer for failing to hand over any money or property, and he may apply to the courts for an order to freeze union funds.

Other provisions in various places prescribe the form, not only of the annual statement sent to the registrar, but also of the treasurer's accounts; or require the accounts to be verified by a statutory declaration or prescribe the date to which accounts must be made out, instead of leaving it to be prescribed in the rules of the union; or provide that copies of the accounts, or of the annual returns, are to be delivered to all members without charge.

The legal regulations of trade union funds adopted in the territories have been inspired by a desire to protect the interests of union members, but in some cases it is apparent that the legislators were also interested in limiting the activities of the unions to those that they thought least dangerous to the public interest. The danger that legislation permitting the registrar to have the accounts of trade unions inspected and audited at any time might have serious political implications was illustrated soon after Trinidad became internally self-governing.

[41] In Kenya, Uganda, Tanganyika and Nyasaland, these provisions apply equally to the accounts of any branch of a trade union.

In 1959, after a campaign in the government party's newspaper against the largest trade union on the island, accusing its officers of misuse of the organization's funds, a compulsory audit was ordered by the Minister of Labour. This action may have been justified on ordinary grounds, but it appeared to the union officers to be inspired by the bitter hostility which the political leaders of the People's National Movement had for the general secretary of the Oilworkers' Union, who had been an intransigent opponent of their party.

Nevertheless, it is difficult to avoid coming to the conclusion that legal regulation is necessary in most of the territories. It is, of course, not only the less-developed countries, with which this book is concerned, that have found it necessary to go beyond the limited requirements in the British trade union acts. The United States has recently sought to protect union members from the misuse of union funds by irresponsible leaders, through an amendment of the law which now makes legally obligatory the comprehensive disclosure and reporting of all financial transactions made by union officers in connection with their union duties.

Registrars have often been far from harsh in carrying out their duties concerning union accounts for the reasons discussed earlier. But there have been many instances where the violation of the law has gone so far that it could not be excused, and penalties have had to be imposed. There may have been some cases where registrars and labour officers have been more concerned with financial rectitude than with promoting effective trade unionism, but these seem to have been relatively few. However, the danger that legal regulation may do more harm than good has to be recognized. The I.L.O. has recently pointed out that 'the governments concerned could give solid encouragement to the growth of sound trade union administration if they would constantly keep in mind the desirability of relaxing such measures of supervision progressively, and as quickly as possible, as trade unions grow in experience'.[42]

Amalgamation and Federation

There has been a tendency in a number of territories for those in authority to view the growth of large unions and general

[42] *The Protection of Trade Union Funds and Property*, I.L.O. (Geneva, 1960).

federations of unions with suspicion. Official opinion has been influenced by the fear that large unions and federations are more likely to be concerned with political activities than are small organizations based upon the unit of employment, or the industry. Experience has largely confirmed the correctness of this assessment of the role of the larger unions and federations, but it is equally clear that unions cannot be kept out of politics by this type of restriction. Although it is a mistake to imagine that unions can be isolated from politics by keeping them small, it has been found desirable, in Great Britain and other countries with a long experience of trade unionism, to regulate the merging of unions into larger units, in order to protect the interest of their members.

Under British law unions must obtain the consent of their members before they can amalgamate. Since 1917, when the conditions to be fulfilled were made easier, unions have been permitted to amalgamate if on a ballot of not less than 50 per cent. of the members of each trade union, the votes in favour have exceeded those against by at least 20 per cent.

The legislation in Northern Rhodesia is, in effect, the same as that in Great Britain. In the West Indies, Nigeria and Sierra Leone the conditions of amalgamation are the same as in the original British legislation, namely that the consent of two-thirds of the total membership must be obtained. Under the legislation of Kenya, Uganda, Tanganyika and Nyasaland, only registered unions may amalgamate on the terms of the 1917 British law, but in Kenya, Uganda and Nyasaland if the bodies amalgamating represent more than one trade or calling they must first obtain the consent of the governor in council or, in Kenya, the minister. Amalgamation is limited in Malaya and Hong Kong to unions within similar trades, occupations or industries. In Ceylon, no trade union to which public servants belong may amalgamate, federate or affiliate with another body, whether of public servants or not, and if this law is violated the union's registration may be cancelled.

In Malaya, since 1948, two or more trade unions whose members are employed in a similar trade, occupation or industry may form a federation, provided that a resolution has been previously circulated to all members of each union and to the registrar, and that a secret ballot in each union has shown that a majority of members voting are in favour. Each federation must apply for registration within a month of its establishment, unless an extension of time is granted, and it will be registered if the provisions have been complied with and it is entitled to register. Similarly, a registered trade union may resolve to affiliate to any existing federation, if it goes through the same process and if its affiliation is approved by the federation.

A federation is subject to all the same legislative provisions as a trade union, and in most of the cases in Malaya, where a ballot must be held, all the individual members of the unions comprising the federation must be given an opportunity to vote. Since 1955 federations of trade unions have been allowed to have political objects and to establish political funds in the same way as ordinary trade unions.

In one further respect Malaya is almost unique. Since 1955 it has taken over the British provisions allowing a trade union by special resolution to transfer its engagements to another trade union,[43] though again the transfer must be to a trade union in a similar trade, occupation or industry. The resolution must in this case be carried by a secret ballot, and, as in Great Britain, the consent must ultimately be obtained of at least two-thirds of the members of the union, unless, after application and after notification of the resolution in the official Gazette and the press, the registrar has dispensed with this requirement.

The Trade Union and Trade Dispute Ordinance of Hong Kong provides for federations, but it does not permit a union to be affiliated or connected with any trade union established outside the colony without the consent of the Governor in Council.

Until 1962 in Tanganyika, any registered trade union could join a federation if, on a secret ballot, half the members of each trade union voted and there was a majority of 20 per cent. in favour. Registered trade unions were not allowed to join a federation if any of the member organizations was a non-registered trade union.[44] However, under the Trade Unions Ordinance (No. 51 of 1962) the Minister of Labour is given

---

[43] Societies (Miscellaneous Provisions) Act, 1940.

[44] The main reason for this provision seems to be to prevent federation with trade unions centred outside the territory. See Legislative Council Debates, Fourth Volume of Session 1956–57, p. 795.

power to appoint any federation of trade unions to be a 'designated federation'. Thereafter no other federation of trade unions is legally permitted and every trade union is obliged to be a member as a condition of its lawful existence.

The laws regulating trade unions described in this chapter have been designed to encourage the growth of unions, their good government and sound administration. While for the most part they have had their origin in the trade union laws of Britain, there have been departures at many points from the British model. Although in many territories the law has been, in certain respects, more restrictive than in Britain, it is only since the achievement of self-government that there have been fundamental deviations from British principles. It remains to be seen whether the more positive laws that have been adopted by some former colonies will succeed in promoting a more effective and efficient trade union movement. It is possible that they might have this result, but it is also possible that they deter the growth of a responsible leadership and a higher standard of union administration.

CHAPTER 11

THE LEGAL REGULATION OF INDUSTRIAL RELATIONS

THE law establishing the right of trade unions to bargain and to strike in most of the territories follows the general lines established in Britain. There are a number of differences, some substantial, especially in such matters as the right to picket during a strike or lockout and the right of employees in essential industries to strike. In certain territories British principles of voluntary collective bargaining have been discarded in favour of ideas culled from other nations, including compulsory arbitration, on the Australian model, and the prohibition of unfair labour practices as developed in the United States.

In all of these territories trade unions are protected, in their collective bargaining activities, against proceedings under the law of torts, though such protection was often missing, as it had been in Britain in the early stages of union development. Section 4 of the British Trades Disputes Act of 1906 provides that no action against a trade union, or against any members or officials in respect of any tortious act alleged to have been committed by or on behalf of the trade union, is to be entertained by any courts, although nothing is to affect the liability of trustees and officials to sue or be sued on matters pertaining to 'property, right or claim to property of a trade union'.

These provisions are repeated in much the same words in the legislation of British Guiana, Jamaica, Barbados, Sierra Leone, the Gambia, Mauritius, Fiji, Hong Kong and Trinidad. Elsewhere there are some minor differences. In Ceylon, Singapore and Malaya, in Kenya, Uganda, Tanganyika and Nyasaland and the Bahamas protection has been limited explicitly to registered trade unions and also to 'probationary trade unions' in Kenya and Uganda. There are some slight changes in the wording of the provisions in most of these territories, which in a few cases alter the scope of the section.[1]

[1] Especially the Malayan Act of 1959. Under this Act trade unions remain liable to be sued 'in respect of any tortious act arising substantially out of the use of any specific property of the trade union' except in the case of actions in contemplation of furtherance of a trade dispute.

In Northern Rhodesia there is no protection in respect of acts done in contemplation or furtherance of a trade dispute unless the dispute has been officially notified to the governor, and either a conciliator or conciliation board has been appointed and has met the parties concerned, or unless an interval has passed without action having been taken by the governor. Until 1958, probably because of a slip in drafting, the Northern Rhodesian provisions were somewhat different in another respect. No action might be brought on grounds of tort against a trade union or a branch of a trade union, nor against any members or officials, *on behalf of themselves or any members* of the trade union in respect of acts committed by or on behalf of the trade union. The words italicized were discussed in 1957 by a commission of inquiry which had received evidence suggesting that those words meant that each individual trade union member was protected against actions of tort in respect of such acts, whereas in the other territories and in the United Kingdom, the protection applied only to the trade union itself, or to persons sued on behalf of the whole body of members. In view of these criticisms the section was amended in 1958, in accordance with the more usual form. By contrast, in the Bahamas, from 1943 to 1958, it was specifically stated that no limitation was placed by these provisions on actions brought against any member or officer of a trade union in his individual capacity.

Interference with the Business of Another Person

In all these territories there is a provision corresponding to s. 3 of the 1906 British Trade Disputes Act, removing personal liability in common law for acts which induce some other person to break a contract of employment, or to interfere with another person's business, or with his right to dispose of his capital or his labour as he wishes, if these acts are done in contemplation or furtherance of a trade dispute.

In the West Indies, West Africa, Hong Kong, Fiji and Northern Rhodesia the provisions are identical with the 1906 Act, as they were formerly in Tanganyika, Kenya, Uganda and Nyasaland. However, the protection in Northern Rhodesia is only applicable if the disputes have been notified and conciliation has started, or if an interval has passed without action having been taken by the Governor.

Elsewhere the provisions are different, and in some respects at least protection may be more limited. In the Bahamas since 1943, it has been limited to 'an act done by a person *on behalf of a trade union*,[2] in contemplation or furtherance of a trade dispute', and it does not apply to any act done in contemplation or furtherance of an illegal strike or lockout.

In Ceylon, Malaya and Singapore, in Kenya and Uganda since 1952, Tanganyika since 1956 and Nyasaland since 1958, the protection, based on the wording of the India Trade Union Act, is even more at variance with British provisions. It reads: 'No suit or other legal proceedings shall be maintainable in any Civil Court against a registered trade union or any officer or member thereof in respect of any act done in contemplation or furtherance of a trade dispute to which a member of the trade union is a party, on the ground only that . . .'[3]

Thus, although the protection covers both individuals and registered trade unions, which have a legal personality in these territories, there is no protection for sympathetic action, nor for any non-unionists who might be taking part in a trade dispute.

Conspiracy in Trade Disputes

The law relating to conspiracy in trade disputes is carried over, with some modifications, from the British legislation of 1875 and 1906. The British Conspiracy and Protection of Property Act of 1875 provided that an agreement or combination to do, or procure to be done, any act in contemplation of or furtherance of a trade dispute was not indictable as a conspiracy if the act, when committed by one person, was not a crime—a crime being defined as an offence for which a penalty of imprisonment could be imposed. It also provided that the penalty for conspiracy to commit a non-indictable offence in a trade dispute should be limited to three months' imprisonment, or the penalty for the crime when committed by one person, whichever was the longer. By an amendment contained in the 1906 Trade Disputes Act, the protection was extended to civil

---

[2] After 1958 'on behalf of a registered employers' organization, or a registered trade union . . .'.

[3] By a slip in drafting, the Tanganyika provisions between 1956 and 1959 referred to 'a trade dispute to which a member of *a* trade union is a party . . .' and were thus less restrictive. This has now been corrected.

actions in respect of acts committed as a result of an agreement in contemplation or furtherance of a trade dispute.

All these provisions are repeated, virtually without change, in Sierra Leone, the Gambia, Barbados, Trinidad, British Guiana and Nyasaland. In most other territories there is no provision that the sentence which may be imposed on conviction for a conspiracy to commit a non-indictable offence is to be limited. In Northern Rhodesia the whole protection is restricted to trade disputes which have been notified; in Kenya and the Bahamas the definition of a 'crime' as being an offence punishable by imprisonment is omitted, with the probable consequence that agreements to commit any offence at all remain punishable as conspiracies. In Singapore and the Bahamas the protection is limited to conspiracies in connection with trade disputes between employers and workmen, whereas elsewhere it appears to cover all trade disputes as defined in the appropriate legislation. In the Bahamas there is no protection against civil actions on grounds of conspiracy,[4] and the Bahamas is the only territory where there is no protection at all for acts done in furtherance of an illegal strike or lockout. Although the legal protection of unions from actions in tort seems to be less broadly conceived in a number of the territories than is the case in Britain, there is little evidence to indicate that legal difficulties have been a significant obstacle to union progress as they were in Britain in the nineteenth and early twentieth centuries. This may, of course, not always be so in the future.

Statutory Machinery for the Settlement of Disputes

British legislation has provided few positive procedures to bring employers and employees together in the first instance by making union recognition and collective bargaining obligatory as it is in the United States; nor has it established any form of statutory negotiating procedure except in the industries covered by wages councils and wage boards. However, since the 1896 Conciliation Act was passed, it has provided for the possibility of official intervention to help in the settlement of industrial disputes which arise in the course of negotiations

---

[4] Kahn-Freund in *The System of Industrial Relations in Great Britain*, Flanders & Clegg (eds.), maintains that in Britain 'the development of the common law has deprived the enactment [eliminating civil liability] of much of its practical significance'. It is not clear if this would be true for the Bahamas.

between employers and trade unions. The Industrial Courts Act of 1919 set up a regular means whereby industry could voluntarily submit disputes to arbitration—the awards of the industrial court being generally accepted, though not legally binding on either side. Under the Conditions of Employment and National Arbitration Orders (in force from 1940 to 1951) and the Industrial Disputes Order (in force from 1951 until 1959), provision was made for the compulsory reference of trade disputes to arbitration, and the awards of these tribunals were enforceable in the courts as implied terms of the contract of employment.

For the most part colonial territories have enacted legislation adapted from these British laws, though in many cases the machinery for voluntary arbitration has been simplified. Special wartime regulations (which are not dealt with here) also often followed British patterns. During the last decade compulsory arbitration has had an increasing role to play. In the dependencies it has been used mainly for the compulsory settlement of disputes in essential services, but in a few territories, mainly after the attainment of self-government or independence, it has been used more extensively, and procedure has sometimes departed very considerably from British precedents in, for instance, the laying down of statutory procedure for negotiations.

Non-statutory Machinery

Malaya and Singapore followed the permanent British provisions closely until self-government, when Singapore decided to take Australia as its model. The Industrial Courts Ordinances of 1940, repealed in Singapore in 1960, but still in force in Malaya after re-enactment in 1948, followed the provisions of the British Act of 1919 with few changes; the main difference being that it was not prescriptive for women to be appointed either to the court or to the panels from which *ad hoc* arbitration boards might be appointed.

A typical enactment providing for voluntary arbitration in other places makes provision for the reporting of trade disputes to the governor, minister or commissioner of labour, by or on behalf of either party to the dispute. The responsible authority may thereupon 'take steps such as may seem to him expedient for promoting a settlement'. One possible step, if both parties consent, is to refer the matter to an *ad hoc* arbitration tribunal, which may consist of a sole arbitrator, an arbitrator assisted by assessors nominated by each side, or an equal number of arbitrators nominated by each side, and an independent chairman appointed by the governor. Certain procedural provisions are made, and subsidiary legislation lays down more detailed procedure for the tribunals. Awards of a tribunal must be submitted to the governor, and are then published. However, in any industry where other arrangements exist for the settlement of disputes by conciliation or arbitration, a dispute must not be referred to arbitration except with the consent of both parties, and then only after there has been a failure to obtain a settlement under the domestic arrangements.

As in the British Act of 1919, the governor may also inquire into the causes and circumstances of any trade dispute, existing or apprehended, and may refer any matters connected with a dispute to a specially appointed board of inquiry, which must look into the matter and report back to the governor. Matters connected with the economic or industrial conditions in the territory may also be referred to a board of inquiry. It is left to the governor's discretion whether a board's report is to be made public and if so, how much of it is to be published, but no information obtained by a board about any individual trade union or business, which is not otherwise available to the public, may be published without the consent of the organization or person in question.

Provisions to this effect have been passed in many dependencies, including Trinidad, Barbados, Jamaica, Sierra Leone, Ghana and Nigeria,[5] and they were at one time in force in Kenya and Nyasaland. In the Gambia and Hong Kong, too, the arbitration provisions apply, although slightly modified, but there is no provision for the appointment of boards of inquiry.

Inspired by part of the British 1896 Conciliation Act, Nigeria has enacted that where a trade dispute exists or is apprehended, the Minister of Labour may inquire into the causes and circumstances of the dispute, and may take steps to enable the

---

[5] In Ghana the force of the provisions has been greatly reduced since the passage of the Industrial Relations Act in 1958.

parties to meet under an independent chairman, who may be appointed by mutual agreement of both parties, or by the minister. On the application of one of the parties, the chairman may, after taking into account existing facilities for conciliation, formally appoint a conciliator who, by negotiation with the parties, must try to bring about a settlement, a memorandum of which must be signed by the parties and forwarded to the minister. Conciliation of this sort is also one of the means which may be used to settle a dispute which has been formally reported.

Any dispute may be reported to the Labour Commissioner or to a labour officer in Uganda, by or on behalf of the parties to the dispute. The commissioner must consider the matter and must endeavour to reconcile the parties. In Kenya any settlement reached under conciliation must be recorded in writing, signed by the parties and endorsed by the commissioner; it then becomes a statutory 'negotiated agreement' and has the same force as an arbitration award. In Kenya, Uganda and Nyasaland an award or an endorsed negotiated agreement is binding on the parties concerned, and is accepted as an implied term of the contract of employment although subject to change because of a subsequent award or agreement.

Provision for the appointment of boards of inquiry into trade disputes or into economic or industrial conditions is made by a number of territories, including Kenya, Tanganyika, Uganda and Nyasaland. In other territories the principles are similar, but practice is different.

Fairly simple legislation in British Guiana provides that where a 'difference', not a 'trade dispute', as defined in the ordinance, exists or is apprehended between an employer or class of employer and employees, or, between different classes of employees, the Commissioner of Labour may inquire into the causes and circumstances, take steps to promote a settlement or, with the consent of both parties, 'refer the matter for settlement to the arbitration of one or more persons appointed by the Governor in Council'. The word 'arbitration' may be rather misleading, however, for the duty of the 'arbitrator' is to inquire into the difference by communicating with the parties, to 'endeavour to bring about a settlement of the difference' and to report to the commissioner. A memorandum of any settlement reached, signed by the parties concerned, must be delivered to the commissioner.[6]

In addition to this the governor may refer matters connected with a 'trade dispute' to an *ad hoc* advisory committee which subsequently submits a report with recommendations for action.

In Northern Rhodesia the emphasis is on the principles of the 1896 Conciliation Act, rather than on the Industrial Courts Act. Under the 1949 Industrial Conciliation Ordinance, provision is made for the registration of conciliation boards—bodies set up by agreement for the purpose of settling disputes within an industry by conciliation or arbitration. Each board must register its constitution with the registrar and furnish the required returns of its proceedings. Conciliation proceedings within the industry concerned must then be conducted in accordance with the regulations of the appropriate conciliation board. If the minister thinks that there is no adequate arrangement in any district trade or industry for submitting disputes to a conciliation board, he may appoint someone to inquire into conditions and to confer with each side of industry and—subject to the Minister's directions—with other bodies, as to the desirability of establishing a conciliation board. A quite new provision is that if the minister thinks that a conciliation board should be established, he can establish one, comprised of representatives of employers and workers, and of other persons appointed by the governor. The chairman is also appointed by the governor.[7]

Under the 1949 Ordinance, where a dispute existed or was apprehended the minister might *either* take steps to enable the parties to meet under an independent chairman, *or* on the application of one of them, appoint a conciliator or a board of conciliation, *or* appoint a board of inquiry, *or* with the consent of both parties (with the usual reservations respecting existing internal arrangements), appoint an arbitration tribunal. In 1958 the choice of appointing a chairman to meet the parties was deleted, and some changes in the provisions for arbitration

---

[6] Although the ordinance is in terms which suggest that the arbitrator's function is conciliation rather than arbitration, nevertheless the Arbitration Procedure Regulations refer to the 'award' of the arbitration tribunal, its publication and interpretation.

[7] None of these provisions appears to have been greatly used.

were made, mainly to enable arbitration to be provided in addition to, as well as in place of, conciliation. The Industrial Disputes Ordinance, passed in Fiji in 1942, to provide for the investigation and settlement of industrial disputes, empowered the governor in council to require the parties to submit the dispute to arbitration, if he was satisfied that the conciliation machinery provided by the ordinance had failed. The decision was then final and binding for a period prescribed or until annulled. This compulsory power was abolished by a new ordinance based on contemporary British legislation in 1958.

Finally, the Bahamas, as usual, has been idiosyncratic. In 1946 there was established a labour board of five members, two of whom were to be members of the House of Assembly who were not office holders. If a labour dispute existed or seemed likely, the board, either on its own initiative or on application by either party, was to make its services available to the parties, and inquire into the causes of the dispute for the purposes of conciliation. Provision was also made for the appointment of a labour officer to assist the board. In 1957 this board was replaced by a labour conciliation board of five members, consisting of an independent chairman, two employers' representatives and two workmen. But at least two of the members had still to be members of the House of Assembly. If a dispute came to the notice of the chairman, on the application of either party, the chairman was to appoint someone to inquire into the causes and circumstances of the dispute and report back. On receipt of the report a meeting of the board would be convened, and the board might then take steps to enable the parties to meet with the members of the board, or to meet under the chairmanship of an independent person. It could then, with the consent of both parties, refer the dispute to arbitration under the provisions of the Bahamas Arbitration Act. Alternatively, the board itself was given the power to arbitrate, on the application of both parties.

Some provisions of this second Act were not very clear, and it, too, was repealed in 1958, when the Trade Union and Industrial Conciliation Act was passed. Under this Act disputes may be reported to the chief industrial officer in writing, together with such other details as he may require. If any dispute exists or is apprehended the chief industrial officer must consider it, and if appropriate arrangements for settlement exist within the industry he must refer it to that machinery unless it has already been used and failed. If such a reference is not desirable he must inquire into the dispute, and take steps to settle it. On the application of one party, he may appoint a conciliator, or act as a conciliator himself. Any settlement reached after any action has been taken under these provisions must be recorded in writing and endorsed by the chief industrial officer; it then has the status of a negotiated agreement. Where no settlement has been reached, the labour board may, with the consent of both parties, refer the dispute to an arbitration tribunal consisting either of one appointed member or of an independent appointed chairman and two other members chosen from panels, one to represent each side. The tribunal's award is submitted to the board and published, but the terms of an award are simply morally binding, they are not enforceable in the courts.

Provision is also made in this present Bahamas Act for the appointment by the governor in council, after consultation with the labour board, of a court of inquiry into a trade dispute; the court's reports are later to be laid before both houses of the legislature for their information and possible action.

The Right to Strike

In British legislation the limitations which have been placed on the right of employees to go on strike in furtherance of a trade dispute, or of employers to impose a lockout for the same reasons, have been of three main kinds. First, there is the permanent restriction on strikes called in breach of contract; under the 1875 Conspiracy and Protection of Property Act a strike in breach of contract is a criminal offence when this is likely to endanger human life, cause serious bodily injury or endanger valuable property; or, in the case of employees of gas, water or electricity undertakings, likely to deprive the inhabitants of a place of their supply of gas, water or electricity.

The second type of limitation was in force between 1927 and 1946 when the Trades Disputes and Trade Unions Act of 1927 defined illegal strikes and lockouts and laid down penalties for declaring, instigating, inciting or taking part in these illegal activities; and at the same time it amended the 1875 Act by restricting the right of public employees to strike.

The third kind of restriction was that imposed under wartime emergency legislation, and in particular under the Conditions of Employment and National Arbitration Order (No. 1305) of 1940, which remained in force until 1951. In this legislation compulsory arbitration was provided as a safeguard to each side of industry in return for the withdrawal of the right to strike or to lockout.

Most dependent territories have statutes based on or adapted from one or more of these provisions, and in some of the more recent legislation, especially in the newly independent states, still further restrictions on strikes have been added. Today the right to strike is extremely restricted in Ghana and in the Colony of Aden, and, to a lesser extent, in Ceylon, Singapore and the Bahamas.

The initial type of legislation to be adopted in the colonial territories regulating the right to strike was modelled on the British Conspiracy and Protection of Property Act of 1875. Jamaica seems to have been the first to provide legislation corresponding to this Act. Under the Protection of Property Law passed in 1905, any employee in breach of contract, knowing or having reasonable cause to believe that the probable consequences of his action would be to deprive the inhabitants of water and light or interfere with the conveying of passengers or freight by railway, tram or coach, is liable to a fine or to imprisonment or both. In 1918 these provisions were extended to include employees of fire services and those with the duty of 'conserving the public health'. Section 5 of the British Act, which rendered anyone liable to a penalty who knowingly endangered human life, caused serious bodily injury or exposed property to destruction through a breach of contract was adopted without significant change.

Barbados also enacted similar provisions fairly early on.[8] In other places the restrictions came much later. The Trades Disputes and Protection of Property Act of Trinidad dates from 1943; its provisions were based on both sections of the 1875 Act and also on the 1927 amendment. However, besides electricity and water services, 'railway, tramway, ship or other transport

[8] Better Security Act, 1920.

services, health, sanitary or medical services, postal telegraphic or telephonic services' were also covered. In 1947 all reference to postal, telegraphic or telephonic services was deleted.

African territories, on the whole, have kept close to the British provisions. In 1947 Nigeria repealed previous provisions and replaced them by a new section of the Criminal Code based on both sections of the 1875 Act. The word 'wilfully' is, however, omitted from the provisions, and the application is to 'any person employed in any undertaking concerned in the supply of electricity or water'. The section refers only to a contract of service, not of hiring; and 'seriously to endanger public health including the health of the inmates of a hospital or similar institution' is added to those breaches of contract which may be criminal.

Singapore and Nyasaland have repeated the provision of Section 5. Malaya since 1949 has done the same, but, somewhat like Nigeria, it adds a prohibition on breaches of contract whose probable consequences will be to endanger 'the efficient operation of any public health service', including hospitals, clinics, conservancy and sanitation services.

The Bahamas has also enacted legislation based on Section 5 of the 1875 Act, which applies 'notwithstanding that a person is acting in furtherance of a lawful trade dispute'.[9]

In some of the territories, especially Nyasaland, Nigeria and the Bahamas, the penalties for unlawful breach of contract have been much higher than in Great Britain, but usually the written consent of the attorney general is required before a prosecution may be instituted. The word 'maliciously', which occurs in these sections, is defined in a different way in each territory; only in Barbados is it defined as it is in Great Britain.

Most of the territories not mentioned in this section either rely on other forms of restriction to prevent strikes in essential services or else, as in Barbados and the Gambia, they have no such provisions. Among those already mentioned, Jamaica, Northern Rhodesia, Nyasaland, Ceylon, Malaya and the Bahamas have essential service legislation based on the principles of the British wartime 'Order 1305' in addition to some of the 1875 provisions.

---

[9] There is no reference in the Bahamas legislation to trade disputes which are not lawful, although there are several kinds of unlawful strikes and lockouts.

Restrictions on Strikes in Essential Industries Based on Compulsory Arbitration Provisions

In many dependencies wartime regulations were made which had much the same effect as the Conditions of Employment and Arbitration Order, commonly known as 'Order 1305' in Great Britain.   These were not often put to the test, and it is difficult to judge their success.   They did, however, have certain consequences, in that in East and Central Africa, and also in certain West Indies territories, permanent enactments have since been made, mainly in order to prevent strikes in certain defined 'essential services' by the provision of machinery for compulsory arbitration.[10]

More than a dozen territories have passed legislation concerning strikes and lockouts in essential services, but an even larger number have no legislation of this kind.   When in 1950 the maintenance of 'Order 1305' as a feature of the statutory machinery of industrial relations was under consideration in Britain, the Colonial Office decided to review the application of this type of regulation in the colonial territories.   After hearing the views of the Colonial Labour Advisory Committee and discussing the matter with the T.U.C. and Overseas Employers' Federation, the Secretary of State for the Colonies issued a circular despatch.   This despatch asked colonial governments to consider the need to take steps to ensure that they had the powers necessary to prevent an interruption in essential services, should there be a complete breakdown in normal industrial relations.

The decision of the Colonial Secretary to send this despatch was influenced by the knowledge that the stoppage of an essential service might do considerable harm to the general public and retard the progress of a colony.   The means available to the authorities in the territories to deal with the effects of a breakdown of an essential service were limited, and might often prove totally inadequate.   It was also believed that the restrictions provided by legislation of the 1875 Conspiracy and Protection of Property Act type would not be an

---

[10] The detailed provisions for compulsory arbitration together with all the other statutory provisions made for facilitating the settlement of trade disputes are analysed in a later section.

effective safeguard. It was, however, pointed out in the despatch that the limitations on the right to strike in essential services could only be justified if the workers concerned were assured of reasonable wages and working conditions, and if there was machinery through which their grievances and claims could be properly ventilated and fairly settled.

Under 'Order 1305' in Britain no employer could lockout, and no worker could take part in a strike in connection with a trade dispute, unless the dispute had been reported to the Minister of Labour, and 21 days had elapsed without it having been referred by the minister to the National Arbitration Tribunal for settlement. The awards of the tribunal, and any other agreements reached after a reference to the minister, became part of the recognized terms and conditions of employment of the trade or industry concerned and could be enforced through the ordinary procedure of the courts.

These provisions have been introduced into essential service legislation in a variety of ways in the different territories. British Guiana seems to have been the first territory to adopt the basic ideas of 'Order 1305', though in the first instance this was not supported by compulsory arbitration. In the Trade Disputes (Essential Services) Ordinance of 1942 it was provided that no employer engaged in an essential service could declare or take part in a lockout and no employee in an essential service could take part in a strike in connection with a trade dispute, unless the employer or the employees' trade union had formally reported the dispute, and the governor had not, within one month of the report, appointed an advisory committee under the Labour Ordinance to inquire into the dispute. The 'essential services' in question were to be defined from time to time by Order in Council, and up to the end of 1954 six such Orders had been issued. These covered all employees of the Transport and Harbours' Department; all winchmen, stevedores, sugar packers, dockmen, slingmen and truckers employed in the Port of Georgetown and New Amsterdam, including the Georgetown passenger transport service; certain sewage, water and electricity workers, and drainage pumping workers, all government hospital employees and the electricity, water and fire-fighting employees at the airport, Atkinson Field.

This ordinance was originally intended to be effective only

until the governor in council should declare the emergency to be at an end, but it remained in force until 1956, when it was replaced by a Public Utility Undertakings and Public Health Services Arbitration Ordinance, whose provisions are hardly less broadly drawn and correspond closely to those in other territories.

Malaya has certain provisions for preventing strikes and lockouts in 'public utility services' but without enforcing machinery for compulsory arbitration. These services were defined in 1940 as:

(a) any railway service;

(b) any section of a government or industrial establishment on the working of which the safety of the establishment or the workers employed therein depends;

(c) any postal, telegraphic or telephonic service;

(d) any industry or government undertaking which supplies power, light or water to the public;

(e) any public health service (which includes both hospitals and clinics, and sanitation and conservancy services);

(f) any industry, government undertaking or service which the government declares to be a public utility service by notification in the Gazette (which notification has a maximum validity of six months but is renewable).

In 1956 the list of services was amended by the addition of fire services, ferry services, passenger transport services, and the storage, transport and supply of petrol or petroleum products.

In any of these services in Malaya it is illegal for employees to strike in breach of a contract, or for an employer to lockout any of his workmen, unless at least 14 days' notice has been given to the other side within the 6 weeks preceding the strike or lockout; it is also illegal to strike or lockout if conciliation proceedings are in progress, or if such proceedings have been concluded within the past seven days. Employers must report any such notices, given or received, to the Labour Commissioner, and penalties are laid down for acting in furtherance of, instigating or inciting others to take part in, or applying money in support of such illegal strikes or lockouts.[11]

[11] These Malayan provisions seem to have been inspired by the Indian Trade Disputes Act of 1947, Sections 22, 26, 27 and 28.

Uganda was the first territory to include provisions for compulsory arbitration in a statute. Its Trade Disputes (Arbitration and Settlement) Ordinance, enacted in 1949, made special provision for what were at first termed 'Disputes in public utility undertakings and in public health and sanitary services', but which in the following year were renamed 'Essential Services'. Uganda was followed by Kenya and Tanganyika in 1950, Nyasaland and Jamaica in 1952, Northern Rhodesia in 1953 and British Guiana in 1956. The Ceylon Industrial Disputes Act of 1950 and the Bahamas Trade Union and Industrial Conciliation Act of 1958 contained provisions on slightly different lines.

No strike or lockout may take place in Uganda in an essential service unless the dispute has been reported to the governor and 14 days have passed since it was reported without the dispute having been referred to an arbitration tribunal. In normal cases the governor will refer a reported dispute within 14 days, and the arbitration tribunal is called upon to make its award 'without delay and where practicable within 28 days'. The awards of arbitration tribunals in Uganda are binding, even where arbitration is agreed upon voluntarily. Strikes and lockouts in essential services in Kenya and Nyasaland are subject to restrictions similar to those in force in Uganda.

In Northern Rhodesia it is illegal to take part in a strike or to declare a lockout in essential services unless the dispute has been reported to the governor and 21 days have elapsed without the dispute having been referred for settlement, not necessarily, it appears, to the tribunal, but possibly to suitable machinery existing within the industry. There are, however, no further prohibitions in Northern Rhodesia, as there are in the other territories. In Jamaica the same provisions apply, except that the standstill period is only 14 days. In British Guiana, on the other hand, it is extended to one month, and, moreover, following British practice, the dispute must have been reported by an employer, or by an organization of employers or workers which, in the opinion of the governor in council, either represents a substantial proportion of the employers or workers concerned, or habitually takes part in negotiations relative to the service concerned.

Y

In the Bahamas no workman may go on strike and no employer may lockout in an essential service unless (1) the dispute has been reported, (2) 25 days have elapsed without it having been referred to an arbitration tribunal and (3) a trade union, of which the striker is a member, or an employers' organization, of which the employer is a member, has decided on strike action by secret ballot after the report was made. It is also illegal to declare, instigate or incite others to take part in a strike or lockout unless all these conditions have been fulfilled. Prosecutions require the consent of the attorney-general. Ceylon goes further than many of the territories in making a strike or lockout illegal in any industry when a dispute has been referred to arbitration.

'Essential Services' in all these laws, except in the Bahamas and Ceylon, are 'services, by whomsoever rendered . . . which are mentioned in the Schedule' to the ordinances. The governor, by public notice, may subsequently add to or delete from the schedule any service he thinks fit, though in East Africa and Nyasaland the notice must be laid before the legislative council of the territory concerned and the council may annul it by passing a prayer to that effect. In Uganda alone, if there is any doubt as to whether a given service is an essential service as defined by the schedule, the chief secretary is to decide on it in his absolute discretion. If a strike or lockout has occurred in Uganda and the chief secretary is satisfied that the parties acted in the reasonable belief that the service was not an essential service, he is to serve a certificate on the parties striking that it is in fact an essential service, and from the date of the certificate the dispute will come within the provisions of the ordinance. In Northern Rhodesia the provisions apply only in certain areas to which they have been applied by Public Notice; so far the application has been to the municipalities and larger townships. Given undertakings in Northern Rhodesia may be, and all the larger mining undertakings have, in fact, been exempted from the provisions of this ordinance.

In his despatch of 1951 the Secretary of State recommended that colonial legislation should restrict to the minimum the number of services scheduled as essential. It was hoped that these would be confined to services necessary to the life and health of the community. However, territorial governments differed in this concept of 'essential services', and there was considerable variation in the lists of services scheduled as essential. Up till 1958, Tanganyika had the longest list. There were 10 services in the original ordinance of 1950, and 5 more were added in 1956. The full list was as follows:

Water services
Electricity services
Health services
Hospital services
Sanitary services
Transport services necessary to the operation of the fore-
    going
Public transportation services provided by East African
    Railways and Harbours Administration
Ports and dock services, including stevedoring and
    lightering, loading and unloading of cargoes from or on
    to ships and despatch of cargo to its destination
Supply and distribution of oil and petrol
Telecommunications, posts and telegraphs
Fire services and transport services necessary to their
    operation
Wireless broadcasting services operated by Tanganyika
    Broadcasting Corporation
Public civil aviation services, including airport and air-
    craft maintenance and civil aviation telecommunications
Meteorological services supplied by East African Meteoro-
    logical Department
Government printing services and transport services
    necessary to their operation

In Kenya the first 6 of these services were included in the original ordinance; 3 others were added later in 1950, and 4 more in 1954. In late 1958, however, amended ordinances reduced the number in both Kenya and Tanganyika to 10.

Nyasaland has 10 services in its schedule. These included the first 6 on the Tanganyika list together with:

Air
Public transport services provided by Nyasaland Railways,
    Rivers and Lakes Services

Transport necessary for the supply and distribution of liquid and solid fuels and lubricants, essential foodstuff and supplies necessary for the maintenance of law and order

Telecommunications, posts and telegraphs

Jamaica also has 10 services, including 8 on the long Tanganyika list, as well as gas and public passenger transport services.

Uganda and Northern Rhodesia are rather a contrast to these territories. The Northern Rhodesian schedule and the original (1949) schedule in Uganda covered only water, electricity, health, sanitary and hospital services. In 1951 Uganda added transport necessary for the operation of these services, and in 1957 it added fire services. So far there has been no addition to Northern Rhodesia's schedule.

The shorter lists of Uganda and Northern Rhodesia are restricted to services whose continuity is essential to the preservation of life and health of the inhabitants. In the much longer lists, however, are included some services essential only to the smooth running of the economy, as well as services which may be essential to the maintenance of law and order in an emergency. There have been strong criticisms of the inclusion of such services in permanent legislation restricting the right to strike.

The need for colonial governments to have powers to enable them to protect the public from the dangerous consequences of stoppages in such essential public services as light and power, water, hospital and sanitation has generally been accepted by all sections of opinion. But the British T.U.C., the I.C.F.T.U. and the I.L.O. have all been much concerned with the possibility that essential services legislation might impinge on legitimate trade union activities. Tanganyika and other territories were much criticized for extending the list of scheduled services far beyond those that could reasonably be regarded as essential. The Colonial Office has also supported the view that compulsory arbitration when extended over a wide range of industries is in conflict with the policy of the British Government to encourage the development of free collective bargaining and voluntary machinery for the settlement of disputes. As a result of pressures exerted from Britain, those colonial governments which tended to schedule a large number of services as essential, amended their legislation, though not always as much as British opinion might have desired. However, since the 1951 despatch certain other defects in the policy then advocated have become apparent. Since the 'essential services' legislation was concerned with stoppages arising out of a 'trade dispute', it could not be effective against politically inspired strikes or stoppages of work not connected with a 'trade dispute'. Moreover, the obligation on governments to resort to compulsory arbitration has enabled unions to force them to make larger concessions to workers in essential industries than was justified on the grounds of economic policy. In the light of these difficulties, opinion had veered round by 1960 to the point where the 'essential service' type of restriction on strikes was thought to be less desirable than the earlier model, the 1875 Conspiracy and Protection of Property Act.

Compulsory Arbitration in Ordinary Disputes

At the moment when the British Colonial Secretary had come to the conclusion that compulsory arbitration had major weaknesses, a trend was already evident in some of the newly independent territories in favour of making all strikes illegal. The governments of these territories fear strikes for both political and economic reasons. Where political opposition has been eliminated they are afraid that industrial unrest may be provoked and strikes used as a means of overthrowing their rule. But even when political factors are not dominant the economic argument against permitting strikes carries much weight. The belief is strong, even among trade unionists, that when a country is trying to pull itself up with its own bootstraps it cannot afford the luxury of strikes.

This argument is, however, based more upon a liking for regulation for its own sake than on either a convincing theoretical or empirical demonstration that economic strikes have had or are having an adverse effect on economic growth. It may well be that the effect of bottling up grievances that would otherwise have led to strikes results in the slowing down of adaptation to change and to the adoption of modern organizational methods and other imperatives of industrial development. The pressures generated by strikes may have a stimulating effect that is more beneficial to economic growth than a deterrent to it.   It would be difficult to prove from the history of the more advanced countries that the prevention of strikes by law would have resulted in an increase in their rate of economic growth.   However, the fact that the case for making strikes illegal is not based upon any proven economic analysis is not likely to influence governments that have decided not to tolerate industrial stoppages.

Compulsory arbitration has, of course, been a feature of the industrial relations systems of Australia and New Zealand for a very long time.   In these countries it was introduced (at a time when trade unionism was very weak) in the belief that it would foster the organization of labour, and at the same time ensure that wage earners received a fair reward for their labours. The establishment of compulsory arbitration in India was based upon a similar set of considerations.

At the time of writing two independent countries (Ceylon and Ghana), one self-governing state (Singapore) and one Crown Colony (Aden) have comprehensive provisions for compulsory arbitration, combined with restrictions on the right to strike which are not confined to any particular class of industry. The provisions are, however, quite different from one another. In 1962 another newly independent territory, Tanganyika, was on the point of introducing some form of compulsory arbitration.

Ceylon

In Ceylon the history of compulsory reference of disputes is a long one.   Under the 1931 Industrial Disputes Ordinance the then controller of labour could, subject to directions from the governor, take steps to enable the parties to a dispute to meet under an independent chairman, make an inquiry as to whether reference of the dispute to a conciliation board was likely to lead to a settlement, and irrespective of the consent of the parties, refer it to such a board.   However, if there were any arrangements for conciliation within the industry the controller of labour could only act after a failure of these arrangements, and with the consent of both parties.   If the board failed to bring about a settlement it sent a report on the proceedings, with its own recommendations for the settlement of the dispute, to the controller. These reports had then to be published, and if neither party rejected them they became binding on both sides until one of them gave a notice of repudiation; strikes were forbidden while the settlement was in force.

The 1931 ordinance thus contained some element of compulsory arbitration, though not all the usual conditions were present, and no very clear distinction was made between the conciliation and arbitration functions of the boards. The ordinance was repealed in 1950 and replaced by a long and rather complicated Industrial Disputes Act, which was itself amended several times during 1956 and 1957. Under the latest provisions the commissioner of labour is obliged to take steps to promote the settlement or any dispute which exists or is apprehended. He may refer a dispute to any internal arrangements existing within an industry or attempt conciliation, or, with the consent of both parties, he may refer it to an arbitrator. In addition, the minister may refer any dispute compulsorily to an industrial court for settlement or, if he thinks it is a minor dispute, he may refer it to an arbitrator appointed by the labour commissioner, or to a labour tribunal.[12]

Where conciliation is attempted, any settlement reached is to be published in the Gazette, and all settlements are binding on the parties concerned until repudiated by written notice. Where a settlement cannot be reached, the conciliator must make a report giving his recommendations for a settlement, and all parties to the dispute must state within 14 days whether they accept or reject the recommendations. If no party rejects them, then the settlement is gazetted and comes into force as though it were an agreed settlement.[13]

When disputes are referred voluntarily or compulsorily to an arbitrator or arbitration tribunal the award is published in the Gazette and is again binding on both sides—in this case for a minimum period of 12 months, after which it may be repudiated

---

[12] Until 1957 a dispute could be referred to a district judge, failing agreement on a joint nomination of an arbitrator. Labour tribunals were established in 1957, with the principal function of adjudicating on disputes between individual workers and their employers.

[13] Under this same Act any collective agreement reached in industry may be submitted to the Commissioner of Labour for publication in the Gazette. If it is published it then becomes legally binding on the parties concerned until one of them repudiates it. In certain circumstances the minister may by Order extend such an agreement and make it binding on employers who were not party to it.

by any party giving 3 months' written notice of repudiation. Finally, there is the compulsory reference of disputes to the industrial court. An industrial court may consist of either one or three persons, appointed from an established panel. Its award is to be gazetted by the Commissioner of Labour; it is binding on both parties and forms an implied term of the conditions of employment. Any party may make application to the minister for an award of the industrial court to be set aside, modified or replaced, and the application must be submitted for consideration by the court, though in the normal case applications will not be accepted within 12 months of the date of the award. The court may then confirm, set aside, replace or modify the award, and its decision will be gazetted and have the same force as a new award.

It is an offence in Ceylon for anyone bound by an enforceable collective agreement, a settlement under conciliation, or an award of an arbitrator, labour tribunal or industrial court to start a lockout, take part in a strike or induce or incite anyone to take part in a strike.

Ghana

In Ghana the provisions are of a different sort. Under the Industrial Relations Act of 1958 and its amendments, compulsory arbitration provisions are made for certain classes of employees in private industry, based on provisions for the establishment of compulsory negotiating machinery, and, again, on the prohibition of strikes and lockouts. A trade union may apply, through the Trade Union Congress, to the Minister of Labour for a certificate appointing the union concerned as the representative organization to bargain with an employer on matters concerning a specified class of employees. The minister, after consultation with the appropriate employers' association, may issue the certificate provided that no other certificate is already in force for the same class of employees. A certificate may be granted, notwithstanding the fact that some of the employees concerned may not be members of the applicant union. Under the terms of the original act of 1958, if any other trade union or an employer made representations to the minister on the grounds that less than 40 per cent. of the employees concerned were members of a certified trade union, then the minister had the right, in his discretion, to withdraw the certificate, and could, if he thought it appropriate, consult with the employers concerned before doing so. However, the 1959 amendment gave the minister complete discretion to amend or to withdraw a certificate.

A trade union to which a certificate has been issued, and the employees concerned, must nominate representatives to a standing negotiating committee, whose constitution and rules must be approved by the minister. All negotiations must take place through this committee. Either party may give notice to the other, requiring them to enter into negotiations on 'all matters concerned with the employment or non-employment or with the terms of employment or the conditions of labour' of any of the employees concerned. The parties are thereupon bound under threat of penalty to negotiate, and to try to reach agreement.

An agreement reached through a standing negotiating committee must have a minimum term of a year, and is enforceable as part of the terms of contract of employment. No rights conferred by such an agreement may be waived by any employee in a class covered by the agreement. The minister may make extension orders applying the terms of a collective agreement to other classes of employers and their employees.

If, on the other hand, either party is satisfied that negotiations in a standing negotiating committee have failed, then the minister may be asked to appoint a conciliation officer; a request from the workers' side being transmitted through the T.U.C. The minister will then appoint a conciliator, unless he thinks the dispute is already being referred, with some likelihood of success, to internal arrangements for arbitration or conciliation. If agreement has not then been reached within two weeks, or the conciliator believes that there is no prospect of reaching agreement, he may report to the minister, who will either appoint a senior officer of the Ministry of Labour to act as an additional conciliator, or will serve the parties with a notice setting out what appear to be the issues between the parties, asking them whether they agree to have these issues referred to arbitration, and notifying them that if *one* of them consents, he has the power to refer the matter immediately to arbitration. If one or both parties consent, the minister then refers the matter to a tribunal consisting of a sole arbitrator, an arbitrator assisted by assessors nominated by each side, or an equal number of arbitrators nominated by each side, with an independent chairman. The award of a tribunal must be forwarded to the minister and takes effect when confirmed by him. Once confirmed it has the effect of a new collective agreement, and is thus binding on the parties concerned.

Employees for whom a certificate has been issued may only go on strike if the party initiating the dispute has given notice that it does not consent to arbitration and if four weeks have elapsed without the minister having directed that the dispute be referred to arbitration on the consent of the other party. Strikes or lockouts in any other circumstances are unlawful; in particular, no strike may be lawfully called with regard to any matter not connected with the 'employment or non-employment or terms of employment or conditions of labour of any of the employees'. In 1960 new and complicated definitions of 'strikes' and 'lockouts' were introduced which cover 'go slow' strikes as well as complete stoppages of work.

The provisions only affect employees in respect of whom a certificate has been issued. They cannot therefore affect public servants, municipal or local government employees or teachers, who cannot have a certificate issued, and, therefore, may in no circumstances lawfully strike. Uncertified unions, or employees in respect of whom no certificate has been issued, have no rights to force an employer to negotiate; their only form of redress is the voluntary arbitration of the 1941 Ordinance.

Singapore

Singapore's Industrial Relations Ordinance of 1960 is based on principles borrowed from Australian legislation, which are different from those adopted by Ghana, but which give the same kind of emphasis to controlled negotiating procedure and enforceable agreements. Under the ordinance it is illegal to strike or to lockout in furtherance of a trade dispute of which the Industrial Arbitration Court has cognizance; this may come about by a joint request for arbitration from the parties to the dispute, or by direction of the Minister of Labour, or by a proclamation from the *Yang di Pertuan Negara* (Head of State) that special circumstances make it essential that the dispute be sub-mitted to the court.[14]

The ordinance enables a trade union or an employer to serve a statutory notice on the other party setting out proposals for a collective agreement, and inviting the other side to negotiate. If an acceptance of the invitation is not given within 7 days the party serving the notice may inform the commissioner of labour. The commissioner or a conciliation officer will thereupon try to persuade the second party to accept the invitation, and if it appears that an employer is to some extent reluctant to nego-tiate because he thinks only a minority of his employees are members of the trade union concerned, then the commissioner is empowered to take a secret ballot of the employees on the question of trade union membership, and to communicate the result to the employer and the trade union.

If there is still a refusal to negotiate, the labour commissioner must report this to the minister, and, subject to ministerial direction, will notify the Registrar of the Industrial Arbitration Court that a trade dispute exists. Again, if negotiations start, but more than 14 days elapse after the serving of the notice without agreement being reached, either party may notify the commissioner, and either he or a conciliation officer may then try to help the parties to reach agreement. If more than 7 days pass after conciliation has begun and the commissioner thinks that an agreement is unlikely, or if he thinks conciliation would be of no avail at all, he must again notify the minister, and subject to direction, notify the registrar that a trade dispute exists.[15]

If, on the other hand, an agreement is reached after negotia-tion or conciliation, a memorandum of its terms must be de-livered to the Registrar of the Industrial Arbitration Court, for examination by the President of the Court. All agreements must specify that they will remain in force for a given period of between eighteen months and three years, and must normally

---

[14] High penalties are laid down for acting in furtherance of an illegal strike or lockout; fines of up to $2,000, six months' imprisonment, or both, may be incurred by offenders.

[15] The minister may always defer the notification of a trade dispute if he thinks further conciliation desirable, and for this purpose he is empowered to direct any person, on pain of imprisonment, and whether connected with the trade dispute or not, to attend at a meeting presided over by the minister or a nominee of the minister.

make provision for the settlement of disputes arising out of the operation of the agreement. If these conditions are not fulfilled the president must refuse to certify the agreement, and he may also refuse to certify it if he is of the opinion that it is not in the public interest. Once certified, however, an agreement has the effect of an award of the Industrial Arbitration Court—that is to say, it is binding on all parties.

The court itself, which is established by this ordinance, consists of a permanent president (who has the status and privileges of Judge of the Supreme Court, and is appointed by the Head of State on the advice of the Prime Minister), and normally, when it is adjudicating on a dispute or on another matter, two members chosen from panels [16] previously nominated by each side of industry. The court must determine the dispute expeditiously, having regard 'not only to the interests of the persons immediately concerned, but to the interests of the community as a whole, and in particular the condition of the economy of the State'. The court cannot, however, adjudicate in relation to certain government employees, except with the express permission of the *Yang di Pertuan Negara*.

Awards of the Industrial Arbitration Court, like collective agreements, must be made for a specific period of between eighteen months and three years, but application may be made for an award to continue in force for a further period. Normally awards must contain provisions for the settlement of disputes arising out of their operation. Both awards and certified agreements are binding on all parties concerned, and in addition the minister may request the court to inquire into the desirability of extending either an award or an agreement to other classes of employers, employees or trade unions. The court may, after hearing all interested parties, give an opinion as to whether any extension is desirable. If the opinion is in the affirmative the minister may then make an order accordingly, if he considers it desirable to do so. Awards may not be challenged in the ordinary courts, but application may be made to the industrial court for their interpretation, or variation, or, in some circumstances, for the variation of agreements.

[16] Opportunity is given for employers and employees concerned in the dispute to select their own representatives from the panel for any given dispute. The employer panel includes three nominees of the Minister of Finance, as representative of the government as employer.

Among many other provisions in this ordinance, power is given to the Industrial Arbitration Court to order compliance with an award or to issue injunctions against contravention or non-observance, though a prosecution for a breach of an award must be pursued in the ordinary courts. It may punish a failure to comply with an order or an injunction as contempt of court.[17] In normal cases no advocate or solicitor may appear before the court, nor take part in negotiations towards a collective agreement, and the parties may be represented only by a trade union officer, an employee of the party or, in the case of a party which is an employees' trade union, by an industrial relations officer of the Ministry of Labour.

There is also provision in this Singapore ordinance for the minister to appoint a board of inquiry into an industrial matter, if he thinks that the matter would not be satisfactorily regulated by the other machinery. Boards may sit in public or private at their discretion, and report to the minister, who will then present their reports to the Legislative Council.

Aden

Finally, in Aden, the Industrial Relations (Conciliation and Arbitration) Ordinance of 1960 made very comprehensive provision for compulsory settlement of disputes by an industrial court. The ordinance was passed as a measure of desperation after the normal procedures of negotiation appeared to have broken down entirely and a very large number of damaging strikes had occurred. Stoppage after stoppage had been called on trifling issues, for political reasons rather than to achieve improvements in wages and working conditions. The object of the Aden Government was not to outlaw strikes in all circumstances, but rather to make the unions adopt a more responsible attitude to collective bargaining. The main principle behind the ordinance is that unions can win their freedom from its restrictions if they provide evidence to convince the court that they are prepared to bargain in good faith. The concluding of a collective agreement would constitute such evidence. So far, however, no union or employer has asked

---

[17] Anyone found guilty of contempt is not only liable to a penalty but is ineligible to be nominated for election as a trade union officer for a period of two years.

for a certificate of exemption, but there has been a sharp fall in the number of strikes, and to this extent the ordinance, ingeniously designed to foster collective bargaining, may be said to be successful; but its adoption aroused fierce opposition from the Aden T.U.C., and it has not received enthusiastic support from employers, so that it is unlikely to remain in effect when a further measure of self-government is granted.[18]

The court established by the ordinance has only one permanent member—a president appointed by the governor, who may at any time appoint assessors nominated by each party to a dispute to assist him in any of his functions as he thinks fit. As in Singapore, the president has the privileges of a judge of the Supreme Court, and apart from a provision empowering the Chief Justice to make rules regulating the procedure of the industrial court, and providing for appeals to the Supreme Court, on a point of law, he is not subject to direction from any other authority.

The provisions for the regulation and compulsory arbitration of disputes apply to all employers and employees in the Colony of Aden, except firstly, those in an industry or occupation where a wages council has been established,[19] and secondly, any cases where a successful application has been made to the president of the industrial court for a certificate of exemption on the grounds that an agreement for the satisfactory settlement of disputes has been concluded between an employer or an association of employers and a trade union.[20]   In such cases the procedure of conciliation and voluntary arbitration under the old Trade Disputes (Arbitration and Inquiry) Ordinance are still open. Apart from these two exceptions, the Crown has the right to refuse compulsory arbitration in disputes to which it is a party, and if it does refuse, then for the purposes of that dispute also, the compulsory arbitration provisions do not apply. In these cases strikes and lockouts are not illegal, nor are they illegal in

---

[18] In fact, consideration was already being given to its repeal less than two years after its announcement following the raising of the questions as to whether or not it was in contravention of the International Labour Code.

[19] A Wage Councils Ordinance was enacted simultaneously with the Industrial Relations Ordinance.

[20] A procedure is laid down for the withdrawal of a certificate on the application of either party if the agreement is not being observed. This involves the appointment of a board of inquiry into the matter under the Trade Disputes (Arbitration and Inquiry) Ordinance.

disputes of which the industrial court has refused to take cognizance because of a failure on the part of employers or employees' associations to negotiate in good faith.

The procedure to be followed is that either party may report a dispute to the labour officer, who must first seek to bring about settlement of the dispute before remitting the report to the industrial court. He is obliged to refer the matter to any existing machinery that the parties might have established, including any joint industrial council they may have set up, unless he is satisfied that these means have already been tried and failed. If there are no such arrangements, or if there is a failure to reach a settlement within a reasonable time, the labour officer must take other steps to secure a settlement. He may act as a conciliator, and may require the parties to appoint representatives to help settle the dispute. A memorandum of any settlement reached under conciliation must be countersigned by the labour officer and forwarded to the industrial court, and is then binding upon the parties for a minimum period of six months, after which it may be repudiated by either party, provided that one month's notice in writing has been given to the labour officer.

If no settlement can be reached under conciliation within 14 days [21] the labour officer must report the fact to the industrial court, giving particulars of the dispute and stating whether in his opinion an agreement can be expected shortly. Should the Crown be a party to the dispute, then it is at this stage that it must state whether or not it will accept arbitration. The court may allow further time for the settlement of the dispute, or it may refuse to take cognizance of the dispute if it is of the opinion that the employers concerned have failed to negotiate in good faith, in which case none of the other provisions apply, and a strike would be legal. Otherwise, the court will proceed to determine the dispute by arbitration. It is empowered to order the parties to attend its proceedings, [22] and to demand the attendance of witnesses and the furnishing of any particulars it requires. The awards of the court are binding upon the parties and must be given a specific term not exceeding two years

---

[21] Or less if the urgency of the case requires.
[22] It may nevertheless hear and determine the dispute in the absence of one of the parties if there is a refusal to attend.

during which time they remain in force.   Appeals on a point of law may, however, be made to the Supreme Court, and applications for variations may be made to the industrial court, though for the first twelve months after the date of the award they will only normally be considered for the purposes of removing ambiguity or uncertainty.

It is an offence in Aden to take part in a strike or impose a lockout, or to advise, encourage, incite or intimidate a workman or employer into striking or imposing a lockout, unless the party concerned is covered by a certificate of exemption from the president of the court, or by a wage council, or the strike or lockout is in connection with a dispute of which the court has refused to take cognizance or has refused to accept for arbitration.   It is also an offence to advise, encourage or incite anyone to refrain from entering into a written agreement, refrain from accepting employment or from offering himself for work which is in accordance with an award;   or to advise, encourage or incite someone not to comply with the award, or 'to retard, obstruct or limit the progress of work to which the award applies', or to 'perform work to which the award applies in a manner different from that customarily applicable to that work', unless it can be proved that the reason for the conduct was unrelated to the terms and conditions prescribed by the award, or was related to a failure by an employer to observe the award.

Part Four

The Development of Industrial Relations

CHAPTER 12

THE PATTERN OF EMPLOYMENT

THE emergence of trade unions and the development of industrial relations in the tropical territories with which this study has been concerned have been closely connected with the growth and pattern of employment. As yet, in most of the territories examined, paid employment extends only to a relatively small proportion of the population, but it has been an important feature for a long time in some places; for instance, in Aden, Hong Kong and Singapore the proportion of the population employed as wage and salary earners is as significant as it is in many of the older industrial countries.

It is clear from an examination of official reports that in many territories there has been a substantial increase in the number of paid employees during the past twenty years. This rise in employment has largely come about through the expansion of industrial activity, public works, retail and wholesale trade, transport and communications and agricultural developments. As the pace of economic growth is speeded up, with the help of international technical assistance and the pressure of rising population, this trend is likely to continue at a faster pace.

In most of the territories the wage labour employed is predominantly male. So far as the African countries are concerned it is only in Kenya, and to a lesser extent in Tanganyika, that any considerable proportion of the labour force consists of women; in none but these two territories and Northern Rhodesia is more than 1 per cent. of the African women in paid employment. There are, however, large numbers of women engaged in trading in West Africa on a self-employed basis, working for profit rather than for wages, and the importance of women in peasant agriculture is very great throughout Africa.

Relatively few Asian women work for wages in Africa, but the proportion of European women in employment is high. Over 40 per cent. of the adult female Europeans in Uganda are employed and over 30 per cent. in Kenya.

337

In the West Indies it is more common than in Africa for women to be employed as wage-earners. They find work on the sugar estates, in banana loading and, increasingly, in the shops, offices, laundries and hotels that are rapidly developing with the expanding tourist industry. In Singapore and Hong Kong women are finding greater scope for employment with the development of industry and services. In Malaya large numbers of women are employed by the government and on the rubber, coconut, oil palm, tea and pineapple estates, and in the tin-mining and tobacco industries. Women are also employed on the sugar, tea and tobacco estates of Mauritius.

I. Occupational Distribution

The distribution of the employed labour force is shown for those African territories where figures are available in the table on page 339. These figures are subject to a good many limitations, but they give some indication of the importance of the relative numbers employed in the different industries.[1] The comparatively small importance of manufacturing is generally evident. Everywhere, with the exception of Aden, Hong Kong and Singapore, agriculture is either the largest, or one of the largest, industries. A greater proportion of the population of the territories is engaged in subsistence agriculture, including the production of cash crops and animal herds, than in any other economic activity; agriculture also employs the largest body of wage-earners.

Agriculture and Forest Products

Employment in agriculture is of three main types—on indigenous peasant holdings, on plantations and on settlers' farms. Peasant cultivators in West Africa, Uganda, Tanganyika, Nyasaland, Malay, Fiji, the West Indies and elsewhere, producing cocoa, cotton, coffee, groundnuts, bananas, rice, tobacco and sugar, rely basically upon members of their own family for labour; but in some places they employ a considerable number of persons in harvesting, and in cocoa farming

---

[1] For example, it is estimated that in Nigeria there were perhaps some 200,000 employees working in small establishments employing less than 10 persons which were not included in these statistics. Thus, the total wage-earning population in 1959 was probably about 700,000. Cf. T. M. Yesufu, *Industrial Relations in Nigeria* (Oxford, 1962).

Numbers of Employees in Different Branches of Economic Activity in Thousands

	Ghana 1960	Sierra Leone 1958	Nigeria 1959	Kenya 1960	Nyasaland 1960	Northern Rhodesia 1960	Tanganyika 1960	Uganda 1960
Agriculture, forestry and fishing	152	2·1	45·5	271·8	85·5	48·4	201·0	61·3
Mining and quarrying	39	6·6	41·2	5·0	0·3	50·2	12·0	5·7
Manufacturing	23	n.a.	32·4	52·3	17·0	26·4	19·0	25·8
Construction	65	11·3	102·9	33·0	21·6	50·6	10·0	30·3
Electricity, gas and water	13	n.a.	16·4	2·5	1·9	2·9	2·0	2·2
Commerce	42	16·2	42·2	39·0	11·9	19·0	15·0	14·7
Transport, storage and communication	40	10·5	47·6	46·4	5·4	11·2	7·0	11·1
Services	117	12·5	144·4	171·3	42·2	94·8	108·0	93·6
Others	—	—	—	0·4	—	—	—	—
Total	491	n.a.	472·6	622·2	189·3	305·3	374·0	244·7

Sources: *I.L.O. Year Book of Labour Statistics. Labour Department Reports.*

especially, a considerable amount of permanent employment is found. These labourers are often not employed on a day-wage basis, and some form of share-cropping is usual.[2] It is doubtful whether there is any form of trade union organization at all among these workers. Agricultural labourers, engaged in individual contracts and working more or less in isolated conditions, have little opportunity for combination.

Where large-scale plantations have been developed, conditions are favourable for wage employment. Plantation agriculture is important in Mauritius, South-East Asia, the West Indies and parts of Africa. It exists on a large scale in Tanganyika, on a lesser scale in Nyasaland, in the Southern Cameroons and to a much smaller extent in the Eastern region of Nigeria and a few other places in Africa. On the island of Mauritius the sugar estates provide paid employment for a large proportion of the economically active population. In South-East Asia substantial numbers of workers are employed on the rubber, coconut, oil palm, tea and pineapple estates of Malaya. In Fiji sugar-cane farming is largely a peasant enterprise, but harvesting gives rise to some paid employment. Plantations growing sugar, cocoa, citrus and pineapple have been until recently the most important source of employment in the West Indies.

Generally, plantation enterprises are owned by large expatriate concerns, sometimes with world-wide connections. These tend to be highly organized undertakings with salaried managements—usually of European origin, though this is slowly changing—employing large numbers of unskilled labourers and smaller numbers of specialized skilled men, paid on standardized rates and supervised in somewhat the same way as industrial workers. Some of the smaller plantations and estates are owned by private individuals or small local companies. An exceptional type is the publicly-owned plantation, such as the large Nigerian Eastern Region Development Corporation, which employs a large number of the agricultural workers employed in the Federation of Nigeria. There are also various production development board and research institute plantations in Nigeria and elsewhere, whose activities are partially experimental. The mainly African-owned rubber

---

[2] See Polly Hill, *The Gold Coast Cocoa Farmer* (Oxford, 1957), for insight into West African contracts in cocoa farming.

industry of Western Nigeria is probably nearer to a plantation industry than to peasant agriculture.

In general, the larger plantations and estates are today likely to provide good conditions of labour, some welfare facilities and fairly good wages for their employees. They can often afford to employ specialist personnel officers, improve housing standards, and provide excellent schools, dispensaries, hospitals and recreation grounds, clubs and institutes. On the smaller, locally-owned plantations and estates, however, management often shows a lack of interest in labour problems, and there is less drive and enthusiasm to improve working conditions, provide better housing and more than rudimentary welfare services. The degree of trade union organization among plantation and estate workers varies considerably. In the rubber plantations of Malaya, Indian workers are members of one of the best-organized unions in South-East Asia. Workers on the sugar estates of British Guiana, Trinidad and Jamaica belong to unions that are quite large and powerful. In Africa unions of plantation workers have been fairly weak, with the possible exception of the union organizing the Cameroons Development Corporation, but considerable efforts are being made by the Plantation Workers' International to build up these organizations in East Africa. These efforts have been particularly successful in East Africa, where in Kenya, Uganda and Tanganyika plantation workers' unions are now firmly established. In Fiji and Mauritius sugar workers are organized in relatively large numbers; the smallholders' organizations are particularly strong and militant bodies in Fiji.

The smaller European-owned plantations and estates merge gradually into the settler farming enterprises. For instance, the European-owned and managed tobacco, tea, coffee and cotton farms of Northern Rhodesia, Nyasaland, Tanganyika and Kenya have developed in this way. However, the more typical settler agricultural holding in Africa is an extensively worked mixed farm, producing livestock, grain and other foodstuffs and usually employing a number of African farm workers, resident on the farm lands. Working and living conditions vary considerably from one holding to another in this sector; relations tend, almost inevitably, to be on a more intimate basis than where employment is on the mass scale which usually predominates in plantation agriculture. Few employees in the smaller enterprises are likely to belong to unions, though they may belong to mass political organizations where these exist. In Kenya a General Farming Union was started in the early 1960's which has attracted some support and appears to be making measurable progress.

Timber production has some of the characteristics of the agricultural industry, but it employs only a fraction of the numbers engaged in the production of agricultural crops. There are some relatively large-scale concerns engaged in the production of timber in Malaya, British Honduras, Nigeria and the Cameroons, but for the most part timber is produced by small-scale units. Forestry and sawmill employees are usually ranked as semi-skilled or unskilled workers, but they often enjoy no better rates of pay than agricultural workers, and frequently their working conditions are far worse.

Fishing must also be mentioned, since it is one of the oldest forms of economic activity and it employs a large number of people in many territories, but normally the work is carried out on an individual or co-operative basis which is not subject to trade union organization.

Mining and Oil Industries

Compared with agriculture the mining and oil industries employ a much smaller number of workers, but the economic importance of these industries is very great. Mining enterprise takes many different forms and there is no really representative size or type of undertaking. In some cases, as in the Rhodesia Copperbelt or in the bauxite areas of the West Indies, large-scale undertakings are controlled by very large mining organizations with world-wide connections, whose headquarters are in Europe, North America or South Africa. Where the scale of mining is smaller, as in East Africa, the enterprise may be in the hands of a medium-sized company which may not be associated with any of the larger and better known international mining interests. In some places there are numerous small mine owners or prospectors; in the Tanganyika gold fields they are usually European and Asian; in the smaller tin-mining areas in Northern Nigeria mainly European and African, and in Malaya Chinese. Recently much of the diamond digging in Sierra

Leone, and to a smaller extent in Ghana, has been undertaken by African licensed diggers, sometimes financed by members of other races. Illegal digging by such syndicates has also become notorious in Sierra Leone. Diamond and gold mining in British Guiana has been carried on since the nineteenth century by negro 'pork-knockers' prospecting individually. An attempt to apply larger-scale methods of mining gold in British Guiana was tried and abandoned in the 1950's. Special cases of public ownership of a mining undertaking are the Enugu Colliery in Eastern Nigeria, which was run as a government department until 1950, and is now controlled by a public corporation, and the Williamson diamond mines in Tanganyika, originally privately owned but recently taken over as a partnership between the Tanganyika Government and the de Beers group.

As with most types of enterprise, the conditions of employment within any one territory tend to vary directly with the size of the undertaking. The largest mining companies usually provide comparatively high wages and often good housing and adequate rations are included as part of remuneration. Among the smaller private mine owners, tributors and prospectors there is always a proportion who lack reasonable conditions of work and housing, and sometimes they are unable to fulfil terms of a contract of labour. In the Nigerian tin-fields minimum wages and minimum conditions of work have been established since 1942 by legislation; unfortunately the standards laid down were not revised frequently enough to avoid difficulties, but in 1956 a Minesfield Joint Industrial Council was established. This J.I.C. was at first only moderately successful, but in recent years it seems to have achieved better results and it is well regarded by all parties.

Trade unionism is generally fairly strong in the mining industry, but it is in the largest mining concentrations, and especially where individual undertakings are large, that organization has been most successful. Strong mineworkers' unions of comparatively long standing exist in Northern Rhodesia, Ghana and Sierra Leone, and the movement is quite strong in Nigeria; though both in the tin mines and in the collieries there has been much internal strife and a tendency to break away, based on tribal antagonisms and on the scattered and heterogeneous nature of the tin-mining industry. In East Africa the smaller scale of the mining industry has made organization more difficult, and trade unions have not become securely established. The bauxite workers of Jamaica and the West Indies are well organized. Before the communist uprising in Malaya the Chinese employees in tin mines were trade union members, but attempts to rebuild union membership among tin miners in Malaya for a long time failed to evoke any positive response. In 1962 there were signs of an awakening interest in unions.

Oil extraction and/or refining is economically the most important industry in Trinidad, Aden, Brunei and Sarawak. Exploration and refining is going on in other territories, and the distribution of the refined products provides jobs on a substantial scale in all of them. As a source of employment the oil industry does not compare with agriculture, but much of the labour employed is relatively skilled, jobs are reasonably secure and the companies are wealthy enough to pay high wages and provide good working conditions.

All the oil companies are owned by British, Dutch or American parent concerns. They are generally managed by European and American expatriates, but most of them are now anxious to promote local-born employees to higher technical and administrative posts. Training schemes and scholarships are available for those who are willing and able to take advantage of the opportunities. The oil workers in Trinidad belong to one of the strongest and most efficient trade unions in any of the British territories. They are also quite well organized in Aden, but unions have yet to develop in Brunei. Oil companies have paid a great deal of attention to the conditions of employment of their workers, and in general industrial relations are usually more highly developed in this industry than in many others.

Government and Local Government Services

It has been traditional, as well as economically necessary, for governments to undertake much of the development of such public utilities as railways, roads, harbours, electricity, telecommunications and water supplies. The building and operation of the railways has almost invariably been the responsibility of the government, and the employment by the government of direct labour on road building and road maintenance and on the construction of houses, offices, prisons and public buildings has usually been considerable. In Nigeria the coal mines are publicly owned and were developed by government enterprises, originally related to the supply of coal for the railways.

Traditionally, therefore, the governments are among the largest employers of labour in these territories. Moreover, apart from the size of their labour forces, the government's policy towards its employees is important in that it often sets a standard which other employers in the territory are expected to attain. Before powerful trade unions emerged, the wages and conditions of service provided by government departments have usually been determined in accordance with standards which those in authority considered to be reasonable in the prevailing circumstances. Employees of the larger European-owned enterprises, and sometimes also the employers themselves, have looked upon government conditions of employment as setting a reasonable kind of national minimum, and private employers have been encouraged to conform to this standard. But even without the pressures of conformity induced by political and psychological motives, the dominance of the government as an employer inevitably compels other employers in the labour market to follow its lead in setting rates of wages and other conditions of work, especially of such grades of labour as are not in abundant supply.

Employment of labour by municipalities, native authorities and other local-government bodies is mainly confined to administration, sanitation and other essential services, including water supplies, road making and repairing. Local-authority schools may also account for some employment.

As the territories have developed the numbers employed in the administrative departments have grown steadily. The civil service has become a major provider of employment for the better educated—both those with secondary education and those who have graduated from universities in Britain or elsewhere overseas.

Teaching in government, local-authority, missionary and private schools has also been one of the most important occupations chosen by the better-educated boys and girls. In the post-war period members of the teaching profession, like those in the civil service administrative departments, have usually enjoyed well-established conditions of employment regulated at the national level.   By local standards, rates of pay and other aspects of employment in these fields have been reasonably good, but they compare unfavourably in local eyes with the standards enjoyed by expatriates working in the country.

The defence services provide a considerable amount of employment in certain territories, such as Singapore, Malaya, Hong Kong and Aden, where there are important military installations.   Changes in defence policy have sometimes had a serious affect on employment, and not unnaturally when this has involved cuts in the numbers employed protest has been provoked and trade unions encouraged.

Trade union organization in public employment has in general been easier than in other employment because of the larger scale of the establishments and because of the fact that it has been official government policy to encourage the growth of trade unions.   This has ensured that governments would be bound to make some attempt to recognize and treat with unions of their own employees.   The Gold Coast was an exception to this general situation, when from 1941 to 1950 restrictions were placed on the right of civil servants to organize.   Similar restrictions were also applied for a time in Nyasaland.   A further reason why unions of government employees were among the earliest to be formed was that the educational standards, status and experience of these workers were relatively advanced.   The system of Whitley councils developed in the United Kingdom has been adopted in a number of the colonial territories, but it has not taken root firmly as yet in many of them.   Unfortunately staff relations in the public service have not been uniformly well handled, and as a consequence the Whitley committees have often gone through difficult periods.

Transport and Communications

In most of the territories the railways are publicly owned and managed either by government departments or government agencies such as the East African Railways and Harbours Board, or public corporations such as the Nigerian Railway Corporation.   Railway undertakings are, of course, large employers, and a fairly high proportion of the employees are in skilled or in responsible positions. Wages and conditions of work are generally up to the average for the territory concerned, and up to the standards set by the government; though in some cases, for example in the Rhodesian railways, for a number of years after the war staff and labour conditions, housing and other amenities seem to have been noticeably sub-standard.

The fact that railways have generally been, at least in some measure, under the control of the government from the beginning, that they have been among the largest employers, with a unified ownership and administration, and that the employment which they have provided has been stable and secure, has helped to encourage the growth of trade unions. As employers, government departments and public bodies have generally been more disposed to recognize trade unions than have some commercial employers. Thus, in almost every territory railway workers have been among the first to form strong and fairly successful trade unions.

The structure of road transport usually shows a marked contrast to that of the railways. Road transport is mostly under private ownership, and is organized on a small scale. In West Africa it is one of the most striking forms of private enterprise.[3] There are government-owned road-transport services in Nyasaland, and in some territories there are municipal passenger services. Bus services are, however, often a private-enterprise venture. The capital required to purchase a truck, which can be converted into a passenger as well as a goods vehicle, is relatively small, and this encourages local enterprise.

The structure of the private road transport industry, especially its localized basis and its generally small-scale organization, has made for great differences in conditions of employment. This type of industry is one in which it is particularly difficult to impose minimum standards; when regulations are applied they can usually be evaded. Trade unions are generally small and unstable where they exist at all. Nevertheless, when, as in Sierra Leone and parts of Tanganyika, fairly large-scale units have developed, they have encouraged the formation of strong trade unions, and sound negotiating machinery.

[3] See E. K. Hawkins, *Road Transport in Nigeria* (Oxford, 1958).

Sea transport is important to most territories, and coastal shipping especially is a fairly important source of employment Inland water transport is also important in Nyasaland, on Lake Victoria—where it is publicly owned—and to a smaller extent in the Gambia and on the Niger, Benue and Cross rivers of Nigeria, where the canoe and steamer services are run by private enterprise. But far more important as a source of employment in all the territories bordering on the sea are the ports. Dock labour is employed by large shipping companies, independent dock labour contractors, large importing firms or public authorities, such as the East African Railways and Harbours Board and the Singapore Harbour Board.

Much dock labour is employed on a casual basis, but in some places, for example, Singapore, Freetown, Mombasa and Dar-es-Salaam, dock labour schemes are in operation. Dockworker's trade unions are important in all the major ports in every territory; in some cases they are the most powerful unions in the territory. In the smaller seaports and in the river and lake ports, where the demand for labour is more seasonal and on a smaller scale, workers are generally engaged casually when required. Conditions of employment are often much inferior to the major ports and trade union organization is usually poor or non-existent.

Air transport, though an important and rapidly growing means of internal and international communication, is not, by comparison with road and rail, a large employer of labour. The significance of air transport as a source of employment is not, however, to be measured merely in numbers. The men employed in this industry are usually highly skilled workers, and many of them have to shoulder a great deal of responsibility. As more and more passengers and freight are carried by plane the importance of good industrial relations to the safe and efficient operation of air services will become increasingly evident.

The rates of pay and conditions of employment tend already to be good by local standards, but the employees of air transport organizations compare them unfavourably with those enjoyed by airline employees in countries with higher standards of living. The comparison is most obvious in the case of air crews, but the effect of the international labour market on the pay of these employees influences other related occupations. Although the industry is young, unions have already been established; they could not yet be termed strong organizations but their influence has been felt.

Other types of employment in communications include postal, telegraph and telephone services, and broadcasting and other telecommunications services. All of them are generally under the control of public authorities or private companies working under conditions regulated by franchise and restrictions, laid down by agreement and law. Employment is normally fairly good by local standards. As in other forms of government service, the employees in the telecommunications services have been among the first to form unions and to seek to improve their lot by collective bargaining.

Building and Civil Engineering Trades

Apart from the government, which is often one of the most important employers of men in the building and civil engineering industries, there are firms of every size and description, as is typical of the building industry almost everywhere. At one end of the scale are the branches of the very large British-owned civil engineering contracting firms, which undertake a wide range of public works, including road and bridge building, hydro-electric works and the erection of large public and commercial buildings. The overseas organizations of these firms are generally managed by expatriates, and senior technical staff are also frequently brought from the home country. The smaller building firms are usually local, although in many cases they are controlled by Europeans or Asians in East Africa and possibly Levantines in West Africa, and by Chinese in Singapore, Malaya and Borneo.

The very smallest jobbing concerns, as in Britain, generally consist of a man working on his own account, sometimes assisted by members of his family. An appreciable proportion of the carpenters, bricklayers and masons in most of the territories are self-employed, or alternate between periods of work on their own account and periods of employment with a building firm.

On the whole, conditions of employment in the building and civil engineering industry tend to be less attractive than in some other types of employment. Work in any one place or on any one project is usually temporary, and for that reason the long-term welfare of the employees, especially in such matters as housing conditions and ration supplies, tends to be given less weight than is given by employers in some other large industries with a large amount of fixed capital equipment. Another important reason is that unskilled building labour is generally in abundant supply, productivity is low and there is, therefore, relatively less incentive for employers to take the steps necessary to maintain a stable and contented labour force.

For much the same reasons as apply in the industrially advanced countries, in particular the more or less casual nature of building work, trade union organization is generally weak among the mass of labourers. And unlike the situation in the older industrialized countries, no strong tradition of organization has so far been developed by the craftsmen employed in the building industry.

Manufacturing

In none of the territories, with the exception of Hong Kong and Singapore, does manufacturing as yet occupy a very high proportion of the labour force. This sector of the economic activity, though rapidly increasing in many places, will probably remain relatively small as a source of employment for a long time in all but a few of the territories. Almost everywhere the typical form of manufacturing industry connected with processing the agricultural or forest products of the territory is in the light processing industries, such as soap and margarine, rum and sugar, plywood and joinery, tobacco and rubber, textiles and clothing. Certain types of processing industry are intimately connected with the growing of export crops; cotton ginning, the preparation of coffee beans and tea leaves and fruit canning. These processes are often undertaken on the estates, or at the headquarters of a producers' co-operative society.

There are breweries and soft-drink plants in some of the territories, and in some territories the assembly of motors and cycles is undertaken, and motor repairs shops are widespread. Fertilizer production and cement manufacture has been undertaken in a few areas, and concrete plants and brick and tile works are fairly common. Boat-building yards, foundries, railway repair shops and light engineering works are to be found here and there. In Hong Kong and Singapore, where wage-earners form a higher proportion of the total population than in other territories, the range of fabricated products of all kinds is rapidly growing.

Printing is fairly important in every territory. There are also the traditional craft industries of gold and silversmiths, blacksmiths, woodcarvers, leather craftsmen and weavers of straw, wool and silks.

Most of the manufacturing industries, even the largest, tend by European standards to be organized in small units of production. Many of the larger establishments, except in Hong Kong, are British owned; there are some American and European firms, but there is also a considerable amount of Asian capital in East Africa, the West Indies, Malaya and Singapore. A small, but growing amount of African enterprise is developing, especially in those industries in which establishments are smallest, the organization of production the least complex and capital needs at a minimum. In West Africa industrialization has sometimes taken the form of a partnership between the government and private concerns; for example, the important textile mills at Kanduna in Nigeria are run as a joint undertaking.

In the larger types of enterprise, where the buildings are modern, conditions of employment are reasonably good by any standard, but employment conditions are very poor in some of the smaller establishments in such industries as clothing manufacture, laundries and woodworking, especially in the large cities. Safety and working conditions in all territories are regulated by factory legislation, entailing the inspection of premises by officials. Laws concerned with safety and hygiene can be enforced relatively easily in the case of the large modern plants, but enforcement is much more difficult when it comes to the small under-capitalized indigenously-owned enterprises, because local employers would often be driven out of business if the regulations were strictly applied. In some cases wage councils or similar legislation have been adopted as a means of establishing and enforcing minimum wages and conditions.

Trade unionism is occasionally strong, especially in the larger enterprises, but it is often weak in the small firms. In certain

AA

territories unions are frequently based on single establishments; it is sometimes inevitable where an industry, such as tobacco processing or soap manufacture, consists of only one factory in the territory.   There is a tendency for amalgamation of the small units to take place, and this has been brought about, as has already been mentioned, by the legislation adopted in certain territories.

Commerce

There is no typical size of firm or establishment in the whole-sale and retail trade.   Undertakings range in size from large expatriate trading companies to the numerous self-employed petty traders in the streets and markets of every town and village in every territory.   In West Africa the bulk of the import and export trade and much of the trade at the wholesale level is in the hands of the large European or Levantine mer-cantile trading concerns.   A similar pattern of ownership, with the addition of Chinese and Indian merchants, prevails in the West Indies.   In East and Central Africa much of the mer-cantile business is in the hands of Asian, especially Indian, concerns employing Asian and African assistants.   Some of the retail outlets and much of the wholesale business is run by Europeans.   In South-East Asia the Chinese have been vigorous traders, and with the exception of some important European establishments they dominate the mercantile busi-ness.

The large expatriate firms in West Africa control some of the major shipping lines, and they handle most of the merchandise imported into each territory.   They control many of the channels of distribution of imported products, sometimes down to the retail level.   The export trade, above the level of small middlemen, is also largely in their hands.   In Nigeria at least some of the export produce itself is grown by these firms on their own plantations, and they also have a share in the pro-cessing and manufacturing industries.   Large numbers of men are employed by these mercantile firms, though employment is of the most heterogeneous nature, and many individual establishments, warehouses, retail stores, etc., are small.

In West Africa and the West Indies there are a number of rather smaller trading firms, under Lebanese and Indian control, which deal in textiles, clothing, hardware and dry goods. These are often family businesses employing relatively few outside the family group. Most of the retail trade in West Africa is in the hands of African traders, many of them women. Although some of the businesses are large, relatively little wage labour is employed and such as there is tends to be characterized by irregular terms of employment in which wages may have only a minor place.

The characteristic features of mercantile business are the personal relationship between employer and employee, and the small scale of the enterprise in many branches of trade. For these reasons trade union organization is rather difficult, but higher education and a degree of political consciousness have made shop assistants and office clerks among the first to organize in many places. Mercantile employees have often provided the leadership and administrative skills for unions of workers employed in other industries.

Personal and Domestic Service

As cities grow, personal service trades, such as catering, hotels, laundries, hairdressing, garage facilities and motor repairs, are becoming increasingly important as employers of labour. In territories where tourism has become an important feature of economic activity, as in Bermuda, the Bahamas and the West Indies, employment in those services has grown considerably.

Employment in domestic service of all kinds has existed for a long time in most of the territories, and in some cases the number of workers engaged in this activity is substantial. By the nature of their employment, domestic servants have a close personal relationship with their employers, and their conditions of service vary very greatly. Despite this there have been many attempts by domestic servants, especially those employed by Europeans, to organize into unions, but their success has not been very great. As in other countries, the most important factor regulating the level of wages and working conditions of domestic employees is the labour market. As the general standard of living rises that of domestic employees tends to rise too.

II. MIGRATION

The supply of indigenous labour available in most of the territories has generally been inadequate to meet the demands generated by European-directed agricultural and industrial enterprises. This situation could only be remedied by the migration of workers on a considerable scale, and an astonishing amount of movement within and between territories has been going on for more than a hundred years.

Permanent Migration

Migrant labour from overseas has been an important feature of the growth of the labour force in the West Indies, Aden, Mauritius, South-East Asia, Hong Kong and Fiji. In the early stages of Caribbean development African slaves were brought to labour on the sugar estates and other agricultural plantations. After the slave trade was abolished, indentured labourers were imported from South India to work for specified periods. It was assumed that on completion of their contract most of these workers would wish to return to their native land. Some did return, most stayed to establish a permanent rural population in Trinidad and British Guiana. The descendants of the slaves tended to migrate to the towns, so that today urban areas are predominantly African, and country areas East Indian, in racial composition. In the Windward and Leeward Islands, Barbados and Jamaica there are few Indians, and both rural and urban populations are largely composed of the descendants of the negro slaves.

After the indenture system was abolished, an employer was legally free to recruit labour, but the worker had to arrive free of debt. Since no written agreement could be entered into and either side was entitled to cancel a verbal agreement of employment at a month's notice, the employer had no legal hold over the immigrant. To obtain the labour that he required, an employer had to offer a rate that would induce men to accept the work offered; thus a market price for labour was established, and this could be bargained over.

Many Indian workers, assisted by an immigration fund, went to Malaya in search of work, and a large number of migrants who had paid their own travel expenses also entered Malaya each year. Between 1920 and 1939 the number of Indians assisted to emigrate to Malaya was 729,261. Those who travelled at their own expense were, until after the first world war, mainly 'members of the commercial classes, traders, moneylenders and clerks'.[4] In the 1930's a large proportion of the unassisted immigrants were labourers; in 1934, for example, some 22,000 arrived in Malaya, and in 1937 the figure rose to 50,000. Many of those who had emigrated to Malaya eventually returned to India, but large numbers have remained to form a permanent section of the population of the Malayan peninsula. In 1938 the total Indian population in the Malay States and the Straits Settlements was estimated to be approximately 750,000.

Numerically the Chinese now far exceed the Indians and almost equal the Malays in Malaya and Singapore. In 1956 there were 2,300,000 Chinese and 740,000 Indians in Malaya; in Singapore 1,000,000 Chinese and 124,000 Indians. The principal reason why the Chinese outnumber Indians to such a great extent in Malaya and Singapore today is that large numbers of Indians have returned home, and the Chinese have stayed to become the dominant economic group, both as employers and wage-earners.

In addition to the migration of Indians and Chinese, numbers of Javanese have moved to Malaya, but they do not constitute an important minority of the population, since they have been assimilated with the indigenous Malays, to whom they are ethnically similar, to form the Malaysian element in the population.

Indian immigrants brought into Mauritius and Fiji, Trinidad and British Guiana to work on the sugar estates have now become most important elements in the population. They are increasing and at a pace which has already given them a numerical majority.[5] This development has caused considerable political tension, and it is a critical factor in the industrial relations in these territories.

Most workers in the African territories are of rural origin and attached to the land in some way, either as peasant farmers themselves or as members of a family whose livelihood is concerned with the land. Probably the largest group of employees is composed of migrant workers who travel long distances, often hundreds of miles, from their homes to the place of employment. They may stay at work for only six months or they may stay for ten years or more, normally without losing touch with

---

[4] *Malaya Labour Department Annual Report*, 1934.
[5] In Trinidad they are still in a minority.

their families or home villages, to which they return at the end of the period of employment, or possibly at intervals during their employment.

In Africa migrant labour is especially important in Northern Rhodesia, Tanganyika and Uganda, and to a rather smaller extent in some West African territories. The number of wage-earners in Nyasaland is a fairly small proportion of the total, but about twice as many Nyasalanders were at one stage employed outside Nyasaland as were employed within the territory. Nyasaland and, to a lesser extent, Northern Rhodesia are sources of migrant labour for the industries of Southern Rhodesia and South Africa; and some labourers migrate southward from Southern Tanganyika. There is also much long-distance migration within all these countries. The importance of securing an adequate supply of labour to meet the needs of the agricultural estates and plantations has been emphasized by the governments of the territories, and many different sorts of measures have been introduced at various times before, during and after the last war, to increase the supply of African labour available for work within each territory.[6]

In addition to that element in the labour force which has migrated from a country far from its adopted land, there is another type of labour which migrates to the towns and farms from the surrounding areas. This type of labour, which is important in Africa in such industries as building, road construction and railway engineering, is never wholly dependent on employment, since a connection with a family peasant holding and the native village is always retained. In the larger centres of employment it is often these local men, who though primarily agriculturalists by family inheritance, form a high proportion of the skilled and higher-grade workers. Among the better-known examples in Africa are the Baganda working in Kampala, and the Luo and Kikuyu of Kenya. The Enugu coal mines in Nigeria have always been staffed mainly by men living within 20 or 30 miles of the mines, and a considerable proportion of the employees of the larger industrial and port towns in West Africa are generally from the local tribes.

---

[6] See P. G. Powesland, *Economic Policy and Labour* (Kampala, 1958); Reports of Labour Departments of Kenya, Uganda and Tanganyika 1945–56; Report of East African Royal Commission, Cmnd. 9475.

Seasonal Migrants

A third type of employee, common to all the territories, is the seasonal worker. Employment may fluctuate because of seasonal variations in the demand for labour; this occurs with the groundnut harvest in Nigeria and the Gambia, cotton-picking in Northern Nigeria, Uganda and Tanganyika, the cocoa harvest in Ghana, the coffee harvest in Kenya, the cutting of sugar cane in the West Indies, Mauritius and Fiji, and the harvesting of rice, citrus and other crops. Because of this seasonal fluctuation, migration to the employing area may take place, and local men may enter employment only at the time when work is available for a few weeks or months in the year. Or it may be that the employees will only present themselves for employment at certain seasons of the year; agriculturalists, for example, only appear when the main work of the farming year is over and the harvest has been gathered in, or during the 'hungry season', the period shortly before a new harvest when the income from employment provides the means to buy food to fill the gap. Migration is not only induced by shortage of food, but also by a sense of adventure or of achieving manhood and by a desire to obtain some cash with which to buy manu-factured consumer goods. This is the type of labour which is employed on the Nigerian cocoa farms and in the tin mines, in agriculture in parts of East Africa and on road-making in many territories.

There are also some seasonal fluctuations in the supply of the rather more settled migrant labour. Labourers intending to migrate for a period of several years will normally not make the journey to work until after the end of the main harvesting season, and will go back home perhaps several years later in time for another harvesting season. In the busiest farming season labour in the centres of employment may be in ab-normally short supply because the drift of migrant workers to and from their homes is far from constant throughout the year.

This tendency for an important section of the labour force, in the African territories in particular, to treat wage employ-ment as a temporary and somewhat exceptional period of a man's life has a number of significant consequences. The in-dividual's stake in his employment is diminished; his interest in his job and in conditions of work do not mean so much to him as they would if he accepted paid employment as a permanent feature of his life.   For much of the time that he is in employment he is involved in adjusting himself to industrial life, and to techniques required in his job.   He has relatively little incentive and often only little opportunity to improve his skill, since the practice of a skilled occupation necessitates a fairly long period of acclimatization and training, at the end of which he may be ready to give up wage employment and return home. Labour turnover is high, partly because the temporary employee wishes to get new experience, and partly because he is inclined always to be looking for better opportunities; this instability of employment reinforces the difficulty of acquiring skills.   Absenteeism also tends to be very high, and so far as trade union organization is concerned, the short-term outlook of the employees and the rapid turnover among the potential membership makes progress difficult.

These characteristics of the employees have their effects on the outlook of the employers too.   The high rates of turnover and of absenteeism and the short period of the normal working life of unskilled labourers may make it uneconomic, if not physically impossible, to make any effective attempt to raise standards of productivity and aptitude.   The fact that a supply of labourers is forthcoming who, owing to their outlook on employment and their accustomed low standards of living, will accept very low rewards, means that the wages in unskilled work tend to be very low, and the incentive for managements to insist on high productivity or to control the usage of labour more strictly are thus lacking.   Lack of interest in the long-term welfare of the employees is influenced by the fact that few individuals are employed for a long time.   Managements are encouraged to use labour wastefully and to do relatively little to reduce labour turnover or rates of absenteeism which they treat as inevitable.

Another important characteristic of many of the men engaging in wage employment in Africa is the fact that not only are they from a rural background, but they are from more or less closed tribal communities in which the concepts of 'work' and 'leisure' found in western industrial communities hardly exist.   In village life productive activities, such as agriculture or building, religious, social or recreational activities, may all be seen in the same light as part of the totality of life within the community, and in relation to community obligations. Within the productive sector of community life there are no strictly regulated hours of work, no externally imposed discipline over output, little permanent differentiation between employer and employed, and only a minor degree of functional difference between specialists in different occupations. There is no conception of what is 'the boss's time' and what is one's 'own time'. Work is not performed for any specific reward: it is done partly for the sake of one's own subsistence in the long term, partly for the rewards which may customarily be expected from the person whom one is helping at a particular time, partly through a sense of obligation to the community and partly in return for the security which membership of the community brings in the event of sickness, disability or old age.[7]

There are many effects which are due to the contrasting conditions found by migrants who enter industrial life in the towns. The sense of obligation to the community is missing, along with the security given by the tribal system. The co-operative spirit in which work has been performed disappears, and the worker is a lone individual, working under forces of discipline imposed by the employer, who regards himself as having little or no responsibility for either the welfare or the activities of his employees at the end of the working day. The only reward for work is the monetary one of wages paid at the end of the month, with the possible addition of free housing or food. Work is strictly regulated and supervised and relations with the worker are to a great extent depersonalized. The individual naturally takes a long time to accustom himself to the changes in conditions, and may never really understand the implications of his new situation, or, so far as he does understand, may resent them. The employer also probably understands little of the worker's outlook, and may make no real attempt to do so.

Though the importance of migration in all its aspects has been stressed as a factor of major importance in the supply of labour in the territories, a growing part of the population is

[7] Raymond Firth, 'Work and Community in a Primitive Society', *Duke of Edinburgh's Study Conference Report*, Vol. II, Background Paper X (Oxford, 1957).

settling down to permanent residence in urban centres. It is from this group of urbanized persons that much of the skilled working force—office employees and those who rise to supervisory and responsible managerial and administrative posts—is drawn. This minority is thus of great importance, and there are clear signs that it is acquiring the attitudes and structured forms of an urban society.

III. The Supply of Skilled Labour

Opportunity to fill the more responsible posts in industry, commerce and the public service has become an issue of major importance for the indigenous workers in all the territories. The advance to independence has made the replacement of British or other expatriate personnel by local-born employees a matter that must be pushed forward with the greatest speed. There was, in the past, a belief among British and European employers that the local-born man was inherently incapable of learning the skills necessary to warrant promotion to the higher levels of responsibility. This opinion may not be entirely dead as a private notion, but as a matter of public policy both private employers and governments have recognized that the advancement of the indigenous worker must be fostered by all possible means.

The greatest obstacle to the advancement of local-born employees has been the limited number with adequate educational qualifications. There are, however, considerable differences in this respect between the territories. The larger West Indian territories of Jamaica, Trinidad and Barbados have attained levels of literacy and educational opportunity that have brought them within measurable distance of the advanced industrial countries. West Africa is ahead of East Africa, but all the territories of that continent fall a long way short of what is required if they are to overcome the shortage of skilled workers and technical and administrative personnel. Africans have an avid thirst for education and great efforts are being made to overcome the deficiencies that exist, but these are so great in some territories, such as Tanganyika and Nyasaland, that it will be some time before they are remedied.

Illiteracy affects the ability of the worker to acquire skills and the supervisor's capacity to give instructions and pass on information. The problem of communication is rendered specially difficult, when, as in Africa, Malaya and elsewhere the worker and management speak entirely different languages. In some cases a *lingua franca* learned in employment provides a means of contact between groups of employees and management. But the very limitations of this kind of language constitute a barrier to the development of higher-level skills and experience that would lead to positions of greater responsibility.

On the whole, it is the better educated men who most frequently seek employment. In Africa mission education has possibly instilled into some children a conception of the value of and the duty to work. Schooling probably gives its beneficiaries an idea of superior status which they can only acquire by leaving their home communities and entering wage employment. Education also tends to inculcate a desire for a way of life that can only be achieved through a regular cash income, since the material goods that are associated with the desired standards can only be acquired by cash payment.

Not only are the better educated community members likely to enter employment, but it is the better educated also who enter the superior kinds of work, the skilled occupations and, especially, clerical and other office work. This is to be expected, for there are many skilled occupations where literacy is at least an asset, even if it is not necessary, and in office work some education is, of course, essential. But apart from this, those with a better education are more likely to treat their employment as a settled state rather than as a temporary and exceptional period in their lives. These men are more likely, therefore, to wish to enter the better-paid jobs, and to desire to train themselves for skilled work. The rising demand for education is not unconnected with the belief that this is an entrance to the westernized world of industry; the educational qualifications required for many jobs in a modern society mean in effect that those who have obtained them have to a great extent turned their backs on the traditional society in which they were brought up.

It is unfortunate that education, which was in the past the gateway into the public services, has become associated with permanent, safe, pensionable jobs, since this association has tended to be generalized. One of the great disappointments for many people in Africa, now that many children have been educated up to School Certificate standard and beyond, is the fact that they cannot be guaranteed government employment as was the case in the past. Before education can be most effectively used this attitude will have to be modified.

In most territories there is a reasonable supply of workers who have acquired the traditional skills associated with building, but there is a shortage of men who have been trained to undertake the more modern types of engineering and electrical work. Technical colleges and trade schools exist in many, probably in most, of the territories. Labour departments have encouraged the development of vocational training [8] and many large firms are now running apprenticeship courses and training schools; but the numbers trained have in the past been small, and those reaching the higher levels of technical skill have been very few. In the engineering and electrical trades the age of the trainee is generally higher and the pace of the course is sometimes slower than would be the case in Britain, but British instructors in modern training departments in the West Indies, South-East Asia and Africa have reported a high standard of work, comparable with the standard they would normally expect from apprentices in the United Kingdom. There is ample evidence that the ability to master modern techniques is not lacking if the training facilities and the jobs demanding these skills can be provided.

Until comparatively recently almost all foremen and supervisors, in most territories, were expatriates. This situation has already changed greatly in the West Indies and South-East Asia, and it is changing in Africa. In Aden, East and Central Africa, foremen and clerical employees are often Asian. This is resented by the indigenous workers who feel that the opportunity to improve their status is restricted. Much progress is being made in the advancement of indigenous employees and there are many examples, such as the Ports Authority, the Enugu coal mines and several large commercial enterprises in Nigeria, where most of the supervisory staff is now of local origin.

[8] Using the T.W.I. system the Kenya Labour Department Training Section trained 1,415 supervisors and 23 persons as instructors in 1960. In addition the section ran courses in job safety for office supervisors.

The problem of promotion to the highest levels of management is rather more complicated. In the first place, there is often a reluctance on the part of the more able employees, in the African territories, and to some extent in the West Indies, but not in Hong Kong, Malaya and Singapore, to enter industry with a view to becoming a manager. There has been, and there still is, a marked preference for graduates to opt for the professions of law, medicine, teaching and the civil service rather than for industry. This attitude arises in part from a preference for government employment, which enjoys a high local prestige, guarantees a good income, provides a high degree of security and offers an opportunity to play an influential role in the political advance of the territory. Many of the bright young men of the territories are attracted by socialist and Marxist doctrines, and they have preferred employment with the government rather than with 'big business' concerns. Since those companies are also associated with the colonialism of the past, and with the domination of 'white' expatriate management, ardent young nationalists have felt some hesitation about seeking employment with them. Feelings of this kind are gradually diminishing as more opportunities for promotion are made available and better conditions of employment are provided. Outside Africa such attitudes have already largely disappeared as the policy of recruiting management from local services has proved to be successful.

Many of the larger companies have started management development programmes for their local-born and locally recruited staff. These schemes often include sending selected students to the United Kingdom for a period of training. Residential training courses have been established in Africa, and there is much discussion about the types of courses that universities might provide. A significant number of students who make their own arrangements go to Britain and the United States to take courses in business administration, personnel management and other types of specialist training that will qualify them for a managerial post when they return home.

Newly independent countries are naturally anxious to see foreign-owned concerns managed by local men as soon as possible. If a high level of efficiency is to be maintained this change-over is bound to take some time, since managerial skill and experience cannot be acquired overnight. From the point of view of good industrial relations it is essential that the process of promoting local personnel should be clearly seen as the established policy, but it is also necessary that good industrial relations should not be jeopardized by a lower standard of managerial efficiency that would have an adverse effect on the mass of employees.

There will inevitably be a difficult period in the African territories while change is taking place. During this time, which should be relatively short in some cases, it will still be necessary to employ numbers of white technicians, foremen, supervisors and managers. The principal problem that has to be overcome is to change the social relationship between persons to one of equality of status and esteem, while retaining the functional relationship which necessarily involves white supervisors and managers having the status and authority appropriate to their role. This basic problem, which has an important bearing on the climate of industrial relations, will be discussed in the following chapters.

CHAPTER 13

THE EMPLOYERS

THE first employers of importance in the tropical territories of the Commonwealth were governments, estate and plantation owners, mining companies and commercial traders.   Later, as governments began to assume greater responsibilities for developing public services, ports, railways and roads, they expanded their administrative organization to become often the largest employers of all.   Only in relatively modern times has industry developed on a significant scale.   As we have shown in the previous chapter, the population employed for wages is still often only relatively small, but it is steadily growing larger.

The attitude of employers towards the labour that they have employed has been very much the same as the attitude of employers towards labour in the older industrial countries. Before trade unions emerged and democracy was extended to wage-earners, labour was looked upon as a commodity; it had to be paid for at rates that would induce it to work, but its bargaining power was low because of its uncertain attachment to employment and lack of experience.

There were, however, special features about the labour situation in the colonies that distinguished it from that which prevailed in the older industrial countries.   In most territories labour was scarce.   In the early period in the West Indies employers were forced by the need to obtain workers, without which the colonies could not be developed, to resort to slavery, and after this was abolished, to the importation of indentured labourers.

Coercion has gone long ago, and today the conditions of employment on estates and plantations sometimes compare reasonably with those found in the best of modern industrial plants or public services.   It is inevitable, however, that the past influences the present, and neither employers nor workers easily live down, or are disposed to forget entirely, their past authority or their past humiliation.

The abolition of coercion and the substitution of economic

persuasion left the employers with the problem of attracting the labour they required.   The simplest solution was to import the skilled workers they needed, and to recruit the unskilled locally. The owners and managers of estates and plantations, the government and its administrators, the directors, managers and technical personnel employed in the rising industries were until recently all white-skinned and mainly British.   Their underlings were often also aliens, Indian and Chinese or would-be-white Creoles and half-castes.   Thus, the fundamental attitudes of employers and workers alike were dominated by the economic and social associations of colour and race.[1]   It would be idle to suggest that these factors have completely disappeared —they have not; but they have been greatly changed with the evolution of the colonies through self-government to complete independence.

Migration has continued to be an important feature of the supply of labour in the dependent territories.   This factor has meant that many employers have had to provide housing and accept responsibility for looking after large numbers of workers who were far from their homes.   The maintenance of discipline among large numbers of workers living away from their families inevitably presented difficulties.   The 'compound' provided a solution to a problem that could only be finally resolved by the permanent settlement of the labour force in towns and villages.

Estate, plantation and mine employers were convinced that they were adequately discharging their responsibility if they satisfied the needs of their workers to eat, sleep and occasionally sing and dance.   The notion that primitive migrant workers had the right to question their decisions never entered employers' heads until trade unions emerged.   When faced by an unruly mob demanding a wage increase, better food or more beer, the reaction of the employer was to damn the agitators, to consider the demonstration an outrage and to send for the police.   So long as there were no institutional arrangements through which workers could express their grievances and

---

[1] Racial prejudice has not been confined to the attitude of white employers; it has been manifested just as strongly by Negroes, Indians and Chinese towards each other in the West Indies; by Malays, Chinese and Indians in Malaya, Singapore and Borneo; and by Africans, Indians and Syrians in the African territories.

resolve them by discussion, the extreme behaviour of both sides was inevitable.

The problems which faced the employer were by no means simple to overcome. Migrant labour was generally illiterate, often could not speak or understand English and was unused to disciplined work. These factors made for difficulties of communication and led to a crude and over-simple evaluation of their qualities as human beings. Furthermore, in spite of low wages, migrant labour was often expensive in real terms and there was little incentive to improve conditions of employment in face of a capricious world demand for tropical products.

The attitude of British employers overseas has changed considerably in the past twenty-five years. In every territory they have been influenced by the social changes that have occurred; by the rising tide of nationalism; by a public in Britain that has changed its opinion about colonialism; and by governments in Westminster that have reflected this social change and given it further impetus.

The fact that many of the large companies operating in the colonies are subsidiary organizations of major British, European and American firms has meant that their industrial relations policies have been influenced by developments in the metropolitan countries. Although in most cases the local companies have a good deal of freedom to shape their policy according to local circumstances, they generally receive advice and directives from headquarters. Men sent out to the overseas branches have inevitably carried with them the ideas and practices which they have learnt in Britain or other advanced industrial countries.

In the recognition of trade unions, the development of collective bargaining, and the adoption of modern methods of personnel management, it is generally the large companies with head offices in London or the other great cities of Europe and America that have led the way. Local firms have often been slower to adapt their policies to the changing tide of events, but they have been pulled along by the larger international companies. Of course, not all the large companies have been farsighted or progressive in their managerial policies, but it must be said quite bluntly that they have generally been more ready

BB

to adopt a modern approach to industrial relations than many local-born employers.

Small-scale employers of British descent have been afraid that to concede to their active employees the right to join trade unions, to settle wages by means of collective bargaining and to enjoy the same status as white persons would be to invite economic ruin and social disaster. For a long time after it was apparent to those able to take a dispassionate view that change was necessary these employers continued to resist the pressures. They heaped abuse upon the British Government, whom they accused of wantonly fostering trade unionism among people who were not fit to exercise such rights. They often refused to recognize unions, and whenever possible they took steps to prevent unions from developing. Gradually under the pressure of events these diehard attitudes have given way to a pragmatic recognition of the advance in status of work-people in the colonial territories.

Non-British immigrant communities of Levantine, Portuguese, Indian and Chinese descent have provided another substantial group of employers, who have made, perhaps, fewer concessions to the new societies that are taking shape. Employers belonging to these groups have not looked upon their work-people as inferior because of the colour of their skins, but their outlook has been dominated by a strong sense of family and community interest and they have often been meaner in matters of wages and conditions of employment. The desire of these employers to use their labour to maximum advantage has not been tempered by the paternalism that has often been a feature of the British employer. As a consequence, these groups of employers are often looked upon with hostility by the local population, which regards them as unjustifiably privileged, and living well at the expense of the native workers. Their position is sometimes attributed to favours which they have obtained from the colonial power; they are thus regarded as enjoying privileges to which they are not entitled and ought to lose on the gaining of independence.

The most difficult employer of all to deal with from the point of view of unions and the department of labour is the indigenous one. There are several reasons why this is so. In the first place indigenous employers are generally small employers; they often lack capital and have to conduct their activities under the most primitive conditions. Secondly, they have no experience of the standards of employment to which Europeans are used. They are, therefore, not aware that they are falling below the standards of employment set up by the large companies, and accepted by labour departments as desirable for all. Thirdly, and this is most important, these small indigenous employers cannot easily be compelled to observe minimum legal standards of employment.

Even when employers in this category are aware that they are called upon by law to observe certain safety, hygiene and wage standards, they very frequently fail to carry out these obligations. The enforcement of minimum standards on small employers is a difficult problem in every country, including the most advanced industrially, and in this respect the difference between the situation in the overseas territories and metropolitan countries is purely relative.

There is, of course, something to be said in favour of the small employer of local origin. Very often the relationship which exists between him and his work-people, although in material terms much inferior to that given by the expatriate employer, contains more of the personal element to which the local worker is accustomed. Time-keeping is more lax; local festivities are more directly observed, and a semi-paternal relationship of employer and worker, which defeats the efforts of the departments of labour, often brings contentment where the material conditions would hardly seem to suggest that contentment was possible.

British experience indicates that the enforcement of minimum standards of employment depends to a large extent on the effectiveness of the trade unions. Where trade unions are weak or non-existent there is no organization to support the work of labour inspectors. It has been pointed out that without unions to observe and report on violations of wage laws and factory acts it is possible for employers to evade their legal responsibilities under these statutes for months or even for years.

The state of trade unionism in most of the territories with which we are concerned is often still too undeveloped for it to play the role of 'police' in relation to minimum standards of employment which have been a feature of unions in the

industrially more advanced countries. There is, then, relatively little pressure on the indigenous employers to raise their
standards. Other factors also come into play to give the small
employers a relative immunity. These employers are often
quite prominent supporters of nationalist movements, and in
this respect they are political partners of the unions. In many
cases the political leaders are reluctant to bring pressure for
obvious reasons. Large employers of a different race and
colour are much easier targets for unions and politicians.

For all these reasons, it is the large firms which are the pace-
setters, since they are the ones which can be persuaded to observe high standards of employment. In these circumstances
the larger companies often feel that they are unjustly singled out
for criticism. Historically, however, it is this type of employer in every country who has been unionized first and who
has been pushed or persuaded into providing the good conditions of employment. There is, therefore, no fundamental
difference in the situation which exists in the overseas territories
and that which has prevailed, and to a lesser extent still prevails, in the more advanced industrial countries.

The Government as Employer

The single most important employer, in most territories, has
been the government, and therefore the standards of employment set by governments have been of great significance. As
large employers, governments have been concerned with obtaining the labour they required for the carrying out of the
services provided by the state, such as communications, public
utilities and social and administrative services. As the major
employers, the governments of the territories were in a strong
position to determine the level of wages and to establish conditions of employment that would secure the supply of labour
which they required at the lowest cost.

In the African, Borneo and Pacific territories, governments
in the past resorted to forced labour when on occasion it was
necessary for the maintenance of essential services; and chiefs
were also permitted to conscript workers in certain circumstances. By the 1930's most governments had come to accept
the view that men should be induced to work by the offer of

wages, except in the most dire circumstances.[2] Colonial
governments were, however, concerned to avoid inflating wage
levels, partly because they believed this was undesirable on
social grounds since the money would be frittered away on
wasteful forms of consumption, and on the economic grounds
that the territories were financially poverty-stricken. Since
governments were often the most important employers, they
could set wage levels within broad limits to suit their own
purposes.[3]

The development of Colonial Office policy favouring the
growth of trade unions and a system of collective bargaining
inevitably altered this situation. Governments in the territories were no longer in a position to determine arbitrarily the
wages and working conditions of their employees. They had
to take account of the views of the emerging trade unions.
Many of those in authority found this change difficult to accept,
and although they had taken steps to legalize trade union
activity they were reluctant to recognize labour organizations
and to accept the duty to bargain with them.

In all territories trade unions are now accepted, but there are
still places where government departments are inclined to hold
the trade unions at arm's length. The Educational Department of the Government of Hong Kong, for example, had, up to
1960, consistently refused to enter into any kind of bargaining
relationship with the Teachers' Union, although this was the
most stable and responsible union in the colony.

In displaying this reluctance to recognize trade unions,
colonial governments were behaving exactly as the British
Government had behaved when faced by the organization of its
own employees before the first world war. It was only after the
British Government had been compelled by political pressure to
accept the findings of the Whitley Committee, which it had itself appointed to report on industrial relations as applicable to
its own servants, that it decided to adopt the standards it
recommended for others.

The behaviour of the Government of Nigeria in this early
period of trade union development was not completely un-

[2] Both I.L.O. Conventions No. 21 and No. 105 relating to the abolition of forced
labour have been applied without modification to every British territory, with the
sole exception of minor services rendered to Chiefs in Fiji.
[3] See Major G. St. J. Orde Browne, *The African Labourer* (London, 1933).

typical of the reactions of other governments to the need to adjust to changing circumstances.   In 1937 wages committees were established for the purpose of reviewing at periodic intervals the rates of wages of daily-paid labour in the employment of the Nigerian Government.   These committees at first consisted of an appointed president, district officers and heads of local government departments, and there was no obligation upon them to consult with any employees' associations.   In 1942 the committees were widened to include representatives of the government's employees; but the government did not trust its employees to select its representatives wisely, and the choice was made for them by administrative officers.   This paternalistic and well-meant behaviour did not meet with the approval of the trade unions in the civil service, which were the oldest and most experienced labour organizations in West Africa.

After the war, when social pressures were again forcing the government to examine its policies, consideration was given to the question of developing a more representative machinery for the regulation of relations between the government and its employees.   An inquiry into the methods of negotiation of issues arising between the government and its employees was carried out in 1947 by Mr. T. M. Cowan, an officer of the British Ministry of Labour and National Service.[4]   The Cowan Report led to the establishment of Whitley councils, based upon the British model, in the Nigerian civil service departments. Unfortunately, neither the Nigerian Government nor the trade unions were ready to adjust their attitudes sufficiently to make the Whitley system work effectively, and it broke down little more than a year after it had been established.[5]   Following a further investigation into the breakdown of the joint bodies by another officer of the Ministry of Labour and National Service, the Whitley councils were reconstituted, but collective bargaining over wages has not developed through this machinery. The salaries of government servants have, in fact, had to be fixed largely by commissioners brought in from outside to look

[4] *Report on Methods of Negotiation between the Government and Government Employees on Questions affecting Conditions of Service in Industrial Departments* (Lagos, 1948).

[5] Another example of the failure of the parties to make Whitley committees work effectively occurred in the case of the disturbances at the state-owned colliery at Enugu in 1949.   See *Report of the Commission of Enquiry into the Disorders in Eastern Provinces of Nigeria*, November 1949 (H.M.S.O. Colonial No. 256, 1950).

at the position and make recommendations every three or four years.

The establishment of Whitley councils on the British pattern in the colonies was urged on the governments of the territories by the Secretary of State in a circular despatch sent out in 1949.[6] In this despatch the Secretary of State pointed out that the success of the Whitley scheme depended upon the readiness of the two sides to make the machinery work. It is on this point that difficulties have arisen; in many cases the governments and civil service trade unions have been highly suspicious of each other.

There have been complaints from civil service trade unions that the governments have been far from good employers. One issue which has aroused some strong feelings is the essential services ordinance, which in many territories prevents government employees, and sometimes those employed in a large number of privately operated but essential services, from taking part in strikes.

Many civil servants feel that governments take advantage of the legal prohibition on striking. It is difficult to assess the merits of this charge, since it is likely that irresponsible strikes might have occurred if the threat of legal sanctions had not been present. The most important sanction that colonial governments exercise, in common with the governments of any other country, is their ability to withdraw previous rights. A breach of discipline can be punished severely by this means, and colonial governments have followed the general practice of warning their civil servants of the risks they run when a stoppage of work has been threatened.

The problem of fixing the appropriate level of salary and wage for government employees has given rise to much dispute in Britain. In this case civil service remuneration has been linked to the movement of wages in private employment, the general principle being that wages and salaries in government service should keep pace with, but not exceed, those paid to non-government employees. It is difficult to pursue this principle when government is overwhelmingly the dominant

---

[6] The West India Royal Commission, 1938–39, had strongly recommended that the governments of the territories should give a lead to others by establishing Whitley councils through which the conditions of employment of their own employees could be peacefully settled.

employer, and this has been the case in many colonial territories.   In these circumstances it is not surprising that colonial
governments have found wage-fixing a problem that has presented them with many difficulties.   An effective principle has
not been discovered, and with the development of trade unions
colonial   governments   have   found   themselves   continually
pushed into the position where they had to call for a commission
of inquiry.   The awards of these commissions have generally,
but not always, provided a temporary solution.   They have
usually recommended that wages and salaries should be advanced to levels higher than the governments would themselves
have been prepared to accept.   Bargaining has commonly
followed, sometimes accompanied by threats of strikes and
serious unrest among the employees of the government.

The determination of civil service wages and salaries is not
any more easily solved by self-government.   It sometimes grows
much worse, as for example in the case of British Guiana, where
awards of commissions of inquiry have incited the unions and
embarrassed the government.   Closely associated with the
wage and salary problem has been the question of staffing the
civil service with local-born and recruited officers.   Since
British expatriate civil servants have had to be compensated at
rates adequate to attract them to overseas duties by the payment of an expatriation allowance, they have generally been in
receipt of salaries in total far above the level paid to the locally
recruited officer.[7]   Furthermore, the locally born man was
limited in his promotion possibilities until comparatively recently.   The differential between local and expatriate salary
grades is the source of continuing difficulties, even after all staff
recruited overseas have been replaced, since local-born officers
are often inclined to feel on grounds of equality that they are
entitled to the same rates as their predecessors.

Thus, the problems facing governments as employers have
been complex, but it is difficult to avoid the impression that in
some cases they have been over-cautious, even obstructive.   A
weakness in the practice of government as an employer has been
the failure to recognize the need to train establishment officers

[7] In this respect it is interesting to note that after independence many of the
territories have paid an expatriation allowance to their civil servants overseas to
compensate them for differences in cost of living, separation from their families
and other factors which involve financial burdens.

and others responsible for exercising, in effect, managerial responsibility in the principles and practice of modern personnel management. However, in recent years there has been an improvement and governments have paid some attention to the need to train administrative officers; but they are still much less aware of the importance of their role as employers than private enterprises.

In spite of the deficiencies of governments as employers, the conditions of employment and the level of industrial relations in government service compare reasonably well with conditions in private industry. They are usually superior in terms of job security, if not in wages, to any but the major private concerns. Employment with the government is, perhaps for this reason, looked upon in most territories by a majority of employees as more desirable than work for a private enterprise.

The Growth of Employers' Organizations

The need for employers in the colonies to take a more organized and positive interest in the well-being of their employees was stimulated by the I.L.O. Conference held in Philadelphia in May 1944. This conference was notable for its declaration of the basic principles for which the International Labour Organization stood, and for the clear decision that after the defeat of Germany, Italy and Japan, the conditions of labour in the colonies would be a matter of major concern. The I.L.O. had adopted conventions of special significance for dependent territories before the war, but the general question of minimum standards of social policy in dependent territories appeared for the first time on the agenda of the I.L.O. conference at Philadelphia.

At this time the British Employers' Confederation, which represented British employers at the I.L.O., had no direct relations with organized employers in the colonies, and lacked knowledge of the problems with which they were concerned. It was therefore necessary, in view of the I.L.O. decision and the prospect of conventions being adopted, that the B.E.C. should be in contact with those who had experience of labour problems in the colonies. In December 1944 the B.E.C. called a meeting in London of a number of associations in the British colonies informing them of this development and asking for their views on the proposal to form a permanent organization to co-ordinate and represent their interests. Most of the replies received were in favour of the establishment of the body suggested.

In the meantime the provisional committee sent out a questionnaire to discover the reactions of colonial employers to the statement on 'Minimum Standards on Social Policy in Dependent Territories' issued by the I.L.O. In due course a series of observations were prepared and sent to the British Employers' Federation for transmission to the British Government.

The B.E.C., in August 1945, invited the provisional committee to suggest names, for submission to the Ministry of Labour, of persons to act as technical advisers to the employers' delegates in the British delegation to the next conference of the I.L.O. The B.E.C. also asked the provisional committee to accept responsibility for submitting names of persons for appointment to the Colonial Advisory Committee.

In September 1945 the Colonial Employers' Federation was formally constituted with the following objects: (1) to represent employers in the British Colonies, Dependencies and Mandated Territories in all matters coming within the scope of the I.L.O.; (2) to provide information on colonial labour questions for the I.L.O., governments, employers and others who might be interested; (3) to watch over all legislative matters and to take appropriate action; (4) to promote and encourage joint consultation between employers; (5) to advise employers on all labour problems likely to affect their interests; (6) to take any action likely to secure the attainment of the Federation's objects.

An executive committee of ten persons representing the geographic areas of West Africa, East Africa, North Rhodesia, West Indies, Ceylon, Malay, North Borneo and Sarawak was elected. The first chairman of the Colonial Employers' Federation was A. R. I. Mellor of the United Africa Company. The foundation of the Federation owed more to Mellor than to anyone else; it was Mellor who had gone to the B.E.C. and persuaded them to support the idea of forming a separate organization which would be a repository of information about colonial labour problems. Mellor also enlisted the support of

Mr. A. Creech Jones, who became Secretary of State for the Colonies, with the formation of the post-war Labour Government, in July 1945. Mellor, an ex-member of the Egyptian Civil Service, was greatly interested in the problems of labour overseas, and as Personnel Adviser to the United Africa Company, concerned with their solution. He was the first to recognize the need for a body that would act as a two-way channel of communication and be a spokesman for the colonial employers in London.

In the first year 17 associations of planters and chambers of mines and commerce, and 10 companies, joined the federation. Affiliation fees amounted to £930, and £868 was spent on the activities of the federation in this first year. Two technical advisers to the British delegation were sent to the I.L.O. Conference, held in Paris in October 1945, and to the I.L.O. Conference held in Montreal in 1946.

The second annual report of the federation criticized the five conventions passed at the I.L.O. in 1947 as 'a clumsy and ill-balanced "charter" for workers in those territories'. In the view of the federation the I.L.O. was seeking to impose standards—already established in the more advanced colonial territories—on others which were not yet ready for them. The I.L.O. decisions were cited by the federation as evidence of the need for a body that would be 'safeguarded against premature introduction of measures in colonial areas, where sound economic and social developments can only be secured by the patient and gradual methods already followed'.

The second annual report of the federation raised the question of a permanent staff, but the decision of the members was against the expense involved. There was some suspicion that a permanent staff might imply that labour problems were of greater importance than some members were prepared to concede. The federation continued to be run on a voluntary basis, largely by the chairman, and a secretary, whose time was loaned by his employers to the federation, for the sum of £300 per year. In 1950, with the work of the federation increasing each year, the question of the appointment of a full-time secretary was again raised. With the advent of a new chairman it was decided to reorganize the federation, and in 1953 Mr. E. M. Hyde-Clarke, the first full-time paid secretary, was appointed.

At the same time the name of the federation was changed to the Overseas Employers' Federation. From this time the federation has grown steadily. In 1958, 39 employers' organizations were affiliated; in 1960 the number of associations had gone up to 50. In addition the federation had 130 companies as members.

In this period the federation, under the guidance of E. M. Hyde-Clarke, who was appointed Director in 1957, has greatly expanded its work. The federation now provides an extensive information service to its members. Every two weeks an O.E.F. Newsletter is sent to member organizations and appropriate bodies. Special advice and information is given by the federation on any issue on which a request is received from an affiliate. During 1959–60 advice was given by the federation, *inter alia*, on the 'check-off', supervisory staffs, wages, cost of living, pensions, provident-fund schemes, joint industrial councils, staff associations, dismissal procedure, wages councils, labour legislation and I.L.O. conventions and recommendations.

Since 1953 the Overseas Employers' Federation has met with representatives of the T.U.C. for informal discussions with the Secretary of State for the Colonies. These meetings have served as a means of exchanging information and as an avenue of exploration of important problems affecting employers, unions and the government. Consultation has not been confined to the Colonial Office, but has also included the Commonwealth Relations Office, Foreign Office, Department of Technical Co-operation and the Ministry of Labour.

The work of the Overseas Employers' Federation has undoubtedly contributed significantly to the development of good industrial relations in British tropical Commonwealth territories. The policy of the federation has been based on the principles of racial non-discrimination and non-nationalism. Although the employers' organizations affiliated to the federation are mainly composed of firms with a British parentage, membership is open to non-British firms.

Apart from the influence of the federation on British policy, especially at the I.L.O., it has given much wise and responsible advice to employers in the colonies and helped them adjust their policies to the rapidly changing situation. Through the

O.E.F., employers in one territory have been able to benefit from experience in another; they have had a source of advice and a repository of experience and information to which they could turn in times of difficulty. However, every affiliate retains its autonomy and is free to reject advice sought and obtained.

The Overseas Employers' Federation, though much the most important body providing employers in the tropical Commonwealth territories with information and assistance, is not the only body in Britain that has exerted an influence.

The Industrial Welfare Society has been running training courses for overseas welfare administrators and executives from private and government establishments overseas for a number of years. The Institute of Personnel Management has developed relations with members and associates in the territories and has encouraged the formation of local associations of labour officers.[8]

The Duke of Edinburgh's Study Conference, held in Oxford in 1956, on the Human Problems of Industrial Communities within the Commonwealth and Empire, broke fresh ground. It brought together, on the most ambitious scale, representatives of industry and trade unions, management and operatives, drawn from Britain and most of the territories of the Commonwealth. The emphasis of the conference was placed on the study of the problems rather than on the passing of resolutions advocating over-simple solutions. The results of a conference of this kind are always difficult to assess, but at the very least, it helped to promote a wider understanding and interest in the problems involved. The need to study the problems with which the Duke of Edinburgh's conference was concerned is a continuing one, and there is a need for industry with interests in the Commonwealth to support university research into these fields more effectively than it has so far done.

Many of the larger business firms are now making considerable efforts to educate and train local-born employees so that they may fill any post that falls vacant. The policy of a large

---

[8] Courses for labour officers employed by labour departments, as mentioned in Chapter 8, have been run by the Ministry of Labour, in conjunction with the Colonial Office, since 1959, and approximately 500 officers have passed through. These courses are still available to the countries that wish to use them after they achieve independence.

and growing number of British concerns is to promote locally born persons to positions of management as rapidly as possible. It is now recognized that the interests of the company and the interests of the community in which it is located must be closely identified. If this identity is not achieved, then the stability of the enterprise cannot be secure. The removal of obstacles and barriers to promotion to skilled, supervisory and managerial grades is clearly an essential step. It is one thing, however, to accept such a policy in principle; it is another to make it effective. There is a tremendous desire to be educated and trained for positions of industrial responsibility, but it is not an easy matter to find the persons with the talents required. In some cases employees have been reluctant to embark on a training course for management, since they feared that this would identify them with a politically undesirable situation. This attitude is, however, rapidly disappearing, and the demand for education is growing at a fantastic pace in most of the territories of the Commonwealth.

In some territories employers' associations are actively promoting courses that will improve the quality and understanding of their managers. The work of the British Institute of Management overseas must be mentioned in this respect, since it is paying increasing attention to the problems of management development in the tropical Commonwealth territories, and in a number of countries it is in close contact with management associations that have been formed. In other cases there is a growing interest in modern managerial techniques, and firms are sending an increasing number of their managers and potential managers overseas to attend training courses. There is a need, however, for more to be done in the territories themselves. Much could be achieved if closer relations were established between business organizations and the universities. There has been a tendency on the part of the universities to look upon the problems of industrial management as outside their sphere of interest. Both the universities and industry have much to gain from academic inquiry into the problems that face business organizations and the community in the developing territories.

CHAPTER 14

THE DEVELOPMENT OF
INDUSTRIAL RELATIONS

THE relations between employers and their work-people in every country are influenced by the factors that distinguish one territory from another. No two systems of industrial relations are exactly alike. The pattern of industrial relations developed in Britain differs from that of Australia, the United States, France, Holland and Sweden. Inevitably then, differences are to be expected between the territories that are the subject of this survey; and in spite of the fact that they have all been under British rule, the systems of industrial relations that are emerging differ in important respects from the United Kingdom pattern. However, in noting the divergences it is important not to lose sight of the features that are common to the systems of industrial relations that have been adopted in Britain and in the less advanced industrial countries.

In one respect the experience of the tropical territories differs hugely from that of Britain, that is in the speed of their economic, social and political development. The system of industrial relations in Britain matured over a long period of industrial growth and social and political change. Most of the tropical territories have jumped from a stage of primitive development to the establishment of modern industry, modern cities and modern systems of social organization in a few decades. The sheer speed of this evolution must never be forgotten in assessing the problems and achievements of the territories.

Industrial relations have become a significant factor with the growth of the employed population. Where the volume of employment is not large, the units of production small, and the processes simple, managerial organization and administration is on a more or less personal basis and relations between employers and employed tend to be informal. As the units of employment grow larger and industrial techniques become more complex, the personal and informal methods of management have to give way to more bureaucratic systems of administration. Communication becomes more difficult, the owners of enterprises become more remote from their managers and the managers tend to be insulated from the bulk of the employees by layers of supervisors. Eventually the problems created by this kind of development compel management to seek the establishment of more formal methods of communication. The professional manager, though separated from the majority of employees by his functional position and his social status, is, therefore, more ready to recognize the need to enter into arrangements with trade unions than was his predecessor, since this is a necessary means of maintaining orderly relations with employees.

The evolution of industrial relations in the tropical territories is closely related to the development of the dominant form of employment. There is, of course, no complete shift from one type of employment to another. In most cases the different kinds of employer exist side by side. The first type to emerge in many territories has been the government official, the small settler and native farmer, Asian, Levantine or European trader, hotel keeper, tailor or other craftsman, employing a handful to a few score of workers. In all these cases the relation between employers and worker was direct and close.

The second type of employment-provider, existing from the earliest days in some territories, is the large-scale plantation drawing on migrant workers. With the growth of government departments, especially public works, the development of mines and processing plants, opportunity for the employment of large numbers of unskilled labourers was increased. It was until relatively recently typical of this type of employment that management was not greatly concerned about the quality of the labour employed and the high rates of absenteeism and turnover that occurred, since the key jobs were all held by European and Asian expatriate staff; so long as the supply of unskilled labour was sufficient the employer was satisfied. There was in these circumstances little contact between employer and worker other than through intermediaries.

In the third category is the clerk in government services. Clerical employees require a higher level of education than unskilled workers and they generally have more social aspirations and social skills. The larger and more highly mechanized firms, usually international companies with experience in many countries, also fall into this group. These firms have required levels of skill and responsibility from their employees that could only be secured by employment standards equivalent to those provided in the advanced industrial countries. The growth of this third category of employment has had a considerable influence on the employment practices in the other categories in the past decade.

In the period before trade unions emerged workers expressed their discontent by lowering their output, absenteeism, high turnover rates and from time to time by spontaneous demonstrations of protest. Since these protest demonstrations were not sponsored by organizations capable of directing them to specific and attainable ends, they often developed into destructive outbreaks of violence which expressed the frustration of workers who lacked the means to secure the redress of their grievances by other methods. Invariably these outbreaks of unrest led to a sharp reaction by the authorities, who to prevent wanton damage to property and danger to life quickly moved to arrest and imprison those who could be identified as leaders. Thus, the immediate outcome of these demonstrations was a hostile response which led to the collapse of the protest movement, but not the elimination of the factors which provoked the expression of discontent.

This phase of industrial relations has been passed through by every country before trade unionism has emerged and been recognized as providing the means through which the dissatisfactions of workers could be channelled and expressed in an orderly process of bargaining for improvements in the conditions of employment. In the colonial territories the large groups of workers brought together to work on the plantations and in the mines indicated their dissatisfaction with their conditions of employment, before trade unions were developed, by mass demonstrations. There were, for example, riots and demonstrations in Jamaica in the nineteenth century and outbreaks of unrest occurred on a number of occasions in British Guiana. Similar spontaneous eruptions of protest occurred in Africa and South-East Asia before trade unions were established. It was in fact out of these demonstrations that trade unionism eventually began to emerge, as was shown in earlier chapters.

In the great majority of territories and industries before trade unionism of any kind had begun to emerge employers were unconscious of any need for direct contact with representatives of their work-people; they were usually convinced that they provided adequate wages and satisfactory conditions of employment. Any suggestion that employers needed to consider improving their relations with their employees was dismissed with scorn as unrealistic and irrelevant. Outbreaks of unrest were generally regarded by employers as the work of agitators and political adventurers.

One well-known exception to this attitude was the institution, about 1930, in the Roan Antelope Copper mine in Northern Rhodesia, of a system of 'Tribal Elders', who were to be the means of contact and communication between the management and the employees. This development, which preceded the emergence of trade unions, was described earlier, in Chapter 2. The Elder system was effective only to the extent that tribal authority could be maintained. When this broke down after the development of the mineworkers' trade union the influence of the tribal representatives quickly declined, despite attempts by management to build up their prestige; eventually they were rejected by a large majority in 1953 in a ballot held at Roan Antelope to determine their future.[1]

There were a number of other attempts to set up some form of consultative machinery in the absence of trade unions, but in the pre-trade-union period the general opinion of managements was that colonial workers were too illiterate, too ignorant of the ways of industry and too apathetic to play an intelligent part in joint consultation, or to grasp the problems which management faced. Managements were, therefore, reluctant to take steps to improve their means of communication with their employees until unrest and the advent of trade unions forced them to consider taking some action. However, managements were not always left to take this decision by themselves. In East Africa, where trade unions developed later than in many other territories, the Government of Kenya encouraged the development

[1] Epstein, *op. cit.*

of joint consultation; by 1950 it was estimated that about one-third of the total number of workers enjoyed some form of recognized consultation. Other governments from about 1950 encouraged employers, to a greater or lesser extent, to set up some form of domestic consultative machinery through which they could communicate with their employees.

The Labour Commissioner of Tanganyika stated the problem bluntly in his report in 1950:

> Our experience over the last few years in this Territory has shown that the vast majority of workers here are at present incapable of comprehending the principles and concepts of trade unionism, and furthermore, that neither they nor their employers are as yet capable of sitting down round the table and thrashing out their problems together.

So both sides had to be taught the basic principles of sitting down round the table. Employers were to be encouraged to set up domestic or tribal councils to handle social problems among employees, and to create some sort of consultative machinery. In 1951 the Labour Department again concluded in its report for the year that consultation at the workshop level must remain the basis of its industrial-relations policy, and it was hoped that the experience gained in joint consultation would lead both sides of industry to see the advantages of the process of sitting round the table rather than hurling accusations at each other or allowing grievances to mount. It was also hoped that this experience would lead to the formation of trade unions whose leaders would be people who had a knowledge of negotiations which would enable them to lead trade unions effectively and constructively. The same view was put forward in the report of the East Africa Royal Commission of 1953–55, which concluded:

> By way of contrast [to the ineffectiveness of trade unions] we have been impressed by some of the recent attempts to build up works councils and joint staff committees. . . . These joint bodies may consider any matter affecting the conditions of employment, including wages. It would be premature to pass final judgement on these experiments, but they should be encouraged, and their results should be carefully watched. They have the advantage that they compel their members to focus their attention on matters about which they are likely to have some personal knowledge, and

they may provide a training in negotiating which may prove to be of considerable value at a later stage of industrial development.

This conclusion, which supported the views of some at least of the governments concerned, was criticized at the time, in international trade union circles especially, for seeing joint consultation as an alternative rather than as a complement to trade unionism—a view of consultation shared, no doubt, by the governments themselves, who tended to treat it rather as a preferred alternative—though never to the extent that they explicitly discouraged the formation of trade unions.

This policy lasted for almost a decade in East Africa. In government departments many joint consultative committees were formed in these territories, though the extent of their success and the vigour of their activities were not reported on. In private industry, of course, governments had more difficulty in persuading employers to adopt the practice, and where it was adopted joint consultation was often treated with some scepticism. Even where it was operated with goodwill, joint consultation in these territories worked under real difficulties.[2] Nevertheless, in conditions where trade unions were not yet effective, joint consultation was an improvement on more casual forms of communication.

Unfortunately, when joint consultation was established before trade unions were effective, conflict almost always occurred when the employees decided to form a union. This development was generally resisted by employers who considered the existing arrangements adequate; they saw the trade union as an unwanted source of friction, and felt justified in refusing recognition of the union as long as they could. When this was no longer possible, employers would try to retain as many functions as possible for the consultative committee and endeavour to restrict contacts with the union as much as possible. The union, on the other hand, was generally jealous of the powers and influence of the consultative machinery, and sought to take over as much of these as possible.

The problem of moving from a consultative system to the acceptance of collective bargaining was evident in a number of cases in both East and West Africa during the 50's, and on

---

[2] See Walter Elkan, *An African Labour Force* (Kampala, 1956), and *Migrants and Proletarians* (Oxford, 1960), Chapter 6.

occasion much hostility and ill feeling were caused during the period of adjustment to the new conditions. In situations where unions were accepted joint consultation has in some cases proved a helpful method of improving industrial relations, but as in Britain, its success has been confined to the exceptional case.

The Impact of Trade Unions

The appearance of trade unions has never been greeted with enthusiasm by employers in any country. There were many reasons why they were looked upon with hostility by employers when they emerged in the colonies. Unions inevitably developed against a background of unrest, and employers almost invariably saw them as a cause of discontent and disaffection among their employees. Since the rise of the unions had often been accompanied by mass demonstrations, strikes, sometimes violence and threats of political intimidation, employers had some grounds for their fears. These were usually shared by local governments which tended to look upon trade unions in their early stages as possibly subversive bodies and a danger to the maintenance of law and order.

Distrustful of their activities, employers generally delayed recognition of the unions and refused to enter into negotiation with them until compelled by circumstances. In many cases efforts were made to discourage employees from joining unions, obstacles were placed in the way of union organizers and appeals were made to the authorities to suppress their activities.

The unions were far from easy organizations to deal with in their early stages of development. They were usually poorly organized, led by inexperienced men who were often more concerned with achieving political ends and promoting their own ambitions than with advancing the development of practical trade unionism. The members were excited by great expectations of high wages, better working conditions and an improved social status. In this inflamed atmosphere the unions were liable to make many mistakes, and to pursue extreme demands which they had not the bargaining strength to carry through. Their leaders, faced with the powerful resistance of the employers, were often intemperate and irresponsible. In this situation when employers sought to be conciliatory their gestures were frequently received with suspicion. Each side bitterly criticized the other, and both assumed that the other party was bound to be acting in bad faith when in fact both were often equally gauche and bewildered by the response made by the other side to their overtures. Thus, weakness and unsureness, a lack of insight and understanding of the methods and problems of collective bargaining by unions and employers, inspired an impatient response from both sides.

Industrial relations in the early days of the trade unions could hardly have been otherwise than stormy. In this first period of trade union activity, before unions and employers had learnt to negotiate with each other, strikes were often called because this was the way that workers usually vented their protest; they had not yet grasped the idea of reserving the strike as an action to be taken only after negotiations had broken down. The reaction of the employers to this kind of pressure, often exercised in an unpredictable way, was to dismiss the strikers and to seek to replace them with non-union labour. This was not always possible, but whether it was so or not, the hostile attitude of the employers to the advent of unions aggravated their behaviour and in some cases provoked a violent response.

The situation was sometimes made worse by the intrusion into industrial disputes of governments, which were naturally concerned about the maintenance of public order and the protection of lives and property. Unfortunately the way in which security forces were deployed and the apparent sympathy of the authorities with the employers frequently led to clashes with strikers which sometimes culminated in tragedy.

Many examples of industrial disputes leading to disturbances and the involvement of security forces during the initial period of trade union development might be cited, and a number of these were discussed in Chapters 1 and 2. In some territories, where trade unions had appeared, stoppages occurred that provoked a hostile response in the years immediately following the first world war. In the 1930's and 1940's there were many strikes in the West Indies, Asian and African territories, which led to disturbances and to clashes with the police. A feature of most of these incidents was the intemperate leadership of the unions, the negative attitude of the employers and the unsympathetic handling of the security forces. The refusal of employers to recognize the unions, their determination not to make any concessions to meet the often extravagant claims of the unions and their eagerness to use the authorities to protect their interests only served to encourage more irresponsible action by the union leaders. In this period the personal influence of the employers on the members of the governments who were responsible for the maintenance of law and order often brought about a conflict within the government and frequently limited the ability of the labour commissioner to intervene effectively. Often governments were pressed to take steps that they would have preferred to avoid, and perhaps could have avoided, had they been less subject to pressure, better informed, better staffed and inspired by a greater understanding of the developments that were taking place.

This phase of industrial relations prevailed in most of the West Indian territories up to the outbreak of the second world war. In Malaya and West Africa it lasted until the late 1940's; elsewhere in Africa and in a number of other territories practically to the end of the 1950's.

Gradually it became apparent to employers that the problems presented by the emergence of trade unions could not be solved by tactics designed to obstruct their growth and development. In bringing about this change a number of factors contributed. The growth in the working population, increasing urbanization, industrial development, advancing education, the rising political consciousness of the workers and the growth of nationalist movements were all important elements influencing the course of events. A great deal was contributed by the governments of the territories, under the stimulus initiated in London, through the adoption of laws modelled on those regulating industrial relations in Britain, and through the activities of labour departments.

As employers the governments of the colonies tended to be cautious and rather slow to come to terms with the unions and the changing social and political environment. As was pointed out in the previous chapter, governments gradually set up Whitley councils, but this machinery did not always work smoothly, and there have been many conflicts over the difficult problem of fixing the appropriate remuneration of civil servants.

The influence of governments on industrial relations has not been primarily through their role as employers, but as legislators and administrators.   In the absence of a system of collective bargaining and under the influence of the advice from London most territories passed protective legislation, including acts to regulate recruiting, contracts of service, payments in kind, to limit the hours of work of women and children, workmen's compensation and minimum-wage legislation.   This last generally followed the pattern of establishing wage boards with power to set minimum wages in the industries for which they were appointed.   Minimum-wage machinery became especially important during the second world war, when it was necessary to protect wage-earners from the effects of the rise in the cost of living that occurred everywhere.   The role of labour departments, as noted in Chapter 8, has been of crucial significance in the administration of these policies in every territory.   However, the extent to which Labour Departments were successful in enforcing the standards established by law probably tended to retard the development of mature trade unionism and stable industrial relations, simply because many workers looked to the department for assistance rather than to the unions.

In some territories special attention was given to the establishment of joint industrial councils on the British model.   The object of this development was to promote good relations between unions and employers and to encourage the growth of collective bargaining by the creation of standing bodies that met at regular intervals instead of only when the union had made a large claim on the employers.

A further development that has helped considerably in the building of good relations has been the establishment in many territories of labour advisory committees.   These committees have helped to bring trade union leaders, employers and government officials together in circumstances where they have been able to begin to learn to understand each other's point of view.

The Growth of Collective Bargaining

The first attempts at collective bargaining were inevitably crude, and as already pointed out, it was some time before employers and unions learned the techniques of negotiation.

In this initial period the unions and the employers battled with each other at arm's length, and labour commissioners and labour officers played an important part in helping the parties to come to terms with each other. Disputes were often settled by the employers making some concession without entering into a written agreement. Sometimes when no solution could be found an outside arbitrator was called upon or a committee of inquiry was established. The legal basis for the intervention of the government in this respect was discussed in Chapter 11. On occasion, when relations had deteriorated to the point where there was a danger of an explosion, a commission was sent out from Britain to investigate and propose a solution.

Gradually in the more important industries employers and unions began to develop an understanding of the essentials of constructive collective bargaining. In the past decade this process has gone ahead with tremendous speed, so that today collective bargaining has matured, both in terms of the procedures followed and the scope and contents of agreements. It is impossible to say exactly what proportion of the working population of every territory is covered by collective agreements. In some territories, for example, in Barbados and a number of other West Indian territories, the majority of wage-earners work under conditions established by collective bargaining. In the African territories, Aden, Mauritius, Malaya, Singapore and Fiji the most important categories of employees have their working conditions determined by collective agreements. There is no territory where collective bargaining does not exist, but in some, such as Hong Kong, Sarawak and Brunei, it is still only in an extremely rudimentary stage of development.

It is also impossible to say to what extent collective agreements are effectively administered. There are the inevitable criticisms from both unions and employers that the other party does not observe the terms of the agreement. This type of protest is a feature of industrial relations in the more advanced industrial countries, so it would be surprising if it did not occur in circumstances where the parties were less experienced and more inclined to adopt extreme attitudes towards each other. While the increase in the number and scope of collective agreements cannot be taken as concrete evidence that the objectives they seek to define are reached, it can be reasonably presumed that if they were entirely without meaning for the parties, collective bargaining would have completely collapsed. There is, in fact, ample evidence that both employers and unions believe that they are entering into agreements that will have meaning, and that both sides will, to the best of their ability, honour the bargain they conclude. One test of the seriousness of the parties is the effort they make to prepare for the negotiations; another is the significance which they attach to a breakdown of discussions; and a further one is the interest taken by others in the terms of the agreement that is signed. Whatever weaknesses there might be in the administration of collective agreements, it is worth while examining the scope and content of these agreements that have been concluded as some measure of the development of the industrial relations system in the territories that comprise the tropical Commonwealth.

Union Recognition

As pointed out earlier, the mere existence of a trade union does not necessarily lead immediately to the establishment of collective agreements. The normal response of employers in every country in the initial stage of trade union development has been to refuse recognition, but this stage has now passed in most territories, though it may continue to be a problem for certain unions for some time, as indeed it still is even in some advanced industrial countries.

It is now a common practice for employers to agree to recognize the right of their employees to be represented by a union and to have a declaration of their willingness to do this written into a collective agreement. The granting of exclusive bargaining rights to one union for the entire labour force of a firm, or an industry, is unusual in the United Kingdom, though it is normal practice in the United States. In this respect American rather than British practice is being followed in many of the territories. It is quite usual today for collective agreements to state specifically which unions the employer recognizes, and it is becoming quite common for an employer to undertake not to recognize any other organization during the term of the agreement. For example, in the case of an agreement made in 1960, between an East African company and an electrical power operators' union, 'it was agreed that the

Company should recognize the Union as the sole representative of workers . . . employed by the Company in negotiations affecting all matters covered by the agreement'.

Agricultural workers in every country have always been difficult to organize, but collective bargaining has been going on for many years between the employers and unions on the sugar plantations of the West Indies, the rubber plantations of Malaya and the banana plantations of West Africa. In the East African plantations collective bargaining is of more recent development. For a long time employers in East Africa resisted the efforts of the union to organize and bargain, but agreements were eventually made in the late 1950's with plantation employers' associations which now give unions the right to organize and protect members from victimization for taking part in union activities.[3]

The right of union officials to enter estates in order to organize the workers employed has been an issue of acute contention in territories where plantations are important. By denying union officials access to the workers, who live as well as work on the estates, it has been possible for employers to resist the attempts of the unions to organize their employees. This problem was long ago overcome in the West Indies, Malaya and Ceylon, but it is only in the past few years that the employers in East Africa have agreed to allow union organizers on their estates.

A typical access agreement made in 1959 between a Plantation Workers' Union and a Plantation Company in East Africa provides as follows:

1. The Union shall supply to the Company . . . the names and addresses of all its paid officials and representatives among the Company's employees and will keep the Company immediately informed of any change.

[3] Cf. The agreement made in 1960 between the Nyasaland Planting and Agricultural Employers' Association and the National Union of Plantation and Agricultural Workers. This agreement states that the Employers' Association accords full recognition to the Union and that it will make every endeavour to ensure that all its members likewise accord full recognition to such properly constituted branches as the Union might set up. In addition, the agreement binds the Association to seeing that no member shall impede the Union in its recruitment of employees. Both parties also agree that they will ensure that all members are acquainted with the law relating to intimidation, and they jointly agree that neither will victimize any official or member of either organization.

2. In order that Union representatives may contact employees on the Company's property in an orderly manner and to educate them in trade union procedure the Company agree:

   a. To allow open meetings to be held on the Company's property during the hours of daylight provided they are conducted in an orderly and responsible manner.

   b. For the Union to make provision for the collection of dues on any day provided that at no time there is any interference with payment of the employees and provided also that the collections are made at a reasonable distance from the Pay Office and after consultation with the disbursing officer.

For their part the Union and their Representatives agree:

   a. That whenever a Union organizer or official wishes to visit an Estate or Department of the Company he will first contact the Company's General Manager or his nominee for permission.

   b. That all meetings at any time on the Company's property shall be conducted in an orderly and responsible manner and shall be confined to the Company's employees.

   c. That the number of Union representatives present at any meeting shall be limited to those whose names have been notified to the General Manager or his nominee.

On the face of it these rules should not be onerous, but there is a certain element of paternalism about them which tends to irritate. The Company is clearly anxious to protect itself from excited and emotional meetings that might result in dangerous consequences. This is a legitimate fear, but it is doubtful if it can be entirely guarded against by rules of this kind. The danger of this agreement is that the employer might be tempted to use the opportunity it provides to bring pressure on the union by denying a union representative permission to visit an estate when he desired to do so; this could greatly reduce the effectiveness of the union and discredit it in the eyes of its members. It is possible that employers would be careful to avoid such a deliberate restriction of the right of a union official to have access to members, but the ordinary problems of communication that are likely to arise when a union representative has always to obtain permission before visiting an estate are certain to give rise to difficulties unless the employer interprets this rule in a sympathetic way.

In some cases recognition clauses in collective agreements stipulate that they are only binding so long as the union can prove that it has a fully paid up membership of not less than half of the company's employees.[4] Some employers have been persuaded that it is in their interest to enter into a 'closed shop' agreement with the union. This is, for example, the case in the agreement between the Grenada Seamen's and Waterfront Workers' Union and Geest Industries Ltd. This agreement, following American practice, also gives the union the right to be jointly responsible with the company for the appointment of the Chief Stevedore, whose functions include the engaging of labour for loading and discharge of ships and the organization of this work.

British trade unions, with certain exceptions, have always preferred to collect their own contributions, but again following American practice, in an increasing number of cases in the territories overseas employers are agreeing to 'check off' contributions from the pay packets of their employees. Ghana and Tanganyika have made the check-off legally enforceable on employers at the request of a trade union. The organizational advantages and problems that go with the 'check-off' were discussed in Chapter 6. This development is mentioned here since it is, in itself, evidence of the growing maturity of industrial relations. In most cases agreements provide that the individual member must give his consent before the employer is permitted to deduct the union contribution from his wage. Thus, the right of the member to refuse to pay his contribution in this way is allowed, and this may seriously limit the effectiveness of the 'check-off' system.[5] There have been cases where it has become an important factor in internal union rivalry, as for example, in British Guiana, where dissident members of the Mineworkers' Union on one occasion sought to bring pressure to bear upon the leadership by urging members to revoke their assent to the 'check-off'.

It is quite common for collective agreements to embody a clause setting out the rights of management as well as those of

[4] For example, an agreement made between Uganda Textile Workers' Union and Nyanza Textile Industries Ltd. in 1959.

[5] In some cases in East African plantations it is said that the proportion of workers agreeing to the check-off was at first not more than 15 per cent. of the total eligible.

the unions.   A typical statement of these rights is to be found in an agreement that was made between the Bustamante Industrial Trade Union, The Trades Union Congress and the National Workers' Union and the Sugar Manufacturers' Association of Jamaica.   After defining the rights of the unions, this agreement states that:

> It is understood and agreed that the Estates shall have the sole right to conduct their businesses and manage their operations, to control and direct the working forces, to introduce technical improvements, to determine the times, methods and manner of working, and type of work to be done, to modify, extend and curtail or cease operations and to determine the number of employees required; to promote, demote, transfer and lay-off employees and to discipline and discharge them for cause; and to decide in its sole discretion all other matters connected with the Estates' business, provided that the Estates agree not to breach any of their obligations under the terms of the agreement.

The adoption of a clause of this kind does not mean that on such questions as the manning of machines, lay-offs and discipline there is no place for negotiation.   Employers ought not to be criticized for seeking to safeguard their ability to manage efficiently, but in some cases anxiety on this score has led them into attempts to curb legitimate union interests.   In this respect employers overseas have behaved no differently from employers in Britain, Europe and America; the history of collective bargaining in the advanced countries has been to an important extent one of extending the frontier of negotiation to matters that were once the subject of unilateral decision by management.   Agreement on what should be an exclusive managerial prerogative has been, therefore, the subject of continuing controversy in the advanced industrial countries; this problem is unlikely to be avoided in the developing countries.   It can be said with certainty that attempts to prevent the unions from questioning managerial decisions which seriously affect the welfare of their members are not likely to be durable.

The Content of Collective Agreements

The subject matter of collective bargaining, which was at first narrowly confined to changes in levels of remuneration, is now as widely extended in the more advanced agreements negotiated in these territories as in any of the countries which have a much longer experience of collective bargaining. The following list of sub-headings from an agreement signed in West Africa in 1960 gives some idea of the scope of collective bargaining today. It is by no means untypical. A similar list of items could be compiled from collective agreements signed in many of the territories.

1. Title
2. Preamble
3. Scope of the Agreement
4. Interpretation of this Agreement
5. Amendments to this Agreement
6. Recognition of the Union
7. Maintenance of Union membership
8. Union Notice Board
9. Permission for Union Meetings
10. Permission to Attend Meetings
11. Constitution of Divisional Negotiating Committee
    Object; Function; Questions Excluded; Membership; Agenda; Meetings; Minutes; Procedures
12. Duties of Employers
13. Rates and Standards of Employment
14. Welfare
15. Medical
16. Educational and General Training
17. Retirement Benefit
18. Employment Procedures
19. Employment and Service Records
20. Apprenticeship
21. Promotions
22. Hours of Work
23. Travelling to Work
24. Salaries and Wages
25. Increments
26. Overtime
27. Height Money
28. Out-Station Allowance
29. Transfer Allowance
30. Acting Appointments

31. Frustrated Work
32. Pay Day
33. Paid Annual Vacation Leave
34. Sick Leave
35. Maternity Leave
36. Holidays
37. Absence from Work
38. Absence during Working Hours
39. Sickness Reports
40. Redundancy
41. Laying-off Procedure
42. Suspension
43. Warnings
44. Summary Dismissals
45. Termination of Employment
46. Grievance Procedure
47. Tools Allowance
48. Loss of Tools

Not even this rather comprehensive agreement covers every matter that might be of great importance to workers.   Housing, for example, is often provided by employers, especially where plantations and mines are concerned.   There is a tendency for employers to rid themselves of this responsibility, which they had to discharge in the past because this was the only way that their workers could be housed, but local governments are often reluctant to take over the responsibility for the management of such properties.   Where housing is an item that is included with the remuneration of the job it inevitably becomes the concern of the unions.   Since they are also matters which lend themselves to disputes, rents and rights and duties of employer and tenant may become an issue of collective bargaining and be regulated by agreement.

Although redundancy agreements are a relatively new feature of British collective bargaining, they have already been adapted to the circumstances of overseas employment.   An agreement made between East Africa Industries and the Kenya Chemical Workers' Union details the conditions under which the employer may terminate the employment of redundant workers.   It entitles every employee to a minimum of one month's notice or pay for a month in lieu of notice. For each year of service up to and including nine years' service redundant employees are entitled to a resettlement allowance of one week's pay. For each year over nine years the amount is raised to one and a half week's pay up to a total of three months' pay. In addition to this resettlement allowance each redundant worker with five years' service receives a quarter month's pay for each complete year of service at the basic rate in the final month of service. This sum is progressively raised for every five years, culminating in a payment after twenty-five years which amounts to two years' pay at the rate of the final month. This rate of compensation is much higher as a proportion of the normal wage than has usually been achieved in the best redundancy agreements negotiated in the United Kingdom.

The redundancy compensation provisions in an agreement made between the Singapore Cold Storage Company and the Singapore Industrial Workers' Union, in 1960, are perhaps not quite as financially generous as in the previous case. Under this Singapore agreement the employer must give a minimum of one month's notice, offer alternative employment if there are suitable vacancies within the firm and pay to each worker the proportion of the annual bonus to which he would be entitled at the year's end and in addition half a month's pay for each year of service, with a minimum of the equivalent of two months' pay.

From the examples quoted it will be seen that collective bargaining has in many cases now reached a level where in terms of the agreements adopted it bears comparison with the standards of the advanced industrial countries. In pointing this out, it does not follow that there are not many weaknesses in the systems of industrial relations that have so far emerged. It is, of course, impossible to judge the effectiveness of collective bargaining merely by examining the results on paper. Collective agreements have to be administered and their clauses interpreted. Investigation of collective agreements in the more advanced countries indicates that the actual situation may often depart considerably from that suggested by the agreement. This is inevitable, since the rules have to be worked by men whose interests are different. Managers and trade union representatives approach the interpretation of a collective

DD

agreement from different angles, and there is, therefore, bound
to be a certain degree of conflict between them.   This does not
mean, however, that a collective agreement is not worth the
paper that it is written upon.   Although collective agreements
in some countries, especially in Latin America, tend to be
expressions of standards it is hoped will be reached at some time,
this is not the tradition of British territories.   In the territories
that have been examined in this survey collective agreements
generally do reflect the actual situation and not merely the
intentions of the parties.   It would, of course, be misleading to
suggest that scope and coverage of collective agreements is as
wide as in Britain.   There is also plenty of room for the more
effective application of agreements signed.   Trade unions are
often still inefficiently organized;   they lack an adequate
number of dedicated competent members who are prepared
and able to accept the responsibility of leadership;   they are
often short of funds and they suffer from tribal, racial and
political divisions.   Nevertheless, in spite of these weaknesses
and many setbacks, a gradual improvement can be clearly discovered.   What is most important is that progress in the task of
building a viable system of industrial relations in which collective bargaining has an important role to play is steadily being
made.

Collective Bargaining and Independence

Governments of newly independent territories are concerned
to see living standards raised as rapidly as possible, and their
desire is naturally to do whatever they can to promote increases
in the wages of workers.   Before the achievement of political
independence low wages were strongly attacked as the product
of colonial rule;   when, therefore, colonial status is ended there
is inevitably an expectation that wage levels will be considerably
raised.   Unfortunately, much as governments might wish to
see this result achieved, independence does not in itself make
this possible.   The problems of wage determination which face
the territories after they have attained independence are no
different in principle from what they were before independence.
It must also be added that these problems which face developing countries are no different in essence from the problems

of wage determination in the industrially more advanced countries.

Although the political leaders in many territories have been inclined to criticize collective bargaining as a system favouring the employers they have generally adopted a cautious policy towards it. While sympathizing with the demands for improved conditions of employment, governments have been well aware that any exertion of undue influence on behalf of the unions would have adverse repercussions in many ways. They have, therefore, in most cases, after independence has been reached, been careful not to encourage extravagant claims. There have been instances where governments have brought some pressure to bear upon employers, sometimes through the appointment of committees of inquiry that they knew would probably tend to favour the claims of the unions. In a few instances the pressure has been less subtly applied, but by and large governments of the territories after independence have not allowed short-sighted political expediency to determine their actions.

There are a number of reasons why the governments of the territories have had to step warily with regard to wages. However much they might have attacked low incomes as a symptom of colonialism, when engaged in the struggle for self-government, the political leaders of the territories are well aware that when in power they are responsible for meeting the governments own wages bill. If wages are pushed up in the private sector the repercussions must be felt elsewhere; government employees inevitably soon demand similar increases, and these may not be easy to finance.

Development planning has also been an important factor making for an awareness of the significance of wage costs. There is nothing which shows more clearly the effects of increased wages on the scope and cost of production than a detailed plan which has to be modified, even perhaps jettisoned, because of wage increases. In this connection the influence of wage costs on the ability to attract capital and increase the rate of investment is generally well understood. An inflationary increase in wages, it is appreciated, is not likely to help in this respect. Governments of the territories have therefore been as much concerned with preventing wages from rising too

fast as they have with lifting them up from their previous low
levels.

The collective bargaining system that has developed in the
territories has been criticized on other grounds as well as on its
efficiency as a system of wage determination.   But so far only
Ghana, Tanganyika and Singapore have felt that they could
not permit trade unions and employers to continue to enjoy the
full freedom of unregulated collective bargaining in case this
led to a dangerous situation.[6]   Collective bargaining in these
territories has been buttressed by a system of compulsory
arbitration and political control of trade union policy, but it is
interesting to note that in no case has collective bargaining been
eliminated.   Although the employers in each territory have
been apprehensive about the way in which issues in dispute
might be decided, there is no evidence that the development
of collective bargaining has been brought to a halt, or that
the agreements and decisions have been ill judged.   The findings of the industrial courts and the awards made have not
always met with the approval of the employers or the unions,
but they do not seem to have been such as to rouse bitter an-
tagonism.

The determination of wages and working conditions is inevitably charged with political implications in every territory.
Nothing could be more political than the attempts made in
Britain and other countries to establish a national wages policy.
Nor can a country be indicted for seeking to regulate the fixing
of wages by the introduction of a system of compulsory arbitration on the model of Australia and New Zealand, or for seeking
to regulate the pattern of wages according to a national plan as
in Holland.

Completely free collective bargaining on the British pattern
is only one of many different models that have been adopted in
the democratic countries of the world.   The United States,
Canada, Australia and New Zealand have all diverged from the
British pattern of industrial relations; it is just as likely that the

---

[6] The compulsory arbitration system adopted in Aden is designed to promote
collective bargaining.   See page 331.   It should be also added that in many
African territories such as Guinea, Libya, Egypt, Sudan and the Portuguese
territories free collective bargaining is not permitted; unions are not allowed to
strike, and in a number of cases forced labour has been introduced as a means of
increasing the pace of economic development.

newly developing countries of Africa, Asia and elsewhere will adjust their systems to suit their own needs.

In fact, this has already happened, as we have previously indicated, in Singapore which has modelled its system on that of Australia. In Ceylon, which has made collective agreements legally binding when registered with and approved by the Ministry of Labour. In Ghana, where collective bargaining has been made compulsory but unions must obtain a certificate from the Minister of Labour before they have the right to represent a class of workers. These are, of course, only the most striking cases; in many other major and minor respects there have been departures from the law and the procedures of industrial relations as they exist in Britain.

There is a danger in countries anxious to develop their economies rapidly that governments, employers and unions will become impatient with the responsibilities of working within the framework of principles which have been embodied within the International Labour Code. This has already happened in some developing territories; the degree to which certain governments regulate industrial relations threatens to destroy the ability of the unions and the employers to settle their problems by independent collective bargaining. It is natural that governments should be concerned to prevent the irresponsible exercise of trade union bargaining power, but if unions and employers are denied the opportunity to learn to appreciate each other's point of view through negotiation it is possible that the long-run development of a healthy system of industrial relations will be seriously jeopardized.

So far, however, in most of the developing territories of the Commonwealth the signs point to the possibility of establishing a viable system of industrial relations that will bear comparison with those existing in the more advanced countries. Whether, in every territory, the pressures of the political circumstances that will prevail after independence will allow the progress made to continue is an open question. If governments refrain from deliberately controlling the trade unions and minutely regulating all the main aspects of industrial relations, then the developments observed have an excellent chance to mature into an effective system of industrial relations. By this is meant a system whereby the vocational interests of work-people are effectively protected by the activities of their own associations. When unions are independent of employers and of the state and government they are able to bring pressure to bear, when this is necessary, to obtain changes in the law and to obtain better wages and working conditions. In turn, the employers are free to develop their relations with unions in the way best suited to the interests of their type of business. The modern state, on the other hand, has a more positive function to exercise than merely holding the ring between employer and union. It has many positive duties that require action that might come into conflict with the decision of management and unions. Where this is necessary and unavoidable the state must take the steps it feels to be essential, but these should never be such as to destroy the ability of management and labour to settle their problems as far as possible independently.

This liberal approach to industrial relations is sometimes criticized on the grounds that under the conditions which are said to prevail in the tropical territories, namely weak trade unionism, political interference, and reactionary employers, the development of a smoothly working system of industrial relations based upon the principles of collective bargaining is impossible. This type of criticism fails to take into account the remarkable progress that has been made. If the development of collective bargaining is judged upon a reasonable time scale, then there are solid grounds for concluding that a viable system of industrial relations based upon the growth of independent trade unions, collective bargaining and the development of mature relations between employers, unions and the state can be and is being created in many territories. The best trade unions are as well led and administered as many in the more advanced countries; bargaining has already reached an advanced level in a significant number of instances; and in most territories, governments, employers and unions are acting with a sense of mutual responsibility.

In focusing attention on these achievements it might be suggested that the weaknesses in the industrial relations situations in the tropical territories are being forgotten. This is not the case, but if we wish to assess the course of future development it is important to recognize the peaks that have been scaled, since it is these that indicate what has already been achieved and what is likely to be emulated when conditions are ripe elsewhere.

The development of a healthy system of industrial relations certainly requires more for its attainment than the negotiation of collective agreements. No matter how advanced an agreement might be on paper, until it is effectively administered it is only a promise of achievement. The lack of an adequate corps of paid officials and lay representatives certainly frequently leaves the workers greatly dependent upon the willingness of the employer to carry out the terms of the agreement.

Many employers realize that not to observe the terms of an agreement to which they are a party, even if the union is not capable of making certain that they do so, is shortsighted. There is a limit, however, to what an enlightened employer should do; it is not within the bounds of possibility for an employer to make the established grievance procedure work effectively if the members fail to use the opportunity that it provides. Here again it is wrong to draw the hasty conclusion that the advanced type of collective agreement, which embodies the procedure and the benefits which are to be found in the British and American agreements, has no meaning in Africa or Asia because it is often inadequately enforced by the union. While this may be true, such agreements have an important educational value, and in due course the unions will develop their organization to the point where they will be able to exercise their proper function.

It is sometimes suggested that unions in the tropical territories are being choked by the kindness of employers, the nursing of labour departments and the resistance of the international and the older trade union movements. There is much truth in the contention that unions in the British overseas territories have not had to overcome the bitter opposition of the type that unions in Britain, Europe and America had to defeat before they won the right to exist. It does not follow, however, that the only way to good industrial relations in overseas territories is by going through the same experience as the older industrial countries. The difference in the history and experience of the tropical territories will lead to differences in behaviour, and it is possible that the unions will be weaker for not having been tempered in the same type of furnace as the older unions, but this is a drawback that cannot be overcome by regretting that the experience of the colonial unions has not been the same as the British.

Others, it must be said, feel that colonial employers have been unduly harsh and repressive. In some important respects this is also true; colonial employers did at one stage treat labour as cheap and expendable. They did not see the indigenous worker as a human being in the same category as themselves, but as a primitive, almost child-like creature, capable only of working under strong paternal discipline.

In spite of this aspect of colonialism, British rule almost certainly conferred more benefits than it inflicted damage, if the advances of modern civilization are regarded as benefits, as they most obviously are by the peoples and leaders of the territories. The objective of every territory is to achieve the same material standard of living as the colonial powers enjoy, and this is to be done by following the path pioneered by those countries, namely the path to industrialization. Economic development and social progress would almost certainly be much less advanced in the tropical territories had there been no colonialism, but this fact is emotionally of far less importance to the indigenous colonial worker than the shame which is felt at having been reduced to an inferior political and social status.

Resentment against white superiority is one of the most difficult problems that many employers have to face in the developing territories today. The problem is not so much that British employers are identified with colonial rule, but the past record of the relations between one ethnic group and another. Industrial relations in the tropical territories are to a large extent a reflection of race relations. Management and workers are not only divided by functional and economic differences but also by differences of colour, language and behaviour patterns associated with racial groups. The conflicts which occur are by no means confined to white and black, but as often arise between African and Indian, Malay and Chinese, Fijian and Indian, Tamil and Sinhalese.

In this situation decisions are often charged with racial implications. Those affecting promotions and dismissals, wage and salary structures, welfare and social policies are only too easily attributed to racial factors. It is, therefore, necessary in this kind of atmosphere to ensure that the fear of racial discrimination is appeased by an appropriate policy, but there is a danger that this might reach a point where progress towards an integrated working community is jeopardized. Some regard must be had for efficiency, and in the last resort it must be on these grounds that decisions are taken.

Another factor of considerable importance to good industrial relations that cannot easily be altered is the barrier which language differences present to the communication of ideas and a common understanding of questions at issue.[7] When trade union leaders have to present their case in English they are often having to use a language over which they have less command than the employer. Even more important is the fact that language differences may prevent managers and workers from ever discussing matters in a face-to-face situation. In these circumstances the acute problems of communication which beset any large-scale organization are made much worse.

Perhaps even more basic than these differences are those which arise from the great differences in the scales of values of workers who have come to industrial employment from tribal communities held together by customs and beliefs that are entirely alien to those who manage. When the accustomed rhythm of life and the social sanctions entailed do not support the behaviour patterns required of an industrial worker difficulties are bound to ensue.

These difficulties are inevitable and cannot be overcome merely by the manipulation of managerial techniques. The adjustment to the conditions of a modern industrial society will gradually develop as employment expands, cities develop and a permanent committed labour force is established. The transition period will, however, last for some time, and it is a responsibility of management and unions to recognize the nature of the problems and to seek their cure by the pursuit of policies that are as sympathetic as the circumstances permit. While it is clear that the methods developed in the advanced industrial countries to cope with the problems that arise out of employment may not always be applicable to the tropical territories, there is much evidence to show that their relevance

7 See W. Elkan, *Migrants and Proletarians, op. cit.* p. 67.

is likely to become more and not less significant as economic progress takes place.

The systems of industrial relations which are emerging in the tropical Commonwealth territories will finally be determined by the same sets of factors that have determined industrial relations systems in other countries.[8]   These are: (1) the technological characteristics of the work-place; (2) the economic factors affecting the demand for labour; and (3) the political and ideological nature of the state.[9]

It is clear from the evidence that we have examined that the technological characteristics of employment in the territories have given rise to problems that are familiar to every other country that has gone through the same type of economic development.   The response evoked in the territories, namely the development of trade unionism, collective bargaining, strikes, procedures of conciliation and arbitration, and the issues in question, namely wages, hours of work, discipline, social benefits, are exactly the same as in every other country.   There is then a vast area of similar problems and similar responses.   Similar, too, are problems which confront the unions in the tropical territories with respect to their proper role in relation to the political stability and economic development of the state. Today unions everywhere are faced with the need to exercise a dual responsibility—one to their members and another to the public at large.   Organized labour is called upon to co-operate with governments and employers to achieve economic and social goals agreed to be desirable.   How far ought such co-operation to be taken?   Should it be to the point where the right to oppose is abandoned and the interests of members are sacrificed to the general welfare as conceived by the political leaders?

If the liberal political state nurtured during British colonial rule fails to survive the pragmatic test of independence and a totalitarian system is adopted in its place it is certain that the industrial relations system will not escape unscathed.   Such a change in the nature of the state will alter the relations of unions and employers to governments, and in the process the proce-

[8] See J. T. Dunlop, *Industrial Relations Systems* (New York, 1958); and Kerr, Dunlop, Harbison and Myers, *Industrialism and Industrial Man* (Cambridge, Mass., 1960).
[9] See Dunlop, *op. cit.*, p. 9.

dures which regulate these relations are bound to be reshaped to suit the new pattern of authority.

Whatever type of political system is adopted in the early period of independence, as the tropical territories develop economically and employment becomes increasingly significant, the basic elements of industrial relations will become more important. It is unlikely that the great mass of wage-earners will, in the future, be any more satisfied that they enjoy a fair wage than their predecessors are satisfied today. They will, therefore, seek to express their demand for higher wages and better working conditions by collective pressure even when every manager is an indigenous person and the majority of enterprises are locally directed. Therefore, the problems that spring out of the relationships between management and managed will not disappear with the disappearance of ex-patriate managers, they will continue in the future as they have continued in every country, irrespective of its political char-acter, where men and women are employed in productive enterprise. It is possible that a solution to these problems will be found which will make trade unions and collective bargain-ing unnecessary, but there is no evidence so far to indicate that this would result in either better protection for the workers or a faster rate of economic growth.

The basic issues that face developing territories in the field of industrial relations and trade union policy are the classic issues of freedom and state regulation that have faced mankind for more than two thousand years. While it is true that freedom of association and the rights associated with it can only be sustained under specific social conditions, those conditions depend for their creation upon a value judgment that they are worth establishing. There is danger at the present that the effort will be given up because a totalitarian system of state regulation is simpler to operate than democracy and it is strongly supported. It is supported not only by the political leaders, who are naturally concerned to avoid the dangers that trade union pressures may bring, but also by some British, American and other outside observers, who have come to the conclusion that the system of industrial relations developed in the ad-vanced industrial countries is too complicated for the less developed territories.

There is no doubt that trade unions in the tropical territories of the Commonwealth are often weak, often badly led, often irresponsible in their demands, but so were trade unions in the advanced countries of the world when they were at a comparable stage of development. The danger that unions may abuse their power is one that has to be guarded against, but this does not mean that unions must be completely subordinated to the state. It is possible to devise methods of protecting the public interest without entirely destroying those rights which have come to be regarded in the more advanced countries of the world as of vital importance. The right to organize might have to be circumscribed to the extent that large numbers of overlapping and weak trade unions are discouraged. The right to strike might have to be limited to prevent the exercise of this power to damage the interests of an employer from being used to an extent that would gravely hurt the general interest. The right to engage in political activities might have to be curtailed so as to prevent the stability of the government from being undermined by extra-constitutional pressure from the unions.

Extreme limitations on the right to organize, to bargain, to strike, to engage in political activities ought to be judged in the context in which they take place. They should be accepted as desirable only in so far as they contribute to the development of economic and social progress that will make such restrictions unnecessary. It is important that the departures from the standards laid down in the International Labour Code should be justified only upon the basis of a short-run necessity and not as ends that are good in themselves. If these principles are followed there is no reason why a strong and healthy trade union movement, capable of promoting the interest of its members and at the same time the interest of the community, should not be developed.

Under the conditions of modern industrial civilization this is ultimately the *sine qua non* of a stable system of industrial relations; without institutions that are capable of representing their interests work-people will lose their ability to advance their point of view and to protest against the violation of their interests in an orderly and rational manner. They will be reduced to an anonymous collection of ineffective individuals whose lot is completely dependent upon the minority which dominates the centre of power. This may be the fate in store for many developing countries, but there is no reason why this must inevitably be so. The temptation for the more advanced countries to take the view that a totalitarian system is right for under-developed countries is one that ought to be resisted. It may well be necessary for the industrially less-advanced countries to develop new procedures for resolving employmental conflicts and determining patterns of remuneration. Collective bargaining on the British, American, Australian or Swedish model may not be exactly right for the conditions of African and Asian territories, but there are no conditions in any country so different from all others that lessons cannot be learnt. The features of industrial relations that arise out of the functional characteristics of employment and industrial organization, economic and technological developments, cut across the boundaries of states and are as important as the differences induced by disparate culture patterns.

INDEX

Acts of Parliament and Ordinances (Great Britain), 265
British *Trade Union Acts, 1871, 1876, 1913*, 178, 265
Conciliation Act, 1896, 307, 309
Conditions of Employment and National Arbitration Order (Order 1305) 1940–45, 308, 314, 316
Conspiracy and Protection of Property Act, 1875, 306, 313, 314, 316, 323
Factories Acts, 185
Imperial Acts Extension Ordinance, 261
Industrial Courts Act, 1919, 308, 309
Industrial Courts Ordinance, 1940, 308
Industrial Disputes Act, 325
Industrial Disputes Order (1951–9), 309
Trades Disputes Act, 1906, 175, 194, 233, 305, 313
Aden, 152, 354
  arbitration, 70, 99, 324, 331 *et seq.*, 402
  British Petroleum Refinery in, 101
  collective bargaining in, 391
  employment pattern in, 344, 346
  formation of unions, 69 *et seq.*
  Industrial Relations Ordinance, 331 *et seq.*
  racial problems in, 100–1, 362
  right to strike, 314
  skilled workers in, 362
  Trades Union Congress of, 100
  unions and politics, 102
  unions, membership of, 123, 276
AFL–CIO, 108
  and ICFTU, 159 *et seq.*
African Bureau, 198
Antigua, 37, 92, 95
  union membership, 123, 126
  Trades and Labour Union, 161

Anti-Slavery Society, 198
Alexander, Simeon, 38
All-African Trade Union Federation, 162, 163, 164
Arbitration, 70, 83, 185, 194, 244, 304, 308 *et seq.*, 391
  compulsory, 308, 315, 316 *et seq.*, 323, 402
Awberry, S. S. and Dalley, F. W., *Labour and Trade Union Organisation in the Federation of Malaya and Singapore*, 72
Awolowo, Obafemi, 103

Baker, Kenneth A., 19, 115
Bahamas, 152, 260, 264, 266, 269, 276, 290, 295, 298, 304, 307
  arbitration in, 312, 319, 320
  right to strike in, 314, 315
Barbados
  Labour Party, 37, 94
  Observer, 31
  Progressive League, 37
  skilled workers in, 361
  unions, accounts of, 298
  unions, legal regulation of, 261, 304, 307
  unions, membership of, 123, 126
  workers' union, 37, 94, 129, 140
Batu-Areng strike, 25
Becu, Omer, 161
Blythe, W. L., 'Historical Sketch of Chinese Labour in Malaya', *Journal of the Royal Asiatic Society*, 7
Borodin, Michael, 23
Boss Boys' Committees, 55, 56, 57, 58
Brentano, Lujo, *History and Development of Gilds and the Origin of Trade Unions*, 6
British Employers' Confederation, 375, 376

413

British Guiana, 9, 10, 11, 152, 157, 223–4
arbitration in, 311, 317, 319
development of unions, in 38, 39 *et seq.*
Industrial Workers' Union, 40, 93
Labour Party, 39
Labour Union, 15–17
Manpower Citizens' Association, 38, 93
migration to, 354
People's Progressive Party, 40, 93
strike in, 1924, 16
suspension of constitution, 40
The Guiana Review, 31
wage-fixing in, 374
British Honduras, 123
British Industrial Courts Act, 1919, 176
British Institute of Management, 380
Brunei, 24, 27, 81, 344
collective bargaining in, 391
unions, membership of, 123
Bustamante, Alexander, 35, 36, 37
Bustamante Industrial Trade Union, 36, 396
Burnham, Forbes, 41, 93
Butler, Uriah, 35, 36, 38
Buxton, C. Rodan, 147

Catholic unions, 87
Ceylon, 175, 184, 393
arbitration in, 314, 319, 320, 324, 326
collective bargaining in, 403
Department of Indian Immigrant Labour, 205
Indian Immigrant Labour Ordinance, 204
unions, legal regulation of, 261, 266–7, 268
unions, registration of, 28, 283, 287
Check-off system, 129, 130, 131, 253, 277, 278, 279, 395
Chief Registrar of Friendly Societies, 261

China, 6, 352
All-China Federation of Labour, 23
Canton, Labour Conferences, 23
Chinese labour, 146, 355
Chinese Seaman's Union, 22
guilds in, 7–8, 22, 24
influence of, 22 *et seq.*, 96
unions in, 98
Chinese Protectorate, 203
Cipriani, Captain, 13, 14, 16, 92
Citrine, N. A., 262, 295
Citrine, Sir Walter, 147, 149
Closed shop, 395
Collective bargaining agreements, 319, 390, 396, 399
in independent countries, 400
Colonial Development and Welfare Act, 1940, 187, 265
Colonial Development and Welfare Fund, 150
Colonial Employers' Federation, 376
Colonial Governments
and Labour Advisory Boards, 227, 228
and legislative process, 232–6
labour policies of, 175, 224
Ministers of Labour of, 221
Colonial Office
See also Secretary of State for the Colonies
and local labour departments, 181, 182
and Overseas Employers' Federation, 378
despatches of, 209, 210, 261, 316, 373
Labour Adviser to, 148, 197
Labour Committee, 176, 189
Labour, Department of, 148
labour policy of, 154, 169 *et seq.*, 172, 188, 189, 285
model labour laws of, 250
officials of, 196
Social Service, Department of, 184, 196
Colonial Labour Advisory Com-

mittee, 189, 190, 198, 226, 231, 316
Committee of Experts on Social Policy in Non-Metropolitan Territories, 1955, Report of, 245, 246
Communists, Communism
and colonial students, 30
and ILO, 256
and Kuomintang, 23, 98
and unions, 87, 95
Far Eastern Bureau, 25
in Asia, 23
in Hong Kong, 78, 98–99
in India, 172, 174
in international movements, 23, 156, 158, 159, 160, 163–4
in Jamaica, 36
in Malaya and Singapore, 24 et seq., 72, 77
in Nigeria, 103
Pan-Pacific Labour Conference, 1924, 24
Compulsory registration of unions, 245, 261–3
and appeals against, 285
in British Guiana, 262
in Jamaica, 262
in Mauritius, 265
in Northern Rhodesia, 233, 263
in Nyasaland, 262
Conditions of employment, 182, 185, 189, 244
Conference on Labour Administration, 1956, 193
Conspiracy in trade disputes, 306–7
Contracts of employment, 183, 187
conventions on, 243, 244
Cowan, T. M., 372
Creech Jones, A., 47, 377
Critchlow, Hubert, 15, 16, 38
Cundall, F., *Political and Social Disturbances in the West Indies*, 9

Dakar, Trade Union Conference at, 158
Dalley, F. W., 72, 152
EE

Department of Technical Co-operation, 200, 387
Depression, impact on labour administration, 207 et seq.
Dominica, 37
union membership, 123
Ducroux, Joseph, 25
Duke of Edinburgh's Study Conference, 359, 379
Dunlop, J. T., *Industrial Relations Systems*, 408

East African Royal Commission, 1924, 175
East African Royal Commission, 1953–55, 195, 385
Education, 183, 244, 246
technical, 360 et seq., 379
Edwards, Ebby, 147
Elkan, Walter, *An African Labour Force; Migrants and Proletarians*, 386, 407
Employers, 365 et seq., 368, 370, 406
and collective bargaining, 401, 402, 405
organizations, 375
plantation, 393
See also
British Employers' Confederation
Colonial Employers' Federation
Overseas Employers' Federation.
Employment
age of, 185, 188, 244
and immigrant labour, 353 et seq.
conditions of, 365
in agriculture, 338
in building and civil engineering, 349, et seq.
in commerce, 352–3
in government: local government services, 344
in manufacturing, 350
in mining and oil industries, 342
in personal and domestic services, 353
in transport and communications, 347 et seq., 344

Employment (contd.)
occupational distribution of workers, 338
pattern of, 337 et seq.
women and children in, 185, 189, 244, 248, 337, 353, 390
Epstein, A. L., Politics in an Urban African Community, 54, 113, 384
Esua, E., 151

Fabian Society, 197
Colonial Bureau, 197
Fiji, 81, 152, 171
arbitration in, 83
collective bargaining in, 391
development of unions in, 82
Indian unions in, 83
Indians in, 355
Industrial Association Ordinance of, 286
Industrial Disputes Ordinances, 1942, 83
Industrial Disputes Ordinance, 1958, 312
labour ordinances in, 82, 83
pattern of employment in, 338, 354
racial problems in, 83
strikes in, 83
Trades Union Congress of, 83, 144
unionism in, 144, 264, 304, 341
unions, membership of, 123
Firth, Raymond, Work and Community in a Primitive Society, 359
Forced labour, 251, 252, 370
ILO convention on, 242, 243, 248
Free Labour World, 164

Gairy, E. M., 138-9
Gambia, The, 42, 123, 157, 180, 261, 282, 295, 298, 304, 307, 348, 357
Gazette of India, 204
Garvey, Marcus, 14, 29
Ghana, 6, 125, 239
arbitration in, 309
check-off system, 130, 278

Ghana (contd.)
collective bargaining, 402, 403
Convention People's Party, 49, 106
development of unions in, 47 et seq.
employment in, 357
Industrial Relations Act, 1958, 51, 272, 279-81, 309, 326
right to strike, 194, 314
strikes in, 48, 49, 145
trade union legislation in, 42, 47
Trades Union Congress of, 48, 49, 105, 107, 144
Unfair Labour Practices Tribunal, 281
union accounts, 298
union funds of, 295
union, registration of, 282, 287
unions and independence movement, 48
unions and international movement, 162, 164
unions and politics, 105 et seq.
unions in, 123, 155, 156
unions, legal regulation of, 261, 272
unions, membership of, 278-9
Gittens, R. A., 151
Glasspole, H. A., 151
Gold Coast, 157
Artisans' and Labours' Union, 18
Census of Population, 1911, 7
Labour, Department of, 210
strike in, 1921, 18
Government Reports and Publications
British Guiana, the Suspension of the Constitution, 41
Census of Population 1911, Gold Coast Colony, 7
Colonial Annual Report, North Borneo, 1947, 80
Command Papers on colonial administration, 184
Commission of Inquiry into the Strike and Riots in Freetown in February 1955, 46

Government Reports and Publications (*contd.*)
Labour Conditions in the West Indies, 32
Labour in the United Kingdom Dependencies, 1957, 243
Labour Legislation in the Colonial Territories, 194
Labour Supervision in the Colonial Empire, 248
Report of the African Commission, 356
Report of the Commission of Enquiry into the Disorders in the Eastern Provinces of Nigeria, 1949, 45, 372
Report of the Commission . . . into the Stoppage in the Mining Industry in Northern Rhodesia in July 1957, 52
Report of the Commission of Inquiry into the Sugar Industry, 40
Report of Rhodesia and Nyasaland Commission, 186
Report of the Royal Commission on Labour in India, 1929–31, 174
Report into disturbances in the Copperbelt of N. Rhodesia, 1935, 54
Report into disturbances in the Copperbelt of N. Rhodesia, 1940, 55
The Colonial Empire, 1937–38, 210
Report of the Commission on Trinidad and Tobago Disturbances, 1937, 209
West India Royal Commission, 1897, 9, 10
West India Royal Commission, 1938–1939, 3, 186, 187
White Paper on Native Taxation, 177
White Paper on the Trade Unions and Trade Disputes Bill, Mauritius, 265
Green, J. F. N., 147
Grenada, 37
Manual and Mental Workers' Union, 138
Labour Party, 138

Grenada (*contd.*)
Seamen's and Waterfront Workers' Union, 395
unions, membership of, 123

Hanrahan, G. Z., The Communist Struggle in Malaya, 24, 25, 26
Hawkins, E. K., Road Transport in Nigeria, 247
Henderson, Arthur, 19, 20
Hicks, George, 147
Hill, Polly, The Gold Coast Cocoa Farmer, 340
Hock, Lim Yew, 75, 96, 97
Hong Kong, 6, 22, 247
and Kowloon Trades Union Council, 78
Chinese societies in, 8
collective bargaining in, 391
Communists in, 78, 98–99
employment in, 346, 350, 351, 354, 363
Federation of Trades Unions in, 78
Machine Trade Benefit Guild, 22
Mechanics' Union, 22
strikes, 1920, 1922, 22; 1926, 23
Trade Union and Trade Disputes Ordinance, 302
Trades Union Congress of, 144
unions, 144
unions and politics, 98–99, 305
unions, funds of, 295
unions, legal regulation of, 301
unions, membership of, 123, 270
unions, nature of, 77, 80
unions, registration of, 271, 284
women workers in, 338
Housing, 183, 188, 398
Hyde-Clarke, E. M., 377

Indentured and contract labour
Chinese, 146, 171
in West Indies, 365
Indian, 100–1, 171, 204–5
Independence
and political movements, 117
movements and students, 29

India, Government of, 172–174
Acts of, 203
emigration from, 203
High Commissioner for, 148, 173–4
Indian Emigration Act, 1922, 172, 203
Indian Immigration Fund, 203
Indian Trades Disputes Act, 1929, 174
Industrial and Commercial Workers' Union of South Africa, 148
Industrial Relations, 195, 245, 246, 337, 367, 381 *et seq.*
legal regulation of, 259 *et seq.,* 304 *et seq.*
Industrial Welfare Society, 379
Institute of Personnel Management, 379
International Confederation of Free Trade Unions, (ICFTU), 45, 52, 62, 64, 68, 103, 104, 107, 116, 133, 156, 158 *et seq.*
and right to strike, 322
International Solidarity Fund of, 161, 196, 198, 234
International Federation of Mineworkers, 165
International Federation of Trade Unions (IFTU), 157
International Labour Code, 241, 247, 252, 255, 403, 410
International Labour Conference, 241, 242, 244
International Labour Organization (ILO), 12, 105, 115, 122, 133, 146, 148, 151, 172, 176, 196, 198, 238, 241 *et seq.,* 271, 272, 300
African Regional Conference of, 1960, 250, 272
and employers, 377, 378
and right to strike, 322
annual conferences of, 254, 256
conventions of, 176, 180, 185, 189, 231, 241 *et seq.,* 245, 247 *et seq.,* 252, 272, 371
Dakar Conference, 1955, 245
Declaration of Philadelphia, 244, 375

International Labour Organization (ILO) *(contd)*.
Director-General of, 242
Forced Labour Convention, 1930, 242, 243, 248, 251
International Labour Code of, 241
Labour Standards Convention of, 242
publications and reports of, 248, 249, 250, 300
Regional Conferences of 244
Reports of, 242
International Institute for Labour Studies, 254
International Trade Secretariats, 165, 166
International Transport Workers' Federation, 165
International Typographical Union of America, 11

Jagan, Cheddi, 40, 41, 42, 93
Jagan, Janet, 40, 41, 42, 93
Jamaica, 10, 11, 29, 199
arbitration in, 319, 322
Bustamante Industrial Trade Union, 36, 396
Cigar Makers' Union, 17
combinations legalized, 17
formation of National Workers' Union, 36
Labour Party, 36, 92
legal regulations of unions in, 259, 290, 304
Longshoremen's Union, 17
Montego Bay Labourers' Benevolent Union, 17
People's National Party, 92
right to strike in, 314
skilled workers in, 361
strikes after 1918, 17
Sugar Manufacturers' Association, 396
Trades Union Congress of, 151, 396
union finances in, 294
unions in, 341
unions, membership of, 123, 126

Jamaica (*contd.*)
Workmen's Co-operative Association, 17
Jayawardena, V. K., *The Labour Movement in Ceylon with reference to Political Factors, 1893–1947*, 176
Jenks, C. W., *The International Protection of Trade Union Freedom*, 245
Joint Industrial Councils, 390
Josey, A., *Trade Unions in Malaya*, 72

Kahn-Freund, O., in *The System of Industrial Relations in Great Britain* (eds. Flanders, Clegg), 307
Katilingu, Lawrence, 109, 112, 113, 235
Kenya, 172, 175, 188, 229, 230, 272
African unions in, 61
arbitration, in 310, 319, 321
Asian unions in, 61
emergency powers legislation, 152
Federation of Labour, 62, 108
forced labour in, 198
joint consultation in, 384–5
pattern of employment in, 338, 356, 357
probationary trade unions in, 283
Railway Asian Union, 62
redundancy agreement in, 398
union segregation, 137
unions, accounts of, 298
unions and politics, 62
unions, funds of, 295
unions in, 123, 145, 341, 342
unions, officers of, 136, 293
unions, legal regulations of, 261, 267, 270, 291, 292, 301, 304
unions, registration of, 281, 284, 287, 288
women workers in, 337
Kerr, Dunlop, Harbison and Myers, *Industrialism and Industrial Man*, 408
Kuomintang, 23, 24
Kwantung Mechanics' Union, 22

Labour Advisory Boards, 186, 187, 227, 228
in Kenya, 229
in Nyasaland, 229
in Tanganyika, 229
Labour Advisory Committees, 390
and Colonial Office, 176, 189, 190, 198, 231, 316
Labour Departments
and Commissioners of Labour, 218 *et seq.*
and constitutional advance, 219 *et seq.*
and labour legislation, 230, 231
effects of war on, 211–14
establishment of, 203, 211
organization of, 218
staff of, 214
work of, 229
Labour factory inspectorates, 183, 189, 244, 368, 369
Labour legislation, 201, 230, 231, 232
Labour officers, 214, 217
appointment of, 211
local recruitment of, 216–17
training of, 192
Labour Party (Great Britain), 174, 181
Labour Government, 1945, 197
Latchmansingh, Dr., 40
Laurent, Dr. Edgar, 19, 20
League of Nations, 12
Lewanika, G., 113
Lloyd, P., 'Craft Organization in Yoruba', *Africa*, January 1953, 6
Loblack, Christopher, 31
Lowe, John, *The Malayan Experiment*, 77
Luyt, R. E., *Trade Unionism in African Colonies*, South African Institute of Race Relations, 28

MacDonald, Malcolm, 32, 181, 182, 209
MacDonald, Ramsay, 175
MacMillan, Professor W. M., 147

Malaya, 6, 152, 184, 227
arbitration in, 308
Chinese Engineering Mechanics'
Association, 24
Chinese in, 8, 26, 71, 74
Chinese Labour Union, 25
collective bargaining in, 391, 393
communists in, 24 *et seq.*, 72, 73,
95
essential services in, 318
indentured labour in, 171
Indian Plantation Workers'
Union, 74
industrial relations in, 389
Labour, Department of, 203, 205,
355
Malaya Seamen's Union, 24, 25
Malayan General Labour Union,
25
Malayan Labour Union, 25
Pan-Malayan Federation of
Trade Unions, 72, 73
pattern of employment in, 338,
346, 349, 350, 351, 354, 363
post-war problems in, 72 *et seq.*
Trade Union Adviser's Department, 72
Trade Union Ordinances, 71, 72, 73,
261
unions and politics in, 95
unions, funds of, 296, 297
unions in, 24, 25, 341
unions, legal regulation of, 267,
268, 301, 302, 304
unions, membership of, 123
unions, registration of, 281, 287,
288
women workers in, 338
Manley, Norman, 36
Marks, F. X., *The Rise and Development of Labour Movements in the
British Caribbean, with particular
reference to British Guiana,
Jamaica and Trinidad*, 10, 13
Master and Servants Laws, 177
Mauritius, 19, 152, 184, 224, 247
Artisans and General Workers'
Union, 116

Mauritius (*contd.*)
collective bargaining in, 391
employment in, 357
indentured labour in, 171, 354
Indians in, 355
Industrial Association Ordinance, 264,
265
Labour Party, 21, 114
National Trade Union of, 20–21
Protector of Immigrants, 207
strikes in, 21, 115, 182, 188
Trade Union Bill, 1926, 21
Trades Union Council in, 115, 116
unions and politics, 114 *et seq.*
unions in, 304, 341
unions, legal regulation of, 265,
271
unions, membership of, 123
unions, registration of, 284
women workers in, 338
Mboya, Tom, 62, 107, 108
McGregor, Roy, 147
Mellor, A. R. I., 376
Migrant labour, 353 *et seq.*, 366, 367
See also indentured and contract
labour
Mineworkers' International Federa-
tion, 234, 235
Minimum wage, 185, 189, 244, 248,
390
Minimum wage boards, in West
Africa, 43
*Minimum Wage-Fixing Convention,
1928*, 180
Ministry of Labour (Great Britain),
150, 176, 189, 198, 261, 317,
373, 379
Mitchell, J. C., 'Africans in Indus-
trial Towns in N. Rhodesia'—
*Duke of Edinburgh's Study Con-
ference Report*, 54
Morse, H. B., *The Gilds of China*, 7
Moutou, W., 19, 20
Movement for Colonial Freedom,
198

Nan-Yang Federation of Labour,
24–25

Natal, 171
Narayanan, P. P., 74
Nigeria, 6, 157, 192, 199, 231, 351
Action Party, 103
All-Nigeria Trade Union Federation, 104, 161
and international movements, 164
application of ILO conventions in, 248, 249
Civil Service Union, 18
employment pattern in, 338, 339, 340, 341, 342, 343, 345, 352, 356, 357
General Strike, 1945, 44
government employees in, 372
Labour Advisory Boards in, 43
Labour Party, 104
National Council of Nigeria and the Cameroons, 103
Nigerian Eastern Region Development Corporation, 340
Nigerian Labour Congress, 103
Nigerian National Federation of Labour, 103
Railway Workers' Union, 42
right to strike in, 315
Trades Union Congress of, 44, 103, 104
trade union legislation in, 42
Union of Teachers, 43, 125, 151, 161
unions, accounts of, 298
unions and politics, 103 et seq.
unions, education of officers, 194
unions, funds of, 298
unions in, 144
unions, legal regulation of, 261, 290, 301
unions, membership of, 123, 126, 268
unions, registration of, 281
Nkrumah, Dr. K., 48, 49, 106, 107, 108, 155, 156, 162
North Borneo, 24, 80, 81, 271, 284, 349
Northern Rhodesia, 19, 157, 175, 186, 233–5

Northern Rhodesia (contd.)
African Mineworkers' Union, formation of, 58
African Mineworkers' Union in, 109, 113
African National Congress in, 110, 111, 113
Amalgamated Engineering Union, 52
and Colonial Office, 184
arbitration in, 311, 319, 320, 322
Boss Boys, 55, 56, 57, 58
closed-shop agreements in, 274–5
Contractors' Labour Association, 57
European Civil Servants' Association, 52
European Mineworkers' Union in, 51, 52, 58
Federal TUC, 52, 53
formation of new unions, 1947, 60–61
Mines African Staff Association, 59
Mine Officials' and Salaried Staffs' Association, 52
Northern Rhodesian Mineworkers' Union, 274
organization of Africans, 53 et seq.
other European unions, 52
pattern of employment in, 342, 347, 356
Rhodesian Railway Workers' Union, 19
segregated unions in, 137
Shop Assistants' Union, 53
strikes in, 57, 181, 188
Trades Union Congress of, 52
Tribal Elders system, 53 et seq., 384
unions and politics, 108 et seq.
unions in, 123, 305
unions, legal regulation of, 261, 290, 291, 301, 307
unions, membership of, 113–14, 273
unions, officers of, 293
unions, registration of, 178, 259, 262, 281 et seq.

Northern Rhodesia (*contd.*)
Zambia National Congress in, 111, 112
Nyasaland, 65 *et seq.*, 175, 180, 186
arbitration in, 310, 319, 321
Civil Service organization, 66
closed shop in, 275–6
early unions, formation of, 65
pattern of employment in, 338, 348, 356
Railway African Workers' Trade Union, 65
right to strike in, 315
Trades Union Congress of, 66
training of workers, 360
unions, funds of, 296, 297
unions in, 123, 304
unions, legal regulations of, 267–8, 271, 291, 292, 301, 307
unions, officers of, 293
unions, registration of, 282, 284, 287

O'Connor, Quintin, 38
Oldenbrock, J. H., 161
Onraet, R., *Singapore: A Police Background*, 25
Orde-Browne, Major, 148, 184, 186, 206, 210, 211, 228, 229
The African Labourer, 371
Overseas Employers' Federation, 130, 150, 153, 160, 198, 239, 256, 316, 378, 379

Parry, Edgar, 46, 216
Passfield, Lord (*see also* S. and B. Webb), 21, 146, 175, 179
Personnel management and welfare supervision, 150, 177, 379
Philadelphia Conference (ILO), 375
Philadelphia, Declaration of, 244
Picketing, 186, 194, 262
Pickles, W., 'Trade Unions in the Political Climate', *Industrial Relations: Contemporary Problems and Perspectives* (ed. B. C. Roberts), 67

Plantation Employers' Associations, Companies, 393
Plantation Workers' International Federation, 165, 341
Polak, H. S. L., 147
Post, Telegraph and Telephone International, 165
Powesland, P. G., *Economic Policy and Labour*, 356
Prakash, A., *The State in Relation to Trade Unions and Trade Disputes in India*, 173, 174
Public Services International, 165
Pugh, Sir Arthur, 147
Punekar, S. D., *Trade Unionism in India*, 174
Purcell, A. A., 175
Purcell, V., *Malaya Communist or Free*, 72

Racial problems, 30, 39, 83, 100, 110, 137–8, 253, 366
Raffles, Sir Stamford, 202
Recruitment of union members, 127, 128
Red International of Labour Unions, 23, 156
Redundancy, 398, 399
Registration of unions, 281
and registrars, 289, 299, 300
and suspension of, 286
Reid, T., 147
Rhodesian Railway Workers' Union, 19
Richards, Alfred, 10, 13, 16
Right to strike, 253, 304, 313 *et seq.*
Roan Antelope Copper, 384
Roberts, B. C., *Trade Unions in a Free Society*, 142
The Trades Union Congress 1868–1921, 147
Rohan, Arthur, 19, 20
Rojas, John, 38
Roper, J. J., *Labour Problems in West Africa*, 18
Ross, W. McGregor, 147
Rottenberg, Simon, 'Labour Relations in an Underdeveloped

Economy', *Economic Development and Cultural Change*, 37
Rozemont, M. G., 116
Ruskin College, 149
courses at, 151

Sarawak, 24, 27, 80, 81, 271, 344
collective bargaining in, 391
union membership, 123
union registration, 284
Secretary of State for the Colonies, 20, 21, 32, 64, 114, 115, 116, 130, 146, 148, 149, 150, 159, 178, 182, 189, 192, 261, 316, 320, 373, 377, 378
Second world war, 389
effects of, 187, 212–14
Shaw, Arthur, 147
Shell Oil Company, 81
Shiels, Dr. Drummond, 147, 175, 176, 179, 208
Sierra Leone, 18, 48, 157, 272
Artisans' Union, 47
Council of Labour, 47
Labour Party, 47
patterns of employment, 343
Railway Workers' Union, 47
trade union legislation in, 42, 261
Trades Union Congress of, 47
union leaders in, 46
unions, accounts of, 298
unions, funds of, 295
unions in, 45–47, 123, 190, 347
unions, legal regulation of, 301, 307
unions, registration of, 271, 282, 283
United Mineworkers, 47
Singapore, 152
arbitration in, 308, 324, 328 *et seq.*
Chinese in, 26, 71, 75
Clerical Workers' Union, 24
Cold Storage Company, 399
collective bargaining in, 391, 402, 403
communists in, 24 *et seq.*, 72, 76, 95

Singapore (*contd.*)
employment in, 346, 348, 349, 350, 363
Federation of Trade Unions, 72, 73
Industrial Arbitration Court, 328
Industrial Relations Ordinance, 1960, 277, 328
Industrial Workers' Union, 399
Peasant Party, 96
People's Action Party, 97
post-war problems in, 72 *et seq.*
right to strike in, 194, 314, 315
Socialist Front, 96
Trade Union Ordinances, 72
Trades Union Congress of, 75
Trade Union Working Committee, 75
unions and politics in, 95
unions, funds of, 295
unions in, 24, 25
unions, legal regulation of, 267, 268, 304
unions, membership of, 123
unions, registration of, 281, 287
women, employment of, 338
Skilled labour, supply of, 360 *et seq.*
Slavery, 365
South African Mineworkers' Union, 19
Spearpoint, F., 'The African Native and the Rhodesian Copper Mines', *Journal of the Royal African Society*, 54
St. Kitts-Nevis, 37
unions, membership of, 123, 126
St. Lucia, 37
unions, membership of, 123
St. Vincent, 37
unions, membership of, 123, 126
Strikes, 31, 194, 388
in Aden, 70, 102
in British Guiana, 1924, 16
in East and Central Africa, 54
in Fiji, 83
in Gold Coast, 18, 48
in Hong Kong, 22, 79
in Jamaica, 17

Strikes (contd.)
in Mauritius, 182
in Nigeria, 44
in Northern Rhodesia, 181
in Tanganyika, 65
in West Indies, 182
right to, 304
Students, 149
Summerbell, T., 10
Sun Yat-sen, Dr., 22, 23

Takoradi, strike at, 145
Tanganyika, 62 et seq., 155, 175, 180, 232
African National Union, 64
arbitration in, 310, 319, 321
check-off system, 130
collective bargaining in, 402
early unions in, 62-63
Federation of Labour, 63
industrial relations in, 385
Labour Department of, 206
pattern of employment in, 338, 342, 356, 357
skilled workers in, 360
Stevedores and Dockworkers' Union, 63
Trade Union Ordinance, 1962, 302
Trades Union Congress of, 144, 145
unions, accounts of, 298
unions, funds of, 296
unions in, 123, 341, 347
unions, legal regulations of, 261, 270, 291, 292, 301, 304
unions, registration of, 282, 287
Technical assistance to under-developed territories, 253-4
Tettegah, John, 49, 156, 162
Times, The, 108
Trades Union Congress of Great Britain (TUC), 19, 39, 64, 69, 84, 116, 130, 143, 155, 157, 198, 234, 316
and international movements, 157 et seq.
and right to strike, 322
Annual Reports of, 156

Trades Union Congress of Great Britain (TUC) (contd.)
Commonwealth Department of, 152
Colonial Advisory Committee of, 146 et seq., 149, 150
Colonial Fund of, 151
grants and assistance to colonial unions, 152, 153
influence on colonial unions, 146 et seq., 155-56
Trade Unions. See also Union Officers
accounts and Annual Statement, 297
amalgamation and federation of, 300 et seq.
and Civil Service, 373
and closed shop, 273-6
and communists, 23, 87 et seq.
and employers, 28, 91
and influence of British TUC, 146 et seq.
and international movements, 157 et seq.
and guilds, 6 et seq.
and political parties, 85 et seq.
and redundancy, 398-9
and social change, 27 et seq.
constitutions and administration of, 289 et seq.
corruption in, 132
democracy in, 139 et seq.
finances of, 129 et seq., 289 et seq., 294
ILO conventions on, 245
impact of first world war on, 12
in Britain, 4-5, 85 et seq.
independence of, 120
in Europe, 5, 86 et seq.
in U.S.A., 5
language problems in, 138
leadership of, 29, 91, 118, 124, 133 et seq., 141, 387
legal regulations of, 259-334
legal status of, 117
officials of, 149, 293, et seq.
organization of, 122 et seq., 350

Trade Unions (*contd.*)
  recognition of, 183, 392
  registration of, 271 *et seq.*
  statutes on, 189
  treasurers of, 294, 297
  use of funds of, 294
Training Within Industry, 192
Trinidad, 9, 27, 92, 152, 344, 354
  All-Trinidad Sugar Estates and Factory Workers' Union, 39
  conference of labour officers, 190
  Federated Workers' Union, 38
  indentured labour in, 171
  Labour newspapers in, 31
  Labour Party, 14
  Oil Workers' Union, 38, 161, 300
  People's National Movement, 38, 92, 300
  right to strike in, 314
  skilled workers in, 361
  Trades Union Council, 92, 141
  Trade Union Ordinance, 1932, 14
  union leaders in, 38
  unions, accounts of, 298, 299–300
  unions and politics in, 92
  unions, character of, 38
  unions in, 341
  unions, legal regulation of, 261, 304, 307
  unions, legislation in, 180
  unions, membership of, 123
  West Indian Independence Party, 38
  Working Men's Association, 10, 13, 16, 92
  Working Men's Reform Club, 9

Uganda, 67 *et seq.*, 175, 272, 273
  arbitration in, 310, 319, 320, 322
  Civil Servants' Associations, 67
  early unions in, 67
  Labour College at Kampala, 68
  Labour Department of, 206
  organization of public servants in, 67
  pattern of employment in, 338, 356, 357

Uganda (*contd.*)
  probationary trade unions in, 283
  Textile Workers' Union, 395
  Trades Union Congress of, 68
  union, accounts of, 298
  union, funds of, 295
  unions in, 123, 341
  unions, legal regulation of, 261, 267, 271, 291, 301, 304
  unions, officers of, 293
  unions, registration of, 248, 287, 288
  unions, segregation, 137
  women workers in, 337
Unfair labour practices, 304
Union leadership, 133 *et seq.*, 387
Union Officers, election of, 292
  qualifications and duties of, 293 *et seq.*
  training of, 149, 150, 151, 158, 163, 194, 246, 254
United Africa Company, 376, 377
United Negro Improvement Association, 29

Wallas, Graham, 179
Webb, Beatrice, 179
Webb, S. and B., *History of Trade Unionism*, 3, 6
Welensky, Sir Roy, 19
West Indies, 9, 27, 33, 186, 224, 247, 351
  and Colonial Office, 184
  and early trade unions, 8 *et seq.*
  collective bargaining in, 393
  commerce in, 352
  education in, 362, 363
  employment in, 6, 354
  Labour Commissioners in, 148
  Labour newspapers in, 31
  legal regulation of unions in, 259 *et seq.*, 301, 305
  Royal Commissions on, 9, 10, 31, 32, 149, 373
  strikes in, 31, 146, 182, 188
  union finances, 130
  unions and politics in, 92

West Indies (*contd.*)
unions in, 190
unions, leaders in, 133, 134
unions, membership of, 123
unions, organization of, 126
unions, registration of, 282, 286
women workers in, 338
Whitley Committee, 371, 372, 373
Councils, 389
Williams, Eric E., 38
The Negro in the Caribbean, 31
Workmen's Compensation, 20, 177,
181, 182, 185, 187, 189, 231,
232, 390
World Federation of Trade Unions
(WFTU), 38, 45, 103, 116, 157,
158, 162

Yesufu, T. M., *An Introduction to
Industrial Relations in Nigeria*, 18,
44, 104, 105, 338
Yew, Lee Kuan, 77, 96, 97

Zanzibar, 123